Alien in the Mirror

Alien in the Mirror
*Scarlett Johansson, Jonathan Glazer
and* Under the Skin

MAUREEN FOSTER

McFarland & Company, Inc., Publishers
Jefferson, North Carolina

LIBRARY OF CONGRESS CATALOGUING-IN-PUBLICATION DATA

Library of Congress Cataloging-in-Publication Data
Names: Foster, Maureen, 1948– author.
Title: Alien in the mirror : Scarlett Johansson, Jonathan Glazer and Under the skin / Maureen Foster.
Description: Jefferson : McFarland & Company, Inc., Publishers, 2019. | Includes bibliographical references and index.
Identifiers: LCCN 2019033375 | ISBN 9781476670423 (paperback : acid free paper) ∞
ISBN 9781476636504 (ebook)
Subjects: LCSH: Under the skin (Motion picture)
Classification: LCC PN1997.U525 F67 2019 | DDC 791.43/72—dc23
LC record available at https://lccn.loc.gov/2019033375

BRITISH LIBRARY CATALOGUING DATA ARE AVAILABLE

ISBN (print) 978-1-4766-7042-3
ISBN (ebook) 978-1-4766-3650-4

© 2019 Maureen Foster. All rights reserved

No part of this book may be reproduced or transmitted in any form or by any means, electronic or mechanical, including photocopying or recording, or by any information storage and retrieval system, without permission in writing from the publisher.

Front cover: Scarlett Johansson in *Under the Skin*, 2013 (A24/Photofest)

Printed in the United States of America

McFarland & Company, Inc., Publishers
Box 611, Jefferson, North Carolina 28640
www.mcfarlandpub.com

For Faith and Harrison—
Thank you for your love

In memory of
Chris Collins (1962–2014)
Mark Mason (1960–2010)
David Rose (1924–2017)
Terry Smith (1972–2012)
Scott Hutchison (1981–2018)
Harris Savides (1957–2012)

Table of Contents

Acknowledgments — ix
Preface — 1

Part I: Watching *Under the Skin*

1. Landing — 5
2. The Foreigner — 10
3. The Monster — 18
4. Fall, to Rise — 27
5. Lonely — 33
6. Quiet — 40
7. Leaving — 52

Part II: The Journey

8. Jonathan Glazer — 59
9. Beast, Birth — 66
10. The Novel — 77
11. The Birth of *Under the Skin* — 90
12. Scarlett Johansson — 100
13. Film4 and the Money-Road to Production — 111
14. Setting the Stage — 117
15. A Camera the Size of a Box of Matches — 130
16. "A Kind of Dreamscape" — 142
17. Forget What She's Done — 152
18. Alchemy — 165

Part III: The World *of Under the Skin*

19. Opposites Attract	181
20. The Alien in the Mirror	190
21. Laura and Her Cousins	198
22. The Family of Non-Humans: Aliens, Androids and Clones	212
Epilogue	228
Appendix	233
Chapter Notes	239
Bibliography	251
Index	257

Acknowledgments

There would be no book without the consent of *Under the Skin*'s producers Jim Wilson and Nicholas Wechsler and director Jonathan Glazer, who, despite the fact that they didn't know me and had little more than a glimpse of what I was up to, put their trust in me. Thank you to Reno Antoniades and Jennifer Fradlin for their aid and their patience through many emails at the beginning of this process. I am grateful to StudioCanal for generously providing me with photos from *Under the Skin*, and to Film4 and FilmNation for photos as well as permission to quote extensively from their interviews and production notes.

Many dozens of people took time from their busy schedules to talk with me about their experiences working on this film—their names and stories are in this book. I'm also grateful to those too numerous to name here—the assistants, agents, and managers in the industry who kindly helped me to connect with the people I was seeking and whose efforts involved persistence and sometimes a bit of detective work!

Though I began writing this book in 2014, the gestation may have begun in 2005–6 while I was immersed in the writing of a thesis on Philip K. Dick's *Do Androids Dream of Electric Sheep?*—a journey nurtured by my excellent advisor Sharon Klein at California State University, Northridge. When I lived in Berkeley, California, in 2007, it was the countless films I was so fortunate to see at the Pacific Film Archive at UC Berkeley—and my job working for the charismatic professor Marilyn Fabe, who had hired me as a teaching assistant—that helped me get through a very difficult year of my life and enabled my adventure deeper into film.

From 2007 to 2013 I taught at University of California, Santa Cruz, and I am indebted to Provost David Evan Jones at Porter College, Provost Lourdes Martínez-Echazábal at Merrill College, Writing Program coordinator Elizabeth Abrams, and Provost Joel Ferguson at Crown College not only for hiring me but for giving me the opportunity to turn my writing courses into de facto film classes. It was a great privilege and an endless pleasure to teach my students at UCSC, and I think of these screenings and invigorating class discussions as the experience that both inspired me to write a long work about film and gave me the confidence to take the first steps.

David Alff is the acquisitions editor at McFarland & Co., Inc., Publishers who thought that my idea to write about a little-known science fiction art film was an interesting one, and I am grateful for his decision, his patience, and his guidance. Invaluable to my research, and lovely places to spend time, were the Margaret Herrick Library in Beverly Hills and the Iliad Bookshop in North Hollywood.

Ingrid Browning LaRiviere, who was my colleague at UCSC and became a dear friend, has given me much support over the years, and a new friend, Aloura Charles, has been encouraging as well as helpful. My friendship with Leonard Durso has survived the ruptures of time and geography, and his dedication and discipline as a writer have always inspired me. For their friendship and support over many decades, I am deeply thankful to author Viki King, to Stan Berkowitz, and to Bruce Foster.

Paul Schaeffer has given me excellent advice and suggestions during this project. For candid feedback, commiseration, perennial (and often quotidian!) support, and above all his friendship, I have relied heavily upon my confidant and fellow author, Jeffrey Lieber. My sister Jackie Schaeffer—a savvy consultant on writing, editing, visuals, and alas, computer challenges—has been there for me from the start with guidance and love.

This book is dedicated to my children, Faith Foster and Harrison Foster. Their help and support in every way, their cherished company and endless (and often life-saving) humor, and their affection mean more to me than anything.

> *Sometimes the fascination of the unknown is overwhelming and electrifying. It is a mystery to me why I'm compulsive about continuing this "making of art," but I find that to keep peace of mind, it has become as necessary as eating and sleeping.*
> —Patti Warashina, from *50 Northwest Artists* by Bruce Guenther, Chronicle Books, 1983

Preface

"A Science Fiction Rhapsody Laced with Thorns"[1]

This quote has delighted and haunted my imagination since I first read it in 2014, months after *Under the Skin* made its controversial premiere. It's from a review in the *Village Voice* by film critic Stephanie Zacharek, and as I write this I realize my response to the quote is a mirror of the quote itself—to be both delighted and haunted is to experience a "rhapsody with thorns."

The poster for *Under the Skin* that lived outside my neighborhood theater tantalized me for weeks before the film opened. Designed by artist Neil Kellerhouse,[2] it's a portrait of Scarlett Johansson that beguiles the viewer in the same way that her character beguiles the men she stalks on the streets of Glasgow. A compelling and irresistible tension between darkness and light, fantasy and foreboding, melancholy and menace—these seductive dialectics drive the poster, Jonathan Glazer's direction, Johansson's performance, and every other aspect of this captivating film. Johansson's face and neck are partly eclipsed in shadow, partly tinted in a rainbow. This image and the black background in which it floats are overlaid with a star-studded cosmos, a fairy dust of tiny orbs across her face. At the time I knew nothing about the movie, and this gauzy portrait insinuated a haunting story of an elusive love, a fantasy, a distant world—or maybe all of these.

The director's narrative style here is to withhold more than he gives, playing on our sense of longing. What fans of this film have in common is that we value that longing more than knowing. We embrace the aesthetic of withholding. In presenting us with opposites that perform a ballet rather than a battle, Glazer robs us of our comforting black-and-white way of seeing, and refrains from offering what it is we think we want.

This powerful approach is both perfectly suited to the story it tells and responsible for the fervor the film inspires. Glazer and his team galvanize the rhetoric of opposites and the aesthetic of withholding to spin a spellbinding and most unconventional narrative about an otherwise conventional theme: a woman's journey of self-discovery. The film is as much about alienation as aliens, and it is ultimately a meditation on what it means to be human—in particular, a human woman.

By the time I saw the movie I'd heard the spoiler, and not by choice—I ran into someone who had just seen the film in New York and spilled forth with *you know Scarlett Johansson's an alien, right?* After that, when I saw the poster again, everything about it said "alien"—but it hadn't the first time. The poster channels the film: Its elements, like the shots and scenes in the movie, are alien once you know the story, but without it they can be interpreted in ways having nothing to do with extraterrestrials. Dreams, metaphors, visual poetry, imagination, science. People who see the film knowing about Johansson's character (the tyranny of the information age) can read the possible cues accordingly, but there is nothing explicit. The game Glazer plays with his audience may be partly a strategy to build suspense, but I believe it's more a function of his art, which has everything to do with suggestion—and nothing to do with revelation.

My science fiction sense of wonder was nurtured throughout childhood with repeated viewings of old films on *Million Dollar Movie*, thanks to New York City's WOR-TV Channel 9. Emphasis upon *repeated*—their weekly feature screened twice nightly on weekdays and three times on Saturdays and on Sundays. A movie as riveting as *Invasion of the Body Snatchers*, my sister and I (and in time, our little brother) would watch over and over, lying on the floor, heads propped on hands, and of course in our pajamas (to distract our parents with the illusion that we were on our way to bed). Then there was *War of the Worlds, Forbidden Planet, Invaders from Mars, Cat-Women of the Moon, The Incredible Shrinking Man, Attack of the Crab Monsters, The Fly* ("the disintegrator integrator will change life as we know it"[3]), and *The Thing from Another World* ("keep watching the skies!"[4]).

The fear and suspense we simultaneously savored and dreaded was complicated by empathy for these people, and also these creatures, caught up in bizarre circumstances. Despite the havoc they wreaked on Earth I felt sorry for the gawky tripod beings in *War* as they withered and died from our earthly bacteria. What would it be like to be a scientist suddenly trapped in the creaking, crackling exoskeleton of a giant crab? What if my father came home one evening and regarded us all—like the sheriff in *Invaders from Mars*—with the cold eyes of a soulless Martian?

After college I began writing film reviews, and later, fiction—two habits I supported by working as a script reader for studios. Writing coverage was a kind of marriage of my two earlier jobs, and it fanned my film desire. What eventually surfaced was a longing to write something more extensive about film—and maybe focused on just one film. Now and then over the years,

Cat-Women of the Moon, 1953, directed by Arthur Hilton. From the author's early science fiction film education. Actors Susan Morrow on left, Carol Brewster right, and William Phipps, who appeared in *War of the Worlds* that same year. Astor Pictures Corporation/Photofest © Astor Pictures Corporation. Special thanks to Eddie Brandt's Saturday Matinee for the DVD.

whenever I saw a movie I couldn't stop thinking about, I wondered if it could be the one. After seeing *Under the Skin* in April of 2014, and chasing it from theater to theater until its first run came to an end, I knew the book I wanted to write. Beyond the science fiction magic, there was the character, her story, and the setting—the charm of Scotland I had found in my countless viewings of Bill Forsyth's timeless *Local Hero*. My pleasure tinged with sadness in the films of Antonioni, and experiencing his cinematic reverence for the landscapes and the people of the Po River Valley of his youth was reignited by the way Jonathan Glazer embraced both the urban and the natural beauty of the country where he shot.

I hadn't pondered it too deeply when I started writing this book—that was a compelling need I wanted to fulfill. But somewhere along the journey a friend asked me, why *this* movie? Wending my way to an explanation I landed on a reason that seemed to underlie all the other reasons, and it's a simple one: my love for the character and her journey. I relate to her. I empathize with her. I believe she has something to teach me.

Part I of this book is a walk through the film, scene by scene. Scarlett Johansson enthralls as an alien who arrives on Earth to prey on humans, but her path takes a surprising turn. Glazer's minimalist rendering of Laura tracks a curiosity that gives way to action, which leads her—for a brief precious time—to experience what it is to be a human and a woman. This section explores how cinematography, mise en scène, music, and the scant use of dialogue poignantly animate Laura's experience on Earth as a mirror of human experience and define what it means to be human across a spectrum of bliss, tragedy, and beauty.

Part II reveals the movie's backstory, the novel by Michel Faber that is dramatically different from the adaptation, the business-end of how the film was made, the long journey of screenplay drafts and reinventions, and finally, the shooting and the post-production. We look at the many challenges Glazer and his team faced using unpredictable covert filmmaking that took the movie to unforeseen places every day, every moment. For the chapters on the shooting of the film I relied mainly on the voices and words of the people who made it. In Part III we take the style, motifs, iconography, and themes touched upon in the first section and more closely explore their powerful contributions to the film, as well as how they both connect it to and distinguish it from its science fiction cousins: movies about aliens. In the epilogue *Under the Skin* is launched, and amidst marketing, distribution, premieres, and festivals, we visit the response—one as full of dialectics and emotion as the film itself.

I felt a certain daunt as to how to go about my first non-fiction book. I was somewhere in my first draft when I attended a Writers Guild event for the 20th Anniversary of *Jerry McGuire*, followed by a Q&A with the writer/director, Cameron Crowe. To one of many people in the packed audience who asked him for advice about screenwriting, Crowe replied, "Write the song that's in your head." I took that advice.

This book is not an explanation of the filmmakers' intent—except for the places where they've stated that intent in interviews—but it is a book that ponders, explores, and deeply appreciates the film for lovers of *Under the Skin*, present and future. It is for fans of Jonathan Glazer and Scarlett Johansson, enthusiasts of science fiction and fantasy, and readers who adore the rabbit-hole journey of delving deeply into the experience of a film. Most of all, I've written it for people who love movies.

PART I: Watching *Under the Skin*

1
Landing

The black of the opening sequence and a menacing white dot racing toward us *appear* as the cosmos, and the series of abstract images that follows as *perhaps* the arrival of a spacecraft. But would anyone seeing this film cold—without the alien spoiler—assume this? This atmospheric visual could be a metaphor, an eerie fusion of sound and image whose meaning is, for now, unknown. And the beguiling white dot marks the introduction into the mix of an element as important to the story as anything we will see on the screen: the work of composer Mica Levi. Glazer recalls that his music supervisor Peter Raeburn, with whom he'd worked for years on most of his projects, played him a tape:

> about 20 seconds of it, and I immediately said "Who's that?" and I said let's try that right at the beginning, and what I got really excited about was the capitalized idea of "the aliens are coming." Let's not pretend they're not, they are. Let's be scared of the white dot. Let's start like that.[1]

That a white dot amidst the blackness qualifies for Glazer as an "establishing shot" calibrates for us his sensibility right out of the gate—and he and his team stay unfailingly loyal.

Feverish, irritable strings accompany this spacecraft's arrival. Levi intended it to "feel like a life form you can't quite understand, but it's carrying on relentlessly, like a beehive."[2] Critic Zacharek hears "a chorus of anxious violins like 1,000 obsessive crickets. This is the music of unease, the sound our neurons might make if we could listen in on their workday."[3]

These sounds also mimic the grunting engine and shrieking wheels of a train; it's future-travel that evokes travel of the past. The evocation is sinister, for as the introduction of trains once facilitated industrialization, rampant consumption, and exploitation of faraway lands and peoples, these travelers are the darkest pioneer-predators of anyone's nightmare come to pass. The entry of a black cylinder into a white orb juxtaposes technology and nature because the spaceship imagery alludes to a human eye. This dialectic, an inexhaustible trope in science fiction that can only become more urgent as our technology intensifies, plays a poignant role in this film. The image also conjures sexual penetration, ironic because intercourse is an experience various characters in the story anticipate but are without exception denied; there are Laura's victims, the Logger who attacks her, the "Quiet Man" who takes her in, and Laura herself. It's a paradoxical aspect of this erotic thriller that is perfectly in tune with the experience of watching it. For all the feverish sexuality in Johansson's appearance, affect, and performance, our experience of her can never for a moment be separated from a spectrum of buzz-killing that ranges from unease to inexplicable queasiness to dread. Zacharek says of Johansson in the later sequences, "her nakedness is the opposite of a sleazy thrill ... she hides both everything and nothing; she's treachery and softness rolled into one."[4]

Although this thwarting of desire is always related to the alien presence, it's not always for the same reason. As for the eye-like imagery of the black insertion into the white orb, it is in fact an eye—a micro-close-up of our alien's human face as it is being "manufactured."

Soon the muffled, staccato syllables of a female voice accompany the train wheel drone. They suggest someone practicing English, and in fact they were lifted from the star's sessions practicing her British accent—*buh-buh-buh, nuh-nuh-nuh no*. And then: *Film, films*. Glazer reports he can't "lay claim" to this little wink to the audience, because it was neither scripted nor a direction from him, but its relationship to the character is meaningful.

> She worked with a voice coach [Paula Jack] who invented this phonetic system of repeating word fragments. So what you're doing is you're watching a parallel of watching your actress in disguise–wig, costume, makeup—and being prepped to go out in the world.... I heard Scarlett saying those words and I thought, I'm going to use that. So "film," is one of the words Scarlett says, but by pure chance. I can't take credit for that.[5]

But he can take credit for using it—so maybe the "wink" is Johansson's.

The pounding music, the acquisition of language, and the insertion/coital image embody what the aliens are up to: the penetration of our world. And the mood is menacing—this mission is no errand of mercy. We cut to a close-up of our alien's newly minted human eye, with an iris that pulsates to the rhythm of the phonetic sounds.

After a high-angle glimpse of a stream winding through an earthly wood in the dark of night, we see the headlight of a speeding motorcycle, and soon streetlights, and then the full moon, all echoing the eye. The eye motif that resurfaces throughout *Under the Skin* is by turns romantic, erotic, increasingly unnerving, and symbolic. The zigzag of the road on which the biker travels imitates the curves in the woodland stream of the previous shot, imaging the way that this alien and his coterie will soon blend into their earthly surroundings—unnoticed.

1. Landing

Laura's "eye" is among the first images in the film. In this scene in the van the Nervous Man says to her, "Something about your eyes..." He seems dazed by her. There *is* something about her eyes, and in the way her alien colleague Bad searches them and the way Laura gazes into mirrors (courtesy A24 and StudioCanal).

The driver of the motorcycle, Bad (Jeremy McWilliams), disappears down an embankment then hikes back up with the body of a woman slung over his shoulder. As he walks along the highway her long hair and arms swing lifelessly left and right—she's an object, like a rag doll or even a sack of flour. His treatment of her is dark—this is not a rescue. We haven't yet been told or shown that he's not human, but there is something *inhumane* in his affect.

We meet Johansson (called Laura in the script, though we never hear her name) in a stark white, anonymous space—it's devoid of architectural definitions such as floors, walls, or ceiling. It could be a white parallel to the introductory black space, except that outer space is "nature" and this feels technological and non-natural; not *space* as we understand it. Although we're witnessing an event that appears to involve humans, the surroundings undermine the human. The sterility of the white context channels the advanced technology that enabled the mission, captures a sense of eerie futuristic science that is a facet of the genre, and finally, suggests a deficit of humanity; instead suggesting something alien. As if both suspended in and trapped by this surrounding white, the highway girl Lynsey Taylor Mackay lies motionless on her back while Laura, who is naked, undresses her.

The young woman's scant black outfit, ripped black mesh stockings, and black hair conjure up a goth gal; her tresses fan out like the branches of a scary tree. Yet she looks innocent. Her face is expressionless and her eyes are inexplicably, and chillingly, wide open. As Laura performs her task she has the same affect as Bad in performing his on the highway: swift and in control, a seasoned professional. Although there is no sexual act, the coarse nature of the girl's capture, the crude stripping of her person, and the blatant objectification may make us think of rape, perversely foreshadowing the culminating attack in the forest. Simultaneously, it feels as though this moment of objectification is not sexual: She's a utilitarian component of a mission in which Laura and Bad appear to be partners. But what is this nefarious mission?

Laura proceeds to don all of the girl's clothing, beginning with her black push-up bra and thong underwear. In dressing herself she exhibits the same familiarity and self-assuredness that she did during the undressing, as she hoists up the mesh stockings and buckles the high-heel boots. She knows the drill. Without a spoiler, as if we didn't read the opening image as a spacecraft (which it isn't), would there be a single reason to think she's anything but a human woman, engaged in some kind of crime, or scam, or cult ritual? She was as nonchalant with her nakedness as she now is when provocatively clothed, in an outfit that seconds before was worn by the girl, who put it on before leaving her home to go out into the world and … lure a stranger?

As the highway girl lies naked, Laura, now fully dressed, stands to her right. In a dramatic two shot/full shot they are black figures silhouetted against the stark white background, a right-sided "L" with Laura vertical as she gazes down at the girl, horizontal on her back. The composition, along with the fact that the girl is now naked and Laura clothed, stresses Laura's dominance and authority—yet earlier when it's Laura who is unclothed, it's her own nakedness that projects and wields authority. Why is this so, when nakedness often conveys vulnerability? Perhaps it is the fact that technically it's not Laura's own body that is bared here; it's a body she is *wearing*, a ruse. Her command over the situation is palpable; if anything, she's extra-insulated by this high-tech human-body armor. The fact that they are silhouetted in the shot rather than detailed both mystifies and intensifies Laura's anonymous power.

We wonder about the identity of this discarded, abducted, or murdered girl—a runaway, or prostitute, both?—but in time it seems feasible that she is in fact Laura's predecessor. When a tear makes its way from her eyes, it punctures a viewer's assumption that she is dead or unconscious, or somewhat more horrific—paralyzed. For filmmaker Angel Herrera, the moment "implies that their fate is inevitable, that they will all get sucked into the human experience. The girl's tear is telling Laura: 'This will happen to you.'"[6] He notes that their white surroundings also connect their fates; this woman's in this inexplicable space, and Laura's in a blanket of snow.

At this moment something piques Laura's curiosity enough to make her kneel beside the woman, and at first we may believe that something is the tear traveling down her face. But after Laura touches the woman and stands again holding her own hand high, a magnified close-up of the tip of Laura's finger reveals that what has captured her fascination is in fact an ant.

Because the next shot of her is a low-angle as she rapidly descends a decrepit staircase, we may think the previous events happened "upstairs"; it's a rational assumption, but it doesn't fit. The staircase is grounded in our quotidian reality, and the white space is enigmatic. Underpinnings of our real world, "rooted in the familiar, the known," give science fiction movies a "recognizable verisimilitude" notes Keith M. Johnston. On the spaceship in *Moon*, for example, which is filled with technology and populated by clones and a robot, "there are Post-It notes stuck to surfaces, Sam counts down the days by drawing smiley faces on the bathroom wall, his bedroom is a mess of clothes and papers."[7] Verisimilitude is comforting, so we're more vulnerable—an impossible white space that we can distance ourselves from is less menacing than a decrepit old building. A quick exterior shot of Bad as he pulls his motorbike from the back of the van reveals the building's exterior, and the visual inference that the weird white space is located within fuels a cognitive dissonance that is exploited again later throughout the film.

When she arrives at the landing, we glimpse through the window in the background, in the right side of the frame, a group of hazy, shimmering colored lights in motion—an alternative, says editor Paul Watts, to "a UFO up in the sky after the staircase. Everyone has a different requirement for clarity … seven lights flashing is all you're going to get."[8] Or perhaps they are Aurora Borealis!

The elegant creepiness of our introduction to Laura is a concert of every cinematic element you can name—action, composition, production design and costume, sound, silence, and editing that are so densely packed into this brief scene (so intriguing and provocative it could stand alone as a short film) that when it ends it leaves you asking, *what just happened?!* In this quintessential queasy unknown, Mackay achieves an acting coup simply through her elephant-in-the-room status—who is she? Is she dead? Is she even human? Throughout the sequence Laura comes to us exclusively in partial body shots, profiles, and 3/4 shots that establish her mystery and detachment and fuel the assurance that she's in command. As she drives the van her partner has left for her, we now have our first full-frontal close-up of her face, and although it's the face of Scarlett Johansson that we know and love, we're now not so sure we love her, and we definitely don't know her. Even though we've just seen everything—her body fully exposed in the previous scene—it is in this close-up that the tense disconnect between the movie star on the marquis and the stranger called Laura begins to set in.

2
The Foreigner

The camera follows Laura from behind on a down escalator and through a crowded mall, her sexuality the focus of this tracking shot. Her predecessor's outfit that Laura now wears is fashionably and provocatively vulgar—high-heeled black boots, torn black mesh stockings with skimpy tight denim cut-offs, and a tailored denim jacket that favors Johansson's trim waist and full hips. Her insouciant demeanor and wiggle-walk speak sex appeal so accurately it appears studied—just as she studied English. She has been meticulously designed and trained, and there's no question that her goal is to lure men to pursue and follow her—just as the camera does in this long tracking shot.

Yet despite her confidence she paradoxically appears vulnerable, and we may feel concerned for her. Although her body is womanly there's a distinctive girlishness to her look that brings a dark edge to the scene, raising the possibility that she doesn't know enough to realize that the men she lures may be dangerous to her. Even though we've just seen her in complete control in the white scene, she now appears less predator than vulnerable teenage runaway. This image of her foreshadows the closing scene in the forest where she also appears girlish and innocent, wrapped in a coat that is several sizes too big for her, desperately running from a man who's discovered her alone, and trapped her. It's all captured in a rear tracking shot of her (as in the mall), a shot which throughout the film recurs repeatedly, becomes iconic, and shifts in meaning as her character changes along her journey.

Laura makes her way through the crowd as a human woman, but there's something a little off about her. Just as Johansson captures Laura's alien-ness in the white sequence through her cold dispassion, she conveys it here in a subtle stiffness of her movement—her hips sway, but it's as if her body doesn't quite fit her. She's not at home in her own skin.

At a mall shop a bright pink sweater catches her attention. She seems to know instantly it's right for her purpose, yet the way she caresses the fabric is an early indication she's both drawn to and curious about humans, their longings, and their pleasures. It is this sweater, along with tight jeans, new black boots, and the woman's black underwear, that she dons for the rest of the film. Apart from the fact that the color alludes to the actress's name, it connotes the passion of Hester in *The Scarlet Letter*—along with the punishment ensuing from that passion. *Under the Skin* may be open to the interpretation that the price the alien ultimately pays is payback for the torture and death of her victims, or for the sexuality that is in fact a role she is playing— in a body that she has borrowed.

In the store's makeup department there are close-ups of five women receiving makeovers, admiring their faces in hand mirrors. There's a sweetness to the shots of the women, who chose pastels, that contrasts Laura's work-mode demeanor as she expertly applies a bright red lipstick to her full, sensuous lips. The makeover women and Laura are in different places on a continuum, from wives re-kindling romance with their husbands, to single women heading off on a hot date, to Laura's bold and blatant, even aggressive, red—but they are all employing sexual power.

The choice to make Laura's introduction to human culture take place in a shopping mall is a canny and interesting one. As Johnston suggests, the familiarity for the audience helps them to receive the elements of science fiction that are profoundly alien. What the mall also offers is the earthling experience that provides sensual pleasures that are part of what piques Laura's curiosity—and that she becomes increasingly drawn to. The mall experience is imbued with sensations related to the human female body that Laura is inhabiting, and the world of touching and feeling that Laura samples in the mall shops in this very early scene forecasts the desires that partly fuel her pivotal decision later in the film. In a shot immediately following, she sits in the van holding a compact mirror. Applying her new lipstick she both emulates the women in the mall and shares in their purpose: to attract.

Laura applies her new lipstick—as anyone might—while looking into a compact mirror, sitting in her van. Hair and Makeup Designer Chrissie Beveridge calls the shade of red they selected "a sort of bright, quite startlingly bright color—for attracting." Beyond its practical function, Laura's lipstick is an early step in her curiosity about, and eventual pleasure in, the world of humans (courtesy FilmNation and A24).

The sounds that travel with Laura as she drives the van into town are machine-like, a pumping or pounding in a one-two rhythm. It's a cold, bloodless perversion of the heartbeat that is the driver of human life—just as Laura's guise is a cold, alien perversion of a human sexual dynamic, about to be performed in the classic "pickup." The sounds represent something robotic about her and her military affect as she heads out on her mission through the streets of Glasgow. Her eyes stare straight ahead. Soon three viola notes accompany the sound, an introduction to the main theme that unfolds here for the first time and then reappears many more times, resonating with a series of critical events—it is the queasy hallmark of Mica Levi's mesmerizing score.

As Laura drives, the camera tracks her point of view; she's targeting with her eyes a series of pedestrians on the sidewalks, or crossing the street. What they have in common is that they are male and they all walk alone, and the sounds and music render these moments both menacing and weird. This series of shots is momentarily interrupted by an outpouring from a soccer game as a crowd of men and women spill out of a stadium onto the street and into the traffic, many wearing the green-and-white scarves in support of their Glasgow team, the Celtic Football Club. Laura appears not at all rattled by them; she's focused on the task at hand, getting the lay of the land. Some of the fans pass by the van so closely that we wince, but Laura maneuvers confidently around them.

That Laura responds as indifferently to the pedestrians as they do to her is one of the subtly alien and alienating moments that occur throughout the film and keep the audience—between the larger, more dramatic scenes—in an almost constant state of unease. Laura mirroring the crowd's nonchalance is a function of her not possessing typical human responses, but the crowd's indifference to her van owes at least in part to Glazer's use of documentary techniques. These pedestrians don't know that the driver of the van is Scarlett Johansson, and most important of all, they don't realize they are being filmed. Glazer recalls,

> I didn't even understand the connection at this point, but I was very interested in this thing of shooting in the real world ... put her in disguise and drop her in the real world, hide the cameras and walk away ... you're part of the lie, part of the conceit. Scarlett's preparation for the role, the construction of the wig and the makeup and the clothes, the artifice of the accent and the immersion in the function of driving and hunting ... it's equivalent to the story we were trying to tell ... the method and the narrative were the same thing. And once that was understood, that concept drove through the whole project.[1]

The people going about their business in the city are prevented from knowing she is Scarlett Johansson because of her disguise; the men she approaches are persuaded by her appearance and manner and working off of assumptions about strange women who proposition them; and the audience knows less than any of them. We could assume through our feelings and experience that things aren't what they seem, but opening that door leads us only to another question: How is it that they seem? All is disguised.

After scoping out a series of lone males Laura finally hones in on one, pulls the van over, and rolls down her window. The flat affect that is her default expression turns suddenly to charm—even more than that, radiance; she's friendly and smiling as she asks him for directions to the M8. It's here that Laura for the first time uses the language we heard her rehearsing in the opening sequence. Writer Jonathan Romney describes how she engages the first of several "marks": "In mundane chat, with an intensely flirtatious tone, adopting a sultry, somewhat posh English accent that tells them, to say the least, she's not from around these parts."[2]

Knowing that she is a foreigner would seem to make the men she talks to a little less concerned about her subtle oddness. This first gent is one of several non-actors filmed with a hidden camera and unaware he is talking to Scarlett Johansson. He gives her directions in great detail, and there are a few chuckles in the audience from those flummoxed by the sound of his Glasgow English. We can make out "gas station" and "left turn" and maybe a few other words, just as we were able to understand a few words when Laura practiced her English in the opening sequence. His regional accent seems a comment on her alien presence. The fact that she repeats some of what he says to her—"Oh, you're going to meet someone" (her "translation" of his reply to her question "Where are you going?")—seems partly for the benefit of struggling viewers who don't understand what he just said. In this case what he said contains an important plot point, as her protocol excludes men who have destinations or people waiting for them, and will be missed and arouse suspicion.

This tense sequence, which introduces us to Laura's mission without revealing it, is driven by the film's sound on many levels. The three haunting notes in Levi's score, the ominous pounding, and the unsettlingly familiar yet foreign language all disorient us. Laura's forays into the streets of Glasgow possess a cinéma vérité realness that is the product of a combination of hidden cameras and sound recorded on location.

Because this man has a date, Laura strikes out. The undertone of menace that pervades their conversation turns darker still in the next shot when, as they say goodbye and the stranger walks on, her warm smile and bright eyes fade into the blackest of looks. It's a horror trope that we love—a character's malevolent intent is revealed when the charm she or he contrived to snare an unsuspecting victim suddenly, in some cases comically, vanishes. "When she's working her wiles, her eyes are bright and reflective: 'I'm far more interested in you than I am in myself,' they seem to say, and weirdly, tragically [for the alien's quarry], she's not even lying."[3] Laura does seem not very interested in herself at all in this early stage, but how that gradually changes shapes the rest of the story.

Have we evidence at this point that she is a killer? Was the highway girl killed by this weird pair, or just knocked out? (She may now be awake and back home, thinking that she got drunk and blacked out. Maybe it's not likely but it's not impossible—the governing principle here is how little we actually know.) The sustained, foreboding strings and the surrounding darkness define her isolation and loneliness as someone on a semi-solitary mission in a strange land eons from home.

While this sense of confinement is captured in mise en scène it's not suggested in her expression, where her default mode is a poker face. We don't know her well enough to ascertain whether her blank look is displeasure at her situation or just her professional, focused demeanor. She is soldierly, android-like, on autopilot. She stops to ask a second man for directions—this time, to the post office—and chats him up. "Do you have family here? … Ah, you do."[4] When she asks a third prospect if he lives alone his answer is affirmative and he accepts her offer of a ride. As they drive along we see through her back window what at first looks like a pair of headlights, but as they diverge we see it's two motorcycle headlights. She notices them intently, and we learn much later that she has more than one biker chaperone.

The fourth man she stops is an immediate dead end when a woman calls out his name, "Andy!"—not alone, he obviously doesn't fit the bill. But the next loner lad on the highway (actor Joe Szula) is distinguished by his long green-and-white scarf (he may well have been among the crowd outside the stadium earlier in her day), his eager responsiveness to her flirting, and his admission that he is out by himself tonight—and lives alone. He accepts her offer of a ride, and his excitement over simply sitting next to her in the van is palpable; she is beautiful, sensual, and she's interested in him. Again we hear the three ominous notes, but for the first time the theme music continues past this prelude, signaling that her failed attempts and false starts are over for now, that this is the man who's in for the full ride. "You have a nice smile," she tells him, glancing at him as she drives, and he replies, "You have a nice smile too."

The fringe-tipped scarf (he is called the Footballer) is draped down the front of his body, and taps the sweetness of a little boy who's been dressed by his mother, who wraps it gently but securely around his neck before she kisses his cheek and sends him on his journey to school on a cold snowy day. This warm piece of clothing adds to our sense of dread over where this van journey will take him, and the homey, comforting scarf, which he tucks into the window as they drive, becomes a noose.

As the Footballer walks behind her, down the path and through the front door of the house where she is staying, his face has a feverish curiosity, and his swagger an anticipation of hot sex. His following her from behind echoes the tracking shots of Laura back in the mall, where the camera followed her from behind as a kind of lure-motif. She can't be resisted; she is compelling. He follows her inside where there is nothing but blackness; what logically would be a dark entry or hallway into a parlor is here a visual continuum to a limitless black void. It's a non-space that mimics the white void of the earlier sequence—something equally unnatural, undefinable, and unsettling. Oddly the Footballer

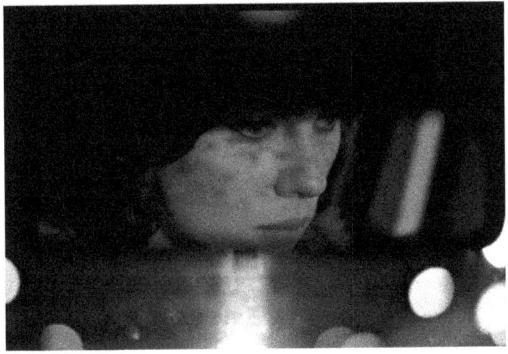

Laura is all business and dull affect when in cruising mode, but when she finds a candidate she really turns on the charm. The darkness and isolation of her twin habitats, the van and the black space, convey a sense that she is trapped—and may, in time, long for escape (courtesy StudioCanal and FilmNation).

doesn't appear the least bit unsettled by his bizarre surroundings. He walks slowly forward, peeling off his clothing and staring straight ahead of him. He appears almost hypnotized—does Laura possess such powers?

It's a bit comical, a man so caught up in a sexual fever that he's either oblivious to or unconcerned about these weird circumstances, the hypnosis of desire. We cut to his POV and see Laura doing the same, a mutual strip tease. Their pieces of clothing fall to the glossy black surface beneath them that also reflects the images of their bodies. The black void, the haunting music, her sexuality as she strips off her jacket and then her sweater, all push the eroticism of the scene into the surreal—like a drug-induced trip, or a dream that has as unnervingly compelling an affect upon the viewer as it is having on the man onscreen. Writer Jake Howell describes how Levi's "piercing strings" and "one-two beat" establish an "overwhelming sense of trance":

> Glazer's representation of seduction is so abstractly manifested that screening the film feels akin to attending an exhibition of video art more than it does experiencing an adaptation of Faber's text. So be it. This is creepy stuff, but horror and beauty share more in common than we'd like to think.[5]

In this indeterminate space it's difficult to say whether Laura is ten feet in front of him, or twenty, or fifty—it's an elastic space. She is designed to induce him to follow her just as the camera does; the man, the camera, and the audience are all under her spell. Now she wears a satiny camisole, and soon she has stripped down to the black push-up bra, tight jeans, and boots. She looks smolderingly back at him over her left shoulder. This gaze at a man while the back is turned to him is a classic provocative look from a romance or a comedy, but her face does not say *come hither*. It's a vamp look from noir or horror, dark-eyed and deadly, that says *come hither if you dare*.

With his eyes riveted upon her as he walks forward, the Footballer, now naked, appears mesmerized. He is also oblivious to the fact that the black shiny surface on which he walks has *turned to liquid,* and as he walks he is sinking deeper and deeper. He doesn't look down at any time or react to this in any way; his eyes remain on her in a series of angle/reverse angle shots. For the viewer, however, it's a series of shockers, intensified by the strings which, because of the accompanying visuals, are now weirder than ever. The complete capture theme that began with the three notes, then progressed as she approached him and lured him into the van, now plays out in full, and the theme's culmination accompanies his demise in a more horrific way than we could have imagined. The first shock is the transformation of what logically appeared as a solid surface into something watery, what critic Michael Phillips calls "the black sea of enigma," and the man's plight "a farewell visit to the world's murkiest spa."[6] *Anatomy of a Movie* dubbed the setting a "liquid floor of limbo death."[7] The next is his baffling lack of reaction to what is happening to him (the hypnosis theory is never more compelling than at this moment), and the third is that Laura, only steps ahead of him on the same path, *does not sink at all* and appears instead to be walking on water. The culminating shocker is that the man, after descending further with every shot, finally disappears under the water and *does not come up*.

Their trail of clothes floats on the "water," Laura walks on it, and the man sinks beneath it. Like the white space and the black space the liquid is now a third non-space or impossible space, something that defies not just our expectations but the laws of physics. Glazer eschews spaceships and other high-tech futurism to convey the alienosity of his science fiction world, and instead morphs what is more familiar to us—buildings, floors, water—into an architecture of inexplicability and dread. Laura glances back at him as if to confirm that he's fully submerged, then turns and retraces her steps, retrieving her clothing as she goes. She's without emotion, as if she's performed this routine a hundred or a thousand times. She then exits off the left side of the frame, leaving the black space empty—and silent.

After this sequence we now know superficially the *how* of Laura's mission, if not the *what* or the *why*. Assuming the victim's disappearance is fatal, she has crossed the line from beguiling temptress to femme fatale. But it can't be more than an assumption, just like the disappearance of the highway girl; there are things we don't know at this point, and *X-Files*'s Fox Mulder, to tap one of countless examples in or out of this genre, came back from the "dead" more than once.[8] To reprise the earlier and ongoing question, is it here that we discover that she's an alien? Like the black-space opening sequence, which we cannot pin down, these images and events could be read as a cinematic device to surprise and destabilize—to distance the viewer, as part of an aesthetic and rhetorical agenda, from anything familiar. There is also a beguiling juxtaposition of the literal and the fantastic that is a motif throughout the film: We open with abstractions of sight and sound as well as a human eye and a human voice; we proceed to a woman undressing another woman in a space that is unreal or surreal; and we continue with two people participating in a seduction that is carried out in an inexplicable blackness into which only one of them is mystifyingly swallowed. Where is this black space? Where does this water begin and end? And could this scenario really take place inside a house?

Credibility is suspended and we give ourselves over to this other world that has encroached upon, and now inhabits, our earthly world. In this way these scenes may be cinematic devices, surrealism, her dream, his daydream, a fever dream—anything but literal. It may also stand as visual proxy for what the entrapped man is feeling and experiencing—again a metaphor. A fifteen-minute acid-trip fusion of dizzying music and jarring visuals is what Kubrick chose to stand in for a cosmic journey through space and time in *2001: A Space Odyssey*—an unmeasurable, unquantifiable event too far outside our understanding. A distant world and its inhabitants also outside our ken is what Glazer knows he's dealing with, and he too invokes this iconic film:

> I always loved the frequency in *2001*, in the monolith, I always loved the idea of that frequency, and just—I don't know what that is.... But it is in my head until this day, here I am mentioning it, because of the fact that it remains ... alien. And if you're going to make a film about an alien, then make a film about an alien. Let it remain alien. Keep it alien.[9]

3

The Monster

Laura's nocturnal hunt resumes—possibly even immediately. She drives with the look of someone on autopilot, who acts and does not reflect. Cinematographer Daniel Landin gives us gorgeous shots of the orbs of streetlamps swimming past Johansson's face as she drives through the Glasgow night; the beauty of one of urban life's simple pleasures is at odds with her mission and with the bizarre enigma we just witnessed in the black space. And with that fresh in our mind's eye we cut suddenly to daylight at the ocean—the familiar place we swim, play, splash around, and feel good—a source of comfort and pleasure. A reprieve from worry.

Laura stands on the beach staring out to sea. When she glances to her left we see what has momentarily grabbed her attention: a family in the distance, a wife, husband, baby, and a dog playing on the sand. There's a towel lying at Laura's feet, and we feel an encroaching dread around the Swimmer who will eventually return to retrieve it. He wears a wet suit (actor Krystof Hádek), emerges slowly from the surf, and jokingly accuses her of planning to steal it—would that her intent were so benign. She chats him up and learns he's from the Czech Republic. "Why are you in Scotland?" she asks. He replies, "Because it's nowhere."

As with previous targets this is an interview, which he not only passes but as a candidate he is perfect: a thousand miles from home pitching a tent on the beach, a wanderer longing to be "nowhere." Darkly that word resonates with the black space that awaits him, a place the audience experiences as the epitome of nowhere. Yet it's poignant because a desire for nowhere connotes a desire to lose one's self, or find one's self, putting him squarely in the realm of "be careful what you wish for." The twist is that at this moment he's far from the urban jungle, the infamous turf of predators; he's in an unspoiled cove on the coast of Scotland. If anything, the threat he's prepared for is a jellyfish sting or a shark attack—not a monster on the prowl, unless it's the one from Loch Ness.[1]

3. The Monster

Their chat is interrupted by an angle on the drama that is unfolding in the distance, where the mother has braved the raging surf to rescue her struggling dog. Her husband has left their infant son alone on the beach to go after her. Now nature doesn't seem such a comfort as we see the waves are poised to swallow up the dog, the woman, and the man in this lonely cove, with tall cliffs whose jagged formations resemble giant teeth. The Swimmer races down the beach and plunges into the treacherous water. Laura watches as the Swimmer gets the man to the shore, but desperate to save his wife, the man pulls free and rushes right back into the water. The exhausted Swimmer, his efforts for naught, staggers back to the beach and collapses on the wet sand.

As Laura approaches him the music begins, echoing the entrapment of her first victim and his fate in the black space. Briefly the camera shifts and deepens focus to show us the baby, who, with his parents both swallowed up by the water, sits abandoned and crying on the beach. Laura looks around for a rock, which she uses to hit the man on the head before dragging him off. A shot of the infant in the upper left corner of the frame as Laura ponders what to do with the Swimmer is shocking mise en scène calculated to place her disinterest in bold relief. Whether or not she's an alien, she is alien to the empathy that we regard as part of what it means to be human. The scene's sense of tragedy is driven by the looming treachery of the cliffs and the waves, the ominous music and the cries of the baby, and Johansson's brilliantly android-like affect. Her calm is contrasted with the many deaths that will result on this beach on this particular day; this cove will turn into a bloodbath. Laura's lure of the first victim to a sea of blackness is too ethereal and visually mesmerizing to drive home the meaning of the event, for us to viscerally experience the obscure horror that is happening. It's in this scene, with her bludgeoning of the Swimmer and her indifference to the drowning couple and the screaming infant, that we experience her as a monster. In an interview with Vanessa Golembewski, Johansson reflected:

> Those emotions are sort of irrelevant to her ... it was really important to kind of wash myself of any of those things, any of those kinds of human emotions ... empathy or fear ... all those things. I had to be liberated of them, and be sort of in a meditative, present state of focus because that's what the role required.[2]

In a brief shot of Laura driving in her van there is, as before, no sign on her face of the drama that has just unfolded. In her performance Johansson creates a kind of bubble around herself; she's clearly in another realm, where everything has a different meaning. Johansson embodies, at every turn, Glazer's guiding principle to "keep it alien." Back at the shore it is now night, and Bad busily dismantles the Swimmer's tent and retrieves all of his belongings. We hear the baby's screams, then see him. The repeated attempts the infant makes to sit up and walk are futile, and the peril of the darkness, the cove that has already swallowed up the child's family, and the encroaching tide only inches away, horrify akin to the iconic baby and carriage hurtling down the Odessa steps in *Battleship Potemkin*. Carrying the tent Bad walks hurriedly down the beach in the direction of the baby, and the framing of this shot encourages us to hope he's about to rescue the child—just as Laura bending down toward the naked girl invites us to think she is drawn in by her tears. The director enjoys the one-two punch, playing us and then delivering the jolt. Even more chilling than the sight of the screaming child inches from the waves is the moment that Bad blatantly ignores the infant, just as Laura had, and reaches instead for the swimmer's towel lying in the wet sand—purging the crime scene of the last of the evidence. The baby's final chance to be rescued is now gone, and the third horror in the sequence is our certainty that within moments, he will drown.

Bad's movements confirm the modus operandi of the mission. His actions and demeanor throughout this sequence, with regard to rigorous focus on the mission to the exclusion of anything that can be construed as human emotion, coldly echo Laura's. Their similarity will become meaningful very soon as her path begins to diverge from his, a result of her extended interaction with, and intimate proximity to, humans—and perhaps also because of her inherent "nature."

After an earlier quick shot of the Swimmer slumped over in Laura's van, the now-empty seat beside her as she resumes driving around could stand in for the empty beach, where all the occupants have drowned. The absence of

Laura stands on the beach watching something quite alien to her: The Swimmer with whom she has just been chatting suddenly dives into the rough sea to attempt a rescue. Just as alien to Laura, moments later, are the desperate cries of the abandoned infant on the sand, which she ignores as she concludes her fatal business with the Swimmer (courtesy StudioCanal, A24, and FilmNation).

her victim in the car also invokes the absence of emotion from Laura throughout and after the cove sequence—it is wiped away and she's moving on to her next prey. Daniel Landin said:

> The affront of her having absolutely zero response to it was to me a kind of epiphany in terms of understanding [the aliens]. But then there's also the beat after that, later on, when she hears a scream from a car which is parked beside her at the traffic light, and you see there's a resonance, something has got through, there's a lingering sense of that moment.[3]

Her silent stillness is accompanied by the child's scream, which we hear and know that she hears, and it actually sounds at first as if it's coming from inside her own van, a phantom that has followed her. The sound along with a quick shot of the child in the next car create the sense that for her the events at the cove are "lingering."

Laura stares at the road ahead, focused on her task, and scans the sidewalk for her next target. A young guy shouts and a car full of young men pulls up at her left; they taunt her. A group of men is of no use to her; she regards them with dead eyes. The mission pushes on, relentless, like the pumping machine sounds on the soundtrack, a mission carried out by a being who is herself machine-like. Critic Geoffrey O' Brien observes:

> Her ride feels like a familiar story that goes on perpetuating itself, from era to era, in one form or another. It could be a serviceable device for a porn film, or a vampire film, or perhaps merely a film about a disconnected person interacting inconclusively with a succession of other disconnected persons. Deep underneath, some medieval tale of a wandering succubus continues to play out ... who seems scarcely to know what world she is on or why she is engaged in this mission. In a condition of wary puzzlement she looks at everything through the windshield.... It all seems filmed under the sign of generic urban loneliness.[4]

Prowling the dark streets once again, Laura spots a slender man walking alone and begins to follow him in the van, then on foot. It's the first time she has pursued someone without the security and the protection of the van, a first step on a journey she can't yet see. Suddenly she's overwhelmed by a crowd of rowdy girls dressed up for clubbing who sweep her along with them as if she were a rag doll.

They want her to join the party, but her utter cluelessness about what is happening is frozen on her face. Here is the vulnerability that she invited by breaking protocol and leaving the van. It's a test, but the unexpected consequence of her action—this encounter with the girls—is also a warning. With a curious absence of her previous agency she appears overwhelmed, and makes no attempt to resist or escape. She reacts as an android whose programming is suddenly inadequate to provide an appropriate reaction; she is momentarily out of commission.

We now know that if it was some supernatural power she invoked in the

Laura is nonplussed by this group of young women who sweep her up outside a club. It's the first time since the mall that we see her on foot outside of her van, and the first time we witness her behavior when something unexpected occurs outside the "script" of her job, where she is in control: she appears quite vulnerable. Costume designer: Steven Noble (courtesy StudioCanal and FilmNation).

black space—mesmerizing or hypnosis—it does not extend to superhuman physical strength, just as she displayed only normal human strength when struggling to drag the Swimmer's body along the sand. Once inside the club she is absorbed into a sea of people, and this black space turns her "at home" black space on its head; with its throbbing crowd of people dancing, blaring music, and pulsating lights, it is palpable that this is as jarringly alien to her as her black space is to us. She flees down a hall and then a staircase that spills her into a dimly lit room full of clubbers. The strobe lights that flash frenetically on the dance floor, and this room that is suffused with a soft, rosy light, signal a radical departure from the black and white spaces over which she had full control—her alien world—and mark both her first contact with and her frailty within the human world. The fact that she selected for herself a scarlet sweater that echoes the light of this room implies a destiny within this human world and a continuation of the vulnerability that will be both a cause and a result of her entry into that world.

With the sudden approach of the slender man she targeted outside (Andrew, played by actor Paul Brannigan), her fear/flight mode vanishes, and she immediately reverts to her seductive charm. He invites her for a drink and she soon asks, "Are you alone here?" It's clear in her face and her voice that she's back on her game as she flatters him, "I saw you on the road." For a brief time they're back inside the strobe-lit club dancing, and then we cut directly to him in the black space where she brought her first victim. Glazer notes,

> Each time you returned to that space you were learning more about it. But you only need to be there three times.... And we kind of understood that we wanted to stay away from alien "stuff" ... which I love in films, but that wasn't what I wanted to do. We wanted to create a space which *felt* alien ... you're doing it using human imagination ... you're then trying to get to places which are kind of more felt than thought. You bypass the intellect. You're trying to get to the inner consciousness of things.[5]

In this medium shot he is topless and his smile is seductive, and he is *dancing*. It's gallows humor on multiple levels—dancing and smiling in the anticipation of sex with this luscious and willing woman, having no clue what he's in for. The moment epitomizes the comedy, and tragedy in this case, of a man lured to his death by his desire: the task of a femme fatale has never been so easy.

The music isn't a continuation of the blaring sounds from the club—it's the hypnotic *idee fixe* of the film's score. It would never be mistaken for dance music, which adds to the scene's macabre humor. Because Andrew's movements as he dances are so perfectly in sync it appears as if he's dancing to the score—which of course he doesn't hear—a hapless soul dancing to his death knell. About this scene editor Watts commented, "The beach scene is a horror show—after that, you need a laugh."

His dance has the effect of blending the film's background score—the non-diegetic music—with the diegesis, the visual world of the film's reality. This familiar theme, because it's as if he can hear it, pulls us deeper into his experience. The music, the way he's dancing, his slight and slender body in contrast with the taller and heftier first victim, his nakedness and something adolescently innocent about him, and the conversation he had with Laura at the club all increase our empathy for him. Her warmth when she tells him "I saw you on the road" and "I wanted to speak to you earlier" approaches affection in the way she reaches out to him, and it's clear she's made him feel special ("You wanted to speak to *me*?"). She is confident in her effect upon him as well as in her control over the situation and in her mastery at simulating human sex games. The pinkish glow of the club room becomes a cocoon of romance and expectation, which only increases our dread over what is about to befall him.

Laura's walking backward and their intense eye contact is hypnotic, as if she is transmitting control through her eyes, and he is responding by walking toward her as if in a trance. Like the previous man's gradual descent into the black water the event appears to go utterly unnoticed by him; there is a long shot of him from behind as he sinks further while she keeps her eyes riveted on him. Once the water is around his chest he begins to gently tread, but it appears an instinctive response rather than a conscious one; his body reacts to the water, but like his predecessor he shows no awareness of the bizarreness of what is happening or of the jeopardy he's in. He focuses only on her; he's oblivious to his pending oblivion.

The comical moment is quickly vanquished by the shock of him disappearing under the water, presumably to experience something dire—presumably to die. The music stops entirely. Seconds of silence creep past as we wait for him to resurface, but he does not. These black water sequences are sexy (sort of), funny, puzzling, suspenseful, jarring, elusive, deeply disturbing, and breathtakingly gorgeous. The menacing blackness raises the stakes, sharpens the edge. The music is a taunting, haunting fusion of eeriness, eroticism, suspense, and surreal menace. The crying strings are soothingly unnerving, and the melody so original that it amplifies our sense that these actions and places are beyond our experience. It doesn't puncture our familiar, it obliterates it.

Whereas the first victim's vanishing under water is our final glimpse of him, here we see Andrew after he sinks beneath the surface. We share his low-angle view of Laura as she picks up her clothing from the mirror-black surface and walks out of sight, her nonchalance making the moment all the more chilling. Her work here is done, and without a second's hesitation she abandons him to his fate. He floats upright, still treading. The sight of Laura walking on the surface into which he sank would be enough to justify the stunned look in his eyes, but there's more: the apparently involuntary jerky movements of his arms and torso for a few seconds, accompanied by sounds of cracking and crunching that emanate from inside his body. The terror in his eyes registers—finally—his awareness of what is happening to him. That we stepped into his nightmare long before he did prolongs and intensifies our horror; this anticipatory dread in the audience is another of the film's finely executed horror tropes.

Next in a series of escalating shocks for him and for the audience is the sudden ghostly appearance of a previous victim, the Swimmer, floating upright toward him. His body is pale and bloated as if he were dead, but his eyes are not. Like the upright corpse of a sea mammal he floats slowly toward the new victim; his grotesque body is no longer his own—he cannot move his arms or legs. His sense of entrapment in his own flesh is palpable for the audience; there is anguish in his eyes. There is a near-absence of sound, a deathly loneliness in this environmental void. Sound designer Johnnie Burn said: "When we are under the void with Andrew, we wanted to really feel the molecules that hold him in place."[6] And we do—largely because is it so very quiet. What's also conjured here is an image of floating in deep space, typically an ill-fated one. The audience and Andrew, gazing at the same horror in the same moment, have a simultaneous realization: that the Swimmer's destiny will also be his own. Yet his final moment is dedicated not to his own existential terror, but to a close-up of his hand as he reaches out through the murky water to place his fingertips on the distended hand of his fellow victim. This bizarre encounter, with its fleeting seconds of empathy between the two doomed men, is juxtaposed with the earlier, startling absence of empathy displayed by the two aliens toward the infant stranded on the beach. Yet along with this contrast, this empathic moment also signals the human journey on which Laura is about to embark.

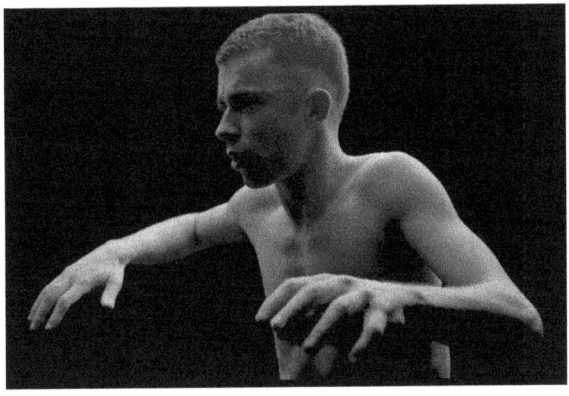

It's in the second visit to the black space that we see what becomes of the men Laura brings there. Here, Andrew (Paul Brannigan), even as he is sinking, seems unaware of his jeopardy. It's only moments later, fully beneath the water, that he begins to feel—and react to—his bizarre and frightening predicament (courtesy StudioCanal and FilmNation).

Every scene in the film in some way interrogates her absence of empathy as an aspect of alien nature, and taps two of the film's powerful themes: What does it mean to be alien? And, by necessity, what does it mean to be human?

In the shots of this compelling bond—and recognition of mutual terror in the eyes of the two men—lies the faintest hope for the audience that one will be able to rescue the other. But within seconds the Swimmer's mute scream punctures any such hope or fantasy of escape. A delicate interplay of the absence of music and the harrowing sounds fuel the tension of the moment. "What happens next is the stuff of Francis Bacon paintings," writes Zacharek,[7] a loss of self that Glazer captures with a stun of image and sound. There's a loud *pop* so shocking that we gasp—and an equally shocking visual of the Swimmer's flesh and bones spontaneously disappearing as he collapses into an empty skin. With a crushed head and the remnants of hands the skin begins to float and dance under the water like diaphanous drapery. Within seconds Andrew meets the same fate, and the two formerly human forms twist and turn in a beautifully grotesque, or grotesquely beautiful, skin ballet.

The next image is a red, lumpy, churning river of gore that races through a black tunnel toward a sideways beam of red light at the end. It's a vertical of crimson aimed at a horizontal and vanishing into it, leaving the tunnel vacant with a final emptying *whoosh*. The beam of red light then expands to bisect the black void of the wide screen; the red river appears to be beamed away, sent off in a montage of beautifully obscure alien imagery. The implication is that these human remnants have been "delivered." This lengthy sequence is a one-two punch: That this gushing gore is the end product of the men's evisceration, and its transport to a distant planet, the home of these aliens, is the goal of this heretofore mysterious alien mission. The next shot is a luminous red star in black space, then a white one. It gives us enough to address what has taunted us since the arrival at the film's opening: Why are they here? What are these bizarre seductions for? *What do they want*? Food? Fuel? Fodder for research?

It's a cousin to Spielberg's take on *War of the Worlds*: human flesh transmogrified for alien survival, those horrific images of blood and guts of captured victims funneled down a machine into an alien version of an ecosystem. It's related to that high-tech industrial, as opposed to "natural," image in *The Matrix*, the sight of Neo strapped and wired in a dark, cavernous warehouse along with countless others: humans as batteries. An early predecessor of all three films is *The Twilight Zone*'s iconic and ironic episode *To Serve Man*,[8] a more literal version of the theme of how humans serve aliens; the title refers to an alien tome presented to humans as a gift, which turns out to be a cookbook. This segment of Levi's score is called, chillingly, *Meat to Maths*.[9]

4
Fall, to Rise

The film's first act ends with this revelation, visually consummating the ritual at the core of her alien mission. Up to this point the story is devoted to a narrative striptease regarding the mission and Laura's role in it, but the focus of the second act is her personal journey. Appropriately it begins with a close-up of her face as she drives on the highway in heavy traffic. A flower vendor approaches her car window, and his sudden, unexpected presence among the cars—jeopardizing himself in the midst of traffic, carrying flowers—has a surreal quality on one hand, yet manages to seem not random but somehow connected to her destiny. He holds out for her one of several long-stemmed red roses wrapped in cellophane—a gift from another driver stuck in traffic—and extends it through the window. Blood from the thorny rose is now all over her hand; she examines it closely.

That the woman singled out by a driver in traffic to receive the gift of a rose happens to be Laura—not by a longshot the woman he imagines her to be—continues a series of seemingly random events in her life (the first was the encounter with the rave girls) that speak to her destiny as one who is chosen for something other than this mission. Strange and unexpected little things are happening because the strangest and most unexpected big thing, a few scenes from now, will transform her life.

When traffic slows she stops again, looks again at the blood on her hand, then looks over at the flower vendor—who is wiping blood from his own hands. She looks once more at the blood on her hand, bringing it closer to her face, almost as if to try to smell the blood, or taste it. Although she already has much "blood on her hands," this lies outside the confines of her mission, and foreshadows both the journey and the outcome of her increasing participation in the human world. The manner in which the blood-stained rose is given to her as a gift from a human who's a stranger to her, and handed to her by another human stranger (the blood is likely his own), extends an invitation to her to join the human race. This first contact she has with human males outside the grisly predator-victim cycle that dominated the first act portends the encounters with men that await her, for better and worse: the kindness of a stranger on one hand, and violence, signified by blood, on the other.

A news bulletin on the radio recounts a Chemistry lecturer at Edinburgh University who washed up on the beach near Arbroath, and his missing wife and 18-month-old son:

> The alarm was raised when he failed to turn up for work this morning. His car was found at the nearby Deer Park Golf Club. His wife, 32-year-old Alison McClelland, and 18-month-old son are believed to have been with him. A police and coast guard search involving a helicopter has been halted due to fog.[1]

Throughout the broadcast Laura sits very still; we see her chest rise and fall beneath her fur coat. When the report ends there is an extended shot of her, eyes moving, reacting.

As she drives through town once again the surprising shift is that she now looks only at women, and the music differs from the earlier "hunt" theme. Next, crowds of both women and men spill forward all around her, as if demanding that she notice them for what they are: not targets or fodder, but human beings. Although immediately following this we see her next victim riding shotgun in the van, Laura herself is distracted. A scattering of reflected lights on the window across her face seem to underscore this, as do the words of the man alongside her (the Nervous Man, played by actor Scott Dymond) who is struck by something about her—"Your eyes," he says, in awe, and repeats it as if he can't explain what he's feeling. But on the path that leads to her house, he looks warily behind him. He's the first of her victims to acknowledge that the decrepit facade and creepy front yard (fine horror tropes) and the sketchiness of their encounter do not bode well.

Yet he follows her through the door. This is another moment that draws laughs from the audience because he's ignoring the signs. His hesitation merges with her affect in the preceding scenes to signal, once again, the beginnings of a change in her. The fact that her attention wasn't on this seduction may in fact be the reason she didn't get the usual eager results from her mark—something is shifting inside her. Writer Kevin Jagernauth commented to Glazer on the film's minimum of dialogue, "the dialogue that is there, tends to be secondary to the sound design and score." He asked the director if he cut down the dialogue during the writing process:

> A lot of that dialogue was there really for people to read.... Once we understood that the way to make this film was to put Scarlett in disguise and drop her into the world ... it was very easy to throw out three pages of dialogue because, her with a guy she had just picked up and who doesn't even know he's being filmed, that dialogue is going to depart from anything you can think of.[2]

The Nervous Man (Scott Dymond), who was dazed by Laura's beauty and her eyes, is having second thoughts as he approaches her decrepit house. The sight of it— and likely a reappraisal of this unnerving scenario—cause him to look warily behind him (hence the moniker). Unlike the eager Footballer he requires a bit of coaxing from Laura. Art Director: Emer O'Sullivan (courtesy StudioCanal and Film-Nation).

The Nervous Man steps through the doorway into blackness as if the physical interior of the house doesn't even exist. We don't need to see what befalls him; his impending ordeal from start to finish has already been revealed. A cut instead to a close-up of Laura in the aftermath, applying her red lipstick, points again to her detachment, but more chillingly because this is the first time we've seen her lure a victim since we witnessed the grisly details of their fate. The imagery of emptied skin and churning gore makes this cut to her makeup ritual especially gruesome.

With this close-up of her on a black background we assume she's still in the black space, but it's a match cut of locales as we pull back to black bricks below, indicating some other black space. Bad stands at her left, then moves behind her, then to her right, and finally he stands before her. There's a face-to-face close-up, an extra-close-up of their features, and another as they stare fixedly into each other's eyes. Is what he sees in the black pools of her pupils something deep within her, and if so, what does it mean? We hold here for a few seconds before he abruptly turns and leaves.

This is the sole shot in the film in which the two alien colleagues share a frame. There's no speaking but their riveting eye contact strongly suggests communication, and it comes on the heels of the awe of her last victim ("Your eyes"). Whether this is communication and whether or not it is reciprocal is worth pondering, as we receive a POV shot from him but not her, as if he is reading *her* mind but not the reverse. Or, informing an ongoing motif that she is objectified—in fact, nothing more than a tool—he appears to scan information from her eyes the way one would download data from a computer. Editor Watts says they called this "the inspection scene." Two notions are fueled here: an alien-android comparison (as if she were a machine that could malfunction or go astray, which indeed she does) and the question of her personal agency, a related theme that's at the very core of the film.

From this moment forward, and for the rest of the film, an escalating digression in Laura's path is masterfully reflected in the visuals, the music, the subtle events, and above all, in Johansson's finely calibrated acting. She is next seen strolling down a city street in broad daylight. The sequence is so refreshing because it's a first. She has opted to leave the van, with its inextricable link to her brutal mission—a taxi to torture and death. In separating from it she separates herself, if only briefly, not just from the mission but from her persona; it's like shedding a uniform at the end of a workday. Apart from its grim connotations the van's two tons of metal protect her from the human world—but also prevent her from fully experiencing it.

The simple human pleasures of a carefree jaunt and a sense of freedom and independence move with her like an aura, but it's abruptly punctured when she suddenly—a real jolt—stumbles and falls face-down on the pavement. Swiftly several people gather round and two men help her up onto her feet—"Are you okay?"—but she doesn't reply, or even acknowledge them. She's stunned by this trauma, an unintended and surely unexpected consequence of her merely dipping her toes into the shallow end of the pool of human endeavor, of going AWOL. As she steadies herself and continues to walk, the pedestrians around her gaze at her in concern, but also perhaps in dismay—there's no appreciation from her, no thank you.

She moves on as though ignoring what's happened, but her affect and her gait are less steady than before as she stares straight ahead of her. The before/after resembles the eager child getting on a bike for the first time and then experiencing the shock, and humiliation, of falling to the ground. She's momentarily deterred, but she'll be getting back on that bike before long.

Here on the sidewalk her openness and courage to try on the human experience, followed by the consequences (the precarious trip and fall on the pavement could be read as an observation that human living is precarious, or as a punishment for overstepping her bounds), foreshadow what's to come as she becomes increasingly curious, adventurous, open, and—by some human standards—reckless. Along her journey there's a tension between the "punishment" reading that the repercussions should serve as caution to her (we fear for her) and our desire for her to have the human experience she is beginning to long for—regardless of the consequences. She had previously and with obvious curiosity (she watched intently) witnessed human compassion in the rescue attempts by the Swimmer on the beach, but on the sidewalk it is she who is the beneficiary of the kindness of strangers, and it resonates deeply as a display of what the film continually posits as a defining human trait: empathy. Daniel Landin recalls:

> We were looking for something that felt cinematic and powerful, but we were also looking for the truth of that transition. And actually the pull between these two ambitions opened up a very beautiful space.... I loved the idea of these people coming to help her. You just think, this extreme predator is in the midst of these things that she has no regard for but they're prepared to lend a hand.... I think it's a really beautiful falling into space, where you allow almost nothing to mean everything.[3]

That the two people who help her up are men ruptures her dynamic with human males, and is a kind of bridge between the film's first half and its second.

Laura as a pedestrian—a fitting double entendre as she strives to engage in a mundane human activity—continues her excursion around town. A long shot of a man with a woman who's sitting on the sidewalk outside a church—perhaps giving her money or just talking with her—further advances the themes of this sequence. A close-up of a young woman standing on the sidewalk as she gazes into a mirror, like a little girl secretly trying on her mother's makeup, echoes images of Laura applying lipstick that we associate both with her deadly allure and with her curious, innocent flirtation with being a human female. Glazer noted:

> If you point your camera at a skip, or a bus, or two people having a cup of tea at a table outside a café, they're all equally relevant to your story. Everything's in play, everything's right, everything's correct, it's the world you're telling the story in. So you're judging everything and then when you pre-cast actors … you've got to match that performance to the truth of the world as it is, so then you have this fantastic barometer for everything…. You have to find unity of all those ingredients … a couple of people have said to me who's cast and who's not cast, and let's leave it at that, that's exactly where you want it to be, because it means the unity of those ingredients is in check.[4]

Her stroll ends but the street sequence continues while she drives, as the camera finds her looking at women and men, families, all of humanity. The foreboding strings are absent here in favor of softer, almost wistful music, and the scene culminates in a montage that's a myriad of faces. This kaleidoscope of humanity is then superimposed on her own face. (See photograph in Chapter 18.) After her venture out into the city, her fall on the pavement, her rescue, and this shot, it is significant that we see no further victims die in Laura's ritual.

5
Lonely

Now it's night, and as she drives on a seemingly deserted street a young male crosses in front of her, approaches her window and begins to speak to her. We think he's a candidate, but the absence of the capture theme at this moment is a cue that this is not what we expect, that it's some kind of detour. Suddenly a group of male teens crowd the van and begin to shake it; one jumps on the hood, another grabs onto the slightly open window as if he could force it downward and get inside. The gang of men as an allusion to a sexual assault foreshadows her fate in the forest, but for now her van is her protection. She slams on the gas and screeches off.

Orbs of white light recur in night scenes throughout the film—headlights, streetlights, the moon or stars in the night sky. It's a motif launched in the opening spacecraft sequence that is carried ubiquitously in her eyes, their significance, and their power. These white images out in the world, whether luminous or diffuse or even ghostly, follow her the way the moon follows us when we drive at night, a guiding light. These lights could be her heart—or surveillance, and convey that she's continuously watched by an overseer.

A man in a hoodie is walking down the street minding his own business. The hooded sweatshirt isn't just a shield against the cold Scotland night, it's protecting him from the world.

She stops the van and rolls down the window. "Excuse me, I'm a bit lost," she begins, and learning he's on his way to the supermarket, asks, "Is it on the way? I could drop you off if you like. Yeah?"

The way he huddles inside his hoodie conveys that there's something he's hiding from her. It's obvious and it's the first thing we notice. Is he avoiding contact because he's on a dark street at night up to no good? Moments after he hesitantly slips into the passenger seat, we see that what he's hiding is his face. Referred to as Lonely, Adam Pearson is another of the few pre-cast actors in the film. His appearance, like the candid moments on the streets of

Glasgow, isn't faked or altered. Laura's failure to react to the stranger's condition as most of his human peers would is striking and piques our curiosity.

She launches a conversation:

> You're quiet. So why do you shop at night?
> People wind me up.
> How?
> They're ignorant.

After accosting him on the street she further invades his privacy, almost comically: "What about your friends? You don't have any friends? You don't have a girlfriend? You've never had a girlfriend?"

At the outset this encounter resembles the previous ones—the loner on the street, the "interview" to gather information—but it quickly veers into uncharted waters. Her invasive questions might be construed as a cunning tool because she knows he's vulnerable, and in fact he is reluctant—a novel challenge that requires a different strategy. That it's a ploy would be an evident reading if it weren't for the previous sequence, which compels us to realize a shift within her—and will explain the change in her behavior for the rest of this sequence—beginning with the deeply personal questions she poses. There's a tension created by not precisely knowing her motivation; is it a ploy or possibly just curiosity regarding a new situation, a new challenge? Mica Levi said, "It felt to me like she was a detective, like she was figuring something out. She's on the hunt."[1] Above all, it is more evidence of her increasing desire for a human experience.

> So you've never thought about it then. When was the last time you touched someone?
> Do you want to look at me? I noticed you looking at me before.
> I have to get back.
> Let me see your hands.

He holds them out and they are small and soft-looking in the dark space between them.

> You have very nice hands ... you have beautiful hands.

She brings them close to touch her face. Her prior scenes with men never involved touching and are scrupulously devoid of intimacy. The tension—between the suspicion that she is playing him to keep him from fleeing the van, and the possibility that she craves an experience of physical intimacy with him—is never greater than at this moment. He takes off his hood, fully revealing his head and features, running his hands through his matted hair. When he lowers the hood, it conveys that he is beginning to trust her. When first in the passenger seat Lonely nervously stares straight ahead of him, answering her questions tersely, or with silence; by the time the camera captures them in a two-shot from behind, he is in profile, as is she, in a shared and equal moment of human connection. After she touches his fingertips to her cheek,

How did that feel?
Cool.
Do you want to do that again? Do you want to touch my neck? Your hands are very soft.

> Casting director Kahleen Crawford said:
>
> We spent some time with Adam talking to him about the scene and what the character might talk about with Scarlett's character—how she might lure him, what would grab his attention and that sort of thing. He gave us some very honest answers and a lot of that is in the film. I think it works so well because you don't know where the scene is going to go or what's going to happen in it, and I think actually some of the energy comes from the fact that it's so real. It says so much about her that she can't really see his difference.[2]

A poignant moment in the 2017 film *The Shape of Water* plays a similar note regarding a human relationship with an alien, only the dynamic is reversed: In referring to her non-human lover, Alisa (Sally Hawkins) says, "He doesn't know what I lack or how I am incomplete. He sees me for what I am."[3]

Laura and Lonely are both inexperienced, and each of them is the outsider. She soon realizes, as does the audience, that she can give them both their first sensual experience. To reflect all that's different for her about this encounter, the shot itself is a departure from any previous one. Inside the van, the low-key lighting, angles, and mise en scène transform this death taxi into a far different and even nostalgic cinematic trope: an old Ford or Chevy enfolding the tentative passions of two inexperienced but curious teenagers, which in a sense they both are. She softly asks him, *Do you want to do that again?*, but as she does so the three foreboding notes of the capture theme, and the ominous one-two beat, rear up. These harbingers of his destiny in the black space are juxtaposed with her sweet invitation to come home with her, and tortuously combine with a close-up of the soft fingers of his left hand pinching the skin on his right, as if to say to himself, *This can't be real*. His instincts are right. If we thought moments ago that his fate, because of her tenderness toward him and a change within her, would be different, the score now suggests otherwise.

At her house the contrasts between this and her earlier encounters continue. Inside the front door we see the details of the actual interior of the house where before we saw only blackness—the walls of the decrepit hall, the stairs—conveying a human habitat, a history. The black space tracking shots from behind are drenched in longing, eroticism, and dread, and the shifting proportion of these elements depends upon the individual scene. Here, because of his nature and her intimacy with him, the dread is tantamount to the longing—and pretty much eclipses the eroticism.

Once the house interior morphs into the black space, there is, for the first time, the briefest glimpse of Laura's actual alien body—dark, glistening, reflected in the glossy surface beneath. There's no indication that Lonely sees it; it's a cinematic cue to her identity for the audience, the only one thus far. We could say the only *explicit* indication, but it is neither explicit nor certain, because the figure we see could be someone other than Laura, another alien, for example, or something imaginary. Next, unlike previous scenarios, Laura faces him as she walks backward, and she isn't a forbidding void away from him as she typically is; instead she stands right in front of him in a proximity we can grasp. "Cold," he says, and she replies, "I won't let that stop us." He looks back warily; he is attuned to what the others were not, to the utter unreality of the events. The profound challenges Lonely would have to overcome to survive in society would grant him this special sense. She says to him, "Come to me."

As she continues walking backward Laura takes off her bra. In a compelling full-shot they stand facing each other in profile, and he is the only victim to whom she has shown her naked body. This fact, the unique man that he is, the way she responds to him, and the recent dramatic changes in her comprise the perfect storm—but for what outcome?

> *Dreaming*, he says, as they stand facing each other. And then repeats it ... *dreaming*.
> *Yes*, she tells him. *We are.*

Not only has she never before spoken in the black space, but her use of the word *we* both asserts her new affinity for human experience and again puts the two of them in a mutual adventure; she too is dreaming, because her experience on Earth is like a dream. At this moment there is another brief medium shot of her alien body which dissolves into a close-up of her human profile, implying that this black alien may indeed be her, and underscoring the duality of her reality and her fantasy. Yet this emerging human persona may for her be more real or more truthful than what she has ever before experienced. We don't know her past. On Earth she is a tool for a space mission, without agency. In *Edge of Tomorrow* Tom Cruise delivers the existential entreaty to Emily Blunt, "I'm not a soldier," and she replies, "Of course you're not, you're a weapon."[4]

But despite all that has been different and surprising about this encounter, Lonely sinks into the black water. We cut directly to a frontal shot of Laura quickly descending the staircase until she stops suddenly, at the bottom, to gaze into a mirror on the landing. The small round mirror on the wall in front of her grabs her attention, as if reminding her of something she's forgotten to do (look in it?).

This attenuated and hypnotic shot is punctured by the sudden buzzing of a fly; she turns from the mirror to look at it, trapped inside the window of a door. From the trapped fly there is a final close-up of Laura's eye, then an abrupt cut to the front door of the house *as she releases Lonely out into the open.*

We ponder what it is she sees, feels, and experiences gazing into the mirror that leads her to this radical action. Until now no one has ever, as the saying goes, come out alive. The transformation in her that threads through this second act of the movie, lushly depicted on her stroll through the streets of Glasgow, is dramatized in her encounter with Lonely and reaches a crescendo as she engages the mirror on the landing—conjuring the idea that it's not the alien world she confronts in the looking glass, but herself. This mysterious, metaphysical encounter is coupled

Laura is intimate with Lonely in several ways that differ from all of her previous encounters with men. Inside the van she touches him, and invites him to touch her. Nevertheless she brings him home and allows him to sink into the blackness—though soon after, she has a change of heart and releases him (courtesy StudioCanal, A24, and FilmNation).

with its aesthetic opposite—the mundane sound and image of an insect struggling to escape—in a one-two punch that leads to the metaphor for her new life: the bursting open of the front door.

There's a fine line between Laura imitating a human and Laura exhibiting human traits, but she crosses it when she frees Lonely. It hasn't been that long since she ignored the wailing infant on the beach and left it for dead. Occurring approximately half-way through the film this surprising event epitomizes the mid-narrative game changer in a screenplay, the action after which the protagonist cannot go back—even if she wanted to. The shift within her has compelled her to sabotage her mission and incur whatever consequences that may involve, for she appears to be no longer interested in—and perhaps no longer capable of—carrying out the mission.

Fittingly, it is just before sunrise. Laura rushes from the front door to the van. We know her usual blank look, her dead, automaton eyes while scanning the streets for prey, but now her eyes are kinetic; she is anxious, agitated, breathing heavily, and in contrast to her usual cruising, driving fast. Her demeanor says she is no longer an automaton—she is emotionally engaged. She is alive. She is likely in serious trouble, and possibly serious jeopardy. But this humanesque adrenalin rush is attributable to something more as well: the exhilaration of freedom.

We see Lonely run naked through a field as dawn is breaking. His youthful body lends him a childlike way of running, and there's a sweetness to it, and an innocence, which in this bucolic setting invokes a primordial innocence, or the grace of humans before the fall. These earliest humans, and this man, and Laura as a newly-born human all share something pure and sacred. It's an idyllic tableau that's fraught with jeopardy on many levels. If he were to be caught naked out in the open he'd likely be hauled away by authorities, or worse, discovered by someone cruel (*They wind me up. They are ignorant.*)—and what humiliation and misery would befall him?

Shots of Bad riding his motorcycle convey instant menace. If we find him more frightening than Laura—although both are engaged in abduction, torture, and murder—it's worth examining as perceptions and presumptions of gender, but it may go mainly to the complexity of Johansson's performance. Gradually we begin to see the cracks in her armor and entertain the possibility that she's not as she seemed, or has changed. In contrast Bad appears stalwart; there's never an indication he could avoid or subvert the mission. And beyond performance and character actions, his attire (created by costume designer Steven Noble) has much to contribute. The image Bad cuts in his black leather jacket conjures an unsettling marriage of two of culture's favorite menaces—creatures from outer space and Hell's Angels. While the former captures our fascination because it's humanoid but not human, the other beckons to the frustrated renegade in us all. The conflating of bikers and aliens has a precursor in Rod Serling's *The Twilight Zone* episode titled "Black Leather Jackets" (1964), where a trio of strangers who frighten the residents of a small town have traveled from a place a bit further off than the interstate.[5] The motorcycle helmet donned by Bad and his comrades evokes another supernatural creature, the giant insect or *The Fly*, amplifying the creepiness of the many shots of him on the highway and adding a touch of visual irony: He's an alien whose disguise as a human biker causes him to resemble a sci-fi monster.

There is tense intercutting here between Laura escaping in the van and Bad speeding down the highway: Which one of them, Laura or Lonely, is he chasing? Just as Lonely is about to cross a backyard fence to what is hopefully a safe harbor, the foreboding music rises up—and Bad intercepts him. It's a surprise, even a shock, and the abrupt termination of Lonely's flight to safety is curiously made more brutal by the fact that we don't witness the moment of capture, or the assault itself. What we see next is somehow worse than that: Bad later shoving Lonely's naked, inert body into the trunk of a car.

The filmmakers' decision to deprive us of this violent closure onscreen has the effect of a final insult to the character of Lonely, who has already suffered far too much. Saddest of all for us, Bad has also undone the good that Laura did in releasing Lonely. As Bad shuts the trunk of the car, a neighbor watches him from her second story window across the street. Significantly, she is the only person in the film to directly witness the aliens' foul play. The window she opens punctures the wall that's existed between the alien activities and the human world—the very wall Laura has also just broken through in releasing her victim and running away in the van.

Driving along Laura no longer has the look of the automaton that characterizes her search for victims, or her dull affect following their deaths. Nor do we see her distinctive and intent black look—her assassin's look. She's anxious and distressed, as well as dazed or even stunned by what she has just done and what she is now doing. Conspicuously absent from this van excursion are shots of potential marks on the street because her mission, by her choice, is over. In contrast she's unaware of anything at all outside the van, and her lack of destination is also palpable: this is about flight. In her aspect and demeanor, her fear is inseparable from exhilaration.

6
Quiet

Laura travels well outside of the city. There's a shot of a cove with green hills in the background, and gentle ocean waves rolling onto the beach. A swirl of fog curls in and licks the shore, a moment so dreamlike it pushes the setting from the tranquil to the mystical. (See photograph in Chapter 17.) This may visually echo the "death beach" of the earlier scene, but contrasting the jagged cliffs, brooding greys, and dangerous ocean of the former setting with a beach that offers pastel tranquility signals a break with her past. If the first beach was a monster devouring anyone who dare approach, this swirl of mist is an archangel of redemption, sweeping up the souls lost on the first beach and restoring the land to restfulness.

The blanket of fog that Laura drives into is like the mist on the beach come to enfold her: she too can be redeemed. Visibility for driving is now close to zero, and it's unclear whether the van has run out of gas or she stops because there's a wall of white covering the windshield. All along she was adhering to a script that confined her but also protected her; now there's no script at all, and the fog awaits like a blank page. The radical departures of the film's second half are expressed across a range of cinematic elements. The mist and fog that introduce this chapter channel her state of mind as well as her change in geography; this phase is a mystery to her. The appearance of the rural environs draws on a science fiction trope in countless films and stories from *Fahrenheit 451* to the final scene of *Minority Report*: the representation of nature or the countryside as the habitat of goodness, versus the city as the petri dish of the pernicious. Like the script she once followed, the van protected her but also insulated and limited her. As a symbol, it's an elegant paradox: Without two tons of metal surrounding her she is more vulnerable than she's ever been, but she is also a free agent—and possibly freer than she's ever been, even on her home planet. In this fog she may, in a sense, be reborn.

Two earlier events that anticipate her eventual abandonment of the van are leaving it behind in order to pursue Andrew outside the club, when the swarm of young women overwhelmed her, and the crowd of teenage boys shaking the van. Each portends a time when it is no longer there to protect her and she must fend for herself. In abandoning the mission and then the van, she forfeits the power and independence afforded by both that were actually only an illusion of power and independence. She exchanges them for the agency of independence and the unknown, its unlimited potential, and its vulnerability.

Once Laura leaves the van on the road we see her almost exclusively on foot—no better metaphor for a path into the unknown, placing one foot before the other in the fog. Signifying that the mission and her life within it are over, the van is absent from the rest of the film. The victim males on the streets are also absent, and the next two times she attracts a man—for good, and then for ill—the willful femme fatale lure that defined her is gone. The friendly and flirtatious dialogue she delivered so proficiently, a language perfected on her voyage to Earth, is no longer needed; from now until the end of the film, Laura says only two words. She's abandoned the communication that was, for her, duplicitous. Her body is never again depicted as a tool of seduction. And the ominous music, beginning with the three haunting notes, is not heard again until it is used as a disturbing inversion of its former meaning—during the sequence in which she is captured.

Laura opens the door of her van and steps out onto the road. Taking the extended time to show us Laura's journey in front of the mirror, Glazer takes another nearly three minutes—also without music, as in the mirror sequence—to track the first moments of her new life. Heading out in front of the van, she moves quickly down the road and disappears into the fog. Shots of Laura standing on the road are intercut with what she sees as she slowly looks all around her, her shoes crunching on the road with each turn of her body: the white line on the highway, then the beach, then the road again. In these close-ups, her face, wide-eyed, intent, blinking only occasionally, is a mirror of her unknown emotion—perhaps wonderment, fear, bewilderment, awe. The sudden loud chirping of a bird causes Laura to break from what surrounds her to look up. Her recognition of the wild creature flying above introduces her engagement with her brand new environment.

From the focus on Laura's face we cut to a panoramic shot of the entire area, and it fills the screen—sky, mountains, and sea in the background, the road cutting across the landscape of open space. Slowly we see Laura, from a great distance, her sweater a pink dot, emerging out of the fog at the left side of the frame, walking along the road. She made a decision; she chose a direction and began to walk. Landin's vista, worthy of John Ford, is more than a pleasure to behold; it is a stunning contrast to the claustrophobia of Laura's old life: the airless black space and the inside of her van. Nothing before this shot so fully expresses her freedom in relation to the constraints of her old life. The expanse of air, water, and land is a world now at her feet, and we can feel her, as she walks across the screen, breathing it in.

We cut for a brief moment to Bad gazing in the same wall mirror that Laura looked into earlier. Again, what is seen is a mystery that we can only interpret through the actions he and she take immediately afterward. It appears as though he now knows that she has jumped ship. Does the alien look into the mirror, or does it look into the alien? In the film *A Scanner Darkly*, one of many of Philip K. Dick's classic interrogations of reality and what it means to be human, Bob Arctor (Keanu Reeves) asks, "What does the scanner see? Into the head? Into the heart?"[1]

Next Laura's seated at a table in a restaurant, and looks around at the other customers—couples, a family with children, everyday people, like the one back in Glasgow that we saw through her eyes. As the scene unfolds it's a confirmation of Laura's new status: She behaves, even if tentatively, as one of the humans who surround her. She has crossed over from the performance of human behavior that she learned for her mission to engaging in the most fundamental human activity, the one necessary for survival: eating. The combination of Laura's soft hair, her candy-pink sweater, and the creamy skin of her face, neck, and cleavage as she slowly lifts the forkful of black forest cake to her red lips visually unifies her with the experience she's about to have, as if everything has brought her to this moment, and it's a delicious moment of anticipation—we want her to have this experience. The fact that she gags on the food and spits it out—and the other diners notice, identifying her on the spot as an oddity—is a reminder of what's really under her skin, and foreshadows the coming experiences. Although the scene opens with an assertion that she can be human, so encouraging to the audience, so thrilling, it closes with a reminder of what she's up against.

A high-angle shot of Laura, back on the deserted road on foot, reasserts her status as an adventurer, a brave wanderer. It puts the cake defeat behind her, but the implications of what just occurred linger in our minds like the mist hovering above the road.

On the road she approaches a corner where a man stands leaning back against a railing, across from a bus stop, arms folded in front of him. The color of her sweater pops in this foggy green landscape (along with the armor of the van, she has shed her fur coat) and the man is directly in her path, as if waiting for her. When she walks right past him he calls out to her, "The bus will be along in a minute." His line is not spoken as a simple statement of fact; it's an invitation. There's something comforting about his assumption that she has a specific destination in mind; because she doesn't, it's an assumption of her readiness, making it not just an invitation to ride a bus, or ride a bus with him, but an invitation to join the human race. She is Dorothy on the yellow brick road, encountering strangers—the Scarecrow, the Lion, the

Laura's verdant surroundings, wet with rain and full of life, stand in stark contrast to the death-driven mission she has left behind. In her bright pink sweater Glazer likens her to an "exotic insect" amidst these pastoral surroundings, but with the help of Quiet (Michael Moreland, foreground) she will begin the curious and pleasurable process of fitting in (courtesy StudioCanal and FilmNation).

Tin Man—whose interactions with her, whether friendly or hostile or neutral, validate her journey and reward her for taking it, for her courage. We can somehow put aside our thoughts of what she's done before as if it's a past life, and become involved in, and fascinated by, this reincarnation of her. There is something fairy-tale romantic in this sequence: that she is a vision in pink coming down the road; that in this high shot as she approaches the man there's really nowhere for her to go but right to him; and the way he stands there watching her slowly come toward him, as if he's been waiting for her all his life.

Laura is silent, but she does accept this invitation—cautiously. She doesn't stand next to him on the corner where he's waiting; instead she sits at the bus stop under an enclosure. Framed within it on all sides she has sought its protection. Like the Swimmer who wandered off to Scotland "because it's nowhere," now it's Laura who's the runaway at the bus station, alone and available to predators like the one she once was.

But how differently she behaves with men when they are not her targets, now that she's abandoned her mission. She is vulnerable and knows it, and acts it. In her post-predator phase there is nothing flirtatious about her. She may be a bit dazed, or vigilant, or just allowing the experience—the change all around her and its unfamiliarity—to sink in.

How much depth, breadth, and range Johansson mines from her character's very limited allowance of emotional response is a testament to her acting prowess that is, as the film goes on, increasingly stunning. It's all in her face—her vulnerability, cautiousness, fear, and bravery—inasmuch as bravery isn't the absence of fear, but the willingness to act in spite of it. She actually has a range of "blank" expressions, what psychiatry calls a dull affect. But now as she rides the bus her face is not any kind of blank; it is fearful, maybe even frozen with fear. It is compatible with the assumption by the bus driver (played by Gerry Goodfellow) that she's chilled to the bone in this cold weather, and she'll "catch her death out there without a coat or hat."

She neither responds to the driver's concern nor acknowledges that he's spoken to her. Her silence with him, and with the man on the road, is in bold contrast with the glib interaction she had with every one of her targets. It's as if the language she learned, intended as part of her programming and specifically to serve the mission, has been forgotten, or no longer applies, or she simply cannot access it outside the parameters of the mission's demands. Or perhaps she is just terrified of these male strangers, as if they could somehow know what she has done.

With the pastoral scenery passing in the window next to her, she is pulled deeper into this foreign place, her new and alien environment. Her anxiety is palpable yet marks her independence and adventurousness—she has jumped on a bus to nowhere. But to further complicate things, it's her first time in a vehicle without being at the wheel—she's not in control. Significantly, she has put her fate in the hands of a stranger, and it's a fitting prologue to the event that follows.

The man from the bus stop, known as the Quiet Man (played by Michael Moreland) moves to the seat behind her to her right. In Laura's face and demeanor, and in her failure to respond to the bus driver's concern, she appears comatose—prompting Quiet to say to her, "Are you okay?" She doesn't reply, and several seconds pass. He asks, "Need any help?" and after another long pause she finally says, "Yes."

It's the first of only two words she utters after leaving her mission, her only words anywhere in the film that are not constructed, and calculated, to lure victims. These words are her only language in the film that's truly authentic to her, that isn't a performance within a performance. Once she says *yes*, the camera is on Moreland for several seconds as he comes to realize that he's taken something on, and doesn't know what that is—and we know he has no idea. But the next several scenes are driven by decisions he makes as he takes charge, benevolently, over Laura's new world.

In the next shot Laura, who has always had men follow her, follows Quiet down a street through a residential neighborhood. At a small market he opens a carton of eggs and checks for cracked ones, a wonderfully mundane detail. Laura tentatively explores the aisles, looking all around her, studying the unfamiliar setting and its unfamiliar goods. Wearing his black jacket she is reduced in both stature and presence inside a coat that's far too big for her, its sleeves extending past her hands, and her vulnerability is captured again— she looks childlike, the opposite of the femme fatale running the show inside the black space. The jacket, lent to shield her from the elements the bus driver warned about, is poignant; once the predator, she is now the protected.

Out on the rainy street he carries a bag of groceries and she follows behind him. She's as comfortable in the downpour as she was in the cold,

In the fog, in the restaurant, and in the two long shots of Laura on the road, she is taking care of business. But here on the bus we see the once-loquacious Laura at a loss for words, looking a little frozen. Whatever alien emotions Laura is feeling, Johansson, within the limited range available to her, exquisitely captures. Finally she turns to face Quiet, accepting his offer of help (courtesy StudioCanal and FilmNation).

neither reacting to the rain nor trying to shield herself from it. The dark coat, unlike her deep pink sweater, now blends her into her earthy surroundings.

In the hallway of Quiet's house, Laura is tentative and apprehensive. That she conspicuously avoids looking in the mirror as she passes it seems to connect with her decision to break with her past, and also fuels an interpretation that a mirror in this film is more than just a mirror. Later, in the living room, Quiet has brought her indisputably, and cozily, into his world. The two of them sit on the sofa eating a dinner he has prepared on TV trays. The homey tradition of eggs and baked beans on toast combined with the slapstick of Welsh comedian Tommy Cooper on the television is about as classic a tableau as you could create in which to insert an alien for comic effect, and it's sweet. We know she's unable to eat the food, but the antics on the screen, which she studies with great focus and concentration, give us a side of her we're seeing for the first time. The opposite of her passive demeanor, it's a look of active engagement; she's trying to figure out what she's seeing and what it means. The laughter from the TV audience, and from Quiet, is the counterpoint that makes the seriousness of her attention all the more touching. She seems intent upon learning something new (and maybe humor itself is a new concept for her). Above all, she appears profoundly curious. Writer Sady Doyle said:

> It's at this point that she becomes an entirely different creature, less predatory *Alien* than stranded *E.T.* Her bafflement as she attempts to eat human food, or watch television, isn't cute, precisely ... but it's hard not to sympathize with her newfound powerlessness and her total incomprehension of the world around her.[2]

Like Superman, who was "disguised as Clark Kent, the mild-mannered reporter for a great metropolitan newspaper,"[3] Quiet is a secret hero—the lender of a warm coat, the cook and server of a nutritious meal, the rescuer of a frightened-looking young woman on the bus. After dinner we move to his kitchen, a tidy room with a warm glow, a habitat of self-esteem and self-care. Low-key lighting enhances its coziness—we'd like to be sitting there, too, and it invites us to imagine what this experience must be like for Laura. On the counter are artifacts of attentiveness that go beyond the necessary— a wooden knife block, cups hanging from a cup tree, a breadbox. They are the small things on which domesticity is built, the defenders against chaos that keep civilization from flying apart in some kind of second Big Bang. They are emblems of a life that is organized and respected, if not standard issue for a bachelor living alone. The truth is that Quiet is more than quiet; he has a melancholic air about him. Perhaps a woman once lived here. Perhaps not so long ago. His melancholic aura may be the climate of a broken heart, and this possibility only endears us more.

The prospect of a lost love rises to the surface as Quiet begins his dishwashing ritual by turning on the radio and Deacon Blue's *Real Gone Kid* begins playing softly in the background. The song itself is melancholic, the memory of a gone woman and the aftermath of her departure from the singer's life.[4] Even if there is no broken heart for Quiet, the comforts of his life, and his nurturing gentleness, seem to be awaiting a partner to share them, and for now that partner is Laura. As he does the washing up she sits in the opposite corner of the room and watches him moving his leg in time to the music. The corner feels like a protected niche for her, a place he's chosen, or that she has chosen, for her own sense of safety. Because she is so still and

Glazer and his team used the term "charting her drift" to describe Laura's journey, which is not so much plotted as it is felt—by her, and in turn by the audience. In this scene in Quiet's kitchen she hears the music on the radio, sees Quiet tap his foot to the rhythm, and begins tapping her fingers on the table. The tune is Glasgow's Deacon Blue singing "Real Gone Kid" (courtesy StudioCanal and FilmNation).

doesn't speak or interact with her surroundings, in this shot she seems almost doll-like. The bittersweetness of Deacon Blue's voice and of the song itself resonate deeply here. To take this riff a step further, listen to the song *Deacon Blues* by Steely Dan, another poignant bachelor anthem.[5] The sweetness in the song both builds on the intimacy of the sofa scene and paints this environment as a safe harbor for her, while the bitterness alludes to the undercurrent of the film that houses the inevitable outcome of her human experience. But for the moment the former prevails, and there is no sweeter or more defining moment anywhere in the film than the one in which Laura *begins to tap her fingers to the music*. This still figure comes to life, the alien Laura is becoming human, and it is music—what more quintessentially human treasure?—that carries her across.

In his small bedroom she stands with her back and hands against the wall, like the corner in the kitchen. The cautious air of the rescued animal is still present, but it has lost some of its edge and almost feels obligatory: there is no going back after the tapping of her fingers. Laura isn't the same as she was a day ago, or even an hour ago. She watches Quiet set a cup of tea on the bed stand and retrieve a space heater from the closet—warmth and more warmth. We hear his *"g'night"* as he closes her door behind him. Amidst the comfort and the nighttime tranquility, the glowing red element inside the heater echoes the red beam of energy that came after the flowing gore of her victims' bodies back in the black space. It's a tiny but unwelcome reality check for an audience being gradually seduced into a romantic dream.

This swiftly transitions to a slow, lavish sequence where Laura examines her naked, human body in a full-length mirror. And as if in defiance of the red beam and its association with past mayhem, the red lighting that lushly infuses this next scene is about sensuality and passion. At the mirror, Laura turns her shoulders to various angles, moves her arms, and touches her body in different places, gently poking. This is a study, a figuring out of what this thing is and how it works, yet the scene is about more than curiosity. This body has functioned as part of her stock-in-trade in her mission of attracting men. But that mission is over, and now this body is, well, still with her—hers and hers alone. What men see when they see it, or what affect it has upon them, no longer matters; their gaze has been replaced by hers, this acknowledgement of ownership, her own interest, appreciation, and perhaps, delight. The bathing of Laura in this blush of light imbues the moment with a sense of fascination and wonder. The strings of Levi's score are soft and sweet. "She's gazing at the thing she's traveling in," commented Watts, "it's the beginning of a love affair."

The strings tense up and quiver as from this red reverie we cut to the menace of night, and a conference of four aliens with motorcycles and black leather jackets. It's a strategy session, the subject of which, we can surmise, is Laura's disappearance. Bad has always been more boss than partner, more controller than colleague. There is no verbal communication, no social time, no physical contact—nothing we can relate to that would reveal something about the two of them together, other than that they've traveled here to pursue the same goal. If we compare their business to a military or government mission, they're certainly not like any two soldiers or astronauts we've come across—there's a conspicuous absence of camaraderie (or an absence of conspicuous camaraderie) because we're bereft of knowledge here. We know nothing of their means of communication, which is why we're left to ponder the possibilities of mirrors, and that strange "inspection" scene, and whether these beings have sex—and if so, how. We don't even know if they have gender—under their skins, they may all be alike. But this much we can see: Laura and Bad may be of the same species, but Laura's not like Bad. Something is happening with her that began with her openness, her innate ability, and now she's an active partner in her own transformation.

The biker cohort promptly fans out in four directions. If Bad always seemed to oversee Laura, his brutal snatching of Lonely earns Bad his name, and now he's positioned as an all-out nemesis, the force that threatens her pursuit of a human experience or portends a worse outcome—her destruction. Or would he reprogram her, get her back on the mission? Which, given how far she has come on her personal journey, would be destruction of another kind.

But we hope he doesn't find her, and soon daylight finds her, with Quiet, walking on a trail through the woods. The long, high-angle shot that enfolds the couple in this setting, the falling rain, and the riders on horseback who pass by, align them with the beauty and majesty of nature, and shift the tone of this couple from an act of kindness to a blossoming romance. He picks her up and carries her across a large puddle, paying no attention to the muck soaking his shoes—someone falling in love doesn't care about his shoes. Allowing herself to be held, to be carried by him in a protective way, allowing herself to *trust* him—which began with her single word *yes* on the bus—is a huge next step. This trust resonates on many levels. It's a hallmark of her human experience, essential to love and an open heart. It is trust in a man, who is a stranger she is coming to know. But above all, it is trust in herself. It's not that she's yielding to him, it's that her trust has empowered her; trust in one's self equals agency, something she was lacking in a mission in which she was merely a tool.

In the background are the ruins of Tantallon Castle. Soon they've arrived on the roof of the castle, and as they're about to enter the tower from the top, a two-shot from inside the dark ruins frames them tightly within the entrance; she huddles against him as a fierce wind whips behind them. Peering down the spooky staircase they appear as two children in a fairy tale, having an adventure. But she's a child *soldier*, conscripted as a killing machine gone AWOL and in search of a human experience that here offers a bit of lost-childhood magic. He helps her down the narrow staircase as the daylight recedes in the background. A shaky camera angle is close on her boots as she cautiously descends. Every tentative step reminds us that nothing in her experience has prepared her for this; she is a newborn. Her hand is in his. The medieval castle in the background evoked the age of chivalry and courtship as she was carried across the stream, and now, helped down the stairs. The experience she is having is part of what she's been curious about from the moment she mimicked the women in the department store and applied that red lipstick.

The motif of her descending a staircase tracks her journey. Near the beginning, all business after appropriating the highway girl's outfit in the white space, Laura comes swiftly down the stairs of a building. Through the window behind her the flash of lights in the sky both establishes the launch of her mission and acknowledges that she is being left behind on Earth—*entrusted*—to do her job. She proceeds to do just that. The four victims we see may represent dozens or hundreds over a period of time, as there is no reference point for how much time has passed or how many victims there have been. Like the black space, time also is elastic. The next time that she comes down the stairs it's a prelude to her release of Lonely, the act that marks her defection from the mission. Here in the castle, emancipated from service by her own actions, it is Laura who follows a man into a space that, although dark, is without menace for either of them—reversing the film's history with stairs, with following, and with darkness. She led her victims to their deaths, but Quiet is leading her to herself. She could not be more vulnerable (as she is virtually trapped in this tower) yet, simultaneously, empowered. As she steps gingerly he guides her with his arms and says, "It's all right, it's all right," and then, "It's okay, it's okay. You did it. You did it." His words resonate as *you did what you needed to do. You left your prison. You made all this happen. You did it.*

The castle sequence is intercut with shots of the four aliens searching for her. They're a reminder that her sortie in the human world may be brief indeed, cut short just as it is beginning. From a shot of one of the bikers tearing down the night highway we cut to a close-up of Laura's face, in her own night. She's immersed in gauzy, rosy light, and the tender strings—an entirely new Levi theme entitled *Love*—intone a unique and what feels like an impossible marriage of romance and eeriness, the passion of an alien. This sequence follows up on her earlier gaze at her body in the full-length mirror; the visual and tactile invitation of her flesh paved the way for the experience that flesh is about to bring her, and the two scenes are suffused in the same rosy atmosphere. She closes her eyes and lifts her face and in these two subtle gestures offers her mouth for a kiss. Her face exudes a quiet ecstasy. We ask how a non-human can achieve this pinnacle of human emotion, and maybe the answer is that it's not human—it is supernatural. It is beatific. The expression on her face captures the essence of her journey, and the essence of the film.

6. Quiet

Laura has willed herself through determination, and at great risk, into this experience—and she convinces us in this scene with Quiet that she is getting something that she wanted before she even knew what it was. She gazes at him warmly and smiles just before he approaches and kisses her. She touches his hand and holds his cheeks. This two-shot of their faces, so close, is the opposite of the shots of her in the black space, and the lengthy remove between her and a man she's brought there that is a symbol of their mutual objectification. Laura has traveled a greater distance than just across the galaxy. They kiss.

She lies back on his bed, wearing the same camisole that lured victims deeper into the black space—another of those visual cues that underscores her reversal. A set, prop, or a costume also performs, and depending upon context, lighting, and affect, they can convey different, even opposing, meanings as they emerge and re-emerge. Wrapped around her push-up bra in the black space, the camisole was trashy lingerie fueling the fever dreams of her captives. When the stark void of the black space gives way to the dreamy darkness of Quiet's bedroom, and her recline causes her cleavage to melt away, the satiny pastel of the camisole whispers and shimmers like the gossamer gown of a bride on her wedding night.

Laura smiles. We have seen her smile previously only in the context of a lure, a performed smile. This is not that. It invites the question that has lingered in the air from the first scenes: What exactly is it that she feels, or is capable of feeling? Our initial question *what does an alien feel?* evolves into *what does an alien emulating a human woman feel?* In this moment in the bedroom her face answers that question, and reveals that the line between what she has been curious to feel or even longing to feel, and what she now is able to feel, has been crossed. In the tapping of her fingers she felt the music, and as she puts her hand around his neck and gazes at him, her face evokes ecstasy.

As he proceeds to make love to her, his physical struggle is evident. This romantic idyll and its dreamy musical score both end abruptly when Laura bolts upright, slides herself to the foot of the bed, grabs a lamp, and shines it between her legs. The moment is sudden, and comical, and sad. She appears stunned. A worried Quiet asks, "Y'all right?" Having avoided her own reflection in the hallway mirror earlier, it's here that she finally confronts it in the full-length mirror at the foot of the bed—staring into her eyes. As in the moment preceding her release of Lonely, there's a sense of either receiving a communication or facing the truth—whatever it was she was avoiding in the hallway.

7

Leaving

The bedroom scene's eerily sensual spell is broken with a cut to the forest that is jarring on many levels. Outdoor light shocks the eyes after the softly lit bedroom. Laura's aloneness out in the open speaks loudly on the heels of her tender coupling with Quiet, and her intimacy with him is extinguished by her fleeing of him. The warmth of their rosy nest gives way to brown and grey, wind, rain, and biting cold. The slow, subtle movements of their bodies are replaced with Laura's shoving of prickly, hazardous branches as she zigzags through the thicket of trees. All of this adds up to the most acute aspect of the spell-breaking: the likelihood that the door has just abruptly slammed shut on her brave and enchanting human experiment.

As Quiet's last words linger in the air unanswered, this sequence is the response. We don't see or hear anything that happens between her stunned gaze in the mirror and her flight outdoors. The omission of footsteps (literally as well as figuratively, for this is how writers refer to these interstitial beats) is a hallmark of the film's aesthetic, a feature that by this point in the story the audience will likely have adjusted to, or resigned itself to. Or not. A different film would be a profusion of information between Quiet's *Y'all right?* and Laura's flight: She runs out of the room, he chases her, calls out to her, tries to stop her, gives up, and covers her with his raincoat—he accepts what's happening, or maybe she has to knock him out; but here we cut to her running alone in the woods in his coat. The shot establishes that she will take the last leg of her journey, the film's third act, alone.

In the coat's earthy color she's a wild animal on the run. As she walks along the forest trail a man approaches Laura and asks, "You've stopped for a ramble in the woods?" Laura's encounter with the Logger (played by Dave Acton) seems ominous, but we're inclined at the moment to find him harmless. For one thing he's in some kind of uniform, so perhaps he's a ranger, a steward of the wild who is helpful to nature lovers who venture in. Also, he seems a bit nervous as he makes small talk with her, as if he's the shy type,

Where the woodland area of Laura's stroll with Quiet feels idyllic, and her time there protected and safe, the forest where she later finds herself is its opposite. With her matted hair and coat misbuttoned, the way a child might do it, she looks lost in the woods and trapped among the trees. The menace intensifies with the sudden appearance of a stranger (courtesy StudioCanal and FilmNation).

comfortable with his solitude in the woods but awkward with social exchanges that are probably rare. "It's a nice place if you want to gather your thoughts and enjoy some solitude," he tells her, and that there are many trails to explore. At face value his attempt at conversation is just a friendly gesture, but it's got that nerve-wracking undercurrent that this entire film is, to one degree or another, never without. There may be an explanation other than shyness for his awkward demeanor: bad intentions. A two-shot of them surrounded by trees underscores that the spot she's in is devoid of an escape route. When he nonchalantly asks her "Are you on your own?" the heart sinks. The words point to trouble for her, and indeed foreshadow it when we recall that it's precisely the question she asked each of her victims prior to drawing them to an inky death. This locale is his domain, one over which he has mastery, one that puts him at an advantage. The shelter where he later tracks her down may be as much his lair as the black space was hers, and we wonder how many other women, hiking on their own, he has molested there.

To his question Laura answers *yeah*, and the heart sinks further. It's the second of the two words she speaks in the film after leaving her mission. What better reminder that she is innocent, guileless (her early persona consisted of nothing *but* guile), and even clueless, not knowing enough to lie in an attempt to protect herself. The calculated dishonesty on which Laura's success as a predator was built is no longer available to her, even at a time when it might save her life. Is it that she is too fearful to think, or that it's too far out of her experience to understand? Or could it be that her newfound trust impairs her judgment, her open heart making her vulnerable?

Her *yeah*, a variation of the *yes* she utters to Quiet on the bus when he asks if she needs help, is a poignant pairing with it. The first affirmation sets off her lovely adventure with Quiet, while the second paves the way for all the dark events that lead to her end. In addition to the similar question, the stranger on the path appears to be detaining her with small talk in an attempt to break the ice, a ruse to make her comfortable with him, though his intent is to do harm—just as she had done with her victims. The feeling of foreboding on the forest trail may be subtle, but it fuels a sense of dread in the audience that she is about to experience the fate of her victims.

As jeopardy encroaches, intercuts of Bad searching for Laura continue with the surprising effect of shifting our perception of him from oppressor to savior. She parts with the stranger on the trail and comes upon a cabin, a bothy, where a sign on the door reads: "Hill walkers are welcome to take shelter here." Despite the welcome it's in this refuge that she will be molested by the Logger for the first time, and we regret that she fled a true shelter—Quiet's home—to end up here. She opens the door on a black space, once again filling the shoes of her victims. She looks all around her then sits cautiously on the edge of a platform where there are two sleeping mats, and she zips up her coat. Is she finally feeling the cold, after showing no reaction to cold or rain earlier? She lies down on her back and soon falls asleep in a fetal position, in the manner of any human person, and she is, in a sense, an embryonic human. A transition to windblown treetops brings us into her dream.

The ferocious wind threatens to topple these towering trees, but the image is as sumptuous as it is menacing. The swaying trees are superimposed on her body as she sleeps, an exquisite double image that merges her own troubled tranquility with the beauty and jeopardy of the forest in a storm. Inherent in this visual paradox is what this film overall, from beginning to end, conveys: that all experience of life and of the world is neither beautiful

7. Leaving

nor terrifying, but both, and the two in a sense cannot be separated. This double image recalls the earlier superimposition of her face with the multiplicity of faces she saw on the street in town, her "immersion" in humanity.

Laura is jolted awake by a man's hand stroking her thigh. From this we cut directly to her running through the woods, her gasps not just for the air she's running out of, but because she's defenseless and she knows it. It's underscored when she attempts to escape in the cab of a logging truck parked on a forest road, its trailer full of the long trunks of felled trees, but she fails—she can't start the engine, can't master it the way she mastered the van. The Logger approaches on the road—it appears to be his truck she's found—and once again she's fleeing through the woods. Her gasps, pants, and outcries when he finally catches her and pulls her down are her only other vocalizations in this human phase, exhortations of the exhaustion, fear, and panic that exemplify her new human-like emotion, a world apart from the cool dominance of her earlier self. The Logger's alignment with the violation of the forest (turns out he's the opposite of a steward) deepens our sense of tragedy and horror as he pushes her down and pulls at her clothing. The music that plays throughout this assault is the sudden reprisal, after a long absence from the film score, of the capture theme, which signals the irony of victimizer-turned-victim.

The logger tears at her camisole, and now there's a third role in this costume's trajectory; from its first appearance in scenarios of sexual dominance, to one of consensual lovemaking, and now to a fragile wisp of fabric to be torn from Laura's body on this forest floor. There is a nonchalance to the man's brutality—underscored by the fact that he's chewing gum while assaulting her—that suggests he's no stranger to this act. The attack, coming so close on the heels of her pleasure with Quiet, both underscores the gamut of human experience she has collected on her brief adventure and juxtaposes the kind of sexual experience a woman would desire with the one she most dreads. As the Logger pins Laura on her back her face drains of all emotion and recalls her default demeanor throughout her mission—a reminder of who she was. We wonder if she even knows what exactly is happening to her. Her point of view in these shots, high above her, is the pale, ice-blue sky as the snow begins to fall. When she continues to struggle, the man shoves her over onto her belly. Then, he suddenly recoils, seeing that his hands are covered with a black, inky oil. He regards them in horror, then a few seconds later sees Laura ten feet or so down the path, staggering away from him, with a gash in her back revealing her black body beneath.

The sight stuns him, and he runs off down the path in the opposite direction. The shot of him examining his black-coated hands is foreshadowed when Laura, after accepting the rose with thorns from the vendor, finds his blood all over her fingers. Whereas Laura appears undisturbed by the sight of the blood, and regards it with curiosity and even fascination, the Logger's horror and disgust are a combination of shock, xenophobia, and humiliation. A completely different reaction on his part to who or what she is could be possible here—curiosity, wonder, and of course empathy and compassion—but if he were a man of empathy and compassion, he wouldn't be assaulting her in the first place. What a different outcome we would have if this man had, instead of a violent reaction upon encountering an alien, a spiritual awakening—an epiphany that would transform him forever.

As Laura stumbles forward after the attack, she holds her hand out in front of her as if, because she is stunned or traumatized, she cannot see. She fumbles for something to grasp onto and finds the branch of a tree. She sinks to her knees, touches her face and her eyes, then gently pulls down before her the human suit, revealing the black alien we glimpsed briefly during the scene with Lonely in the black space. What we now see close-up a creature that melds earthly-life evolution (her skin, though not scaly, seems more reptilian than mammalian) with earthly wildlife (she appears of nature, of the forest, gazelle-like). She is a being of exquisite grace.

The alien pulls her head down in front of her and it rests on her forearm, facing up. We would expect to be looking down at a mask here, something dead behind the eyes, inanimate. Instead, in one of the film's most disarming moments, her human face is looking back up at her, soft and palpably alive, conveying tender emotion. Far from inanimate, the face of Laura blinks twice as it gazes up into the alien's eyes. The alien cradles Laura's head in her arm as a human would an infant, her eyes wide and full of affection, sadness, and mourning. It's the end that answers the beginning of the love affair noted by Watts; it is the summation of her human experience. She stares for a long moment into Laura's eyes, another of the film's extended, lingering shots that captures a crucial moment in the story.

Our affection and sympathy for the alien that was Laura are now at their deepest, as deep as the absence of connection we may have had with her early in the film. She is the opposite of what she was then: agency has replaced duty, empathy eclipses insensitivity, and she has experienced the transformative power of human connection, of trust, of love. It is at this most private, poignant, and revelatory moment that the Logger rushes up behind her. Cautiously, he gets only close enough to her to douse her body with gasoline. The shock comes not only from the horror of his act but in the way that it rips into the tender moment immediately preceding; once again Glazer demonstrates that one of his most powerful devices is juxtaposition. And there's a one-two punch—the horror of the visual, and the realization that he has come back to end her life. The threat of assault has escalated to the threat of death.

The alien, her human body left on the snowy ground, gets up and once again staggers forward. The Logger, several feet behind her, drops a lit match on the ground that ignites the trail of fuel until she is set on fire. There's a tracking shot of her from behind as she flees, and her body is rapidly engulfed in flames. She stumbles out of the trees and into a clearing in the woods. Although on the one hand her fate seems inevitable, the pure white, snow-covered meadow that awaits just a short distance ahead of her presents to us a glimmer of hope—hope that she would know that her answer is to drop down and roll to smother the flames. But she doesn't know, and she doesn't do it. Of the virtually countless moments in the film that remind us of her alien nature—as an advantage, or a limitation, or just a difference—here is the final one, and one of the most poignant: the alien moment that disables her from perhaps saving her own life. The very next shot presents her last possible salvation—Bad, standing in the snow looking all around him, searching for her. We have the feeling he is very close by, but he's still too far, and too late.

Her charred black body, slowly becoming a mound of ashes, lies in the snowy clearing. Smoke wafts up from her in a black column rising in the sky. Pan up to the treetops and the grey sky above as the snow falls down, the flakes looming larger as they approach. This POV shot tells us that she is still conscious; this is how you would see snowflakes falling if you were lying on the ground gazing up. Watching the scene, you can practically feel them touch your face. The shaft of smoke in the sky becomes an amorphous shape that dissipates as it drifts off to the left. It then collapses to the earth—as will her remains—to dissolve in the place that was her adopted home, and become part of its matter and energy in the eternal cycle. Her perishing is the quintessential human one; ashes to ashes. The culminating shot, of the snow falling to the clearing amidst the treetops, gives us the last thing she sees before she loses consciousness and dies. Her final experience on Earth is beautiful, tranquil, and accepting. It's an image of peace.

PART II: THE JOURNEY

8
Jonathan Glazer

Glazer's alma mater is Nottingham Trent University in central England, about a three hours' drive from where he grew up. The school had its origins in the Nottingham Government School of Design established in 1843, and focused on architectural design, including courses in Draughtsmanship and Architectural Ornament. In 1904 students began carving in marble and in stone; in 1912 classes in pottery, gold, silversmithing, enameling, and letter cutting in stone and marble were introduced.[1] By 1934, a new millennial craft that had cajoled its way into the art establishment became part of Notthingham's curriculum: photography. Painting and sculpture were added in the 1960s, and by 1981 they were one of 45 universities in Great Britain offering fine arts degrees. Glazer, a north London boy born in 1965, found himself going off to college at Trent Polytechnic—as Nottingham was called in the 1980s—to major in theater. After the university awarded him an honorary doctorate in 2017, he told the *Nottingham Post,*

> This is where I learnt what I know and set me out into the world. I think what I had here ... was a freedom to think and experiment with no sense of career. It was about being in the moment of what we were doing and a valuable part of my life. There is a tornado of memories here. I designed a play—that was the first individual project. It was loose, it was theatre design and it was lighting, puppetry and I learnt how to direct here.[2]

In 1993, a job with a London production company Academy Films gave Glazer the opportunity to develop and expand those theater skills for the screen, and a new "sense of a career" did not hurt his penchant for experimenting; it gave him the space to indulge it. His admiration for the work of Stanley Kubrick that echoes in *Under the Skin* took the form of winks even in his earliest work—in the opening moments of the video for Blur's *The Universal* (1995), Glazer's camera zooms out from a close-up of lead singer Damon Albarn's face sporting black makeup on his right eye (no fake eyelashes, but heavy on the eyeliner), recalling the iconic gaze of Alex (Malcolm

McDowell) in *A Clockwork Orange* (1971). The multiple Kubrick references here are enough to make the video an homage to the master—he later included *2001: A Space Odyssey* in his list of top ten films.[3] The stark white club where the band is playing resembles both *2001*'s space ship interior as well as the space station, and also invokes *Clockwork*'s Korova Milk Bar, also in the Anthony Burgess novel. Near the end of the song the three white-clad band members (Graham Coxon, Alex James, and Dave Rowntree) march behind Albarn toward the camera just as Alex's droogs follow him along the water before Alex brutalizes two of them and tosses them into the marina.

In the director's first music video, Massive Attack's *Karmacoma* (1995), Glazer playfully includes a full shot of two young girls, identically clothed, standing together in a hotel corridor—like the Grady daughters haunting the Overlook Hotel in *The Shining* (1980). A Palm Pictures DVD about Glazer's work has a recurring motif of the director consulting a street person (played by Paul Kaye) on creative decisions. When he's stuck on what to do with his new music video for Blur, Kaye reminds him of how he'd told him to rip off *The Shining* for Massive Attack and tells him to go into the store and "rent *Clockwork Orange* and do exactly the same thing." As payment, Kaye demands Glazer's socks. Riding an escalator Glazer sees Kaye heading down the other side and shouts out that he needs to cast "a hard man" for a film, and Kaye shouts back "Ben Kingsely." "Gandhi?!" Glazer replies, and Kaye calls back, "If he gets nominated for an Oscar, I want a pair of trainers."[4]

Walter Campbell, co-screenwriter of *Under the Skin* and longtime collaborator, admired the way Glazer's 1996 video for Radiohead's *Street Spirit (Fade Out)* makes unexpected sense of some seemingly disparate pictures—"when things you think won't add up, add up perfectly."[5] In composer Thom Yorke's own reflection, "Its lyrics are just a bunch of mini-stories or visual images as opposed to a cohesive explanation of its meaning."[6] Yorke describes how the darkness at the song's core made it necessary for him to express it in fragments as opposed to "cohesively" in order to "detach my emotional radar from that song, or I couldn't play it…. I'd break down on stage."[7] As Yorke sought to evade a connected narrative out of necessity, Glazer both utilized and repurposed the episodic nature of the Radiohead lyrics in a series of images that render (as Campbell observed) another kind of cohesion; in Glazer's words, "dream imagery, so you connect it in your head like you would the scenes in a dream. It has its own logic. You let it take you where it takes you."[8]

These scenes work individually and in concert as a precursor to *Under the Skin*. The video makes sumptuous use of Glazer's affinity for black-and-white photography, which he used in several ads and videos of this period, and which fuels the neutral palette of his second feature film, *Birth*. The scheme dominates *Skin*'s alien environments to emphasize their nonearthliness, and is exploited to achieve the realism of urban Glasgow. Much of the film's poetry is the monochrome of mountains and fog, night highways with painted lines or glowing headlights, and skin luminous in the darkness. What we have is color photography that's black and white with a vengeance, as Glazer rations color like a miser, preserving its power for the deep pink of Scarlett's sweater, the blood on her hands from the rose, the red of her lipstick.

The black-and-white effect of *Under the Skin* informs its visual power and its emotion, and the same is true in *Street Spirit (Fade Out)*.[9] The black and white is dreamlike because our world is color, and reality can seem too fake when it's pushed. But a black-and-white dream isn't the opposite of reality, it's an alternative to it. Here Glazer pushes black and white instead; its saturated effect is claustrophobic (despite its desert setting) as is the palpable weight of the humid air from the gathering storm, trapping us in a small area defined by grey metal campers under a heavy night sky. The actors' movements feel confined; Yorke runs but never gets far, Johnny Greenwood leaps forth from a trailer only to go back inside. A frantic dog, mouth foaming, is chained to a pole. When a bucket of blood is thrown it vanishes upon hitting the ground—even that gets nowhere.

A counterpoint to this darkness and melancholia lies in images of nature that emerge from the night's heaviness: a flight of birds, a galloping horse, a tree against the sky full of stars, and a flash of lightning to follow the opening sound effects of rainfall. A group of three dancers in flowing black nun-like drapery make exquisite balletic leaps into the air and descend just as gracefully in slow-motion that is used throughout—for example, in Yorke's defiant leap into the air as if to transcend, to break free. In an early shot his features cry out as he pulls at his own hair in anguish; later, he has a face of bliss. A young boy stands up to the tormented dog, and it backs down; the boy comes face to face with an enormous dragonfly that hovers before him, as if the two are communing.

Yorke says, "The image I had in my head when I wrote the song is from a book by a guy called Ben Okri, when he talks about a world child, a spirit taunted by people who are trying to kill him off, and send him back to where he came from so he can't affect the human race."[10]

The plaintiff strains of the music and of Yorke's tenor are dirge-like yet irresistible; the visuals are poignantly dismal yet breathtaking. All of this video's elements exemplify Glazer's gift for marrying the dark and light—and foreshadow the tense, tortuous beauty of *Under the Skin*.

The director's short-form work, which is ongoing through his feature film career, offers a tour of his recurring motifs and the themes they invoke. The claustrophobia of *Street Spirit (Fade Out)* rears up in a variety of other confined spaces, particularly long, rectangular ones such as narrow motorways, cramped rooms, or hallways—like the corridor in *Karmacoma*. In *Virtual Insanity* (1996) the cramped interiors can't contain the dancing of Jamiroquai, whose unbridled kinetics defy both the size and the whitish sterility of spaces that seem defeated by his gift. Glazer's second project with Radiohead is *Karma Police* (1997), which opens from the point of view of a car driving on two-lane blacktop in the darkness—as if through a tunnel—as its headlights find a solitary man fleeing the car. Similarly, *Rabbit in Your Headlights* (1998), a collaboration of composers UNKLE and Thom Yorke, sends French actor Denis Lavant sweating and ranting as he runs undaunted through a tunnel full of traffic. Honking, hollering drivers knock him down but he repeatedly gets up and forges on—the final car to hit him explodes in a cloud of smoke behind him.

A Song for the Lovers (2000) opens with Richard Ashcroft's back to the camera, framed by three rooms of a railroad-style apartment and a doorway at the end. Moment to moment he's boxed in by the dimensions of mirrors and hallways; a close-up of his face is constrained by the camera frame. His odyssey concludes with the camera pulling back from him through the multiple frames of doorways and walls—echoing the absence of the lover alluded to in the song, and the intensity of his solitude. While the men in the previous videos are victors over their surroundings, he appears captive. The theme culminates in Glazer's exhilarating *Odyssey* (2002), a commercial for Levi's jeans where the protagonists—a man, and then a woman—defy their containment inside a building by bursting through a series of contiguous rooms and corridors, wall after wall, finally through the towering trees of a forest, and out to the open sky. The ad's tag line is *Freedom to Move*. The sound track for this video also alludes to the work of Kubrick—it's the darkly triumphant *Sarabande* by Handel heard throughout Kubrick's *Barry Lyndon*.

Glazer's video for *Into My Arms* by Nick Cave & The Bad Seeds (1997) eludes the many varieties of production design that trademark his other work before or since. But two of his recurring visual motifs are critical here—the black and white and a sense of entrapment. The song is a spiritual exploration in the form of a love poem. It speaks reverence and adoration for the loved one while positing the divine in that love, rather than in an omnipotent higher power. Rather than build an environment, Glazer accompanies the intimate music with a gallery of intense emotion: close-ups of people on the verge of tears, or convulsing in sobs, their features quietly desperate or contorted in anguish. The darkness of the atmosphere combines with the close-ups to create the sense of human beings trapped with their torment that the viewer also experiences.

Yet at the same time, the visuals may be cathartic for those on screen as well as the audience—a release from that trap of suffering. In the video the shots of this diverse group of people are intercut with clips of Cave's per-

Director Jonathan Glazer frames his cinematographer, Daniel Landin. Their collaborations include the artful adverts Levi's "Odyssey" (2002), "Ice-Skating Priests" for Stella Artois (2005), Sony Bravia "Paint" (2008), and *Under the Skin*, which earned Landin 13 nominations and awards for images that are by turns haunting, terrifying, and romantic (courtesy Alexander O'Neal).

formance, which may convey that each individual is reacting in real time to the deep emotion in Cave's voice and in his lyrics (as opposed to the reverse, that the song illustrates their suffering) that stir something profound within them, and liberating. Cave has said that the band requested that some performance footage be cut into the video as a relief from the imagery on the screen, which Cave found "grim and dismal." For him, "*Into My Arms* was, even though it's melancholy in its way, a very uplifting song. It's about spiritual love, or it's about temporal love and spiritual love, and it's a song full of hope, and, I think, one of The Bad Seeds' more uplifting songs." He found the video to be an example in the genre where powerful images eclipse the song, which is "forgotten about."[11]

It may be easier to argue that the video simply reflects the song differently from the composer's vision than that the song has been "forgotten," but from the perspective of the artist it could be the same thing. Watching and listening to Cave perform the song at the piano (accompanied by a bass) does lead to different emotions than watching the Glazer video, and to different ideas—a very different experience. But this could also be said about Blur's *The Universal*, or Radiohead's *Street Spirit (Fade Out)*, or most videos by anyone, as it goes to the artistic controversy regarding music videos that is as old as the genre itself—ever since MTV changed forever, for better or worse, the way music is delivered to its listeners. "I'm not even that particularly committed to that art form of the video" said Cave at the time, "and all it represents."[12] Illustrating a work that was composed only to be heard can be like adapting for the screen a book created to live only in the imagination of the reader—just as Glazer adapted Michel Faber's novel. Interestingly, Thom Yorke's reaction to his audience's response to the song *Street Spirit (Fade Out)* at concerts is the opposite of Cave's reaction to Glazer's video interpretation of *Into My Arms*. Cave embraces the spiritual aspect of his song and regards it as one of the band's most uplifting. In contrast, Yorke expressed this sentiment about *Street Spirit (Fade Out)*:

> All of our saddest songs have somewhere in them at least a glimmer of resolve ... "Street Spirit" has no resolve.... It is the dark tunnel without the light at the end.... It drains me, and it shakes me, and hurts like hell every time I play it, looking out at thousands of people cheering and smiling, oblivious to the tragedy of its meaning.[13]

Walter Campbell was creative director at Abbott, Mead and Vickers BBDO Advertising when Tony Kaye[14] the director he sought to hire for a new Guinness project, was unavailable. Campbell called Glazer. "I loved the work he was doing in music videos. The choices he made, the artists he worked with ... he also had an amazing sense of pace and tone. We discussed other people, but Glazer was the only one I was interested in."[15] Searching for an approach, he thought of friends who were Guinness enthusiasts. "I'd seen how deeply they would engage looking at the pint being poured. I'd see how their imagination was firing at the thought of it."[16] Focusing on anticipation within the Guinness ritual, Campbell came to the line "Good Things Come to Those Who Wait," a theme that would drive not only this advertisement, but a perennial campaign for the brand. It's more meaningful when you know that the company claims it takes one minute and 59.53 seconds to properly pour its legendary brew.[17]

Amidst research for another Guinness ad called *Swimmer* (aka *Swim Black*) Campbell saw a photo of a Hawaiian surfer gazing at the ocean who "had that same look in his eyes, a sort of longing and satisfaction combined...."[18] Guinness's brand marketer Andrew Fennel expressed that he'd been working with surfers in Cornwall and would love to have an ad in that spirit. Another image the *Swimmer* research brought forth was British artist Walter Crane's fantastical 1892 painting, *The Horses of Neptune*. In its stunning panorama of white horses galloping in white water, Campbell found the visual key to the ad he wanted to make. The copywriter was Tom Carty. Of the challenge Glazer said, "You're putting together two elements which have no reason to belong with one another—the horses and water—and to have them become the same thing it was just ... very, very difficult to put together."[19]

Called Guinness *Surfer* (1998), the black-and-white ad (cinematography by Ivan Bird, who would later shoot Glazer's first feature) opens with a 23-second close-up on the face of a man (professional longboard surfer Rusty Keaulana), 16 of which are silent until the narration begins. His gaze out to sea is charged with longing, and in the attenuated silence the sense of anticipation that Campbell sought is realized. From the moment four surfers crash into the water with their boards, Glazer intercuts their plunges below the surface with the horses' galloping legs in the water, and the men's triumphant rides in the curl with the horses' trouncing of the waves. The theme of expectation gives way to a triad of nature celebrating humans, creatures, and the spectacular sea. All these images—and the passion and determination in the men's faces—find an uncanny partnership with the hypnotic, pounding drums of Leftfield's *Phat Planet*, which had yet to be released but was brought in by the ad's music supervisor Peter Raeburn. It delivered what Campbell had wished the music could evoke: "the sound of the blood in the surfer's head when he's on the waves and he knows he could die."[20]

Glazer's Academy Films and many of his same colleagues reunited for the making of the 2006 Sony Bravia ad entitled *Paint*, a prodigious technical feat involving scores of hard-hatted crew members and 70,000 liters of environmentally-friendly paint. It was shot at a vacant and headed-for-demolition housing project, including a multi-story high rise, in Queen's Court, Toryglen, in Glasgow. Here Raeburn employs Rossini's *The Thieving Magpie*, which is heard in *A Clockwork Orange*—its fluttering strings and winds a sardonic counterpoint to the brutal scenes they accompany (including the "droogs at the marina" sequence discussed above). Its triumphant flourishes satirize Alex's exhilaration in his violent pastimes. In the Sony ad, however, the eruptions and explosions of paint are simpatico—and synchronized—with both the lyrical fluttering and the dramatic flourishes of the music, and here it is the beauty of color and of editing that are triumphant and exhilarating. "What we're looking for is quite visceral," said Raeburn, "but the music is quite balletic."[21] His words could also describe a sequence on which Raeburn and Glazer collaborated nearly a decade later in *Under the Skin*—the demise of the victims under the black water, which merges the visceral and the balletic in both visuals and sound.

9
Beast, Birth

Glazer greeted the millennium partnering with Louis Mellis and David Scinto to adapt their stage play *Gangster No. 1* for the screen. The project ran aground over a disagreement with the producer around casting, but the trio found their ticket to the movies in the ravishing and profane heist movie *Sexy Beast*. According to Glazer, of all Mellis and Scinto's possible projects this was the one the playwrights were most eager to do. He remembered reading somewhere that they had "encouraged" him to direct it, but that doesn't quite capture it—"As soon as they put it in front of me, I was going to do it. It was just dynamite writing."[1]

"Our first indication of the film's uniqueness is how little attention is paid to criminal detail," writes Brian Eggert, "how this entry in the buoyant British crime subgenre revolves not around the much-discussed heist, nor even around shootouts or the criminal organization." Instead what drives the movie are its imagery and "introspective character examination—the depths of its characters and their innermost fears and lows."[2] Actor Ray Winstone plays a safecracker emeritus who is terrorized back to work by a maniac criminal (Ben Kingsley). Winstone said, "Instead of going into it making a gangster film, I went into it making a love story."[3]

The visuals are by turns what Eggert calls "dark David Lynch imagery" and glorious flourishes that light up the film's dream sequences. Near the beginning of the film retired bank robber Gal (Winstone) and his wife Dee-Dee (Amanda Redman) are aloft in a flying embrace—they recall the airborne lovers in Marc Chagall's delightful *Over The Town* (1918) that portrays the artist and his wife Bella soaring over the village in "a celebration of their love."[4] Gal's devotion to DeeDee is expressed in all his actions and words—"I love her like a rose loves rainwater."[5] But it's in the dreams and fantasies that we experience it as breathtaking, and (literally, as above) transcendent. It's the depth of their passion that establishes from the beginning what Glazer has up his sleeve, so much so that no amount of profane screaming or bloody violence can topple it. "In a way," said Glazer, "it was trying to be a film that wasn't about a gangster."[6] A film with the word *sexy* in the title doesn't always deliver, but this one does—literally, figuratively, ironically—and however you want.

Gal's emotion also reasserts (in case further evidence in needed) Glazer's deeply romantic side. In *Sexy Beast* neither romance nor violence relents (until the end) and the exhilarating duel between—or wild balance of—the glorious and the brutal thrills the soul and fuels the roller-coaster pacing. Glazer had been concerned about having too much that was "told, rather than shown. That can be tedious … we needed to cut certain chunks out of scenes in order to make the film move as it needed to."[7]

As it turned out, the editing (it was cut by John Scott and Sam Sneade) is not only free of chunks, it busts any chance of even catching one's breath. The film's dual climax is a flare-up of match cuts. We're thrown back and forth between the spectacular robbery (underground tunnels, blasting through walls, and water gushing like a dam breaking) and the murder of its mastermind, Don (Kingsley), at Gal's home by the four people he has savagely tormented from the beginning. Dynamite blasts a wall and water surges in a tunnel as a boulder crashes into Gal's pool; the robbers bust their way in just as the fatal blow crushes Don. With his death the audience is treated to a paroxysm of revenge—and relief.

Along the lines of show-versus-tell, the visually-driven director was prepared for the challenge of a script he called "dialogue intensive." Fittingly, his way through was a visual one: "I had to be architectural about it." He approached the first act as if Gal had shot it, "like holiday snaps, just so simple." For DeeDee the shooting was to be "curvaceous and fantastical." In the second act, when Kingsley comes on the scene, Glazer wanted it "angular" and "abrasive and spare."[8] In his book *The Visual Story*, author Bruce Block describes a frame in Gal and DeeDee's living room with the two couples and their nemesis, Don. "The architecture of the house and pool create the basic linear motif for most of the film. The sparse set dressing makes the architectural structure seem even more important."[9] The tension of the visuals (cinematography by Ivan Bird; production design by Jan Houllevigue) captures the command of Don, the intimidation of the couples, and their sense of entrapment.

In the caper sequences, however, Glazer felt free to move about and "enjoy the paranoia of the camera," and instead of repetitive tracking, "allow the words to do all the dancing."[10] That dancing, when it spins into profane screaming, is the bailiwick of Kingsley. Words on this page can't do his scathing, obscene, assault-rifle insults any justice—they can only be fully experienced as a deluge that blares at you from the screen. When Kingsley read the script, "The role of Don Logan, exquisitely written … leapt off the page,

For *Sexy Beast*, Ray Winstone (pictured) said, "Instead of going into it making a gangster film, I went into it making a love story." Ben Kingsley saw in the ferocious Don "the grief and rage of the unloved child." The result is an unorthodox and unique caper movie as romantic as it is suspenseful. Striking cinematography by Ivan Bird. 20th Century-Fox/Photofest © 20th Century-Fox.

grabbed me by the throat, and insisted I play him." For all Don's coruscating abuse of Gal and Deedee, and their friends Aitch (Cavan Kendall) and Jackie (Julianne White), Kingsley sees beyond to "the grief and rage of the unloved child."[11] Eggert said:

> Glazer's evident enthusiasm behind the camera exemplifies Gal's impassioned, unpretentious love for his wife ... what makes *Sexy Beast* unforgettable and distinct within its subgenre is its human quality. The sincerity of Gal's affection is as potent as Don's vile nature in *Sexy Beast*'s skewed polarization of romantic and misanthropic men, and this conflict, uncharacteristic in a British crime film, remains the picture's lasting quality.[12]

"A Sublime Undertow of Feeling"[13]

The spritely notes of a flute, like a hummingbird flitting from flower to flower, follow a man jogging on a snow-covered path through Central Park. Imagine this scene with a brooding musical accompaniment—the stark contrasts of the snow against the silhouetted trees and the black-clad runner— and the resulting mood would foretell the scene's outcome. Instead, for the opening scene of *Birth* (2004), composer Alexandre Desplat seduces us with the exhilaration of being alive on a brisk winter's day—there are even festive bells among the strings. At first a brief voice-over conveys that this man has a good life and knows it, but later the orchestra expands its reach like a grey cloud slowly taking over the sky. We don't see the man's face as we follow at a distance from behind, and unlike the rear-tracking shot from *Karma Police*, this man isn't fleeing: he's running toward his future that isn't to be. He collapses. During a long silence we watch the tunnel from the outside, and when the flute resumes, a newborn baby in a pair of loving hands emerges from water. Roger Clarke said: "As Sean dies unnoticed on a cold winter's day, in the darkness of a tunnel with snow piled brightly beyond it, where does his spirit fly? This is the essence of the story."[14]

A decade later, Sean's widow Anna (Nicole Kidman) has moved on with her life and become engaged to Joseph (Danny Huston). But her past resurfaces in the form of a 10-year-old boy (Cameron Bright) who implores her to believe that he is her dead husband. (The sudden absence of music—a lengthy silence that connects Sean's death with the newborn baby—proposes an answer to Clarke's question above.) Anna is both distraught and appalled at what she can only assume is a macabre prank, and her fiancé as well as her mother (Lauren Bacall) are enraged at what they know can be nothing but that. But young Sean's intimate knowledge of his namesake and their life together—and the intensity of his inexplicable bond with Anna—persuade her to believe the impossible. The passion revived within her after years of grief, and the anguish and jealousy Joseph experiences watching this (and fearing she is losing her mind), makes for the film's deepest emotion: what each is going through is unfathomable. Glazer's subdued style in *Birth* makes the film's more dramatic moments shocking: Joseph's rage and frustration amidst this perverse love triangle lead, after an outburst at a party, to his desperate spanking of the boy.

The film appears to be a reincarnation story, but maybe not; Anna has her heart broken a second time when in the end young Sean admits he has fabricated all of it. The film ends with a rear-tracking (recalling the opening shot of Sean in the park) of the couple on their wedding day, trying to restore their lives to normalcy—although Anna has just plunged, quite sadly and in her wedding gown, into the ocean. Like M. Night Shyamalan's *The Village*, a story set in a remote enclave that is apparently terrorized by creatures, *Birth* is not science fiction but ultimately a drama based upon an apparent lie. It's a genre shape-shifter, but the promise of the supernatural is only partly a ruse; in the case of each film, the paranormal lure both turns the film into a thriller and delivers emotional challenges for its characters that are so extraordinary they might as well be supernatural.

Key cinematic elements in both films fuel the sense of a haunting presence. In *The Village* James Newton Howard's score and Hilary Hahn's wistful yet urgent violin create an atmosphere fraught not just with suspense, but with the sadness of lives not fully lived—the plight of all the village's inhabitants. Desplat's score is romantic and flirts with baby and nursery imagery, as if teasing us, and Anna, with reincarnation. In other, darker moments, it holds the characters in the lingering grip of the past, reflecting what Kidman describes about Anna: her love for her dead husband is so powerful that "she's not free."[15] Glazer describes the first time we meet Anna, at the cemetery. "She really spends the whole film saying goodbye. She never really leaves that cemetery."[16]

The heaviness of the past informs the look of the film. Its monochrome photography has a stillborn, funereal effect, and the upper west side of Manhattan exteriors and interiors alike are solemn and seem frozen (assisted by the wintry setting) in a time that's not now. Anna and Joseph's apartment, and the scene where Anna meets her mother for lunch at La Caravelle, recall the paintings of Vermeer (the darkly elegant production design is by Kevin Thompson). In pre-production Glazer had been seeking a "somber" quality for the film, recalled Director of Photography Harris Savides. "Finally, we saw one location photo—the lobby of the Waldorf-Astoria, dark marble and warm colors. And Jon just said, 'that's it.'" *Birth*'s otherworldly pall, Savides says, was achieved by lighting from overhead and through muslin, and "we also had to underexpose the film quite a bit."[17] *Quite a bit* is elaborated upon in a *Filmmaker Magazine* tribute to Savides, who passed away in 2012. The article's author Zachary Wigon called *Birth* the cinematographer's "greatest work":

> Savides underexposed the film two stops, and then pulled it two additional stops, netting a total underexposure of four stops—which seems to have sent the head of every camera nerd on Cinematography.com (is there anybody else on the site?) spinning fast enough to power the electric grid of a major metropolitan city.[18]

The archway of the tunnel in the park, in which adult Sean falls to his knees, frames his final moments and becomes his sepulcher. Savides's gift for capturing nonverbal brilliance has quietly intensified many films, including Gus van Sant's *Last Days*, Noah Baumbach's *Margot at the Wedding* (in which Kidman also stars), and Sofia Coppola's *Somewhere*, a movie with so little talking the script comes to "about 30 pages—the rest was in [Coppola's] head," said star Steven Dorff.[19] Beyond its cinematographer and minimal dialogue, *Birth* has a third kinship with Coppola's film, which was released in 2010—the critical casting of a pre-adolescent co-star to play opposite an anguished adult protagonist. Elle Fanning was eleven when she was cast as Chloe, Dorff's eleven-year-old daughter, who is thrust on him by his estranged wife Layla (Lala Sloatman) when he's on the brink of a crisis and helps him save his own life.

Her pre-pubescence is perfect, for she is not too young to be aware of his problems, but not yet the teenager who would be more immersed in her own and burdened by the confusions of sexuality. For *Birth*, Glazer had initially bypassed Cameron Bright, who was nine at the time; he'd imagined a boy of twelve or thirteen for the role. It was Carrière who persuaded him to cast a child and avoid the extra layer of adolescence and its complications. In Bright, Glazer found "something very adult ... and something very vague, which allows Anna to imbue him with what she wants."[20] Bright performs an extraordinary balancing act of committed love and an undertone of eerie obsession, which Kidman of course shares.

A lengthy close-up of Anna's face at the opera makes us believe in the profoundness of the effect Sean is having upon her. Two times Joseph leans in toward her, interrupting her reverie, and she winces both times. As if to seal it, and shut out any reality that is not her own, she finally closes her eyes. This close-up lasts nearly 2.5 minutes. Asked how this sequence was described in the screenplay, screenwriter Milo Addica recalls, "It wasn't. That was all Jon."[21]

A similar lingering moment with her husband Joseph is shot through a window, gradually culminating in a close-up that captures his ordeal, elimi-

In Glazer's film *Birth*, Anna (Nicole Kidman) grapples with a boy's shocking revelation that he is her dead husband reincarnated. This close-up of her lasts nearly two and half minutes, by the end of which her face tells us that she believes it. Anna's internal journey here is not specified in the script; screenwriter Milo Addica says, "That was all Jon." And of course, Kidman. Photographer: James Bridges. New Line/Photofest © New Line Features.

nating any need for dialogue or action. Huston recalls, "I read the script. I knew that Nicole Kidman was attached to it, and that Lauren Bacall, a family friend, was also to act in it, so the whole package seemed extremely thrilling to me. And I was delighted when I received the call that in fact he wanted me for the film."[22] On working with Glazer, Huston said,

> He's always trying to photograph the inner workings of the mind. He's somehow able to film one's heart and one's soul. It's in a way a very precise, meticulous way of capturing images, but they are more than the image itself. Somehow you have the feeling that the drama, the story, the music, is able to carry the moment, so as an actor you don't have to ... *perform*.[23]

Writer Milo Addica recalls, "Jon fought for Danny Huston. There were people who wanted to replace him. But he wasn't afraid of playing the role. Some actors didn't want to be upstaged by a 10-year-old boy. Or feel that his was less than a starring role, that it was *her* movie."

Glazer didn't have to seek out Nicole Kidman—she read the script, wanted the role, and came to him. Screenwriter Jean-Claude Carrière recalls, "We gave the script to Nicole at ten in the morning and she said yes at four in the afternoon."[24] Carrière:

> She was perfect for the film. Jon and I had the feeling that we needed another week or so to add more, and she gave us a week of work freely without getting paid. She came with us to the festival. She is a fantastic professional, you can ask anything of her, she is never in bad spirits.

Glazer said: She's "Nicole Kidman, mate ... she's coming from another place. It's as if she's in this amniotic fluid."[25] There's reciprocity in Kidman's description of her director: "He has to feel it—he's almost like an actor, because he has to feel something. And if he can't feel it, then he can't shoot it."[26] There is a theme regarding Glazer's process in the responses of his collaborators— "He doesn't stand on a block of truth and certainty," said Carrière, "trying to impose what he sees and what he feels ... that's what I like about him."[27] For Savides, Glazer "kind of reacts to a performance and then builds on that. And watches talent do something—that spawns an idea—and the performance morphs into something that comes out of the actor. It's a very emotional, very private process."[28] All of this was ideal for Kidman's approach to acting. "You're allowed to grow and change and move within a structure rather than it being mapped out. I'm not very good at someone saying 'do this, be this, and do it now.'"[29] When asked what risks he felt might cause him to fail, Glazer replied, "They were constant. Daily ... it did feel like we were kind of jumping off a cliff and building our wings on the way down."[30] Savides said: "A scene can be written as one thing. But I learned, early on ... it ended up being something else ... it's not easy making a movie that way, but somehow it ends up being more organic, more real."³¹

Toulouse-Lautrec Slept Here (and So Did Jonathan Glazer)

The original idea came from Jonathan—producer Jean-Louis Piel brought him over to meet me. Jonathan told me the idea about a boy pretending to be the reincarnation of a dead husband of a woman. That was the beginning—I found the idea interesting. He made several trips to Paris, he lived in my house, we became friends, we worked and the producer was there to write down notes. Step by step, we arrived at the script.

Piel had produced a number of films including *Shanghai Triad* (1995) and *Chinese Box* (1995), two movies starring formidable Chinese actress Li Gong. In 1982 he had worked on *Antonieta*, written by Jean-Claude Carrière and starring Isabel Adjani and German star Hannah Schygulla. Glazer appreciates powerful female leads, "actresses like Liv Ullman and Bibi Anderson in Bergman's films, or Hannah Schygulla in Fassbinder's films. They're often more interesting than men."³² Carrière first met actress Schygulla on Volker Schlondorff's *Circle of Deceit* (1981). "For fifteen or twenty years she was Germany itself," says Carrière. It's a tribute to the excellence of Kidman's performance that Carrière feels that had the film been made in those years, Schygulla could have played the role.

Carrière's Paris home near Pigalle is a former brothel once frequented by Toulouse-Lautrec, who transmuted into art the daily lives and intimate relationships of the madams and prostitutes who confided in him. Carrière's list of collaborators is distinctly international, from Miloš Forman and Abbas Kiorastami to Wayne Wang, Andrjez Wajda, Hector Babenco, Anna Maria Tatò, and many others. His longest and best-known creative partnership is with the Spain-born Mexican director Luis Buñuel. Perhaps their most acclaimed film outside of *Belle du Jour* (with Catherine Deneuve, 1967) is *The Discreet Charm of the Bourgeoisie* (1973), credited by critic Melissa Acker with "paving the way for later generations of experimental narrative filmmakers such as David Lynch and Pedro Almodovar." The movie's "playful form, exquisite irony, and magical ambiguity,"³³ a penchant Carrière continued to explore, flows through *Birth*.

"I was extremely interested to work with Jonathan because I had seen his commercials," said Carrière. "He masters the art of the image. Also to work with a British filmmaker. We are neighbors but we are totally different! I like to work with people of different countries, and cultures, who see things differently." Regarding his proximity to Glazer during the writing process, "I'm used to that. For the writer the fact that the director is there facing you is essential. To have the director there to talk, explain, show, draw, present." The script remained true to the premise Jonathan had at the outset, although

> from the beginning, I was against the idea of a "real" reincarnation—I said to him, "It's not as though any of us knows someone who was reincarnated and came back to tell us about it." So, step by step I placed it a little away from his original idea. Another woman comes and says, "Joseph was not in love with her, he was in love with me," and then the boy had to admit his lie.

Carrière's admiration for Glazer is in part that "he has a sense of an elliptic storytelling. He is asking from the audience more than other directors. He's leaving some empty spaces, some empty moments where somebody from the audience could bring in something ... the people who really love it add something to the film."[34]

Glazer's work with Carrière had brought him a long way from his years-old "seed" paragraph they had started with, yet for Glazer the story was still evolving. He had invited writer Milo Addica to the UK to work on what was to be his next film after *Sexy Beast*, which was *Under the Skin*—but as they began, Glazer gave Addica the script for *Birth* to read—and they ended up working on that instead.

At the time Addica was fresh off an Oscar nomination and awards for *Monster's Ball* (2001) which he co-wrote with Will Rokos. Back in 1995 Addica, an actor living in Echo Park, met Rokos when they performed in a play together. In their personal lives and in their careers, both men were struggling. They thought about writing together, and "began kicking ideas back and forth" to see where it could lead. "We both had difficult fathers. I had read the book *Death at Midnight* [by Donald A. Cabana, 1998], the memoir of a prison executioner, and gave it to Will. We became interested in making a movie not from the point of view of the condemned, but from the reverse perspective."

The subject matter was beyond difficult. "It's hard to write about the human soul," says Addica, a task he would confront again in *Birth*. "Who are we? Who am I? What's my connection to this material? You try to bring some sort of arc to what you do." Then, there is the audience—you're asking a great deal of them. "A lot of people aren't open to feeling, and you have to sort of sneak it in." They kept working on the script. In the meantime *Dead Man Walking* was released later that year, and a few years later, *The Green Mile*. "People told us, you'll never get your movie made now," because of the similar death row setting—though the emphasis was very different. When they began submitting the script, "Nobody wanted to make it. They told us, 'No audience is going to the movies to see a racist bigot.'" It would appear that the casting of Tom Hanks had a great deal to do with bridging that gap. The film was produced by Lee Daniels, who has no fear of pushing audiences past their boundaries—he has since made *The Woodsman, Precious,* and *The Paper Boy* (the last two he also directed).

Milo recalls a meeting when he first joined *Birth* with Glazer and Carrière at Covent Garden Hotel in London. "Here I am, talking with the other screenwriter on the project, trying to find common ground. I was pretty adamant in my approach," he admits. "It became a heated debate." The venerated French screenwriter, he recalls (with just the right balance of respect and writer's balking) "was taking me to school." During the *Birth* process Glazer also consulted longtime collaborator Walter Campbell. "I think I see a different side of Jon," says Campbell.

> He can come to me when he needs help and he's frantic and stressed. But even when he doesn't know what to do, he knows the effect he would like the story, scene, moment, sentence to have. He still hunts for it. His questions are very focused, his intent is very clear.[35]

"I wasn't interested in making a paranormal story," says Glazer. "It was a conduit for this love story."[36] It is comparable to *Under the Skin* in that the science fiction elements—extraterrestrials, the harvesting of humans—aren't more than a catalyst for sending Laura on a journey. The role of the paranormal in *Birth* raised the question—"How to approach the idea of reincarnation? Treat it delicately," was Milo's thought. "Flatten the drama, make it look easy. You don't want to preach."

The writers also had to walk a tightrope between the allusion to lovers (existing in Anna's memory) and the physicality of a woman in a bathtub with a boy—and that tension is part of the brilliance of that scene. We can't deny what we fear to see, but there is also what we feel: their deep love for one another in the past, which has bled into the present. Glazer has said that it was not his intention to make a "salacious" film, but he is not surprised by the controversy that erupted in the press. "I'm aware that it is the ultimate taboo in many respects," he says. "But for me [the bathtub scene] was an important part of the story—it was essential for [Kidman's character] to be confronted by that absolute no-go area. The context of that scene is sacred in a way."[37] It is the dovetailing of two risky terrains—the taboo and the supernatural—that galvanizes this tense scene, poising Anna for her leap of faith.

After an incident leaves the boy covered in blood and dirt, a second bathtub scene follows his confession to Joseph that he has "lied" about being Sean. Anna confronts him. Addica recalls hashing out with Jonathan a way into the scene: "Why don't we just slip him under the water?" The gesture of the boy sliding downward, as if trying to hide himself from Anna, reminds us that he is a child, and reveals his shame. But is it shame over the lie? Or is he ashamed of an affair he had while married to Anna, forcing him to withdraw his claim that he is Sean in order to keep the affair secret and protect her? This assumes that he is indeed the reincarnated Sean, and seeing him beneath the water asserts this by referring back to the water birth scene—the ten seconds which imply the newborn received Sean's soul. As this is a Jonathan Glazer film, nothing is explained or concluded, but Addica's view stands in contrast with Carrière's—"I think the boy *is* Sean."

Glazer:

> We aimed to make something robust in which every question leads to another. I'm not a Buddhist and I don't believe in reincarnation; I don't think I could do a film about it if I did. I was more interested in the idea of eternal love. I wanted to make a mystery, the mystery of the heart.[38]

Glazer & Addica: A *Birth* Mini-Montage-Documentary

Glazer: "Milo turned up and stayed to the bitter end, helping me through the whole thing. Helping to split the atoms."[39]

Addica: "He'd say, it was rubbish, what you gave me today was rubbish."[40]

Glazer: "His dedication was remarkable."[41]

Addica: "We kept hearing … this is not going to work."[42]

Glazer: "I wasn't really ready, though. The script wasn't ready. I hadn't worked it all out."[43]

Addica: "I became defensive for Jon, protective of him. We were joined at the hip."[44]

Glazer: "Basically, we were rewriting while we were shooting."[45]

Addica: "We'd finish shooting at around 6 p.m. then write into the night, one time until 3 in the morning."[46]

Glazer: "I hope it resonates with people. I hope they feel it. I hope it moves them."[47]

Addica: "I was constantly being told what we were trying to do was inconceivable."[48]

Glazer: "It's a very difficult piece to pull off.... It's a knife edge.... But the studio was afraid I was making haiku."[49]

10
The Novel

Writer Samuel Wigley:

People who saw *Birth*, and saw beyond a surface farfetchedness to its sublime undertow of feeling, knew to be excited about the next Jonathan Glazer movie. The wait ends, nearly a decade later, with another birth of sorts: a Kubrickian pre-title sequence that begins with a pinprick of light in the middle of darkness ... Michel Faber's 2000 source novel delayed revealing its enigmatic protagonist's extraterrestrial origins but—with the secret already out in the ether—this otherworldly opening makes it apparent from the start.[1]

Book critic John Messer called Faber's novel "a wildly imaginative, scorching, bizarre, and insidious first novel."[2] Jonathan Glazer departed from the book as much as he depended upon it, but in essence he ended up in the same place: all the adjectives Messer conjures above apply to Glazer's film. While the two works of art have these elements in common, the film is more beautiful than insidious, more intimate than scorching, and as relatable as it is bizarre. It's true the film is stealthy, but it also approaches us head-on with matters of the heart.

When a book is adapted for the screen, the inherent differences between the two mediums can drive the digressions from the original work. In *Blade Runner* Ridley Scott focuses upon the conflicts between the human world and the plight of the androids. This plot is not only action-heavy and highly cinematic, but it contains the central themes of Dick's novel about what makes us human. Scott chose not to include the religion of Mercerism and how it affects people's lives in this future world, and the Penfield Mood Organ[3] that they use, like a drug, to alter their emotions and cope with their dystopian world, two threads that are important in the book but might bog down the film or overcomplicate it. He also omits a lengthy sequence that takes place in a parallel world of androids—a piece of business that could easily be a foil to his subtler exploration of whether or not Rick Deckard is human.

What we ultimately see on the screen is Glazer's vision of the story. The source is respected (or it wouldn't have been embraced in the first place) but allegiance must be to the vision and, by necessity, to the film medium and what it requires.

> Isserley always drove straight past a hitch-hiker when she first saw him, to give herself time to size him up. She was looking for big muscles: a hunk on legs. Puny, scrawny specimens were of no use to her.[4]

Faber's debut novel nearly won the UK's prestigious Whitbread Award, and its opening sentence surely wins the bait-and-switch award. Isserly (the protagonist) is driving on a picturesque road in the Scottish Highlands. She "might catch a glimpse of his buttocks, or his thighs, or maybe how well-muscled his shoulders were." And once he's riding shotgun in her car, she's "savoring the thought of how superb he'd be once he was naked."[5]

The film's black opening and the white-space "weird science" lab cue us that something less ordinary than seduction is underfoot. But refraining from cues (except a vague reference to Isserley's odd body) Faber plays with us a little—"Yes, she wanted him,"[6] and the hitchhiker's admission, "My ex-wife—doesn't want anything to do with me. I don't exist anymore as far as she's concerned."[7] Here is the author's dark sense of humor: Isserley wants him, all right, but for what? The man thinks his assurance of availability is what Isserley wants to hear, but he doesn't know why that's true (like Laura, she avoids victims with partners waiting for them). And the irony of *I don't exist anymore* is seen when, within a short time, it becomes more or less true.

> Then the middle finger of her left hand flipped a little toggle on the steering wheel.... It was the icpathua toggle, the trigger for the needles inside the passenger seat ... one needle in each buttock.... He lost consciousness and his head lolled back into the padded hollow of the headrest.[8]

Another author smile here, for they pass a lorry labeled "FARM FOODS"—and a *farm* is exactly where this hitchhiker is headed. Isserley will drive him to her headquarters, where his unconscious body will be taken by her male colleagues to an underground facility and be *processed*.

The set-up of the novel is recognizable; it's the details that will distinguish the two works from each other in tone, plot, and ultimately, themes. The two protagonists do the same job, but the differences between them are both literal (what is made visual in the film, and what is revealed narratively in the book) and metaphorical (what is explicit in the book's narrative that is left open to interpretation in the film).

Isserley is not an alien who wears a human skin; she is an alien who has been surgically altered to appear—to men who aren't looking too closely—as human. Her extraterrestrial race resembles what we call animals—they walk on all fours and are covered with fur. To make her pass for a human woman, her employer, Vess Industries—the owners of Ablach Farm, which makes men into meat—reconstructed her spine so that she could walk upright, removed her sixth finger, mutilated her ears, and, of course, amputated her tail. She shaves her skin frequently and wears thick glasses to conceal her bestial eyes. For her daily outings she dons a pair of trousers and a low-cut top, with no bra. To compel men to ignore anything they find odd about her looks, Vess Industries enhanced her with large, smooth, upright breasts that she pushes forward to lure her victims into the front seat.

Enduring daily exercises to maintain her upright body, Isserley suffers constant backaches and leg pain, and endures humiliation by alien colleagues whom she knows regard her as a vertical and denuded freak. She spends her days searching for *vodsels* (the aliens' word for meat; *human* is the word they use for themselves, while *vodsels* are considered *animals*). But she doesn't regret accepting the job with Vess Industries, an escape from her plight at the New Estates—a subterranean habitat for the less fortunate in society. Men she'd been with found her beautiful and swore they wouldn't let it happen to her, but they had all abandoned her. Had she stayed, "She'd have been shambling around spiritlessly … in underground corridors of bauxite and compacted ash. She'd have been working her guts out in a moisture-filtration plant or an oxygen factory.… Instead here she was, free to wander in an unbounded wilderness swirling with awesome surpluses of air and water. And all she had to do in return, when it came right down to it, was walk on two legs."[9]

While in the film we are left to speculate about Laura's past and why she may have ended up in this position, the novel gives us a few pieces to build on. Isserley's description of the New Estates evokes the underground hell of the laborers in *Metropolis*. And the reference to oxygen makes us wonder if this species finds itself without breathable air as a result of environmental neglect, or a cataclysmic event, or perhaps forced to colonize a planet without oxygen and make do.

Isserley's cruising protocol differs from Laura's—seeking hitchhikers only there's no asking for directions, a guise which lends itself to Glazer's shift from the Highlands to Glasgow, where solitary men can be easily and frequently found.[10] A key difference is that Faber includes extended interior monologues of the men riding shotgun. This one, as all of them, first notices her body:

> That's why this car was heated like an oven, of course: so she could wear a skimpy black top and air her boobs for all to see—for him to see … She had thick, fluffy hair, mouse-brown, hanging straight down so that he couldn't even see her cheeks.… She was a weird one all right. Half Baywatch babe, half little old lady.[11]

The hitchhiker's description of his driver is comical because he doesn't seem to realize he's describing an animal—which she is. This woman is more than "weird," and his cluelessness is translated in the film to scenes that also prompt laughs, where men lured to bizarre places appear oblivious to their surroundings—as they are here to Isserley's surgical enhancements. These passages don't do much to endear us to these victims—not that they deserve to be butchered for it—but Isserley's sad tale moves the sympathy dial in her direction. In the film, it's somewhat the opposite. We assume the men's lust, but without their explicit train of thought, what's otherwise conveyed is their cluelessness, and even sweetness.

Isserley and Laura deliver the men, but neither dirties her hands; both are essentially kidnappers. Here the film takes a detour, however, in having the men follow Laura into her house as opposed to spiking them with a knockout drug. The sequences of the victims walking behind her, through spooky gardens, into decrepit hallways and mysterious dark spaces, all without flinching, puts an erotic as well as mystical spin on a horror trope. That they appear mesmerized is captivating and suspenseful, hypnotic and creepy—and because of the cinematography, production design, and music, it's also beautiful. Glazer's diversion here from the novel is lushly cinematic and full of mood, but not exclusively: It also creates opportunities for the motif of lure-and-follow, which is threaded through the film, and the trope of the femme fatale, which teases and is played with, interrogated, and reversed. It lays the groundwork for Laura's human adventure. Like Isserley's conversations in the car, it's performative—and it's also the early stage of Laura's path to self-actualization.

With language we begin to separate Isserley from her onerous (to us, if not her) task—or perhaps connect her more deeply to it:

> Lately, she suspected her feelings were getting swallowed up, undigested, inside purely physical symptoms. Her backache and eye-strain were sometimes much worse than usual, for no real reason; at these times, there was probably something else troubling her.[12]

It's double-edged when Isserley learns that the owner's son Amlis Vess is arriving soon to inspect the operation. She is confident that she's too good at her job to be let go and sent back to the horrific New Estates, but it then occurs to her that "she would have to do this job forever." She wonders if they'd ever find anyone else willing to do it, because "no-one could be as desperate as she had been."[13] Soon Isserley is awakened by a frantic banging on her door. It's her colleague Esswis to tell her that four vodsels had escaped—and have to be found immediately.

Animals and Humans

It's in Chapter 5 that the animal-human allegory begins explicitly to unfold. The author has said that as literature his novel is not an "argument," although "I do have strong feeling on these issues."

The trouble with our carnivorous society is that we have millions of people eating vast amounts of meat but not wanting to take moral responsibility for how it's produced. Animals can be cruelly treated ... as long as it all happens in secret and the result is disguised in a neat supermarket package.[14]

Amlis Vess is unprepared for what he discovers while touring the processing facility, and he's come not on assignment but of his own volition—out of curiosity. The sight of the *monthlings* in their pens—the workers' name for the vodsels that had been captured, processed, fattened to 250 KG, ready for slaughter and the cargo ship—distresses Amlis, and he sets four of them free.

When Isserley and Esswis head out to search she knows what's at stake. "The thought of a shaved, castrated, fattened, intestinally modified, chemically purified vodsel turning up at a police station or a hospital was a nightmare made flesh."[15] It would go beyond just shocking people—it would put the mission at risk. Following some rustling sounds and using a flashlight, they discover one hiding in the thicket. "It had the typical look of a monthling, its shaved nub of a head nestled like a bud atop the disproportionately massive body.... Its mouth opened wide to show its cored molars and the docked stub of its tongue. 'Ng-ng-ng-ng-gh!' it cried."[16] When Isserly angrily confronts Amliss about releasing the vodsels, his reply is that he doesn't believe in what the company is doing. Already detesting Amliss—she thinks of him as a rich spoiled brat—Isserley is troubled by the fact that she's attracted to him. When he discovers her in the dining room eating meat he reminds her, "We're all the same under the skin."[17]

Amlis begs her to accompany him to the subterranean levels where the livestock are kept; there's a question he needs her to answer. Isserley is claustrophobic and still has nightmares about the New Estates. Down in the livestock area "there was a stench of fermenting urine and feces, a few spidery contours of wire mesh sketched in by feeble infra-red bulbs, and, swaying everywhere before them, the firefly glints of a swarm of eyes."[18] In his graphic descriptions of the vodsels in their pens Faber spares no details—he wants us to cringe, and then remember that these are members of *our own species*. Their tongues are cauterized to stop their speaking, they are castrated, and fattened in a month's time to over 500 pounds.

What Amlis brings her down there to see is a vodsel scratching five letters in the dirt on the ground—the word *mercy*. There are moments when the author's "animal theme" is as funny as it is repellent or shaming. Faber shoves our noses in our treatment of animals which we justify because they taste so good—far preferable to sacrifice the critters than sacrifice our morning bacon or backyard barbecue. His satire is even-handed; Amlis's defense of animals can sound like the rant of your vegan brother-in-law. Isserley is as resistant as any of us when confronted with our anthropocentrism, our animal-kingdom hierarchy. She dismisses his arguments as sentimental anthropomorphizing. The fact that these male victims have language—or that she's had long conversations with them in her car—doesn't even touch her conviction that they are *food*.

Faber's allegory is a reversal of roles for two different species, but is also striking as it applies to groups within one species, specifically the human race. Once a culture makes the determination that it is superior to other cultures—if we define what is superior as *ourselves*—then we define much of what is unlike us as inferior, or undesirable, or possibly evil, or even threatening to our survival. At its most benign it's pride; then chauvinism and nationalism—a slippery slope to oppression, bloodshed, war, and genocide.

In this regard, Faber's novel is about societies; it's a political novel. Glazer chooses not to delve into the humans-as-food allegory. But issues of empathy and xenophobia, and questions of what we are and what we owe each other, are imbedded in Laura's arc. Early on, our shock at her ignoring the crying infant forces us to reflect on her absence of empathy and our own humanity. Putting her on the receiving end of human kindness when she falls on the sidewalk triggers the theme from a different angle. Later Laura herself will become a victim of a lack of empathy and of xenophobia. Amlis's statement to Isserley, "We're all the same under the skin," can also be a question—"Aren't we all the same under the skin?"

The animal question in the novel is compelling in its own right, but its most emotional role is the one it plays in Isserley's journey. In the film, we track the subtle but significant glimpses into Laura's psyche, moments that signal there are changes within her. In the novel we have a direct pipeline to Isserley's thoughts, and soon after being reassured by her that she has no regrets about accepting the job, leaving home, and having her body disfigured, we begin to hear notes of internal conflict triggered by Amlis's visit.

Isserley becomes defensive about the job she's doing even before meeting Amlis, because his freeing of the vodsels is a radical condemnation of her, and it's only exacerbated by the *mercy* incident. She worries about further rebellious acts from Amlis, but what she's really concerned about is something going on within her. When Amlis asks her what the word scrawled in the dirt means, she stops herself from saying it out loud:

> For her to speak the word at all dignified it with the status of being a word in the first place.... At a stroke, she would be dignifying the vodsels, in [Amlis's] eyes, in both writing and speech. But isn't it true, she asked herself, that they have that dignity? Isserley pushed the thought away.... She looked straight into Amlis's eyes, to add the power of conviction to her denial.[19]

The word *denial* here as a rejection of Amlis's point of view may also refer to Isserley being *in denial*. On the road in pursuit of fresh meat, she ponders the nature of her victims, particularly the unemployed ones "skulking

At first Isserley resists Amlis's empathy for the "animals" they harvest, but eventually a change is evident when, for the first time, she feels remorse over a victim. Later a man she picks up alludes to being reincarnated as a "wee beastie." This photograph was taken during filming of *Under the Skin* after the crew—and Laura—left the city for the countryside (courtesy Alexander O'Neal).

at the peripheries of the herd.... In a way, the vodsel community itself seemed to be selecting those of its members it was content to have culled."[20] Apart from being another Faber satirical aside (her thesis echoes a common observation of hunters, which is in fact what she is) as well as a statement about societies' abandonment of their less fortunate, Isserley's Darwinian rationale for her activities feels less like a justification than its opposite: proof that she is beginning to doubt herself. Her brushes with a sense of bonding with humans, expressed in the novel in thoughts, are a version of nonverbal moments in the film—Laura's staring at the human blood on her hands, for example, or her desire to take a stroll among the people in downtown Glasgow.

It's at this point that Isserley picks up a hitchhiker who pulls a knife on her, orders her to drive to a secluded spot, and assaults her. "Her genitals, she knew, were buried forever inside a mass of ugly scar tissue caused by the amputation of her tail. But the scar-lines themselves might resemble the cleft of a vodsel's sex. 'I don't see nothing,' he grunted."[21] Seconds later, Isserley forces her fingers into the hitchhiker's eye sockets, killing him.

Isserley's attack, since it occurs while she's on the job, comes off as an occupational hazard, whereas the assault on Laura poignantly refers back to the person she no longer is. The moment when the hitchhiker discovers the absence of her genitalia (a verbal moment) becomes in the film a cinematic moment (Quiet's futile struggle to penetrate Laura) and Isserley's poignant thoughts about the mutilation of her body are translated to Laura's abrupt and also comical grabbing of the lamp to inspect what is—or isn't—between her legs. The man's realization about her alien body offers Isserley the opportunity to gouge out his eyes and save her life while in the film, it's what brings Laura's rapture to an abrupt end, sending her to the forest where a rapist—and the end of her life—awaits. It's the opposite. The details of all three sequences are also a reminder of the contrasting moods of the book and film overall—the former more blunt, pragmatic, and realistic; the latter mysterious, romantic, and tragic.

Two-thirds of the way through the novel Isserley's internal struggle is increasingly evident. Her resentments from the beginning, the conflicts with Amlis that put her on the defensive, and finally the brutal attack, have pushed her to react to her life and her plight. Something new is coming over her, surrounding her like the mist along the Scottish coastline. Back out on the road, her car parked by a jetty, she reflects. "The sea would either take her or it would leave her be.... Something important was eluding her. She would wait here until it came to her. She would wait forever if necessary."[22]

Isserley spends the night in her car, and when she awakens she says aloud, "If that's the way you want it," taking her survival as a sign that she is not meant to die here, or now. She lingers, musing on the tide, the surrounding nature, and "the little molluscs that people—that vodsels—collected. Whelks. That was the word. Whelks."[23] When her own pleasure in nature is interrupted by—and aligned with—an awareness of vodsels' enjoyment of nature, she catches herself referring to the vodsels as *people*, and corrects herself as if to deny it. Her recognition of a vodsel word also recalls the word that she and Amlis saw a vodsel scratch into the ground—*mercy*. At this moment Isserley flips the icpathua toggle, and watches the silvery needles erupt and squirt their poison into the air. Then she begins to cry.

A Fiery End

> "It's disgusting the way they treat humans ... it demeans us as much as them." —Planet of the Apes 2001[24]

Faber starts the next chapter repeating the novel's opening sentence that begins "Isserley always drove past a hitch-hiker when she first saw him...."

Next, also from the opening, "Puny, scrawny specimens were of no use to her." He immediately repeats it: "This one was puny and scrawny. He was of no use to her," and on the next page yet again—"Isserley always drove straight past a hitch-hiker...."[25] We sense from his repetition and syntax that Isserley has pushed herself onto auto-pilot, perhaps as a means of pushing away not only the trauma of the attack and what she was forced to do to save her life, but the burden of having to think about that life, about going forward. We also realize that although Isserley's years on her job have contributed to deaths of countless men, she likely has never before killed a man with her bare hands.

Here the author devotes six pages to the next hitchhiker's reflection about Isserley: "She was driving like a robot.... She was in some sort of trouble, some sort of distress. She might even be in shock."[26] As William (significantly, the author gives this hitchhiker a name) rides along with Isserley, his stream of consciousness unfolds in puzzlement and humor, and finds its way to a poignant statement about humans and "the death of trust."[27] His use of the word *human* is ironic and also funny, because the one who has prompted his musing isn't human in the first place—and she believes *he's* the one who isn't human. Faber likes to play with the word, and *animals* and *primitives* as well, as if all three seem on some level interchangeable, and the world would be a better place if we could acknowledge it.

William's vilification of lying is also ironic because he's unknowingly the victim of another lie—namely, that Isserley is merely giving him a ride. Isserley was recently a victim of someone else's lie—a rapist pretending to want a ride. This sequence is in a sense transmuted in the film to the scene on the bus with Laura and Quiet. William's thought—*She might even be in shock*—captures Laura's affect while riding the bus. In the novel William wonders if he should ask Isserley if she's okay. Quiet, concerned about Laura, asks, *Are you all right?* And then, *Do you need help?* Laura's reply signals her trust and opens the door to her human experience. Quiet, trusting her, has nothing to fear (unlike the men who previously trusted her, when there was good reason not to) and opens that door.

But Isserley isn't ready. In contrast with William's concern for her, she is thinking: "He was obviously a male of the species.... A vodsel the same as all the other vodsels, one of billions infesting the planet. A few parcels' worth of meat."[28] But her disgust is also for her job. Just before triggering the icpathua needles, sending William to his fate, she wonders if this is the way she will spend the rest of her life. Then, her tears begin to flow. She doesn't know why, but she does know "something inside her is trapped."[29]

Isserley believes that the remedy for what ails her is a visit to the Processing Hall, a place she avoided. Three stories below the ground, it's an industrial space that features a contraption known as "the Cradle," which is a grain chute that resembles a giant gravy boat (more of Faber's mordant humor). After witnessing the tongue cauterization and castration of a new arrival, Isserley then asks to see the fate of a monthly. Approaching the Cradle he is pushed off balance and his enormous weight topples into the chute.

> Isserley had edged closer, aching to see his face.... Sedated though he was, the vodsel struggled ... with his own memory. It seemed to him he'd seen Isserley somewhere before. Or perhaps he merely recognized she was the only creature in the room who looked anything like him. If anyone was going to do anything for him, it would have to be her.[30]

The pens are in a dark, underground space. The underwater evisceration of Laura's captives may be quicker than the "processing" of the novel's men, but it is no less grotesque. When Andrew sees the Swimmer floating in the black depths, and reaches out to touch him, it echoes the vodsel's desperate glance at Isserley. She recognizes his long eyelashes and the reader recalls the day she picked him up on the road. In moments the man's throat is slit. Isserley screams "Yes!" but she faints, and later finds herself with Amlis Vess, who has brought her out for fresh air. His trip is ending, and has confirmed what he dreaded: that although his father had reassured him simply that "this stuff grows, we harvest it and ship it home," his father's lucrative industry is based on "terribly cruelty"[31] They argue their opposite views and finally Amlis persuades her to take him for a drive in the countryside. They come across a flock of sheep, Isserley's favorite earthly creature. When Amlis asks if she's tried them for meat, she is appalled at the thought of eating furry creatures that walk on all fours, creatures like them.

The changes in Isserley are not subtle but verbal and clear, and like Laura's cinematic signposts they lead to a decision from which there is no turning back. For Isserley that moment comes closer to the end; it's what might be the beginning of the third act in a screenplay, rather than the midpoint pivot of the film. Shifts within Laura are provided through Johansson's acting and gestures and through visuals—though not a word is spoken about who is she is, where she's from, or what she suffers and desires. In contrast Isserley's rage and longings from the beginning are apparent—at least to the reader. Laura is a product of a cinematic vision; Isserley, a literary one.

From this point forward Isserley, and the novel, hurtle toward the end. The next hitchhiker she picks up, Pennington, is himself a predator repulsed by his own actions. During their conversation she finds him different from the others and is alarmed at the thought that she might actually like him. Pennington realizes he doesn't want to hurt her, and eventually asks to be dropped off, but Isserley flips the toggle before he can get out—then she whispers, "I'm sorry, I'm sorry."[32]

That night Isserley has her usual nightmare that she's being led to a dark underground place, but then it's not her, it's a dog trapped inside a vehicle out in the wilderness—Pennington had told her he lived in a van with his dog. She thinks she might rescue Pennington, but she knows that by now he has already been mutilated. The next day Isserley gets back on the A9 to search for his van, finds his dog inside jumping back and forth on the seats, barking in a frenzy, and releases him. Her fondness for Pennington, the empathy that causes him to resist his chronic compulsion, her later regret, and the rescue—all of this is conflated in the film within Laura's experience with Lonely. After this, just as Laura flees, Isserley decides to never return to Ablach Farm. She plans to live off the land. "Her car was nestled in a bower of ferns near the edge of a loch … she waded into the icy shallows and washed herself.... She hoped the shampoo froth wouldn't do any harm to the things that lived in the loch."[33]

Off to buy food and fuel, Isserly is accosted by a hitchhiker—agitated and begging her to stop. To get rid of him she agrees to give him a lift to meet his girlfriend who's in labor. Soon he's on the subject of religion—how he can't believe that his church will think of his baby as a bastard. "'Where I come from,' she replied carefully, 'religion is … dead.'" He tells her that reincarnation appeals to him. "Everything's goat a soul, and yi cannae destroy a soul. Plus yi get tae huv anither try—dae better next time.... Who knows, eh? Ah might come back as a wumman, or a wee beastie!"[34] His words are his last before a rattle that has been plaguing Isserley's car acts up, she loses control of the steering, and crashes into a tree. When she awakens she believes her spine has been shattered. The hitchhiker is no longer in the seat.

A woman locates the hitchhiker some distance off, lying on the ground. "He's alive," she calls out. Isserley begs the woman to take him with her, but she says he shouldn't be moved, and that *Mercy Hospital* is nearby—recalling the word scratched in the ground by a doomed captive. The woman leaves to call an ambulance, but Isserley does not want to be found. As her tears fall, she remembers the device installed in the car—the "suicide pill" that will blow it—and her—into a million pieces. All it took was the courage to press the button, and the faith that the connection was still intact. Her hand shaking, she reaches forward. "Here I come."[35]

Although the book is very different from the novel, Glazer has said, "I feel like they're connected in spirit."[36] Author Michel Faber told interviewer Gabriel Diego Valdez:

> The film is indeed experimental and, quite apart from admiring its intrinsic merits, I'm relishing the fact that such a thing has infiltrated the marketplace and reached moviegoers who might not otherwise have got detoured so far outside their comfort zone. This is analogous to what I tried to do with the novel, which lulled readers into thinking it was a conventional horror-thriller before taking them on a very different ride altogether.[37]

It's interesting to see the aspects of Isserley and her experience that Glazer retained, those he left behind, and those that perhaps remain as echoes.

After Isserley leaves the farm, she's at a gas station filling up and she's hungry—and takes a chance on a packaged meal labeled "Hot Dog" (while thinking there's something weird in eating "dog" having just saved one from death). Later, crouching over in the grass near her parked car, she vomits it up. As with Laura's gagging on the cake, this physiological reality poignantly symbolizes, and foreshadows, the defeat of their assimilation into the human community. The grim darkness of the bowels of the New Estate, an atmosphere that's called up in Isserley's nightmares, her claustrophobia, and her dread of the dark, is echoed in the black space that Laura must always return to.

On the TV in Isserley's house, she hears the news report that the police are searching for a man who has gone missing—looking at the photo on the screen, Isserley recognizes the red-headed hitchhiker she had abducted. Another photo shows him with his family—two toddlers. Laura is in her car with the radio on when news of the disappearance of the family at the beach is announced. Isserley's response to the news is to reprimand herself for taking this particular man, a sign that she's losing her edge. The broadcast in the background while Laura sits in the driver's seat, the camera on her face, says everything the director wants; that she is hearing it, that she's conscious of the aftermath of her deed.

When Isserley is watching TV, her avoidance of dialogue about love is typical of her sentiments throughout the book—she misses the way men prized her natural body back at home, and resents their forsaking of her; she rails against Amlis's spoiled life, naivety and privilege, but she desires him; she has dreams and fantasies of orgasm, but her body in the shower is nothing but a reminder to her that she was surgically robbed of any possibilities. When Laura gazes at her naked form in the full-length mirror in Quiet's home—the human skin that is the film's equivalent of Isserley's transformed, human-ish body—she seems curious, not at all repulsed, admiring. The close-ups of Laura, when Quiet kisses her and soon makes love to her, bask in her bliss.

Isserley's heart and psyche are afflicted with acrimony; she has fantasized about mutilating the mouths and genitalia of the surgeons who maimed her in the same way her colleagues mutilate the vodsels. Laura's inner life is mysterious, but we sense no sign of rancor. Fittingly, Isserley's sensual longing is tinged with the bitter and the bittersweet, whereas Laura's is blossoming and tinged with beauty. Laura's desire may be a quest to find a facsimile of her sexual past, or she may have no sexual past—her longing may be that of a virgin. There are similarities between the women and their experiences, but the differences are aligned with those of the novel and the film; Faber as something more of a realist, and Glazer more the romantic.

Isserley's affinity for her natural environment is a saving grace. The awe

Amlis expresses when she shares her countryside with him reanimates her own feelings about snow, about sheep. After his departure she regards the fog as another miracle Amlis would have cherished: "A tide of white haze lapped at the grassy shores of the motorway."[38] There are no words for Laura's thoughts or feelings about nature, but as with the sound of the radio broadcast, a presence creates a notion. After she leaves the city, a bank of thick mist awaits her on an empty country road, and coastal fog curls up to surround a cove like an embrace—like Isserley's white haze lapping on the highway.

Nature delivers both women to the close of their experiences. For Laura, the forest, the snow-covered ground, her body burning, and a shot of plumes of dark smoke that dissipate into the sky. From below, the falling snow is perceived as the last thing Laura experiences in her life—her dying is a thing of beauty. Late in the novel, Isserley contemplates the vastness of the sky. "Nothing that happened on the ground could ever compete with the grandeur of what happened above ... she had made a sacrifice, and had gained the whole world forever."[39] We watch as Laura's remains ascend to the clouds. In the seconds before Isserley blows up her car, she wonders where she will go: "She would become part of the sky.... Her invisible remains would combine, over time, with all the wonders under the sun."[40] This is in Glazer's film.

Author Michel Faber said:

> Isserley's actions hurt us—get under our skin—precisely because we identify with her and want her to be OK. Feeling disapproval for Hollywood-style "baddies," or compassion for people who are presented in a very sentimentalised way, is easy. But in real life, we are challenged to feel compassion for people we dislike or fear, and to reject evil behaviours in people we love. That's much tougher than taking a theoretical stand.[41]

11
The Birth of *Under the Skin*

"Read this. Let me know what you think."[1]

Jonathan Glazer's career from the beginning looks and feels like a journey toward, and prelude to, *Under the Skin*. The commercials and music videos yield countless *aha* moments around the sights and sounds he was trying on. These are stand-alone works that are fully realized as art, but in addition we're watching him in his laboratory, experimenting, boosting it further, evolving. Relentlessly pushing the visuals and music to tell the story and seeing how far that could take him underlies both the emotional and aesthetic success of *Birth*, and with *Under the Skin* he's pulling out every stop, seeing just how much he can get away with. It's the eclipsing of the cerebral by the senses, the seduction of the viewer into gradually letting go of their addiction to language and, above all, to exposition.

A sublime step on this years-long journey, *Birth* is a bridge to *Under the Skin*—not only in Glazer's style and sensibility, but in the realms of genre, story, and character. *Birth* is not science fiction but it plays in that field, as Glazer had done early on in the surreal tone and imagery of *Street Spirit (Fade Out)*, the fantasy of the Walter-inspired (both Campbell and Crane) *Surfer*, and nearly all of his work—from the color explosions of *Paint* to the dream sequences of *Sexy Beast*. He flirted with science fiction for a decade before finally plunging in full-throttle with Faber's book about creatures from outer space. For both director and star, *Birth* was something of a genre Trojan horse. Kidman said it wasn't the reincarnation aspect that drew her to the project, because she saw that "he was trying to make a film about love."[2] *Under the Skin* is also a film that is less about the paranormal than the very normal: one woman's journey. But it took Glazer many years and multiple drafts of the script to uncover what would become the essence of the film, its driving force.

A peregrination of a dozen years began in 2000–2001 when Jim Wilson at Film4 Ltd. in London received a copy of Faber's novel from a William Morris agent named Bill Contardi.[3] As a production executive at Film4, Wilson had just shepherded Glazer's *Sexy Beast* (about to be released) as well as (among others) Lars von Trier's *Dancer in the Dark* (2000), a documentary about the Sex Pistols called *The Filth and the Fury* (2000), and earlier at Fox Searchlight, *The Full Monty* (1997).

The book also crossed the path of producer Nick Wechsler, whose company Industry Entertainment had a first-look arrangement with Film4. "Jeff Sommerville, development executive in my office, brought me the book," he recalls. "I read it, I loved it, and I reached out to the author through his agent Sylvie Rabineau. We made a deal and optioned the book,"[4] and going forward the two companies collaborated to make the film. "I had been looking for an unusual first-contact movie," says Wechsler. "I knew this would attract an interesting filmmaker—and it did."

Wechsler's producing credits included Gus van Sant's gritty breakthrough feature *Drugstore Cowboy* (1989) and Darren Aronofsky's unflinching *Requiem for A Dream* (2000), the follow-up to the director's low-budget horror/psychodrama *Pi*. Later Wexler would make *The Road* (2007) with Viggo Mortensen, based on the post-apocalyptic Cormac McCarthy novel. In the same year as *Drugstore Cowboy* Wechsler produced Stephen Soderbergh's debut feature, the game-changing erotic thriller *Sex Lies and Videotape* (1989). He recalls,

> Ann Dollard was Steven's agent. She had just signed this young man out of Baton Rouge who had written a few scripts. He was fresh and a new voice. There was something about his short films, he was the star, they had a raw comedic edginess—so I asked Ann to introduce me. I said, "I'd like to be a part of trying to get you off the ground." He wrote the script in three weeks after a breakup with a girl. That script was a darker version of what you see on the screen.

"I like doing movies that first of all are distinct artistically, if possible," says Wechsler, "that take me by surprise or lead me down a different path." As a team Wilson and Wechsler, given their penchant for coaxing an audience down the rabbit hole of their fears and fantasies, seemed fated to be drawn into Faber's marriage of the bizarre and the profoundly human. Believing the story was intensely cinematic, Wilson felt it could be "something an innovative director might be drawn to, because it would allow them to push the envelope, in terms of film language,"[5] arguably Jonathan Glazer's first language. Wilson gave the Faber novel to Glazer who liked the central character, and "seeing the world through her eyes—her being an alien.... I remember being very taken by that."[6] Wechsler says, "Through my pal Jeremy Thomas, who produced *Sexy Beast*, I'd heard all about Jon—and when it was suggested by Paul (Webster, head of Film4) to give it to Glazer, I thought it was a great idea. Jon was intrigued and met me in LA, and we agreed to do it together."

To write the script the team chose author Alexander Stuart, who had recently adapted for the screen his own controversial novel *The War Zone* (1999), a Film4 project and the directorial debut of actor Tim Roth. Roger Ebert called the film "brilliant and heartbreaking…. The movie is not about incest as an issue, but about incest as a blow to the heart and the soul—a real event, here, now, in a family that seems close and happy."[7] Faber's book one year later was a finalist for the prestigious Whitbread Award for a first novel, and Stuart's book had received the Whitbread Prize for Best Novel; the honor was short-lived, however, for the controversial nature of the story became controversial among the judges, and the award was quickly withdrawn.[8] In the film world, however, where controversy is often courted rather than dreaded, *The War Zone* debuted at Sundance, was nominated by the Independent Spirit Awards for Best Foreign Film, and earned a score of other nominations and awards.

While Stuart was in London working on *The War Zone*, Paul Webster, at that time the head of Film4, gave him Faber's book and said: "Read this. Let me know what you think…."

> I read it on the plane home to LA and told him I loved it, and was back in London to meet Jon in a couple of weeks. Film4 flew me to London from LA as he was readying his first film…. They screened it for me and it blew me away. I'd just worked with Ray Winstone on *The War Zone*, and I loved his performance in *Sexy Beast*.[9]

Stuart recalls his work with Glazer on the early drafts of a screenplay for *Under the Skin* as "a weird and fabulous journey for me, in territory both unknown and imagined—drawn both from Michel Faber's novel and the landscape of my own father's childhood in northern Scotland." Although the script "changed enormously" from the time he worked on it, "I still feel a curious sense of ownership even when I see still images from the film."[10] An example of this intimate connection can be found in a single line from one of Stuart's very early drafts, "The whole forest trembles in the wind,"[11] an image that lingers powerfully on screen in Laura's dream at the bothy. Stuart's screenplay was a "faithful adaptation"[12] and fundamentally one cinematic step away from Faber's novel—in essence a bridge from the book to the screen. Glazer liked the script, yet "I knew then that I absolutely didn't want to film the book. But I still wanted to make the book a film."[13] Wilson and Glazer, in the thick of the screenwriting phase on *Birth*, decided to send the Faber novel to writer Milo Addica. He read it and arrived in the UK for a meeting.

Glazer asked Addica what he liked about the book. "It's about hitchhiking at night," he told him, and the director agreed. On its surface the reply seems almost flippant, until you think about a premise that involves darkness, encounters with strangers, and the embrace of the unknown. The final film evolved from this kernel—even more than from the premise of flesh-eating aliens. It's a risk-taker who hitchhikes—and the same is true of the driver that stops.

Jon expressed to Milo his desire for something "explorative" with the new draft of the script—it was to be the next stage in moving away from the novel. Addica's version brought the town—the community and the neighbors where Laura was living during her mission—into the mix, an area which had not played a role in Faber's novel. Laura is confronted by a rival alien who has come to replace her, which is a kind of precursor to the image in the film of Laura's "predecessor," and the notion that she is one in a long line of replaceable recruits for this job.

Near the end, "when Laura accompanies a man into his home, he discovers she is an alien when he spots a tear in her human skin. He reacts by burning her to death using a homemade flame thrower," said Addica. "He's a guy who would have gone to see the movie *Alien*, and that's how he responds to her." This scenario of Laura's end—which in some form or another involves fire in the book and in various stages of the script—most closely resembles the one that ended up in the film. But at this point *Birth* was the more pressing issue, and the writer and director shifted their attentions. When *Birth* was finished, and they met again to work on *Skin*, "I think we hit a wall," recalls Addica. "He wasn't sure what he wanted.... I was following his direction, I think I hit a wall as well." Milo returned to the U.S. Wechsler remembers,

> I worked on every draft—Stuart, Addica—all of them could have been really interesting films.... We would labor over this every year, except when Jon was on *Birth*. Jon was close to loving the earlier drafts, but something was holding him back—they didn't speak to what he really had inside his head. So each time we had to blow it up, start again, look for another writer.

By 2005 the project was enjoying new support from the UK Film Council (first from development head Jenny Borgars, and later Tanya Seghatchian) and from BFI's Sally Ann Caplan. Sometime near the end of 2006 Glazer re-teamed with Walter Campbell, who recalls that Jon asked him to write up something he could read to the folks at Film4. "Jon said, 'I'm trying to make a political horror film.' So I wrote 14 or 15 pages—paranoia and isolation, mythology and all those things, and sent them, thinking maybe this will get the wheels turning." Wilson says that Film4 and UKFC were "blown away."[14] Campbell's starting point diverged from that of the two previous screenwriters, and he chose not to read the novel. Instead, lengthy conversations with Glazer were the springboard—that had always been their modus operandi, the way they were accustomed to collaborating. "John and I do like kicking ideas around," says Campbell.

> We care where we end up, but we don't set off with that agenda in mind.... With this project there were a lot of very strange conversations ... about things like existence. It was this weirdly indulgent sort of stuff ... sometimes not really having anything to do

Producer Nick Wechsler, whose Industry Entertainment had a first-look deal with Film4, brought *Under the Skin* to Claudia Bluemhuber at Silver Reel. His many credits include the post-apocalyptic drama *The Road* (2009) based on Cormac McCarthy's novel. In this photograph the boy (Kodi Smit-McPhee) provides sustenance for his ailing father (Viggo Mortensen). Dimension Films/Photofest © Dimension Films.

with the story ... almost like taking a very scenic route to where we wanted to go to achieve something with the film.[15]

Their 2008 screenplay is an adventurous departure from the novel that involves not a singular alien protagonist but an alien couple who arrives in the Scottish Highlands and moves into Ablach Farm (the locale in Faber's book) as a farmer and his wife—Raymond and Laura Flynn. Faithful to a key element of the novel's premise—aliens arrive on Earth to harvest humans as food—the screenplay builds on earlier drafts (particularly the involvement of the community in the plot), at the same time mining the story's potential for the visually dazzling and disturbing.[16]

Campbell and Glazer's opening-sequence description of the alien's metamorphosis to appear human is radically different from the novel's, in which an earthly furry animal is surgically modified to look human. The leaving behind of this animal-alien moves beyond a visual difference to an important diegetic one, for it's an aspect of having also left behind, somewhere between the novel and 2008, the human/animal allegory that drives Faber's story.

This draft's opening sequence also paints the distinctive tone and cinematic signature for the movie that was eventually to be. The blackness of outer space that conveys the alien arrival becomes the black setting for the alien transformation—and later the mysterious blackness in which their mission is carried out. From the blackness there is movement—"something is articulating itself into form.... Intricate structures start to grow, conjured like some abominable spell ... plumes or spikes flourish with explosive urgency." Suggesting ominously the intelligence of this alien form, "It's as if it's expressing that it can become anything." Details emerge—"a writhing web of tendrils" and a "ragged meandering arterial system that weaves itself into the shape of arms and legs and a torso." When formed, a "male" steps into a hollow form that awaits him. Then, "the back of the female form is peeled outward along the spine, splayed in anticipation." The female, like the male before her, "climbs into the flesh like a ballerina stepping into a tutu." While the setting anticipates the spectacular black water sequence in the film, "abominable spell" and "explosive urgency" invoke the evisceration of the victims. Their de-composition is in a sense the opposite of this "creation" yet akin to it; it's the filling of a skin, rather than the emptying. The splaying of the female to receive its animated form is also the opposite of the scene we see in the forest, when the Logger tears open Laura's skin to reveal her alien form beneath.

In the final film, the black humanoid introduced in the beginning of this draft is seen only in the briefest of glimpses, and saved for a big reveal and a very emotional one—in the climactic scene in the forest, when Laura removes her covering and holds in her hands her human countenance. The alien being's morphing through the various states in the 2008 script—the "sudden gleam of a spike," a triangular form "shocking in its geometric progression," and a "writhing web of tendrils"—is eliminated. Instead of thinking of what is under Laura's skin as a "repulsive and viperous form"—or non-organic, non-sentient "gleaming" product of a cold technology—we have in the movie only the image of a humanesque being, a possible relation to us, and an object of empathy—the element upon which the film's poignant ending is dependent. In the movie, versus the earlier draft, the difference between the alien and the audience is rendered as truly skin-deep.

In this mid-journey draft, the alien couple's exposure to and interaction with townsfolk (in contrast with both novel and film, where there are almost no witnesses) introduces a layer of science fiction devices that doesn't exist in the book. Their ubiquity in the genre doesn't diminish the suspense we're dreadfully and gleefully accustomed to in monster flicks. For example, the "nobody believes me" trope (Kevin McCarthy's futile attempts to warn people about the "pods" in *Invasion of the Body Snatchers*) yields a local named Wystan, whose tale of spotting "a wee man in a black diving suit" in the forest gives his buddies at the pub a good laugh, and causes his trusted former school teacher to assure him it was a dream—or too much drinking. At a pub Raymond is accosted by a young local who senses the off-ness about him—"You're not from Cornwall," she says menacingly. The alien couple is repeatedly harassed by four teenage boys who are also on to something suspicious, and one confronts Raymond with "You're a wrong one. Something rotten wi yee." In other science fiction/horror tropes Raymond has a close call with law enforcement when the body of an escaped victim (like Lonely in the film) is found on Ablach property; he fends off curious visitors (one is a pastor who would like to see Laura dress less seductively) with lies, and he murders a poacher on his property—but Raymond is too canny to be caught.

The couple is jettisoned from the story in later drafts, once Glazer decides that Laura's perspective, her experience, and her personal journey will drive his film. Laura's alien overseer Bad in an abridged way later takes Raymond's place, and Bad's far more limited role in the story allows—along with other deletions and changes—for the film to achieve Glazer's governing aesthetic: a movie that is less verbal and expository, and more mysterious to the viewer—who must do much more of the work. The significance of mirrors in Laura's alien world—and in the control over her behavior—is more explicit in the 2008 draft, where Raymond himself gazes deeply into mirrors, eventually orders Laura to "stay away from mirrors," and actually smashes one; in the movie, the power of mirrors is suggested only subtly, left to be inferred by the audience.

Other literal elements in this draft that are also later abandoned: an alien (black humanoid) is depicted dining on red (human) meat, and an alien in the form of a bird "tells" Raymond when Laura flees the farm. But by this draft, although more drafts and five years remain before the film is shot, Campbell and Glazer have several critical elements they will retain: the drowning of the family at the cove, and four of Laura's victims (the Footballer, the Swimmer, Lonely, and her romantic liaison with a precursor to Quiet). There's also a scene like the follow-up to the nightclub sequence, where a throng of drunken Scottish women pour out of a stretch limo and accost Laura outside her van, recruiting her to join them at a club—and later one says, "Look at her, she looks like a film star." And then there is the black-water demise of Laura's victims.

Campbell tells a story about a job he once had:

> I had sold hardware at markets all around Ireland. I heard this story about this guy there that always fascinated me ... a big tall guy and heavy-set, but something in him looked fragile, and sensitive. After that he wasn't seen in the markets anymore, so I asked, "Whatever happened to that guy?" and they said, "He just walked into the sea one day," and this idea attached itself to me. The idea of these guys walking into the black—and in that, for me, there was something very interesting and poetic, and hypnotic—and I thought "What about this?" What about this experience of willfully walking into this darkness? I thought it might work in the film in a very beautiful way.

Yet in this draft even the black space is more literal, not the elusive non-space of the film: a staircase down into the water is visible, and the black space, along with a tunnel, are located in a barn on the farm.

There are also the early stages of Laura's evolution along her journey. After killing the Swimmer with a rock Laura returns home, and washing the sand from her hands, gazes at the whirlpool of water running down the sink—which matches the notion of the whirlpool at the ocean that swallowed up the family. "We're seeing a burgeoning," Campbell and Glazer write in the script's direction. "The meaning of the event she witnessed connecting with her. She looks away." This moment isn't in the film, but others are that are more understated; Laura sitting in her van while the news of the drowning plays on her car radio; Laura examining the human blood the rose has left on her hands. In the 2008 script, Laura's encounter with a disfigured man serves, as it does in the film, to accelerate her "drift"; after releasing him her face reveals "enlightenment ... pure tranquility," and precipitates her flight from Ablach, from Raymond, and above all, from the mission. In this phase the scene has more dialogue, including Laura's reference to the man's face—the effect in the film of having her not acknowledge this in any way, verbal or otherwise, underscores her indifference to it, aligns the two as outsiders, and serves the goal of leaving as much as possible in the film unsaid. Also left behind in the fullness of time is that Laura's release of the man from her house is witnessed by the teens' ringleader, Fanning. The elimination of all these community connections streamlines the film's narrative toward Glazer's singular goal of Laura's personal journey, which is not woman versus society, nor woman versus God or nature, but woman challenged by, and challenging, herself.

This script's last scenes have elements in common with the film's finale. After Laura's romantic encounter comes to an abrupt end, her alien identity is discovered by a tow-truck driver, who sets her on fire, and as her last act before dying, "the beautiful, gentle face looks up at the black alien head looking down. Hunched over her 'self,' in an extraordinary separation. The inside looking at the outside, the outside looking at the inside." The idea had captured Glazer's imagination and became a kind of subtext, a lingering feeling, for the remaining versions of the script.

Raymond discovers her and grinds Laura's charred remains into the dirt with his boot. Soon after he returns home, a portal in his bedroom wall, beyond which is black space, delivers a brand new "Laura"—identical to the previous one—so that when authorities arrive to question the couple, the matter of Laura's disappearance can be averted. Again the aliens dodge the bullet, but the story's end belongs to Fanning and the boys, who return to Ablach Farm determined to prove the bizarre foul play they suspect. Unlike the closing sequence in the final film, it's a scene that—not suggesting intent here!—invites a sequel.

By November 2011, a month after shooting began, the screenplay leaves behind the alien couple and their interaction with the community, focusing entirely upon Laura's journey. But what is most interesting about this 2011 script[17] are the many differences between it and what we eventually see on the screen—illuminating the changes that were made afterward, either during the filming or in editing. A critical difference between this shooting script and the final film is how dramatically the amount of dialogue between Laura and her victims has been reduced. For example, there are five pages worth of conversation from the time Laura stops to talk with the Footballer to his sinking into the black space. It's nearly all gone in the film, most notably lines where Laura expresses (disingenuous) concern over whether she's safe giving him a ride. He replies, "I think you've got it all back to front love, it's the ones that give you the lift you're meant to worry about. I'm the one that's meant to be frightened. Do you see, the question is, am I going to be safe with you?" The ironic exchange, which telegraphs the scene's outcome, is exactly the kind of thing Glazer would get rid of—but he doesn't stop there. He cuts virtually all the talking: the scene's story is told visually.

Walter Campbell, who came on board mid-journey as co-screenwriter on *Under the Skin*, recalls that Jon had expressed to him, "I'm trying to make a political horror film." Campbell wrote up "14 or 15 pages of paranoia and isolation, mythology, and all those things"—a pitch very well received by Film4 and the UK Film Council. This photograph was snapped on location in 2011 (courtesy Alexander O'Neal).

When she picks up the Nervous Man, three pages of dialogue, including lines that describe his anxiety over entering her decrepit house—he sees someone behind a curtain and fears getting "jumped"—are jettisoned in favor of a single glance behind him as he approaches the house (see photograph in Chapter 4). At least two places in the script, including Laura's meeting with Andrew inside the club and her conversation with Lonely, have the writers indicating "Improv From Here"—aligning with Johansson's comment in interviews that Glazer often recoiled when he heard the scripted dialogue.[18] Here she asks

Lonely to "look into my eyes—look into me." In the film, instead, we have visual cues about her eyes, and Nervous Man's observation about them is far subtler than Laura's dialogue in the script. One of many examples in the script of Glazer's commitment to eschewing the on-the-nose when it comes to the aliens' nature is the deletion of two incidents that show a "hissing gas" escaping from their bodies—when Bad is cut, and when Laura is attacked. The sweeping changes in dialogue and the cutting of explicit details can be summarized as an ongoing and relentless paring down, like the dropping of baggage that weighs the film down and keeps it from taking flight to Glazer and Campbell's vision.

12
Scarlett Johansson

From the age of three Johansson wanted to act. Her mom (Melanie Sloan, later her manager) was a film buff who introduced her to all types of movies—and Rodgers & Hammerstein musicals. "I was a big ham, I suppose.... I wanted to be Judy Garland in *Meet me in St. Louis*. I wanted to be Rosalind Russell in *Auntie Mame*. I made people pay to see the shows I put on."[1]

Her 2014 interview with Barbara Walters is peppered with home movie clips of Scarlett at eight singing *I Enjoy Being a Girl* and offering an introduction—"This is a new tap-dancing step that I made up"—before confidently tapping across the room. Here's a child who is not just talented and full of charm, but who appears to possess—not a wish, nor a dream, but *knowledge*—that she will one day be a star. We believe she knows this the only way she can possibly know it—because in her heart, she already is. The Walters segment also includes video of her audition at age nine for the film *Jumanji*. She didn't get the role. Rejection is what happens "most of the time" to an actor, she told Walters. It didn't change things. She had a craft to hone.[2] In an earlier interview she told Sanjiv Bhattacharya in *New York Magazine*, "I was one of those kids who used to stare in the mirror until I made myself cry."[3]

How the starry-eyed three-year-old traversed three decades to be featured on *Barbara Walters Presents: The 10 Most Fascinating People of 2014* seems on many levels to have little to do with *Under the Skin*, but may have everything do with it. At least part of the actor's fascination Walters attributed to the fact that Johansson had "conquered the all-boys club of superheroes" as the character Natalia "Natasha" Romanova aka Black Widow from Marvel Comics, "the world's biggest action movie franchise."[4] A celebrated actor bringing the character of a female superhero to global cinema is a stride for audiences and for actresses alike. Johansson's role in *Under the Skin* places Laura (in her unique fashion) in a lengthy series of roles the actress has chosen, and continues to choose, that portray female empowerment.

Johansson was born and raised in Manhattan and attended PS 41 in Greenwich Village. Her first audition was a voice-over for Kitchen-Aid, and she got the job, but it was her first and last commercial—because her voice was so deep. "I was this blonde, kind of small, enthusiastic kid, and then I'd open up my mouth and people would go, 'Oh, do you have a cold?'" She says she was "terrible at selling things" and "really bad at improvising…. I'd get so overwhelmed." After one particularly discouraging rejection she was (and not the first time) crying on the subway ride home, and her mom decided that from then on commercial auditions were out for the seven-year-old.[5] She studied at the Lee Strasberg Institute for a year at age eleven, and graduated from the Professional Children's School (PCS), where alumni include Joan Blondell and Ruby Keeler, Christopher Walken and Carrie Fisher, Yo-Yo Ma, Malcolm-Jamal Warner, and Macaulay Culkin.[6]

Her first feature role—for which she may have auditioned around the time of her *Jumanji* call—was a small part in Rob Reiner's *North* (1994), starring Elijah Wood as a boy who emancipates himself to go off in search of better parents. "I needed a 9- or 10-year-old girl to be the daughter of Faith Ford and John Ritter," recalls casting director Jane Jenkins. "I only saw a handful of kids. Scarlett had a perfect look for their child, and read the lines well. I brought her in to meet Rob Reiner after I had auditioned her—and BAM! he thought she was perfect and she landed the part. I do remember meeting her way back then, because she came in with confidence and was assured—not a quality many young children have."[7]

The young actress quickly gained momentum. Two years and three films later her dramatic prowess in the indie *Manny and Lo* (1996) earned her, at age 12, an Independent Spirit Awards nomination for Best Female Lead, and when Robert Redford directed her in *The Horse Whisperer* (1998) he commented that as an actor Scarlett was "13 going on 30."[8] Such was her presence in these emotionally demanding roles, yet her comedic gift brought to life the surly teenager Rebecca in *Ghost World* (2001), its title a poignant descriptor for the adolescent experience of "the loneliness of finding oneself in a world where life is not always easy or definable."[9] Directed by Terry Zwigoff and based on the graphic novel by Daniel Clowes, the film is dark, irreverent, and demonstrates Johansson's precociously droll humor. The deep voice that caused her to tank her commercial auditions was a boon in her turn as Thora Birch's sidekick, delivering to perfection lines like, "Most people are okay, but mostly I just feel like poisoning everybody."[10]

Launched by *North* Johansson's youthful career had flourished. As a child and then a young teen she was on screen every year during the decade ending in 2003, when her adult metamorphosis came in the form of two intriguing and wildly disparate roles—*Girl with the Pearl Earring* and *Lost in Translation*. The former, a period piece directed by Peter Webber based on the bestseller by Tracy Chevalier, is the story behind the portrait by Dutch painter Johannes Vermeer (Colin Firth). Johansson plays Griet, a young housekeeper in the artist's family home who captures his imagination (and he, hers) and becomes the muse for his masterpiece. In one scene at a window, he prompts her past her quick dismissal of clouds as "white" until she discovers the yellow, blue, and grey.[11] In awakening her to truly seeing the world, he also awakens a new awareness of herself, and an unfamiliar desire.

Johansson recalled that she felt increasingly, as filming progressed, that "the Vermeer character was this untouchable, mysterious man, this genius, and my character was completely longing, and obsessive, and in love with this man. It was physically heartbreaking, that's how apparent it became."[12] Just after Vermeer brings Griet to realize that there's more to see in the sky and in the world than she previously thought, there's a shot of her face with the subtlest of smiles. We sense her reacting to this revelation as well as the one growing within her that we've yet to see, and she has yet to understand. In a later scene Vermeer sends Griet to another room to take down her hair, which is pulled back and hidden in a cumbersome housemaid's cap, so he can bring his model closer to what's in his mind's eye. She's alone in the room as she stands removing the cap and her auburn hair softly unravels around her shoulders. When the door unexpectedly opens and she sees him looking at her, it's more than a metaphor implied by her "letting down her hair" to him; in her face is the stunned expression of what she feels for him. Johansson's intense presence in these moments of silence and stillness is something she draws on deeply years later in *Under the Skin*.

Webber said, "If I'm going to take a girl and repress her, put her in a situation where she's not allowed to be herself.... I don't know anyone else who can do the amount of storytelling she can in her close-up. Her thoughts just run across her eyes ... that's acting."[13]

"I constantly struggle," Johansson admitted in a 2003 interview for *Lost in Translation*. She watches herself on screen and says, "God, why did I make that choice? Or why did they use that take? Or what's wrong with the intonation in my voice?!" She finds acting "a very strange profession. You're manipulating your emotions all the time. It's very unnatural, going against the grain." The saving grace may be that "as you get older you have more things to pick and choose from, and you know yourself better and better."[14]

As a teen Johansson could and did play much older characters, making her passage to adult roles a practically seamless one—in fact, she went back and forth with ease. At fifteen she played eighteen in *Ghost World*, and with Griet she played approximately her own age of seventeen.[15] When Sofia Coppola decided to cast her as a 24-year-old in *Lost in Translation*, "everybody said, 'She's too young,'" Johansson recalls, but "she was there for me from the get-go."[16] Coppola said, "I just liked her from that movie *Manny & Lo*, and [even though] she was seventeen, I had this idea of her being this young Lauren Bacall–type girl. I loved her low voice."[17] "What Johansson accomplished isn't typical," observes producer/actor and former casting director Edmund Gaynes (and another child actor graduate of PCS). "Early adolescence is the most common time for an actor to lose his or her career. Many finish for good at 12 or 13, others don't get past 18 or 19. For some that's a life choice, but for most they just don't make the transitions—from child to teen, or teen to adult. To go right through—without interruption—is rare."[18]

"The more you know what you want, the less things upset you," Bob Harris (Bill Murray) reassures his new young acquaintance Charlotte (Johansson).[19] No doubt his advice holds some wisdom for her, but the truth is that although he's over twice her age he's as lost as she is—a bittersweet common ground for the two protagonists in *Lost in Translation*, who meet on a brief stay in Tokyo. Far from Griet's quiet, demure girl who knows her place in her patriarchal culture, restless Charlotte is bristling at her own time and place; educated, emancipated and outspoken, all that is expected of a young, modern woman, she is wondering why she feels so bad. Her rock band–photographer husband John (a pitch-perfect Giovanni Ribisi) is mostly not around, but when he is the disconnect between the two relative newlyweds is palpable.

There's a bit of the sarcastic Rebecca from *Ghost World* in Johansson's humor throughout, as in a hotel lobby encounter between the couple and movie star Kelly (hilarious Anna Faris), who's there promoting her new action film, and with whom John probably had some past diddlings. When Kelly implores the two to look her up so they can meet for drinks ("I'm under Evelyn Waugh ... get it?") and then takes off, Charlotte tells John, "Evelyn Waugh? Evelyn Waugh was a man." "Aw come on," he tells her, "she's nice. Not everyone went to Yale, you know. Why do you have to be like that? Always playing on how stupid everyone is." Charlotte tries to defend herself—"I just thought it was funny."

A standout scene for Johansson comes early in the story, a poignant window on Charlotte's character as she navigates her difficult emotions. After roaming all day, trying to take in the city, she's back at her hotel, and makes a long-distance call to her friend Lauren. She is clearly distraught, but she's on her own here—her friend is distant in more ways than one. Ed Gonalez wrote "Charlotte struggles, even weeps, to see the meaning buried beneath all the kimonos, local religious ceremonies, Karaoke bars and strip joints."[20] Planting her in the luxurious Park Hyatt Tokyo with all its blatant luxury and surrounding her continuously with the magnificence of the city is Coppola's way of not only putting her character's melancholy in bold relief, but confronting her with the responsibility of her own life. That message is underscored by Lauren's distracted dismissal of Charlotte's crisis (Charlotte hangs up the receiver as Lauren's blithe "love you" hangs in the air) and by her husband's emotional absence. The phone call is one of the existential moments in this deceptively comic film, and the ingénue Johansson is wrenchingly up to the task. The connection between Johansson's character and Murray's—with the age difference, it could have been awkward, or worse, lascivious—couldn't be more natural and convincing. "You can't really gauge the chemistry unless you do tests before you start shooting," said Coppola, "and I don't think they even met before we did, so I just picked someone I liked (Johansson) and hoped that it worked ... it's just something about how Bill is that it never came off as lecherous. Maybe because he's such a kid. And Bill is so lovable."[21]

"That fresh young thing?" "She's fresh all right."[22]

Johansson's performances in these two 2003 releases, marked by restraint and by depth of character held in subtext, were followed by roles that opened the emotional floodgates for her. *A Love Song for Bobby Long* (2004) and *Match Point* (2005) gave her a different type of challenge in the opportunity to go full-throttle, outwardly expressing the frustration and rage of characters who find themselves tethered to personal demons. The first film is a pivotal moment for her, "a coming of age tale both for the actress and her character" notes critic Tanya Chesterfield. The teen "holds her own" opposite John Travolta, in a performance that is both "stunning" and "subtle and heartfelt."[23] The film's director/writer Shainee Gabel recalls that Johansson was only fifteen when she met her, as the five-year-journey to the film's release began. "She's a joy to direct," said Gabel. "She'll try it five different ways and each one of the five will be the perfect version of what you're looking for."[24]

When Pursy Will arrives to live at the New Orleans home of her estranged mother Lorraine, who has just died, she discovers two squatters: erstwhile English professor Bobby (Travolta) who is served his wakeup vodka and orange juice by former student Lawson (Gabriel Macht). Bobby leans up in bed just enough to take a sip of his drink, and then announces that they don't plan to leave.

> PERCY: You know, Lorraine thinking I'd share this shit-hole with two alcoholic strangers. I mean you are alcoholics, aren't you?
> BOBBY: But we are not strangers.

Pursy stays because she has nowhere to go, nothing to lose, and a heavy burden of curiosity about her past, of which she knows little—including who her father is. In the early scenes Johansson plays Pursy's resentment and rage at the mother who abandoned her as armor that's toughened her to the world.

Scarlett Johansson is directed by Shainee Gabel in *A Love Song for Bobby Long* (2004), which Gabel also wrote. As a teen actor Johansson held her own opposite mature, veteran male costars; here with John Travolta, with Colin Firth in *Girl with the Pearl Earring* (2003), and with Bill Murray in *Lost in Translation* (2001). Lions Gate Films/Photofest © Lions Gate.

She is *stinking* surly, but it doesn't phase her neighbor Cecil (Dane Rhodes), who lets her know that Lorraine named her after *purslane* because she thought of her as golden. It's a *weed*, Pursy tells him, and when he replies, "So are dandelions, but that doesn't stop kids from making wishes on 'em," he's letting her see that he knows who she is. In contrast is Pursy's strained relationship with Bobby—neither of them knows who he was exactly in Lorraine's life, and who Pursy is supposed to be. Johansson and Travolta capture their complex emotions in a scene that starts off with their usual verbal sparring before suddenly blowing up. Pursy baits him, mocking his has-been life and his constant boozing. He pushes back that it's time for her to carry her own weight, and she pushes further—"Maybe you'd rather I pick up a few dollars bringin' friends home, didn't Lorraine have to do that for a while? Huh? Most junkies do."

Appalled at her disrespect Bobby loses it, then throws it back at her once more—"Ever had two men at once?" Johansson as Pursy reacts instinctively here—out of shock on top of fear—as she throws a drink in his face and kicks him in the groin. She is breathless and trembling as she spits his own words back at him, "You're supposed to be the senior male, huh? Grow up!" Then she cries out, frightened, and as if just realizing it, "I'm just a girl!" The scene is a tour de force of writing and directing, of acting and spontaneity and timing, and—for both veteran and freshman—of star power. Johansson's performance is also the third time in as many years that she's held her own onscreen with a much older male star. "She's a very generous actor," Travolta said of her. "She did give me off-camera what I needed.... Meryl Streep has often said it's just as important if not more important what you do off camera, because that completes two performances. I think Scarlett knows that innately."[25] "If there is such a thing as a natural, it's Scarlett," said Gabel. "It's very rare. I feel fortunate that she latched on to this script in the way that she did."[26]

Following her ingénue in *Lost in Translation* with a teenager in *Bobby Long*, Johansson breaks out with a raw adult performance as the struggling—on many levels—actress in *Match Point* (2005). Offering distinctly uncharted territory for her, the movie is also a rarity for the filmmaker—Woody Allen's very few flat-out dramas in his fifty years of filmmaking include *Interiors* (1978), the later *Cassandra's Dream* (2007), and more recently *Wonder Wheel* (2017). The story is set in and around contemporary London. Exploring the mansion of a wealthy new client, former tennis pro Chris Wilton (Jonathan Rhys Meyers) follows the sound of ping pong and discovers Nola Rice (Johansson) playfully gloating over a victory. "So, who's my next victim?" she addresses Chris as he enters, and invitingly suggests, "You?" But her playing is no match for his.

NOLA: Did anyone ever tell you—you play a very aggressive game?
CHRIS: Did anyone ever tell you you have very sensual lips?
NOLA: Extremely aggressive.[27]

Johansson's first scene in the film, the seductive and fateful meeting of two fetching and determined social climbers, has dialectical tension. She is a touch angelic in her wispy blond hair, pastel lips, and glowing skin, a delicate gold chain adorning her neck. The afternoon light through gauzy curtains falls softly on her demure little white cotton dress—even the stuffed animals surrounding her signal a sweetness and innocence, all of it in sly contrast with her apparent cunning and her cool authority, her baiting of a handsome stranger with a facetious thousand-pound wager. Johansson's coyness is a silken glove, with slight tilts of her head, her perfect pauses and mannerisms, how she lights her cigarette so close to Meyers's face and breezily exhales the smoke. Then there's her cagily laconic timing: her eyes follow the ball to where it's landed, and then she looks back at Chris. Will she resent his display of skill, clearly intended as a dare? She breaks into an altogether friendly smile, and looks him up and down. All before finally responding several seconds later; and we wonder, who's getting taken in here? Add her sultry voice and it's easy to be reminded, as was director Sofia Coppola, of another ingenue in command of her game, newcomer Lauren Bacall in *To Have and Have Not* (1944).

It is just a game, but the stakes quickly escalate. At their next chance meeting, after an audition downtown goes badly for Nola, she steers Chris toward a bar, and here Johansson offers a truer glimpse of Nola than the confident gamer; brooding and self-deprecating (she's merely "sexy," she tells him, while her sister is "classically beautiful"), melancholic and fatalistic, and drinking too much. Her lost soul-ness heightens her sensuality even as it shouts "easy mark" to Chris, played with a velvet ferocity by Meyers. Their feverish mutual attraction soon trumps the fact that both are poised to marry into the same wildly rich family. The afternoons of clandestine passion begin—and continue once Chris is married—until finally Nola discovers she's pregnant.

In Nola's requests that Chris "do the right thing"—abandon his loveless, mercenary marriage and be with her instead—Johansson moves from the voice of moral reason through the increasingly anxious and desperate to the frantic. "Watching her downward spiral is a grueling testament to her acting chops," said critic Lexi Feinberg.[28] Lying in wait outside Chris's office on a busy street she pounces; her screaming accusations pierce him like poison darts as he struggles to hijack her into a taxi. It's mainly in these later scenes that Nola's character calls up comparisons with American author Theodore Dreiser's dark realist novel *An American Tragedy* and its adaptations,[29] in which a pregnant girlfriend becomes for a man a problem to be solved in a most violent manner.

Because a murderer goes unpunished, the message construed from *Match Point* can be that life is without meaning—in depicting that "evil can subvert justice," writes Luca Badaloni, "Allen reached the pinnacle of nihilism."[30] A scenario similar to *Match Point*'s plays out in Woody Allen's earlier film *Crimes and Misdemeanors* (1992) but the director does not embrace this frequent comparison, asserting that the previous film is about religion, whereas *Match Point* is a story about luck.[31] In both cases the murderer is a man whose wealth and power are threatened by a woman who has neither, and it's easy to catch yet a third message (apart from the obvious gender issue) which is that the film is about class; the "rich get away with murder" (see *The Great Gatsby, Chinatown*, and so many others). Yet another interpretation is that in a Darwinian struggle for survival (however that word is defined, in nature or society) the strong prevail over the weak.

In any and all of these spheres—the amoral versus the moral, the lucky versus the unlucky, the ruthless versus the vulnerable—Johansson's acting furiously pushes back. In a performance that moves from the lushly erotic to the shrill, from indignation to rage, she is relentless against all the forces she knows are working against her—existential, economic, evolutionary—and she is not backing down. In a fury Johansson delivers Nola's last stand on the street as she demands to speak to his Chris's wife. If gold-digging were truly her core she'd accept when Chris pleads with her to either have an abortion ("No! I've done that before.") or let him support the child, but this is about more than money, and what the actress so desperately embodies here is a woman's determination, after past mistakes or ongoing frailties, to redeem her life, to save herself. Nola's eventual role as the film's "moral center" is ironic, for in the early scenes she is just as amoral as he is—and convincingly plays his equal in her willingness to marry for money as well as cheat on her benefactor.

Johansson and Meyers "bring a seductive and intoxicatingly youthful sexuality to their adulterous social climbers," wrote Michael Koresky, "without ever losing sight of the repulsive selfishness upon which this morality play hinges."[32] She may be as breezily brazen as he ("Who's my next victim … you?") but when she becomes pregnant their game of money and lust is forfeited for much higher stakes. Andrea Chase said: "Johansson's Nola is an emotional whirlwind, with each painfully intense emotion emphatically effervescent across her face in quick succession."[33] It's as much about economic survival for her as it is for him; she has no faith that her acting will support her and little faith in herself in general, and that's why taking this singular stand—in which she does have complete faith—is vital to her. At this point the story and her character appeal to the most passionate of all the film's dialectics: emotion versus cynicism. Because Chris chooses the latter, there's "no triumph of love"—which Badaloni cites as another component of the film's nihilistic vision[34]—and Nola, though she fights to the death, loses.

Johansson views herself as "an actor for hire,"[35] available for a spectrum of roles that make a variety of demands upon her talent. Her diverse career bears this out. After her dark creation of Nola she shines in two comedies for the same director, *Scoop* (2006) and *Vicky Christina Barcelona* (2008), and does a delightful turn in the ensemble cast of Ken Kwapis's *He's Just Not That Into You* (2009). She played the bratty star DeeAnna Moran in *Hail, Caesar!* (2016) from the Coen Bros., who had cast her years earlier in one of her teen roles, Birdy Abundas in *The Man Who Wasn't There* (2001).

Johansson launched Natasha "Natalie" Romanoff in Marvel's *Iron Man*

2 in 2010, and what this means fiscally is that a film of hers can bring in as much as $1.4 billion at the box office globally, but it's also significant in a very different way: Of her nearly 50 feature films, over a third fall into the genre of science fiction and fantasy. Laura is far from the archetype superhero of Black Widow, but she is curious and courageous, a risk-taker who confronts the utterly unknown. In Spike Jonze's futuristic *Her* (2014) Johansson creates a complex, empathetic "character" using only her voice as the operating system of a computer that belongs to Theodore (Joaquin Phoenix) who falls in love with her. Jonze:

> The timbre of her voice is beautiful. It's the person inside the voice, it's her intelligence, and it's her wit.... How do you define charisma, true charisma? She's obviously beautiful, but you take that away and she's just as captivating. She's got that thing, and combined with the emotional depth of where she's willing to go—she really went there in this incredible way.[36]

A few years later and into the farther-future she plays a cyber-human known as Major in the live-action remake of the Japanese anime *Ghost in The Shell* (2017). Anthony Lane finds irony in the fact "if anything preserves unnerving quiddity and strangeness of the Japanese movie, it is Johansson"[37]:

> Major slots into other recent roles of hers, in *Under the Skin, Lucy*, and *Her*, to create a buzz of impatience with the merely human. Lay aside racial identities for a second: think alternative species, digital personalities, robots—otherness of the most radical variety. Such is the zone that Johansson patrols.[38]

Johansson's "patrol" in these roles is a distinct purview within the realm of courageous females inside the genre of fantasy and science fiction, and her work on this terrain is as touching as it is philosophical. She is as adept at creating a restrained quasi-human or non-human affect as she is at manifesting the earthy fury at the opposite end of the acting spectrum, Nola in *Match Point*. She captures, within this alien affect, or her voice alone, or some alternative demeanor, a complex character with a deep longing. Major struggles to reconnect with the remnants of her human past while carving out whatever sense of agency she can as a cyborg-human governed by a corporation. In *Her* Samantha explains to a devastated Theodore why she must leave him behind: "It's in this endless space between the words that I'm finding myself now. It's a place that's not of the physical world. It's where everything else is that I didn't even know existed."[39] The possibilities she aspires to are as unfathomable to her as the human world is to Laura, and Samantha's farewell is heartbreaking in its expression of a "consciousness" trying to define and to endeavor what is possible—what lies outside of what she has experienced or can even imagine. Johansson conveys this through words exclusively, and in the case of Laura, with almost no words.

In an interview with David Poland, Johansson pondered his comment that her two recent films, Joseph Gordon-Levitt's *Don Jon* (2013) and *Under the Skin* seemed "off the map" for her, or not "conventional movie star choices." She responded, "I'm not sure what's on the map, exactly":

> I've been extremely fortunate to be involved in the Marvel universe for a few years. Which I think ... makes it seem that I've had a little bit more of a mainstream career than I've really ever had ... the films are usually kind of independent productions, and so more than really trying to find a film of a specific size or budget, I've in the past couple of years been able to enjoy doing a wide variety of different types of films, and different types of characters.[40]

Johansson recalls the script Glazer initially sent her as a "two-hander" about an alien couple, focused on their relationship, their attempts to blend unnoticed in the Scottish community, and the townspeople's impressions of them—as opposed to the alien perspective in the film they ultimately made. Over the months and years she "was always checking back in—'What's happening with that Glazer project?' I probably just stalked him until he got sick of hearing from my agent."[41] During that time Glazer and Campbell were honing an entirely different version of the film. Finally Glazer had a draft that he knew was the film he wanted to make, and sent it to her. He remembers clearly the phone call where they decided to make the movie together. "We spoke, and she really got it. It was really in response to that draft" and "enthusiasm for the journey of this character," he recalls. "Something clicked."[42] "For me," Johansson said, "it was becoming more of an opportunity for Jonathan and I to be the kind of two-hander in this." And, "I don't think I was convinced I could do it until Jonathan was convinced I could do it."[43]

"You try and cast people who are perhaps at the right time in their lives to inhabit that character," said Glazer, "and whether they're ready to inhabit that, sort of fearlessly." He believes "it's a lot to do with timing."[44]

"Her first role was an uncredited skit on the Conan O'Brien show [*Late Night*], the same year that she did an off–Broadway production with Ethan Hawke—a play called *Sophistry*," notes journalist Nadine Mendoza Province. Films followed, and of Johansson's turn as Grace MacLean in *The Horse Whisperer*, Mendoza says, "If there was such a thing as being 'born to act, this film demonstrated it."[45]

13
Film4 and the Money-Road to Production

The rendering of Glazer and Campbell's script for *Under the Skin* featuring the alien couple was the first version taken to market to secure financing. Brad Pitt was now attached to play the farmer, Raymond, attempting to blend into the rural life in the Scottish Highlands while his partner spent her days on the road trolling for prey. The budget that had been calculated by Anita Overland, their line producer at the time, was about $43 million.[1]

They took the film to market in 2008, but even with Pitt's hefty star power they "still couldn't raise that much money," producer Jim Wilson recalled. They'd been asked by potential backers to pare the budget down by about ten million dollars, and they spent the next year scraping away at the costs, reducing them by that amount and more. "We wracked our brains," said Wilson.[2] When they were down to about $33 million, Wechsler recalls, "We came very close to getting it," however

> I didn't feel good about one of the financiers that was an important part of the equity. They kept putting language in the contract that I didn't feel was real. Instead of "We will finance" it said "We will try to secure the financing"—it was fakery in the bakery. Bryan Lord at CAA was Brad Pitt's agent, and I felt I just couldn't present it to them as real enough, so I had to call Bryan and say, "This is no longer happening." We would love to have done it. Brad really wanted to work with Jon, he was a huge fan of his.

"Agents at CAA were very helpful in getting us into a room with the right actresses," recalls Wechsler, and "everybody at WME [William Morris Endeavor] were really good allies at helping to figure this out," among them Mark Ankner, who "helped at one stage with trying to secure financing for the film."

Campbell remembers their earlier email pitch to Pitt "to get him on board," where they had "enthused about how we saw him in the film, and how we wanted to make moments of cinema with him that wouldn't be seen anywhere else, and how we wanted to go through that process working with him in a very different way." In the aftermath, said Campbell, "I was haunted by the notion of having to cut ties with Brad Pitt given the nature of that pitch."

In time Film4's Tessa Ross had another approach in mind. After joining the parent company Channel 4 in 2000, Ross later became successor to Paul Webster, the head of Film4 who oversaw the acquisition. Andreas Wiseman writes of a snowy night in December 2009 when Ross invited Glazer and Wilson over to her house. Ross wanted to know if they could only make the film for the budget they had failed to raise—or if they were willing to "reimagine" *Under the Skin* at about half that cost.[3] It's easy to picture Ross's demeanor and her approach to Glazer on that night through a comment she once made about David Rose, one of Film4's founders, and the example he set for her. "When I was at British Screen, I watched David work with such grace and so much wisdom, and yet the wisdom was never forced down people's throats. I thought, 'That's how to do it,' where every decision you make is not about you and your career, it's about the talent that you're supporting."[4]

Glazer was hesitant to cast a star, but he did for a while consider starlings—during a "casting session" one of them befriended the film's line producer Anita Overland (pictured), who did the original budget. The $43 million it would take to make the 2008 script could not be raised, but when Film4's Tessa Ross asked Glazer if he could reimagine the film at a far lower cost, he took the project on a very different path (courtesy Anita Overland and Sarah Jane Wheale).

This new incarnation of the film required rebuilding of the screenplay—and sacrifices. Campbell recalled:

> I think the most difficult part of the process for me was when the first iteration hit a production rock, and the deal that was done came apart ... losing and stepping away from so many images and moments and beats in the story does take a bite.... But the challenge to reimage those transitions through the story did

carry me on, and I knew those images I was having to remove would find a place in other stories.

Yet it was in this reimagining suggested by Ross that Glazer discovered the entirely new approach that would ultimately be on the screen: the story of a singular female alien, and more importantly, told from her point of view. The paring down of the budget paradoxically resulted in an exhilarating expansion of the film's "molten core," as Glazer has called it, its *raison d'etre*.

When Glazer began considering actresses for what was now the only lead role, he wasn't necessarily seeking a celebrity. "I wanted a barmaid from the Holloway Road! I didn't want a movie star. And I was really conflicted about that, for obvious reasons."[5] After a couple of years of "stalking" Glazer, as Johansson jokingly put it, she landed the role in 2010, and without a male co-lead would carry the film's new narrative.

As Head of Production at Film4 Tracey Josephs looked after the physical production, and was closely involved in the original financial deal negotiations when development first started. She oversaw every aspect of the long pre-prep process, the pre-production, the shoot, and post-production through delivery on behalf of Film4, who had provided the development funding for the project as well as production finance. "We had a longstanding relationship with Jon having fully financed his first feature film, *Sexy Beast*. Jim was a creative exec at Film Four Limited, as it was known in those days, before leaving to become an independent producer—so the relationships go back a long way."

Although Film4 had funded development from the start, they were not in a position to help bring *Under the Skin* to the screen at its original price tag of about £32M or even for the later whittled-down figure. Josephs remembers that the company's entire annual budget for making films was about 10M pounds. Of that lengthy whittling process "what I recall is that every time it came down, it was always still a bit too high," but in late summer of 2010 Josephs made a call to Alex O'Neal, a line producer with whom she'd had a long relationship at the studio. Josephs and O'Neal both had a background in music videos, and "Jon was a legend in that world," says O'Neal. They got together with Wilson and Glazer, and as Jim began describing the situation, O'Neal realized his task would be "to crowbar quite an ambitious idea into a small budget."

> At the time I was doing a lot of £1M film budgets in UK. Jim was piecing together new financing for about £7–8M [about $11M] and I was brought in to help figure out how to pull that out. Jim explained the film's earlier incarnation and budget, and with a highly-paid actor [at the time, Pitt] everything else upscales as well.[6]

Credited as Co-Producer on *Under the Skin*, O'Neal says that line producer is closer to what he did on the film, his typical role of "working with directors, writers and producers and with physical parameters"—the creative and the budget/logistical side—to "bring the two together. In the initial state, before I have a crew on board, it's the script and how to shoot it, the where and how of it. Sometimes this is done over coffee in a café in one afternoon, but this took months." He describes the script as "intrinsically uneven," in that although there was "nothing complicated about the story" itself, there were other important factors: the creation of a new camera, innovative and unconventional shooting, a degree of visual and special effects, and locations all over Scotland.

Film Four Limited, also known as Channel Four Films or Film Four International, was owned by the television station Channel 4 in the UK. In 1998, Channel Four's rebranding as Film4 encompassed its newly launched digital TV channel along with its existing film division. That division's debut film in 1982 was *Walter*, directed by Stephen Frears, starring Ian McKellen as an abused man with learning disabilities. The company's support of daring films and filmmakers over the past three and a half decades has brought to audiences Neil Jordan's *sui generis The Crying Game* (1992), Clive Owen's breakout performance in the coruscating *Croupier*, directed by Mike Hodges (1998), the trenchant realism of Danny Boyle's *Trainspotting* (1996), and *Slumdog Millionaire* (2008), with *Slumdog* accomplishing that rare triumvirate of unabashed honesty, critical acclaim, and global box office success. Addressing an audience of writers for *26*, Tessa Ross describes the path to realizing *Slumdog* and her mandate at Film4:

> It's the best example, because it's a film that nobody wanted to co-develop with me, nobody wanted to finance, and everybody said a film in Hindi will never work. Well that's true, if you look at what's happened before—that's absolutely true. But it really wasn't true when we believed in the various talents that were involved in that film.[7]

This mandate made possible Miranda July's indie gem *Me and You and Everyone We Know* (2005), and the brutally heartbreaking *Shame* (2011) and *12 Years a Slave* (2013) from director Steve McQueen. Film4 persevered for a dozen years to see *Under the Skin* through to the end of its rocky road, yet Tracey Josephs recalls that the duration "was well beaten by *Carol*—that was 20 years." The peregrination of *Carol* from the Patricia Highsmith novel *The Price of Salt* (1952) to Todd Haynes's 2015 film starring Kate Blanchett and Rooney Mara earned more than 200 nominations in all, and over 70 awards. One of its six Oscar nominations was for Best Adapted Screenplay (Phyllis Nagy) and the award went to Emma Donoghue's script (adapted from her novel) for *Room*—another Film4 production that year.

Josephs mentions Yorgos Lanthimos—Film4 backed *The Killing of a Sacred Deer* (2017) and two other features—as "another auteur filmmaker who does it totally on his terms. That's what Film4 does—in the mix, it supports a filmmaker's vision." In Lynne Ramsay's *You Were Never Really Here*

(2018) Joaquin Phoenix portrays a damaged war veteran turned violent private investigator/hit man hired to find a 14-year-old girl who has fallen into the sex trade (Ekaterina Samsonov). "The film drop-kicks you into a cosmos of pain, depravity and blunt-force trauma," wrote critic Tim Robey, "with only the faintest flickers of light at the end of the tunnel. It's not an experience to relish, exactly, but it's still one that's fully capable of blowing you away."[8] Also produced by *Under the Skin*'s Jim Wilson (as an independent producer), it's a movie that makes us grateful that films like this, in these times, can get made. Film4's chief Tessa Ross shepherded many such films during her tenure, and is well-known for nurturing first-time feature directors—among them Stephen Daldry (*Billy Elliot*), Steve McQueen (*Hunger*), and Joe Cornish (*Attack the Block*, produced by Wilson).[9]

Ross describes Film4's unusual recipe: "Everything we do is funded by advertising on Channel 4—we don't depend on a penny of public money, but we are entirely public owned. We go out and earn all our own money every day ... we're a brilliant piece of the public service broadcasting in the UK—that's how I would see it."[10] She recalls the original vision of David Rose and Jeremy Isaacs for Film4, "to take the values of what was then a very new public service channel, Channel 4, and those values were of taking risks, of nurturing talent ... of challenging preconceptions. And taking those values to the [creative] community in this country—the talented people who wanted to make feature films."[11] Ross made these remarks to the audience at a BAFTA ceremony in January 2013 where she was honored with the Michael Balcon Award for Outstanding British Contribution to Cinema. Presenting her with the award, Danny Boyle affectionately called Ross "the Paul Scholes of the British film industry"—likening her to one of the most lauded and beloved footballers in English history. At that time *Under the Skin* was nearing the end of its lengthy chapter in the editing room, where much of the movie's ultimate magic—as is the case with so many movies—was realized. After the BAFTA ceremony, interviewed about Film4 and the company's slate for the coming year, Ross mentioned that a highlight was "Jon Glazer's first film for a very long time."[12]

After nearly a decade in development, and a lengthy saga of "estimates all over the shop," recalls Josephs, money from a number of sources met the film's new budget crafted by O'Neal, and *Under the Skin* was ultimately made for $13.3M or roughly £8M.[13] Film4's share was approximately £1.6M.[14] BFI Film Fund was also one of the financers of the film. "We acted as Executive Producers overseeing both the creative and physical production, and therefore monitored preproduction, the shoot, and the edit," according to BFI's Fiona Morham. "Chris Collins was our Senior Executive at that time. Sadly, he has since died of cancer. He was very supportive of Jonathan's vision."[15] Collins had been Senior Production and Development Executive at the UK Film

Council and continued when the council was absorbed by BFI. Their contribution to the budget was slightly under £2.2M.[16]

Glen Basner, head of FilmNation Entertainment—still in its infancy—joined the team and brought the project to the American Film Market in 2010. He felt confident that other distributors "would be desperate to be a part of this film, just like we were. Scarlett gave the film a commercial backbone and people responded very viscerally to it."[17] Basner's conviction was rewarded—they pre-sold the film for about $4.5M (about £2.8M). Two more excellent movies of the alien kind were in FilmNation's near future—*Midnight Special* (directed by Jeff Nichols) and *Arrival* (directed by Denis Villeneuve) both released in 2016.

Another young company—Silver Reel had only recently opened its doors in 2009—was eager to take a chance. "It was Nick Wechsler who brought the script to us," recalls Silver Reel partner Claudia Bluemhuber. "We had worked with him on *The Host*," a science fiction thriller directed and adapted from Stephenie Meyer's novel.[18] Wechsler said: "We'd gotten to know each other, she'd responded to a few of my scripts." He brought her *Under the Skin* when "she was in the early stages of her company." Said Wechsler, "She just got it." Bluemhuber remembers:

> We loved the script, but mostly we loved Jonathan Glazer. We were big fans of *Sexy Beast* and *Birth*. Jonathan as an auteur was what attracted us in the first place, and the opportunity to make another film with Nick Wechsler. Jon was pushing the boundaries of filmmaking—we thought of him as a huge talent. We loved his work. We regarded *Under the Skin* as a prestige project and an art film, not a highly profitable venture, but mainly we wanted to work with Jonathan. It might not be a huge box office success, but we believed it would last long and really be inspiring to other filmmakers. We believed it would open doors.

Creative Scotland, an organization that supports filming in the country both financially and with location services, contributed £300,000 to the production. With their help, a team of adventurous investors, pre-sales, UK tax credit loans, and gap finance, the business of raising money could now make way for the business of making *Under the Skin*.

In the end, the opening credits would read:

Film4 and BFI present
In Association with Silver Reel
In Association with Creative Scotland and FilmNation Entertainment
A Nick Wechsler / JW Films Production
A Film by Jonathan Glazer

14
Setting the Stage

The Look

Asked what she is most proud of about *Under the Skin*, BFI's Fiona Morham responded, "the production value." In a film with so little dialogue there is far greater responsibility on the look and the music to do the telling, to deliver the ideas, the feelings, and the emotion. If there was to be a governing principle for the look of *Under the Skin* from the beginning, it must be inseparable from Glazer's intent for his main character and the viewer's relationship with her:

> I wanted the audience to be with her all throughout the film. To understand her ... to feel her, in a way ... and by watching the movie, I think we get almost disconnected from the notion of reality, because we take the alien's viewpoint. We're alongside her, we look at things through her eyes.[1]

DP Daniel Landin asserts "one of the strong tenets" of the film is that placing Johansson in that Glasgow environment (unfamiliar to her while she is anonymous within in it) is "putting an alien on Earth"—the two are in a sense congruent. They sought an extremely low profile while shooting—"footprints on the ground that were very light"—to be achieved through hidden cameras, and none of the huge equipment trucks, cables, blockades, and fanfare associated with shooting in public places would play an essential role. "The fundamental alien existed in the way she was placed by Jonathan, and our mission was essentially to capture that, allowing the alien quality to be within her interaction with the environment."[2]

The degree to which Laura's alien nature is expressed through Johansson's presence in the Glasgow environment, unfettered by the filmmaking process in the way that Landin describes, can't be overestimated. In combination with Johansson's powerfully restrained performance a portrait is painted of a stranger in a strange land, a kind of "alien aesthetic." Although, "The aesthetic wasn't important to me in this film, actually, the aesthetic was that there was no aesthetic," Glazer said. "The word we kept using was 'unadorned' ... things that were witnessed and found.... I thought, the truth of it—if there was any, if we captured that—that would be the beauty."[3]

"We looked at all sorts of paintings," recalls production designer Chris Oddy. "We were looking at Bruegel, we were looking at Hieronymus Bosch. We were looking at various ancient paintings, a lot of Baroque, and then looking at our landscape and trying to feed that back...."[4] Landin recalls that he and Glazer also drew inspiration from Kurosawa's *Roshomon* and the films of Andrei Tarkovsky, particularly *Andrei Rublev*.[5]

In 2007 artist Simon Duric was working as a storyboard artist on commercials and on small press magazines and books in the fantasy genre, when one day he received word from Jim Wilson, who had seen his illustrations online.

> I was a huge fan of Jon's music videos and commercials and of his previous films.... I'd also heard that Jon had been circling an adaptation of *Under the Skin*, so I asked Jim: "Is this *Under the Skin*?" If I remember correctly I embarrassed myself by waffling on about how much I loved the book (I did) and how I'd read it maybe 9 or 10 times (I had) and was currently re-reading it (I was) and how the book was in my bag right now (it really was.) I dashed over to Jon's office in a taxi and the first thing I did was get out the copy and show him—and then beg to work on the film.[6]

Duric began working in Glazer's studio with the director and the film's co-writer, Walter Campbell. They spent long hours talking about the film, and Glazer showed him photographs and paintings that inspired what the director called the "poetic realism" he was seeking for the film. Jon would talk about a character at a particular point in the story, for example, and where they were emotionally. What he needed from Simon was images to "convey the mood and tone of the film" for prospective financiers. Duric said:

> Back in the day, I'd worked with my own hand-drawn illustrations that I would then manipulate with photographic elements in Photoshop, but Jon wanted something more natural and impressionistic. So I showed him some of my more "sketch book" work—mostly hand-drawn pencil stuff—and that was the "look" he wanted. I think I did over 25 to 30 in the end, on A3 [11.7" × 16.5"] in a two-week period—it was intense! Jon was very interested in the "internal"—I got the feeling he wanted to be able to look at the drawings and feel the character in that moment. That was a challenge.

Duric recalls working on images relating to the "imploding" of the two men in the black void. The story and the script changed a great deal after the timeframe when he was working, but a handful of his images resemble what appears in the film. He recalls rendering Laura inside the house where she lured her prey. The image he is most proud of refers to a scene near the end "where the alien faced herself after the attack in the woods. I'd worked hard on it—maybe doing 15 or 20 drafts just on the expression on her face—because it felt like such a beautiful moment in the story. I was really happy with it."

Scouting Begins, Casting Continues

> I dug my heels in about shooting it in Scotland, because, from reading the book, it had the atmosphere.... It felt so right, I could see it. I could never remove it from there, and I never wanted to.[7]

Glazer has said that he would not have considered shooting the film in another country and trying to pass it off as Scotland; the alternative would have had to be setting the story elsewhere—not what he wanted. He calls the country's landscape and the weather "extraordinary," along with "the light and the four-seasons-in-a-day that Scotland is famous for. There's a wilderness there, and there's also something mythic about it ... the unguarded, real beauty of the people who live in Glasgow that brightens the edges of this wilderness."[8]

Eugene Strange, who happens to be Scottish, was the location manager on *Under the Skin*. His first job with Jonathan was back in 2006 on the Sony Bravia *Paint* commercial, which was also shot in Glasgow and had in common with *Under the Skin* Dan Landin and Chris Oddy, editor Paul Watts, music supervisor Peter Raeburn, and sound designer Johnnie Burn. As two film projects made in the same city by mainly the same creatives they stand at opposite ends of a spectrum—a (literally) splashy ad for a global mega-brand and an arcane science fiction thriller. The former celebrates technology as an achievement and a pleasure (in the product as well as the advert) in an apotheosis of color and exuberance through about as public a display as can be imagined. The latter, focused on the personal, the internal, the subtle, and the painstakingly gradual, hides in plain sight. It's the demolition of a high-rise building versus the "light footprints on the ground" alluded to by Landin. The two projects are a joyous testimonial to the range and diversity of talented people facing specific challenges that tap into different sides of themselves as artists. Each is a glorious walk on the wild side.

Paint was Eugene Strange's first job in the city and he "fell in love with Glasgow." He and Jon began talking about *Under the Skin* about two years later in 2008, and after a couple of trips to get a feel for the country, Eugene began scouting in June of 2011. "I loved exploring Scotland. It's a special place for me and for my wife, Anna—she was my driver for much of it, before the 'grownups' showed up. It was just us driving around the countryside."[9] Later his main collaborators were Jon, Chris, and Dan. In six months he put 19,000 miles on his car. "Indicative of the film, we tried to traipse the length and breadth of the country looking for the perfect locations. I was an alien too in the scouting and prep, I had a skeleton of knowledge ... it was a process of research, knowledge gleaned through other people, and a sort of intrepidness." A key location was the forest to be used for the final sequence where Laura staggers from the woods to the clearing, a place where they were going to positions themselves for that last scene. Strange recounts that:

Under the Skin's location manager Eugene Strange put 19,000 miles on his car over six months' time in 2011: "We tried to traipse the length and the breadth of the country looking for the perfect locations." One they were seeking was a "buzz-cut" forest edge, to be used for the film's final sequence. They finally found it at Drimsynie, near Lochgoilhead (courtesy Kate McConnell/Asylum Models & Effects, Ltd.).

> We wanted something "harsh" in terms of when you're cutting down trees, deforestation gives a straight edge—a machine-scalped feel they wanted—lots of trees in a line giving a kind of beanpole, buzz-cut look. We finally found the forest literally through just the process of driving around, literally thousands of miles, speaking to a lot of foresters who looked at us strangely when we asked for this. Then one day I saw it and texted Jon and Chris "Found it! Found it!" and within a day or two they were up from London.

The prized location was Drimsynie Forest (near Lochgoilhead), and it was summertime.

Actors, Non-Actors and Unwitting Actors

"When Jim Wilson rang I immediately said I'd love to do the job," recalls casting director Kahleen Crawford.[10] She was an ardent admirer of Glazer's work, and when they spoke "he was very keen that I read the script then call back to say if I was up for casting it, but I just kept trying to explain that it would be a yes regardless!"[11] They didn't know one another prior to the film,

The Drimsyne location after the snow (courtesy Kate McConnell/Asylum Models & Effects Ltd).

but Kahleen, a Glaswegian, was based in the city at that time, an asset for a film so intimately tied to the locale and its residents—she cast many of the roles locally. She had read the novel years before, and admits she makes "quite a calculated choice" whether to re-read (or read) source material.

> I prefer to take pointers on whether to or not from the director. The script inspires thoughts and ideas about the characters and the book can inspire others, and sometimes they can be in contrast to what the screenwriter/director are heading towards. On occasion I have waited until I was done on the job and then read the book!

With Scarlett set in the lead, Kahleen "was excited to see what she'd do with the role. I was very much absorbing Jonathan's positivity regarding her casting. He knows what he's doing." With regard to finding actors compatible with Scarlett on screen,

> That's tricky as it's not necessarily something you focus on until close to decision stage. There are so many criteria with casting any role and you want to be open minded. That means perhaps you take that into consideration most of all when you have whittled the pool down to 3 or 4 performers. Really my goal was to get to what Jon was describing around how he saw the character tonally, their energy, characteristics, any skills

required. Or even go off and bring someone totally different to the table, but who I thought might excite him.

Scarlett's role in the story also made the "compatible" issue less important.

> With the other roles we were creating a world that was very separate from her character, so in a funny sort of way I didn't actually have to think about her when we were casting everyone else. I thought about her as a professional and a woman having to come to set and work with people who weren't experienced with filming, or course. But I didn't think about her character or casting to fit her character.... We did think about it visually ... but essentially she's so removed from their world that it gives you a bit of freedom.

For the role of Laura's predecessor, "the scene was so important to Jon because it was part of the opening sequence of the film, and he really wanted to set up the sense of the one who had come before Scarlett, and the idea that she would meet a fate like that herself. I can't tell you how many women we saw." They'd received audition tapes from France, Spain, and Australia, all over the world and "we just couldn't quite crack it." They settled instead on the idea of someone who would be more of just a body double, but when Lynsey Taylor Mackay went in for it Jon called Kahleen to say the search was over—"She's perfect."

When time was nearly running out to cast the alien known as Bad, Kahleen and colleague Caroline Stewart had a brainstorm to recruit the famed Swedish "Ghost Rider"—notorious for daredevil stunts, taunting police, and keeping his identity secret.[12] They recruited their associate Danny Jackson to help with research and a Skype interview with Jon was arranged—but "just as quickly as we found him he evaporated, never again to reply to us." Enter Jeremy McWilliams, a world champion motorcyclist from County Antrim, Northern Ireland. When he got the call for the job, he suspected his friends of playing a joke on him. "At first, I thought it was a wind-up and was waiting for one of my friends to walk around the corner at any moment." The job appeared straightforward, but once weather intervened maybe not so much: "They wanted me to turn up and ride a motorbike really fast through the Highlands of Scotland in really awful conditions, in snow, ice and rain." As one of several non-actors in the film, McWilliams admits "it was handy that there was no speaking."[13]

Dave Acton, another non-actor who played the Logger, came into view because he owned one of the locations under consideration.

> We were looking for something to bring a difficult scene to life, and we didn't know quite what we were looking for, but again, we knew it when we saw it. He went through really extensive auditions. There was one day in particular when he was with us for three or four hours. We had to get him to push me around a bit. But I had to make sure Dave would be comfortable, because it's quite upsetting taking part in something like that—it can be quite difficult for the actors involved.[14]

For the role of Lonely, Crawford recalls, "Jon was very keen to cast someone that [Laura] wouldn't register 'physical difference' with but who to the audience's 'human' eyes would be considered so." They pondered actors and also non-actors with facial variations, and received a great deal of help from a UK organization known as *Changing Faces*.

> We quickly discovered that very few people wanted to step forward for something like this. Acting isn't for everyone, but we also found that a high proportion of people with a disfigurement didn't welcome the attention, or even perhaps welcome a lens being pointed at them. Some people wrote to us saying they could never put themselves in that position, but they were excited to hear that someone was casting for the role.

Adam Pearson was relaxed about the prospect of an audition with Jon. "He was actually hit by a taxi and broke his leg on the way to meet Jon for the first time—it was terrible! But he's a very determined man and so we arranged for a hospital bedside meeting, and he and Jon hit it off."

Scottish actor Michael Moreland had fifteen years' experience in TV and film when he came in to read for *Under the Skin*. He was under consideration for a different part initially and "in the audition room we really pushed what we did in the sessions to explore another [different] character" until they decided to go in another direction for that other part.

> But it became clear there was something about Michael that was pulling us toward looking at him for the Quiet Man.... He had a gentleness—maybe read as a touch shy?—and an understated warmth. Also, he's a skilled performer who—I hope I'm not misspeaking here—isn't afraid to let down any guard he might have and connect with the other actor. And I think this was a connection that had to be carefully judged and played, given it was a particular moment in Scarlett's character's journey. Also, you just sort of want to point a camera at Michael. We found him very watchable.

Walter Campbell recalls that Scarlett Johansson had been one of the early suggestions of Glasgow-based casting director Des Hamilton, "but it took a while for the idea to become a reality." He says Hamilton "worked very hard with Jonathan investigating the breadth and depth of the casting potential in the process." Part of that process was a series of auditions in a car, experimenting with the scenario they'd created for the story, with Jon and Walter "literally crouched down in the back, while [Des] would play the part of the men being picked up," and the actress would play the part of Laura driving the car. Campbell said:

> This very immersive acting out of some of the moments really allowed me to see how strange it was to have these traps acted. When they acted attraction, it always felt odd—not bad, just somehow unreal ... [yet] there were moments when the chemistry in the conversations did become something real.... I mean, there was a real connection ... it was what wasn't being said that felt potent, and that consolidated all my instincts for the need for real interactions in the pickup scenes, and all my certainty that the real gold dust would only be found in the hidden-camera notion and the truth that would reveal.

On the path to casting his lead role, Glazer remembers, "I was meeting up with Scarlett every now and then. We didn't even talk about it when we first met. We must have met three or four times over quite a few years."[15] During that time the film was still in its earlier incarnation with an alien couple. Wilson recalls, "When we realized we needed to reduce the expense of this film so we could make it the way we wanted to make it—to be free, creatively—it became obvious that the actress needed to be someone we could mount a film on."[16]

At the time Jon's favorite of Scarlett's film performances was in Woody Allen's *Vicki Christina Barcelona* (2008). But her work in a music video resonated with him for the role of Laura:

> She's on a photoshoot and she's being made up, and ... spoiled rotten by everybody.... She gets into a car with a big bunch of flowers ... and they wave her off, and she waves them off, and the camera goes with her in the car, and her face just drops. And you see the whole thing was her artifice, it was her pretense.... I saw her as the character, absolutely, in that moment.... If there was one shot in everything she's ever done that confirmed it for me, it was that.[17]

Johansson said:

> It's very rare to come across an opportunity like this, to play a character who goes through the kind of transformation that Laura does ... It's such a beautiful, poetic story, and it's incredibly touching to me.[18]

Shooting Begins in Glasgow

Viewers vary with regard to when they realize that Johansson's character is not human, but it was in fact the director's intention to reveal it right out of the gate—he'd decided to "play bold with the novel's twist." Jim Wilson wasn't keen on the notion, but it was Jonathan's idea to make it a virtue, to say, "Let's tell the audience right away that she's synthetic, that she's not real, and that will inform everything we see from that point on."[19]

"Originally, you would see her whole body being made," says Glazer, referring to the 2008 version of the script. "But I realized that we didn't need all that. The alien eye was the core of it. If we were going to hit one note with that image, then that was it."[20] It was a dual expression of "less is more"—the smaller budget and a more minimalist approach onscreen. As far back as 2005 Glazer was working with Tom Debenham, Rachel Penfold, and Dominic Parker, whose visual effects company One of Us started up in order to do very early visual development on *Under the Skin*. Debenham recalls,

> We had talked about spending months in a warehouse for this sequence. It ended up being more abstract and it's better for it. What I deeply admired about Jon is that

although he got beat back may times he never got beaten. He was never defeated. Nothing was a compromise, everything was progress—it was necessary.[21]

Oddy recalls "it was John's wish to shoot the film chronologically through the story"[22]—and with only a few exceptions, that's what they did. It's not typical for films to be made this way—actors' schedules, access to locations, and other factors usually force production to occur largely out of sequence. "Shooting in continuity, it all felt very real," recalls Debenham. "Everybody was along for the journey that Scarlett's character was taking, the alien immersed in the city—we tagged along with it and it was like we were participating in it. The extreme weather, snow, ice, and from town into country—that felt like part of the journey for us." Extreme weather, however, wasn't part of the strategy. "We planned to shoot in the summer," remembers Alex O'Neal. "After many discussions over how we wanted to avoid shooting in winter in Scotland—which was the absolute worst time—of course that's when we ended up shooting." Two months of filming began in late October.

The headlight of Bad's motorcycle glows in the blackness as it roars

Shooting begins on *Under the Skin* in the city of Glasgow in October 2011, ten years after the producers first optioned Michel Faber's novel. Danny Leigh titled his 2014 article for *The Guardian* "Why Did This Chilling Masterpiece Take a Decade?" There are many answers to that question (courtesy Daniel Landin).

toward us from a distance down a winding country road. It's disarming because of its stark contrast with what we've just seen—the opening cryptic series of unearthly tech images now abruptly juxtaposed with something earthly and entirely familiar. But we can't be comforted by the familiar because we're still disoriented by what's gone before—and the juxtaposition is jarring. Glazer is a step ahead of us—and he'll stay there for the rest of the film. Debenham calls this shot "an amazing science fiction image," and it's uncanny how something like a guy on a motorcycle can end up being exactly that; but in this context the sense of alien menace is undeniable. This was one of the few scenes shot out of sequence, actually a year later in additional photography—a road outside Wanlockhead, known to be at the highest altitude of any village in Scotland at 467 meters. The open road, the intense altitude, and the speed of the champion cyclist all inform that sense of menace. "We loved it because it's quite dark there at night," recalled Strange, "and we shot at dawn." Said pro cyclist McWilliams, "Being in a film was a little surreal," but he got a kick out of "just turning up and seeing your dressing room: Jeremy McWilliams: Bad Man."[23] Stunt coordinator Gareth Milne recalled:

> He rode that Ducati on slippery greasy wet roads at night. We had to lock down the roads and make sure there was no other activity, and he was right at the limit all the time. They were live roads but we locked them off at all the junctions 2 or 3 miles at a time—which he covered in no time flat. I've never seen anything like it! It was great working with him.[24]

After Bad retrieves Laura's predecessor from off the roadway, there's another jolt in an abrupt cut from this dark night sequence to a blinding-white interior. Bad's rough handling of the Highway Woman is replicated in Laura's treatment of her, and his black menace is quickly followed by a white one in a sterile space devoid of nature at night—and of anything else. One of the sequences shot later on in London, the "white void" is the third in the trio of opening scenes that establish an unsettling alien eeriness—without ever showing us an "alien." O'Neal said:

> Jon had this very specific vision of a 360° space all around the actors. We had never really addressed how to shoot black or white spaces until it was time. It was more expensive than we thought—it scared the hell out of Film4. Chris Oddy designed a "bouncy castle"—a giant soft box all around the actors. The floor was on a raised rostrum, full of air pumps puffing air into it that stayed inflated around them.

The unsettling essence of this white void and our inability to fathom it as a "space" works in tandem with Laura's disturbingly dull affect regarding the woman lying on the ground. The location used here is a condemned council building in Ibrox, about to be torn down—just as in the Sony *Paint* shoot, which was also a condemned council building in Glasgow. "We were right where we let off ... and it was not that far from there," notes Eugene. "The continuity wasn't lost on us."

Outside the building Bad again mounts his motorcycle, turning over to Laura the white transit van that will be her home for most of the film. Wearing the girl's clothing, she drives off. "Johansson finds herself in a bustling shopping mall. After the quiet stillness of the opening scenes, the Buchanan Galleries, 220 Buchanan Street in Glasgow, suddenly appear as disorienting as the interior of an anthill in a nature documentary."[25] Johansson's descent on the escalator is captured via concealed camera, and from this moment the movie's signature undercover filmmaking plays a critical role. Debenham describes their cinematographer's disguise for the sequence:

> Dan was dressed as a cleaner and he had his camera hidden inside a bucket with a mop. Stuart Howell's camera was hidden inside a paper bag. In a different part of the shopping mall on the weekend I was following Scarlett around in the makeup department, being very quiet with a minimal crew. We were incredibly exposed, we didn't look like a film crew.

Makeup and hair designer Chrissie Beveridge, who is Scottish, had worked with Matt Damon since about 2003, and met Scarlett co-starring with Damon in *We Bought a Zoo* (2011). The star asked Beveridge if she would work with her on *Under the Skin*. Beveridge doesn't think that people in the mall recognized Johansson per se, although

> people would look anyway, people were staring at her. We did everything in our power to protect her, naturally. We did shoot in the clothing section of Debenham's Department Store and she was looking around at the clothes, and nobody had a clue that it was her. You feel relieved when you manage to shoot what you needed. It went well.... We thought someone would be bound to recognize her, but on the whole we were very lucky. We got away with an awful lot.[26]

Here in the department store Laura selects the sweater that will be her uniform on this mission. Steven Noble was the film's costume designer. Glazer recalls:

> Part of our task really was to create a disguise, something that would stand out to an extent, but at the same time blend. I think we wanted the costume, the look, to feel slightly outside of things ... in the pink sweater walking through that landscape as kind of like an exotic insect on the wrong continent, she shouldn't be there.[27]

In the store Laura selects a shade of lipstick and applies it in the mirror. Beveridge calls the shade of red "a sort of bright, quite startlingly bright color, for attracting." The main goal was to create a look that was entirely separate "from the Scarlett Johansson that we know—which is light hair, off the face, never fringe or bangs." Hence the thick bangs and the brunette hair, which Beveridge describes as "a very dark ash brown that photographed black." The wig has been called "shaggy" and "untamed"[28]—that seems apropos as an echo of the original character in Faber's novel who was literally an animal, a sort of wolf. "The goal was to keep her from being recognized by bystanders," said Beveridge, "but I also feel it helps us immerse into her fictional character, to distance us from her as a celebrity persona." Scarlett's eyelashes were tinted, and her "thick brows were strengthened and darkened with makeup to balance up the dark hair and the strength of the lips." It's a powerful statement on the canvas of what Beveridge calls "the most beautiful skin tone—ivory, alabaster—a bit of yellow—creamy, and very pleasing to the eye."

First Assistant Director Nick Heckstall-Smith recalls:

> Our first covert shoot was the department store where she's choosing clothes and makeup. It was a new experience for all of us, and a bit nerve-wracking. At the end of it we breathed a sigh of relief I think, and Scarlett came to me and said, "Are we going to be okay?" I replied, "Yes," slightly with crossed fingers! I think it reassured her, and made me make sure that she was always okay, along with the rest of us.[29]

The filming at the shopping center sets the tone and the stage—the stage being the city of Glasgow and its environs—for the rest of the film. Eugene said:

> The key thread through it all was that it be real, seeing her in real-life situations, whether her driving or in the football crowd or the shopping center "for real," to capture "real" Glasgow and real people and not using extras. [Among the crew] our reluctance at the start was that we wanted to film in the conventional way with total control of a situation, especially with a big star like Scarlett. Then we got used to the fact: We're going to do this for real.

Glazer's governing principle—the integrity of Laura's journey—meant the sense of the real needed to be achieved, maintained, and never compromised. This principle would both drive the technology needed to film her story and become inseparable from it. Jim Wilson knew that traditional filmmaking wouldn't cut it:

Over 400 cast and crew worked on *Under the Skin*. While some wandered the streets covertly filming or secretly recording, sinking into black goo, running naked across a field at dawn, or getting set on fire, others had to hold down the fort. Pictured here is production manager Livia Burton, hard at work inside the production trailer, but dressed for the Scotland weather (courtesy Alexander O'Neal).

14. Setting the Stage

The conventional way to shoot driving scenes is by having a rig on the front of the vehicle that you mount the camera onto, or you tow the car on a load, so its wheels aren't actually on the road. But we couldn't do it that way. You can't be incognito on the streets of Glasgow if there's a camera stuck on the front. We had to work backwards from that ethos and think "Okay, so how do we do this?"[30]

Technical supervisor Louis Mustill with One of Us recognized that the challenge was "Jonathan's desire to film in a very natural way."[31]

> You don't want 70 people, big cameras, huge lights—all that stuff—getting in the way of the story. So the question was: How do you fit enough cinema-quality cameras in a small space in a way that doesn't ruin the scenario and make the actors behave in a completely unnatural way? We looked at just about everything that was available—from things that were off the shelf all the way up to cutting edge very small high-quality cameras—and we couldn't find anything. So we started to consider coming up with some technology of our own.[32]

15

A Camera the Size of a Box of Matches

Alex O'Neal recalls the early conversations where "we talked a lot about hiding lots of small GoPro cameras, 300 quid each, hidden inside. We considered a 'time-slice effect' with 10 or 20 cameras, thought that was a solution." Tom Debenham recalls:

> Although we'd previously worked with Jon on multiple commercials where he used various cameras, this one needed its own flavor. Myself and Louis Mustill were brainstorming, trying to figure it out based on experience with other cameras. I'd used a Dalsa on a short film and liked it very much. It's no longer made, it was short-lived—it predated the RED camera. The Dalsa utilized a particular sensor called a CCD, with a more analog response to it that lends something more film-like than digital. I wanted something that had a very similar flavor to that but could fit into small spaces.

They utilized the CCD (charge-coupled device image sensor) in creating what they called "the One-Cam," which was very much conceived for this film.[1] Cinematographer Daniel Landin said:

> It's essentially about the size of a household box of matches in which you could fit a 16mm lens. It has a very good quality image. The image we generated we ended up liking so much, we would have shot the entire film on that camera if we could have made it rugged enough to withstand all kinds of weather.[2]

A film budget's limitations regarding time and money (which are often the same thing) are relentless. Film4 had footed the bill for the project's development (optioning the novel, paying for the script, and other costs) and financed (along with others) the production itself, but the costs of R&D for the One-Cam were another matter—a separate and unexpected expense. "There was a certain tension trying to convince Film4 and completion bond that we were going to shoot the film on this new thing. We needed to spend more tens of thousands to make it work," recalls co-producer O'Neal.

> Film4 wasn't going to pay for developing a camera. Film4 is always an incredibly wise voice of reason. They would hesitate about expenses, but then, they wanted Jon to

achieve what he wanted. If you choose to spend too much money on some part of the film and it starts to run out of money, the first part of that will come out of your fee. Jim and Jon were prepared to do that.

"I think Jon ideally would have liked to shoot the entire film on the One-Cams," says O'Neal. Some scenes, such as the black water studio sequences, were shot with an Arri ALEXA. "The team was able to achieve an incredible synergy between the two formats, providing the creative freedom Glazer needed to realize his vision."[3]

Neil Calder represented Film Finances Inc. UK—the "completion bond," or guarantor, "responsible for delivering the film on time and on budget for Film4. They are hugely supportive of filmmakers," says Calder, who received daily updates from O'Neal on how the project was going. "He did a great job managing it." Asked if he ever got nervous, Calder replied,

> Always. It was an unknown quantity. Jon had a reputation for being bullish and wholly focused to get what he wanted. That was nervous-making. But we don't want to hobble anyone creatively—at the end of the day, everyone agrees to the schedule. When you start straying off it or introducing new material, that's when we have to step in and say "Look, I'm responsible for this, I'm not some loose cannon!" We had a tight budget and a tight schedule.[4]

Innovative technology enabled not only the film's key themes but the modus operandi and anonymity so essential to the plot. With the new tiny camera underway the twin challenge would be Scarlett's van, in which the eight One-Cams would be hidden. "A huge amount of work went into rebuilding the van to make spaces for these cameras," recounts O'Neal. "It used to be a 16-seater minibus—we ripped out all the inside for this huge installation to make a studio control room. Chris Oddy designed all this." Glazer explains how the eight cameras had been built into the van's dashboard and behind the headrests. The cameras were wired into the back where "behind the bulkhead I'd be sitting in a chair with eight images on it from the eight camera feeds. I'd have the DP [Landin] sitting next to me, two guys doing digital imaging [Louis Mustill and Arron Smith], the first AD [Heckstall-Smith] and the sound man [Nigel Albermaniche]". The white transit van that we see from the outside is not the same "mobile studio" van towing the generator—that's a different van. That the vehicle from which Laura witnesses the world is not the one seen from the outside seems apropos of the film's themes. Glazer notes:

> We made sure the cameras were built into the van in such a way that they wouldn't be seen—not only by the people who got in the van, or the people she spoke to, but also Scarlett herself. Normally an actor is going to be very aware of where the camera is, and because Scarlett didn't actually know, she was completely immersed in the function of driving, looking and hunting. She was in the real world. For me that was the apex of the whole experience, the invisibility that we had, which enabled us to just watch the story unfold—write itself, somehow.[5]

"We had 16 mikes in the van," recalls Albermaniche, "outside and in, top to bottom, under the seats, to capture every aspect of sound because we only had one take, one chance—and we wanted to get as much from each person as possible."[6] He recalls,

> Driving in the van there was an amazing atmosphere on the streets—you can hear it on the soundtrack. You hear the world, you hear Sauchiehall Street, you hear Glasgow, you hear the people, you hear the footballers—absolutely unique. I found I noticed people more, I noticed sounds more, atmospheres, more of everything around me—because we had to get everything we could.

Only One Chance

It was stunt coordinator Gareth Milne who taught Johansson how to drive the transformed, fully loaded, mobile-studio transit van—and she was learning to drive this cumbersome vehicle "on an English road, whilst acting!" says O'Neal.

> They couldn't get a big enough generator inside the van, it would be too noisy—the only solution was a towable generator 6 × 4 like a trailer on a hood at the back of the van. She wouldn't drive slowly, she was quite fearless, she wanted to go for it. She was

The inside of a 16-seater minibus was ripped out to free up space for a mobile "studio control room" designed by Chris Oddy. Seen here behind Scarlett Johansson are two of eight One-Cams hidden in the van, tiny cameras created by Tom Debenham and the visual effects team at One of Us. Behind the "bulkhead" sat Glazer, DP Landin, 1st AD Heckstall-Smith, and sound recordist Nigel Albermaniche (courtesy Daniel Landin).

Also in the back of the van during filming were Louis Mustill (left) and Arron Smith (right, at computer inside van). The two were with One of Us at that time, then later formed Artists and Engineers. "They were both instrumental in the development of One-Cam," says Debenham, **"and supported the fragile prototype system during the shoot under very difficult circumstances"** (courtesy Alexander O'Neal).

> driving full-speed around corners towing a generator with one wheel off the road. I'm not sure what the crew in the back thought, but she scared the hell out of me.

Strange describes Scarlett "on the wrong side of the road for her, and no police escort, with a film crew in the back, picking up real-life literal strangers. That realness that we tried to capture worked so well because it was done for real." Johansson describes the "covert side of it" as "an experience I'd never really had before."

> When you're working that way, you just have to be open to anything, and because of that you really do allow yourself to be vulnerable. Which is terrifying but it's also very thrilling at the same time. I certainly discovered a lot about myself and my limits.... I became incredibly self-conscious, because I was suddenly totally aware that I had this secret that nobody else knew about. But once you get over that, it's beautiful, because things happen in an organic way that could never happen if they were scripted.[7]

Jim Wilson says of Laura's cruising, "We used to call it 'the Tiger on the Prowl.' She's hunting, and so she's finding out if the person is a suitable victim.

Are they alone? Will they be missed? She would have to go from, 'I need to find the post office,' to 'Do you live alone?' or 'Are you busy right now?' or 'Are you going to work?' It was a strange kind of verbal gymnastics."[8] After a scene, if the footage was a go, "an assistant director would jump out of the van, run up to them and explain what was going on—that we were making a film, they were being filmed at that time, and would they sign a release form for it? Of course, if they didn't sign it, we couldn't use the scene."[9] Although the completion guarantor isn't involved in the issue of securing the releases, Calder says he used to have that job when he was AD on films for Ken Loach.

> Sometimes it's a bit free-flow, and you get people and say "Hi, you want to come over and walk through a shot for half an hour?" Sometimes they don't want to give a real name, so they'll take the cash and put down a phony name. Quite often you put up notices that say "You may be filmed." They can stop you from trying to show the film if they're on screen and you don't have the release form—but it rarely gets to that.

Regarding the men, "they were very surprised by it," Landin recalls. "It was in a fairly seedy area. There were some quite bizarre scenarios."[10] Producer Claudia Bluemhuber was on location for some of the shooting and witnessed that "many of the men would run away. Not the behavior they expected from men after a beautiful woman invited them to get into her van—but they probably felt it was creepy." Wilson called it "an interesting snapshot of male psychology when faced with an assertive female presence."[11] Debenham also recalls at least one man who fled—"When he was told he'd just been in a van with Scarlett Johansson, he freaked out and ran away. I wasn't there but I think he was tracked down. We were immersed in taking a lot of risks." Johansson said: "It was terrifying. Not because I was afraid that I would be found out … but of how people would react in general." She realized she was like the character herself in "being the only one who was in on it" yet never knowing exactly what was about to happen:

> Part of the experience … was actually having to just abandon a lot of these very human instincts that we have of protecting ourselves and wanting to protect one another. That experience helped me also to find that kind of reset stage that the character was in, just totally abandoning that fear and being very present. It was a therapy, I guess.[12]

In an interview with Scott Tobias after the film's release, Jon shared that he felt there was "no way" the impromptu, incognito filming was going to fail—it was more a matter of the quality and quantity of the footage they would get. Tobias called this "faith in mankind," and Glazer replied, "It is, and I think that's precisely what the film was about."[13]

Laura's first foray onto the streets of Glasgow shows us what she's up to through a series of shots of all types of men with one trait in common: they are walking alone. Suddenly there's an outpouring of people onto the streets, fans clad in the green and white of the Celtic team leaving the stadium in

Ibrox after a match—an occurrence that was not serendipitous. Heckstall-Smith has a soft spot for the scene—"It was partly my idea and I researched it, and planned the shoot. It was risky! But we got it—and I think it works well for the film." Eugene Strange recalls:

> We made sure Celtic was playing that day and the route she would drive would be entwined with crowds, and we timed it exactly. It was Jon's idea of where we could get that [shot] of her surrounded by men and prey ... driving slowly through the throngs of men ... looking out the window, looking for prey.

"Surrounding" Laura with prey is a succinct visual cue not just of her mission but of how readily that mission would be accomplished, how blithely unaware her potential victims are. Only later can we appreciate the irony of how cautiously she maneuvers through the crowd lest she hit someone, or even kill them.

Landin observes, "Because of the restrictive nature of car work, you end up having to repeat the scenes several times. Jonathan really wanted to retain the spontaneity of the performance particularly with non-actors."[14] The necessity or even just the tendency to repeat scenes (think of directors known for shooting dozens of takes) starkly contrasts the impossibility of redoing a scene, for a spontaneous scene by definition can't be redone. Eugene recalls:

> So many times through the movie we had a kind of catchphrase—"under the skin of your teeth" or "by the skin of your teeth"—because you had only one opportunity to get what you needed—her on the escalator, or driving through the crowd at Celtic park, or the nightclub—so many times you have only one chance. And of course when you pick up a stranger you have just one opportunity and you make sure you get it.

"The covert filming took a lot of planning," said Heckstall-Smith, "whether it was at the shopping center, on the Glasgow streets, in a nightclub, at a football match or outside a dockyard, it had to be given a lot of thought."

> We had to be sure we were kept hidden, but also get the shots we wanted with more than one camera at a time. We had to make sure that anyone who was featured signed a release form on the spot—but again, not reveal to others that we were filming. Planning had to be very, very precise yet also, at times, suddenly fluid—in response to what was presented to us. Each of these was challenging.

Glazer's pursuit of authenticity for the covert shooting took many forms. Second assistant director Mark Murdoch gives an example:

> For the very first day of the shoot, Jonathan had written a part for a supporting artist to be someone hitchhiking, who delivers cars for a living. He wanted someone who really did that job. It seemed unnecessary—but then when the artist arrived on that day, Jon spoke to him, had breakfast with him, and discussed what it was like doing that for a job—hitchhiking around the country picking up and dropping cars. The man, understanding why he was there, then became totally natural—and believable. That's when I sort of got it.[15]

Part II: The Journey

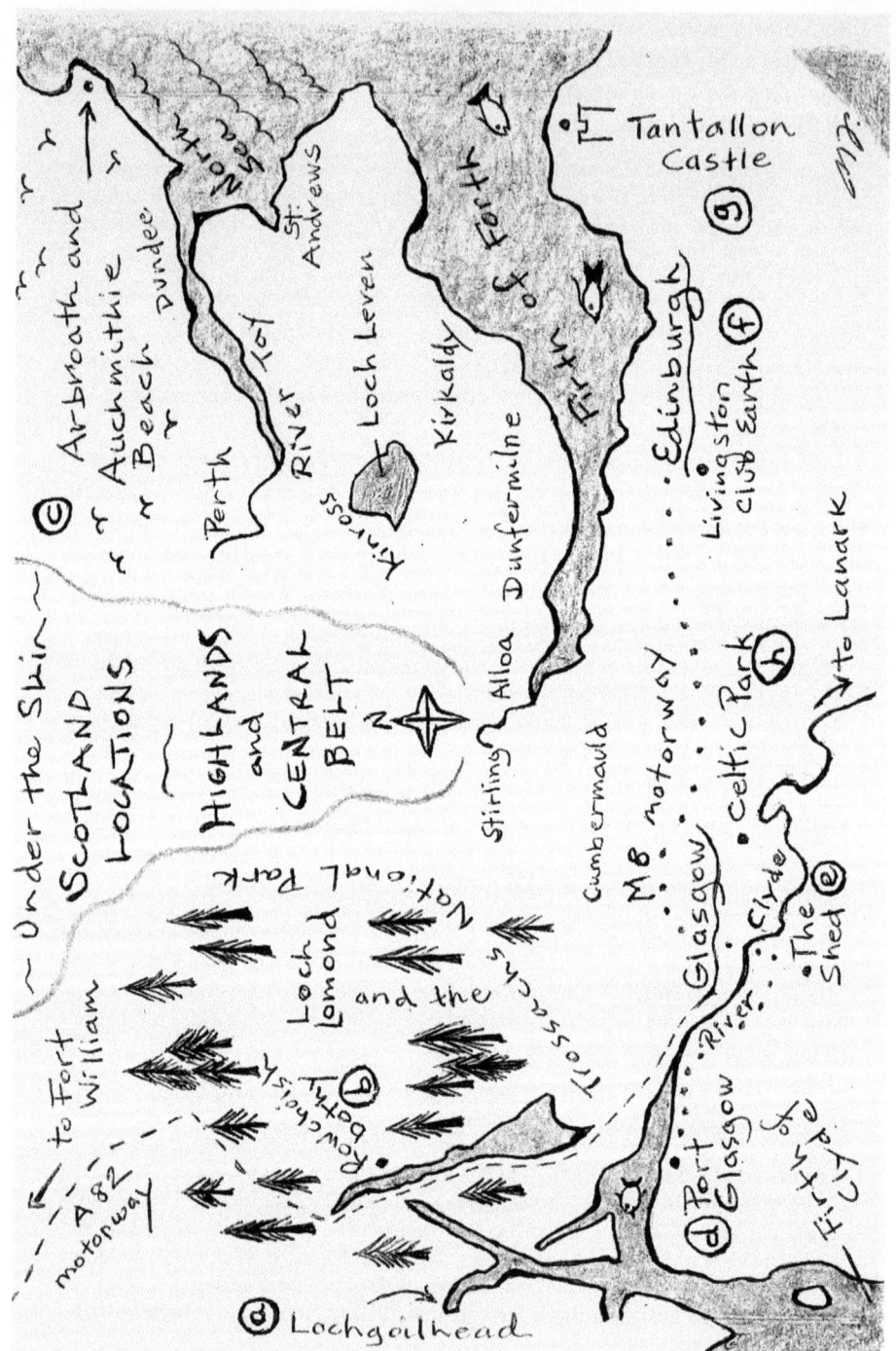

Such an actor would be meeting Scarlett for the first time when the scene was shot, "the thought being if they hadn't previously met," says Murdoch, "when she picks them up in the van their reaction to her would be more effective. The overall greatest challenge was retaining secrecy. We went to great lengths to keep out of the public eye, but also to get natural performances from the cast and the supporting artists."

With men who had not been previously recruited, however, the assignation was spontaneous. The unsuspecting Glasgow man who ended up being Laura's "first victim" onscreen was 29-yeear-old Kevin McAlinden, who approached the van after Johansson stopped and rolled down her window, saying she was "lost.... I'm looking for the M8." As he began giving her directions she launched her ominous interview—"Are you walking? Where are you walking to?"—and of course the proto-lethal, "Do you want a lift?" "Eh, aye, why not?" McAlinden responds. In the van she continues, "So what do you do?" and he answers "Electrician," which was the truth. McAlinden said he was "'stunned' when he got out of the van and was approached by a crew member. The man said: 'Do you know who that was who brought you home? Scarlett Johansson.' I knew instantly it was the truth. It all fell into place. Afterwards, when I told my family and friends, they accused me of being nuts. But I had the last laugh when they saw the film trailer.'"[16]

In this scene the streets are wet with rain, and the sky is fading blue with streaky grey clouds—it looks like the last of the sunset. The orbs of lampposts sparkle in the background as McAlinden approaches Scarlett's window. In scenarios where there was insufficient light Landin would "augment street lamps and position our extra sodium lights on top ... and fundamentally, we didn't really change the visual nature," so that people who were "walking by weren't aware there was a film going on." He calls it "a minimum touch"—only what was necessary to enable filming—"we tried to let the real environment dominate."[17]

Albermaniche recalls one man who got into the van, and "there was an LED light and a couple of microphones sticking out that weren't well hidden," but they went unnoticed by the guy because "he was so focused on her, and the eye contact, so enticed by her ... that he never looked up once!" The story

Opposite: (a) Tip of Loch Goil in Drimsynie, the forest location of the final scenes. (b) The woodland cabin where Laura stops to rest, on the east shore of Loch Lomond. (c) The rugged beach location where Laura meets the Swimmer. (d) The town that seemed the ideal place for Quiet to live. (e) For the club interiors, we're inside The Shed in Glasgow. (f) It's outside Club Earth where Laura, following a lone man she has spotted, is swept up by a group of young women. (g) The ruins of Tantallon Castle overlooking the North Sea. (h) Celtic Park, the vicinity where Laura navigates her van through the crowd of pedestrians leaving the football game. Port Glasgow to Auchmithie (drive) approximately 127 miles. Rowchoish bothy to Tantallon Castle: 110 miles (drawing by author).

echoes the men in the black space who don't know that they're sinking to their doom. He recalls an incident that echoes the 2008 script:

> One of my favorite moments which didn't make it into the film—Scarlett was trying to speak to different guys ... and a guy came up to her and said, "You look like a movie star." We were all worried because we thought we'd got caught! She said, "Why do you say that?" and he said, "Because you're gorgeous."

Debenham describes the first time they shot in the van with eight cameras simultaneously, for 30 minutes—yielding four hours of footage in one take. "We're all in the back of the van sweating bullets knowing that this could never be repeated, and we'd never run them that long before. It did work and we got away with it—more like getting away with it rather than being in control, not ideal!" Johansson wore an earpiece that enabled Jon to "prompt" her during her conversations with the men she approached. The point of shooting with that many cameras, Debenham explains, was that "you can cut seamless, and being able to cut at that many angles amplifies the reality for the audience. Being in a moving vehicle is such a familiar thing for most of us, that when it seems real it makes it a very powerful experience, like you're experiencing something that is really happing—which you kind of are."

The next passenger in the van is the man known as the Footballer (Joe Szula) and is the first to be taken "home," and although we see him sink we won't know what precisely befalls him until a later scene. After the Footballer Laura procures her next victim in a different kind of watery grave. Eugene Strange describes their search for just the right kind of picturesque, "classic" sandy beach where a family would go swimming:

> We looked at beautiful beaches on the west coast that might have worked, and the water might be choppier there. Then in our search we came across a raggedy beach, a pebbly, rocky beach on the east coast rather than the west. A rough beach like nothing else we'd seen. Jon loved the wildness of Auchmithie! But the most important thing about the beach scenes was that the water be rough enough.

Glazer recalls they visited the beach several times to make sure they'd get the waves they wanted—and never did see them. But there were magnificent waves on the day they finally showed up to shoot. Said Eugene, "We were blessed with a bit of bad weather." It disappeared just as quickly when they were finished shooting and, says Jon, "It went back to the pond it was before."[18] They arrived at Auchmithie, on the North Coast of Scotland near the town of Arbroath, with a crew that numbered about 70.

Asked if he found anything "scary or nerve-wracking" during the shoot, Heckstall-Smith replied he was "always scared and nerve-wracked when Scarlett drove the van. I was concerned for her safety. Although she was a very confident driver, I felt detached being in the back of the van."

> The beach scene with the drowning family was very, *very* nerve-wracking! And one of the most dangerous situations I've ever been in. The sea gave us perfect conditions for

15. A Camera the Size of a Box of Matches

Glazer and Landin during shooting at Auchmithie Beach, near Arbroath on Scotland's east coast. The choppy waters Glazer sought were more likely to be found on the west coast, but "Jon loved the wildness of Auchmithie," said location manager Eugene Strange. "A rough beach like nothing else we'd seen." The previously calm sea erupted in waves on the day of shooting, as if on cue (courtesy Alexander O'Neal).

the scene, but was very rough and we had to monitor things carefully. It was also nerve-wracking another way in that the shooting order for the days was dictated by the conditions of the light and the tides and so on, and had to be scheduled very carefully.

Given their tight schedule, the four days that were set aside for the beach sequence was substantial. Strange explains that "a big chunk of time was allotted because of the built-in unknown of the water." Nick "was relieved that it went as planned, and successfully. Luckily Gareth Milne controlled everything very well, but there were a couple of heart stopping moments." A woman desperately struggling in the water was rescued by Milne, who was standing on the beach. "I had told her earlier to give me the sign if she was in trouble," he recalls, "and she gave me the signal—fist above her head—and I went in."

A different sort of momentous event at the beach was witnessed. In the scene we see the baby (played by Ben and Oscar Mills) make several attempts to stand and walk. Campbell recalls that "as it got dark, the child stood up and took his first steps on film."

Cameras in Backpacks

The team visited Club Earth in Livingston about 15 miles outside of Glasgow—and loved it. But they ended up splitting the location, using Club Earth for the exterior (where Scarlett is swooped up and carried off by a group of reveling girls) and shooting the interiors at The Shed in Glasgow. That second venue "had some corridors, a sense of her getting lost in it"—perfect for the sequence where Laura becomes overwhelmed by the mob on the dance floor, and flees into what seems like a maze of rosy-lit hallways and stairs. For Mark Murdoch, "possibly the singularly most exciting day was the club scene. We spent a day rehearsing the camera moves inside the closed club. News broke we were shooting on a Friday night in a club. We came up with dummy cameras with lights on to attract the attention of the public." The production rented the club for two nights but it was of course still open for business. "The adrenalin for everyone was really high, shooting in such a public place, but secretly," says Mark Murdoch. "We were all in it together. It was a buzz." Dan Landin describes the prep:

> We relit the interior of the nightclub with our own lights, which all had to be seemingly no different ... because the people who were going there were regulars and went there every week.... Once the scenes started we couldn't change anything, because the public were involved and we couldn't make ourselves known by adjusting equipment, so everything had to be worked out in advance. Although this limited some of our control, the energy the real club and its clubbers brought made the scene unlike a staged one.[19]

"We retired to a little back room, the club opened, the people flooded in and we waited for it to get really full," says Wilson.[20] At that point Johansson and actor Paul Brannigan quietly merged into the crowd, their movements filmed by crew with cameras hidden inside backpacks and beneath their jackets. "We looked for various situations where you could squirrel a camera away and hide it," says Debenham. "In speakers, in the corner of the bar. Stuart [Howell] was following Scarlett around on the dance floor. It was a pretty exposed situation."

The club "was one of the most pressurizing, crazy things we ever came up with," says Albermaniche. "We rigged a mic on Scarlett's ear" to pick up anyone who talked to her, and another mic picked up the club's music "so we could replace it with different music."

> I wore a massive *Matrix*-style coat, put my mixer in my left and right pockets, earphones in my ear, and walked around the club. I hid a mic in my rucksack. One of my assistants, Andrew Quinney, hid in the actual mechanical section of the DJ booth so that he could

control all of the speakers, so we could get as clean a sound from Scarlett as possible. With Chris Oddy we had the idea of breaking off the bottoms of beer bottles and putting mics inside them!

They were required to post signs outside the club (and outside the mall as well) that they would be filming inside. "People tend to not notice those things, but I got challenged and questioned a few times, and she did get spotted a few times." Bluemhuber says, "In the club it got uncomfortable. People realized either who she was or at least that she was famous, and it became hectic. They had to get her out of there." Heckstall-Smith feels that of all the locations—the mall, the streets—"the nightclub was especially tricky given that we were there for more than one night," giving the public an opportunity to figure it out, "and more vulnerable than other environments."

"We did have to retreat once or twice," says Debenham. But "we would go back in and bizarrely, it would be different. People had either forgotten or moved on. There'd been a hubbub about it, so we'd be a bit judicious." Strange remembers when they drew attention.

> I think [it was] towards the end of the multiple takes of this action. And Scarlett was an attractive clubber, and there were always older men perched around trying to film her—maybe one of the last takes people started to notice something because we filmed there many times, left, went to a safe area and then slipped back into the club. But for what they achieved—[it was] 90% filmed before anyone had an inkling.

Once again they'd gotten the footage they needed "under the skin of their teeth."

16
"A Kind of Dreamscape"[1]

The black space is cryptic and uncanny in and of itself, but for the two victims plucked from the most familiar circumstances—a swim at the beach, out dancing at a club—the setting takes on an extra dimension of the fantastical, as if they've been abducted to the opposite end of the universe. The grotesqueness to which the novel's victims are subjected is modeled on modern factory farming, where the aliens are the farmers. Glazer went in another direction. "It was very much about having the ambiguity of the alien in the film. I didn't want to show the nuts and bolts of it."

> It became about what that space implied—this alternate dimension. That's the horror of it, I think. The why and the wherefores of that are not interesting to me. I wanted it to be something you would have to intuit. I didn't want it to be literal. I wanted to feel lost in that space. I didn't want to have any barometer, any compass, or to feel like I knew where I was. I wanted to be in an alien space. And so we ended up creating a kind of dreamscape for that, because the furthest we can get away from our reality is in dream space.[2]

For science fiction scenarios the go-to is digital, "but Jonathan didn't want it to be done with computer graphics," says Jim Wilson. Instead of placing his actors before a green-screen, he wanted it to be "real for the performers."[3] Glazer recalls:

> You can do it more cheaply and more easily with computer graphics, but it won't have a soul. It's just zeros and ones. By actually filming it, you understand it as being real. I wanted to take those men and give them a physical experience, then shoot that experience. Again, it's something that adds to the viewing experience. You feel it.[4]

After wrapping up the location shooting in Scotland just before Christmas of 2011 they took a break, recalls O'Neal, and then started pre-production on the studio work. For this they headed to Elstree Studios in London, where the first *Star Wars* was filmed, and Action Underwater Studios in Basildon, the facility Glazer had used for his watery underground heist in *Sexy Beast*. "What Jon wanted was to have the character walk towards Scarlett on a black surface and gradually start sinking," says O'Neal, "and he was insistent that we had to do this for real. Chris Oddy designed the set as basically the whole studio floor covered in this black shiny glass." Chris said: "Jon's idea was a joining between the [alien] world and ours." Beneath this surface was a tank made of glass painted black, an area of about 60 by 80 feet, and a device to regulate the water level when someone descended in order to prevent "the Archimedes effect"—in other words, a flood.[5] "Chris was a revelation," says O'Neal. "Not

Here the crew pre-lights the black void set at Elstree Studios in London. They also shot at Action Underwater Studios in Basildon, where Glazer filmed his heist sequence in *Sexy Beast*. For the submerging of victims in *Under the Skin*, "Jon was insistent we had to do this for real," recalled Alex O'Neal. Chris Oddy designed the set, with a shiny floor of black glass (courtesy Daniel Landin).

only did he come up with really creative ideas, but also sometimes clashed with Jon creatively. Often you have 'yes men'—Chris was a unique take on that."

"I didn't want it to look like water," said Glazer. "To me, they're in this weird kind of amniotic gas."[6] To that end, recalls O'Neal, "We tested loads of different black goo to fill up the tank to the level of the glass," so the men could "walk onto a platform that would sink him into the black goo. There was a problem of how to control the goo and not drown your actor. Rachel [Penfold, of One of Us] came up with a very practical solution to go into a lift [hydraulic platform] and have him sink."

> You have to know when to stop doing it physically, where to draw the line, because if you're bent on it and do too much it ends up being much more work and much more expensive than if you'd just done effects to begin with, because you have to digitally undo what you shot. You can't always tell up front how that's going to work.

The film was "visually ambitious, and always punching above its weight." As Debenham describes it:

> The essences became clearer and clearer over time because of the limitations of the new budget. The psychological strangeness of men walking into the black floor was a collaboration of the practical and of visual effects, very much a collaboration of One of Us, Asylum, and Chris Oddy. We all knew there were going to be aspects of each other's worlds that we would be completing.

Covered in Silicone, a Phobia of Water

Depicting the men's fate after sinking into the blackness evolved over time. Chris Oddy remembers "thoughts we bandied about" of humans excavated from bogs whose skin had been mummified. They then envisioned that what might happen to the men in the alien world would be something like a "consumption" of them, leaving behind only the skin. Where "one character meets another who's been there for a while and they have become disgorged, bigger, and bloated."[7]

Creating a skin suit for the actors that could function in the water was the task of Asylum's Kate McConnell, while Senior Special Effects Supervisor Mark Curtis looked after most of the other live action effects. Jon and Chris were of course close collaborators, and Kate credits her colleague Annie Toop, who "was my right hand for the whole thing. She stuck with me to the end."[8] Kate worked "with a team of people at Asylum on all things *Skin*: Laura's fully body skin, various swimmer skins in the black void, and a silicone body burn suit." She admits her official title "Prosthetics Supervisor" "seemed closest for the purpose of the credits but it's not quite right. We used a lot of prosthetic processes and materials to achieve the effects, but never in a conventional way. We're down as prosthetic because a lot of silicon was used—

I was covered in silicone for about a year!—but it was a case of pulling lots of disciplines together." McConnell recalls:

> What Jon wanted was a weightless environment. Having decided on underwater as a way to achieve a weightless look, we then had to find ways of removing the effects of water—everything gives it away that it's underwater. To counteract the green of the water, we painted Krystof [Háydek] bright pink. Hair starts wafting around and holds air bubbles that you can't erase. We were able to do it with Paul [Brannigan] because his hair was short, but Swimmer's hair was long. Annie made the brilliant discovery that very fine tungsten wire, the width of a hair, unlike real hair does not hold air bubbles under water. So a hand-punched wig of tungsten wire was made.

A suit had to be designed that would enable the "bloating" process that Oddy describes, just prior to the body being "disgorged." McConnell said:

> He wore a very thin silicone skin—very loose to look like he was being processed—over a fitted body suit threaded with tiny airlines. Small air bubbles were released through the air tubes to make the skin's surface ripple from inside the suit. So he had to wear this tungsten wig, and a full prosthetic body. They both had to learn to "body breathe" with the divers who were standing by, who would give them air and then back away from the shot. The actors learned signals for the divers who would then come over with the air.

"A lot of it was nerve-wracking," admits McConnell. "I have a bit of a phobia about water so that whole section was a bit traumatic for me." Despite this McConnell is "pleased and honored" that she did the job, and especially values the people she worked with. In the tenser moments during shooting "the gallows humor came out and there was a very large part of that I enjoyed—lots of surreal moments." She recalls one such moment:

> Krystof was suspended in the water about ten feet down for about an hour at a time. Now and then he'd close his eyes for a rest break and relax for a few minutes, just because it's warm and your senses are muffled and you're weightless. It's quite a soporific, and he was also keeping his eyes shut because of the chlorine. Once we were trying to talk to him and he didn't respond—he had fallen asleep.

Neil Calder also visited the set:

> I really enjoyed the creating of the void in the studio floor. When I was there when they did it for real, it looked fantastic. As they walked down it had to look seamless. I thought that was a highlight, to see the thought and design that went into that shot. It was extremely complex, and Chris did a fantastic job. And he was able to deal with Jonathan, to get him what he wanted, and with practical solutions.

"It's always a bit funny when you've got people under water," says Calder. "They call through microphones so the cameraman and the people in the water can hear it, and they give instructions—they call it 'a God voice.'"

For the "flayed bodies under the surface" sequence, Debenham explains, "The prosthetic body and the hollow suit was the practical aspect, and the digital version was overlaid. We used both visual effects and special effects and we would sort of paint between them. It was an unusual way of working—you're deciding to do not one or the other but both, getting the flavors right and getting the audience immersed in the experience of not quite knowing what they were looking at."

> Large-scale special effects can become banal and don't affect us. You inhabit those bodies [in the black water] because you experience and relate to them, you're not immune to them ... people are so tuned in to the reality of real people and performances, and *Under the Skin* is a testament to that. You have to keep fighting for things so you don't lose the essence of that.

What follows the victims' flesh and bone being emptied from their skin is the rushing river of red gore, about as "practical" as you can get—Asylum's solution was what Debenham calls "a vat full of stuff they prepared that slid down a ramp." That redness is abstracted into a red beam—another example of *not quite knowing* what we're looking at—but a good starting point is the sequence's title on Mica Levi's score, which is "Meat to Maths."9 The beam results in a red light that Debenham says was achieved by "firing a laser straight into the camera lens that burned a hole into the negative of the film."

The Swimmer (Krystov Háydek) donned quite a different wetsuit for the black space. Kate McConnell and her team at Asylum Models & Effects Ltd. created this costume with air tubes that caused the "skin" to ripple and sag as the Swimmer's body underwent its horrific conversion. Asylum's Mark Curtis also supervised other live action effects (courtesy Kate McConnell/Asylum Models & Effects Ltd).

What we see at the end of the sequence, when we're looking at the center of the red light at a black hole, can't be done with digital cameras—it was kind of organic working with lasers, all camera and editorial. There was a massive amount of thinking behind "Meat to Maths"—the decision was [to keep] abstracting, keep people wondering. With the laser hitting the lens, something is happening and you don't know what it is. That was a glorious day of experimental filmmaking.

A Year Later, a Reunion

When Laura lures her next victim into the house (the Nervous Man, played by Scott Dymond) his fate needs no further illustration. A close-up of Laura in the darkness applying her signature red lipstick in the compact mirror is a bridge between Nervous vanishing into the darkness and the sudden emergence of Bad from darkness. Her sensuous applying of lipstick is a ritual she has embraced and as a motif seems to signal her desire to look, to act, and to feel as a human woman does. Next there is an inscrutable moment the crew has dubbed "the inspection," where McWilliams circles Johansson as she stands in the darkness, then gazes deeply and at great length into her eyes. "In the movie I look after Scarlett," said McWilliams. "I clean up after her, remove somebody. I kill the ones that she lets go."[10] This scene and the scene immediately following—Scarlett's trip and fall on the street—were written and shot a year apart. Stunt coordinator Gareth Milne—whose daughter Sian was also on the crew, as Johansson's stunt double—recalls the "reunion":

> It was just like *Groundhog Day*. One year later we turned up at the same location with the same crew, everybody to a man who'd been on the first shoot. I'd just gotten back from somewhere when the call came in—"Get Sian and come up!"—and it was like we'd just shot there yesterday. It was a really strange experience, as if nobody had gone away. It's not unusual to have reshoots for even as much as 8 weeks—but this was a new scene, new material.

Laura's sortie downtown on the heels of Bad's inspection may seem audacious on her part, an act in defiance to his proprietary role. The two scenes were created amidst postproduction; Watts recalls Jon's concern that they still needed a moment to "immerse" the character into the human world, and show her in a new and different light. The sidewalk scene is that key moment, and also prefigures her permanent leap, soon after, into that human world. What made sense to Glazer was "to have her be strident and certain, confident—everything we've seen her be up until that point in the film—and then see her miscalculate. Like we all do … the point of the scene really was to feel that fallibility."[11] In order to maintain the tone they'd pursued from the beginning, "Scarlett had to walk down a real street in Glasgow and fall flat on her face," says Wilson—and with real bystanders to boot. "We couldn't have extras because they would look like actors. I said, 'We'll never get away with it. People will recognize her, and our cover will be blown.' But we did it."¹² "It made sense why we needed to do it on a real street," O'Neal knew, "but how the hell do we do it and not give the game away? For a fall you'd normally have a pad on the floor and lots of people around, and have a stunt double do it, but Jon said no—Scarlett has to do it for real."

> That was a whole other ballgame of madness, one year later. Sian did all the tests for the street fall. To rehearse we went to Goodge Street in central London and I hid in a doorway with my iPhone. Sian had been practicing with Gareth prior. In central London it looked brilliant, but passersby completely ignored her when she fell, and walked on! Not one person helped her! Sometimes they glanced over their shoulders then kept going. It was a real gamble—if they're like this in London, what are they going to be like in Glasgow?

O'Neal notes that in London the sidewalk was wider, and the people maybe farther away from Sian. Johansson recalls that in Glasgow, between the multiple takes, they would let some time pass "for life to kind of settle again."

> Some people would just stop and look at you, and continue to walk on. Others would come rushing, and in another take people would take pictures of you with their camera phone and not help. All kinds of strange things. And then unbelievably kind, real acts of human kindness, people genuinely concerned. The dichotomy was fascinating.¹³

For Murdoch,

> What was impressive was how Scarlett embraced the experience. The scene of her falling over in the street—we shot maybe five takes, the crew nowhere to be seen. We obviously took precautions, but ostensibly she was just falling over in the street to see how real people reacted. Likewise being the primary professional actor in the film—it must have been quite difficult.

Debenham was "dressed as a tramp on the street with a camera in a suitcase. Another person was behind a shut window and another in a window above, another with a camera in a shopping bag."

> We would parachute into these kinds of alien situations and observe them first hand. Jonathan inspired us to engineer these scenes. Everything was a risk—technical, emotional, or creative. Jon always wants to take risks because the creative prize is that much greater when you're pushing what you're doing. There are ways that he works with actors. People trust him.

After Laura ventures out and gets her battle scars, we see a collage of countless people in the city, shots now not of just men but women and girls in all walks of life in all kinds of everyday activities. "Not actors," recalls Paul Watts. "All candid. It's like she's gone on a holiday." Albermaniche recalls: "We had people with microphones everywhere!" The crew became "human microphone stands" in constant contact with him. "If someone was close to bagpipes, or to a unique conversation, we could move them closer. We had

Camera crew members Ian Mackinnon and Derrick Peters calibrate the One-Cam that's attached to a bicycle for covert shooting on the crowded streets. One-Cams were hidden in coats, in backpacks, and in cleaners' pails. For Scarlett's stroll on Trongate, Debenham recalls dressing "as a tramp on the street—with a camera in a suitcase. Another person was behind a shut window and another in a window above, another with a camera in a shopping bag" (courtesy Daniel Landin).

to solve problems on the go. Johnnie Burn had a facial so he could get close and hear the conversations."

From a shot of a young girl gazing at her face we go to a close-up of Laura's own eye. As hundreds of people's faces fill the screen like Polaroids in the earlier-mentioned "kaleidoscope" effect, Laura's face emerges from the center—the symbol of her immersion in the human world, foretelling the next chapter of her journey. The inspection, the trip and fall, and the immersion of Laura in the faces of humanity compose a mini-arc for her character that emboldens her for her next encounter on the street.

Adam Pearson plays Lonely, the one and only victim Laura decides to release. Pearson is an activist who visits schools and gives talks to raise awareness about physical differences. "I think I have quite an arresting appearance, for want of a better term. I am very rarely invisible anywhere I go. People will kind of stop, stare—a lot of it is just curiosity."[14] Pearson's illness is known as neurofibromatosis. "Scarlett's willingness to adapt to working with a non-actor was crucial," says casting director Crawford. "Jon really pushed hard to get to this vision for these scenes, but was also incredibly open-minded about exactly how he'd get there. The scenes are ones a lot of people ask me about after they watch the film." Paul Watts recounts that "what was shot in the backyard with Bad and Adam was a long struggle and a beating," its cruelty intensified by the presence of a backyard swing. "But all of this is cut, leaving only Bad's carrying him to the trunk." Heckstall-Smith recalls shooting the last part of sequence:

> When Adam Pearson's character was kidnapped by Bad he was driven off in the trunk of a car. We cut, and the car was driven back to its start position. We just opened the trunk, and Adam sat there, naked, as it was driven backwards. It was a most surreal moment and I have that image etched in my memory, especially as it was in a very modest, neat and tidy housing estate where the locals didn't quite get what was going on.

Pearson describes his role in the film in relation to Laura, who's "on a mission to pick up, seduce, and kill these men. About halfway through the film she

a/ Buchanan Galleries, and
b/ Debenham's Department Store – she shops for clothes and lipstick.
c/ She cruises in the van on the streets around George Square. At the intersection of S. Frederick and Cochrane St., we see the City Chambers Building and Piper Whisky Bar.
d/ Cruising on Sauchiehall St., the old BHS store visible in the background. The street was a treasure-trove of sound.
e/ Trongate: Strolling east toward East Wynd she trips and falls, and passersby, unwitting that she is a movie star shooting a film, help her up. TJ Hughes and "Scotland's Biggest Leather Store" signs seen in background.
f/ Today: For the 2014 Commonwealth Games, The Glasgow City College Building was wrapped with the words "People Make Glasgow." In white letters on a bright pink background, it faces onto George Square. Building wrap by Redblu.
g Glasgow Royal Concert Hall.

"Strolling Glasgow City Centre: A Few Locations" (drawing by author).

picks up my character, and it kind of humanizes her. For the first time in the film she realizes she's 'human.'"[15] Of all the sequences in the film, Johansson recalls their tender moments in the car as "one of our most difficult scenes." Because Pearson was a non-actor she appreciated that "it was hard to get him to let his guard down," and that he was "protecting his vulnerabilities. Trying to find the kind of key that would unlock that was difficult, but once we had it—and it felt like that with a lot of the scenes—once the door was kind of pushed open a little bit it just kind of swung open, and suddenly everything fell into place."[16]

For Glazer,

> The point was to reinforce the idea that she doesn't see what we see. She's not interested in what we're interested in. She doesn't define him by his appearance, and he warms to her for that reason. My biggest fear with that scene is that people would feel pity for that character, and I didn't want that. What I was trying to convey there is a sense that there is something deeply frightening inside her and something deeply beautiful inside him. That's a powerful dynamic.[17]

On the more practical side, Adam notes, "I had to run through a field in Scotland naked at 3 a.m. in November. It was so cold."[18] What's more, says Crawford, he did this "about eight or ten weeks after surgery on the leg break! Adam was searingly honest, and unafraid to push himself for the role both physically and emotionally." About the challenges Adam has faced off-screen he says, "I think when you go through things you build a lot more empathy for people who are going through or about to go through the same thing."[19] The openness that is the result of that empathy drives the candor and the depth of Pearson's performance.

17

Forget What She's Done[1]

The character, the story, and the film itself pivot on Laura's encounter with Lonely and its aftermath. Once Laura is out in the world on her own there is no more need for hidden cameras, because she is no longer hidden inside her mission. "If we were going to be travelling alongside her throughout," said Glazer, "I felt it was important to get to a point where you could forget the first half of the story. You could forget where she's come from. You could forget what she's done."[2] For her second half the director was inspired by Jean Renoir's *La Grande Illusion*, whose characters have been prisoners of war. Once they are liberated "you're in barns and meadows, and you almost feel the wind on your face," because before that you were imprisoned right along with them.[3]

The open landscape where Laura now finds herself is a reflection of this. Strange describes the spot where she leaves her van behind—located on Scotland's A82, which "runs from Glasgow to Port William and beyond."

> The idea was to capture the real epicness and wildness of Scotland. On the edge of the Rannoch Moor—a wild part of Scotland that runs from Black Mountain estate—it feels prehistoric, you can imagine the dinosaurs wandering around there. I spent a lot of time looking for this wild spot that would give you this epic vista. In the edit, the mist was added to the scene to add to the feeling that she was alone and lost, and didn't know where she was.

The establishing shots of Laura's almost mystical environs at the onset of her freedom include a captivating image that was actually photographed later on in the production, during a bad snowstorm. Strange recounts joining Tom Debenham and a small crew to brave the elements and go out to shoot:

> We knew we'd found some good stuff, though we never knew it would appear in the film…. That one swirling loch shot was captured, literally the wind blowing the water at such an angle that it created this Catherine wheel of mist and water. We knew that swirl was pretty special, a "lady of the lake" ghost-like feel. Tom shot it.

This is the "Catherine wheel" of mist captured at the beach by Debenham, after the crew was evacuated from the forest and a small team took off in jeeps to "shoot the storm." During the edit this footage was placed in a series of shots that establish Laura's locale after she frees Lonely and drives off—a visual cue that she has left the city, and her mission, far behind her (courtesy StudioCanal and FilmNation).

The winds were crazy and "it took four of us to hold the camera down," Tom remembers. "We were ankle deep in water."

Just prior to Laura's closer encounter with Quiet, she takes the advice he's called out to her, and waits for the bus. Chrissie Beveridge has a somewhat unorthodox souvenir of that scene.

> We were standing in the freezing cold at the bus stop, talking about animals and dogs. Scarlett is a great dog lover—I don't know how it happened, but she ended up giving me this 12-week old puppy, a miniature dachshund. I love him to death. Helen [Barrett] denies she was in on it, but I don't believe her. Charlie is his name. I brought him to *Lucy*—and to *Avengers: Age of Ultra*—so Scarlett could have a visit.

On the bus Laura is unresponsive to the concerns of the driver (played by Gerry Goodfellow) about her being out without a coat, but she utters a tentative "yes" to an offer of help from the man known as Quiet (Michael Moreland). The next series of scenes unfolds on his turf. "I love the scene where they go into a little supermarket," says Wilson, "and she just walks around the aisles. It's a real shop, and there you have Scarlett Johansson pretending to be an alien, and she's walking past the Hobnobs. It's incredibly British and parochial, and there's something wonderful about the juxtaposition."[4]

Eugene describes the search for the neighborhood where Quiet would live. He, Jon, and Chris had in mind "a newish town, a postwar 60s feel, not a quaint little village—but meant to feel like the Highlands."

> But we didn't have the money to go up in the Highlands, we only had money to shoot for two weeks outside of Glasgow with an overnight crew. So we had to find somewhere that felt like it was remote, and we came across Port Glasgow, and you do feel like you're further up-country in Scotland … it worked visually, and it had the shops and the architecture that we were after.

The problem was, the interiors of Port Glasgow's small council houses didn't have the room for all their equipment—with the covert One-Cam days behind them, they were now dealing with the usual cameras, lights, and crew. Although they had the option to use the town's exteriors and switch to interiors at a different location, Strange says, "It was too much 'against the real.'"

> So we ended up shooting in a modest-interior house after all. The geography and the style worked really well—we were seeking remoteness and a good fit for the character. Their little walk among the blocks really sets up the intimacy of the encounter. It's cozy. It didn't feel right that we jump to a "fake" interior after that walk.

As a production designer Herrera noted the tightness of the guest room and wondered, "Where is this camera fitting?! They got such a good shot of the room—that camera is tucked away!" Eugene remembers that Jon also wanted a fireplace in the house, to get a shot of Scarlett with it "because it's all about her discovery and discovering her senses. But we persuaded him," he laughs, "that it could be an electric fire." A key scene in Laura's discovery takes place in the kitchen of Quiet's house, as she sits at the table while he does the washing up after dinner, tapping his foot to the song on the radio—and she begins tapping her fingers. Johansson recalls:

> The transition she makes is like that of a butterfly—she starts off as this kind of amoeba, part of a mass, and she's cocooned. Then suddenly she transforms into this colorful creature, who is experiencing all these new and different things.[5]

Laura's brief romantic idyll with Quiet unfolds in nature, and their walk in the woods that takes them to a castle. Oddy looked at pictures of all of Scotland's castles—every one. "We wanted it to be a ruin, but still have its form," recalls Eugene.

> Tantallon Castle was nowhere near Quiet's house, but we always felt the castle had to be coastal, because we wanted them to be buffeted on the ramparts up there, and we wanted her to be freaked out by it, and scared—and it felt quite overwhelming for her. I always wanted to find something that had character. It was epic when we found it. The views from it!

As Laura and Quiet stroll through a wood, the wind rustling in the leaves and the clip-clop of horses on the trail enhance the cocoon of nature around them. Their romantic idyll continues as he carries her over a large puddle—a chivalrous act—with the medieval ruins of Tantallon Castle in the background. This frame in the movie is actually a snapshot Strange took during location scouting. Editor: Paul Watts. Sound Designer: Johnnie Burn (courtesy Eugene Strange).

The Storm

Strange was tasked with finding an "eden or a Shangri-la" type of setting for Laura's final episode. "She was to lay by a loch, a remote or beautiful spot, secluded. We looked at Isle of Skye and Loch Marie, quite remote and wild and beautiful parts of Scotland for this 'Eden,' for two or three weeks." This recalls the nature setting that Isserley, in the novel, dreams of making her home after fleeing her mission. They were scouting in June and July, but soon he received an email from Jon and Jim saying to forget the whole idea because they'd be shooting in November and it would be far too cold for her to be in the water. The weather, though, led them to a new approach they felt was more interesting.

> If she was going for a walk in the woods, it made it more believable that there was an evil man in there who had something to do with the woods ... so instead we decided on the forest spot where she'd get lost, and lose her bearings, and that guy would come across her, and then she comes across the bothy, and he discovers her there. Then we found this amazing bothy and it all started to fall into place.

Eugene thinks of it as "a conceptual and creative journey you go on when you start searching for one thing and end up looking for something else—the creative affects, the location, and vice-versa." The bothy they spotted—on a website where hikers upload their photos—was Rowchoish. They had a picture of it but no location, yet "miraculously we did manage to find it," says Eugene. "It was a known spot, but behind dense forest and really hard to get to." Although it was close to Glasgow and their main base, "it was about two and three-quarters hours to drive around another body of water to reach it," recalls Chris, "so what we did was put a jetty on one side of [Loch Lomond] and got a boat across the loch from another jetty" in a town on the other side. "It ferried everyone across" and took only ten minutes.[6] A time saver for sure—but not without its drawbacks. Eugene recalls:

> Seventy crew by boat ... the day of filming it was cold and dark. It was really muddy and the whole crew had to scale a slippery hill carrying their camera boxes ... a 5-minute walk from the shore, long cable runs and equipment ... all on the same day before we lost the light at around 3 in the afternoon. I got a lot of grief from my fellow crew members. "Couldn't you have found someplace else?!"

Near the end of the shooting, when they were filming the scene with Laura and the Logger at the edge of the forest, the weather got serious. "We knew the storm was going to hit us—and soon after our call time," said Heckstall-Smith. "I didn't want to go up to the location that morning, but we did. About an hour or two after we started the storm hit quickly." "Heavy snow and gale-force winds," says Jim Wilson, "and I'm not exaggerating."

> It was technically a hurricane, the strongest to hit Scotland in 100 years. Do I regret it? No. Because genuinely, I feel that without that weather, the forest wouldn't have looked the way it did. But it was definitely the most difficult part of the shoot, and we were in the forest for nine or ten days. At one point we had to suspend filming because 100 mph winds were making these big pine trees bow and bend like balsa wood. Equipment was being flung over.[7]

Tracey Josephs happened to be there that day, with Neil Calder. "He's tough, he's very pragmatic, and supportive of production," says Josephs, "but will put his foot down when he needs to. It was clear we had to get out of there, they wouldn't be able to get the trucks out." Calder remembers, "Tracey and I were saying they should pull the plug."

"I ordered the immediate evacuation," says Heckstall-Smith. "Not only because of the risk in the woods, but also the dangers of travelling back to the hotel. Some thought it a good idea to continue filming.... Jon! I got a bit grumpy." Gareth Milne believes the combination of "weather and locations" to be the biggest overall challenge they faced. Over time,

> It rained, it got cold, then it snowed, then it snowed again, and then it *really* snowed—dumped about a meter—and in that same day we had a hurricane. Pine trees cartwheeling themselves down the mountain! There were conditions where you would say

17. Forget What She's Done

"Nobody in their sanity would go filming in that." Dear Jonathan! It was one of the few days in my whole career when we cancelled shooting.

At the time Alex O'Neal was in a "makeshift production office in a bar at the bottom of the hill."

We were watching the news and suddenly BBC is talking about a "weather bomb" about to hit Scotland! We were sitting there saying, "It really is getting very windy out!" There was a hard-cut edge of the forest and the whole crew was on the other side of that edge. You could see the roots of the trees pulling out of the mud. Inside the forest they couldn't really tell—we saw it from the outside. The equipment trucks had to be left up in there, it was too muddy to drive them down the hill. We got everyone out in 4x4s. We were sitting in the bar and suddenly these four-foot letters from the bar went flying.

Film4 production manager Tracey Josephs was on set the day the storm hit. "It was like a typhoon on the loch," she recalled, but "Jon always pushes the envelope. He's a very sweet guy, everyone wants to do their best with him, he pushes himself very hard ... he is mainly concerned with getting the shots. He goes with the pace and has to think things through. It takes a long time but he gets there in the end, and he takes everyone with him" (courtesy Alexander O'Neal).

Calder recalls, "The landslide closed the road. The trees were in rows packed closely together, lifting the ground and all the roots being entwined together, the whole ground was lifted by the force of the winds."

What was funny was for about two hours or so all the cell phone batteries had gone, and there was no power, so we were back to the stone age with no phones and no laptops, and people were sitting around playing cards and chatting, planning for the next day.

"We got back to the hotel and regrouped," says Heckstall-Smith,

knowing the day's filming was abandoned. We were under a lot of pressure at that time because we were backing into a stop date for Scarlett, so to lose time was damaging. Jon and others wanted to go back out and "witness" the storm on film. I had to point out that there was a red warning issued and that people were advised to stay indoors, and anyone who went on that shoot had to do it on a voluntary basis and be aware of the dangers. I didn't go, because I didn't feel my presence as an AD was required for that sort of shoot, and to be honest I was exhausted—and fell into my bed!"

"Nick is a good AD," says Calder, "and Jon did not want to stop filming! But Nick made the right decision. At the end of the day it is his responsibility, and the producer's, to say, 'This is dangerous—I'm getting my crew out of here!' Sometimes a director will push and push—ask for another ten minutes, then another ten minutes, just one more shot—so someone has to say, 'This is crazy!'" But there were shots remaining that needed to be done. "Calder is 'very experienced,'" says O'Neal, and not easily rattled. "After cancelling the shoot, Neil rolls up his sleeves and says, 'We need someone to go in and direct and second unit.' The following day we hired a second camera, a RED camera, and split the crew up. We had a small crew to shoot Scarlett's character coming out of the woods."

In the meantime, Debehnam recalls the mood when they "decamped back to the hotel. 'We can't be not filming!'" Although the shoot was officially canceled, "it was agreed," Josephs remembers, "that Jon could go out with Eugene and four or five crew. It was freezing cold. Treacherous. Everyone else was banned." Milne recalls: "I've never seen so many people go back to the hotel and force the bar to open and proceed to drink it dry. Jonathan went off to shoot the storm while the rest of us got drunk!"

Said Calder, "We looked at the weather and we saw we lost a half day's work. The budget was very tight—splitting the crew enabled them to finish. It cost more money but it was a less bad outcome. Sometimes these things happen, that's why we have contingencies."

"We asked for volunteers to go out filming in the storm," recalls Tom, "and we got into a couple of Land Rovers with a minimal camera kit."

> We went to the woods and got the windswept trees. It was a pared down, wonderful filmmaking experience. Those extremes of nature felt somehow part of the story, and being in the middle of that and experiencing that felt as visceral as being in the night club. A different kind of war zone. That was the extreme for me—being in that war zone.

Editor Paul Watts used these windswept trees in the bothy scene, "in her dream sequence where she was in the middle of nature, and affected by that. That's the visual image that became overlaid on her face." Jim Wilson calls it a "key audiovisual moment, where this character—whom you've never seen sleep—rests like a human being would. We dissolve through her these images of trees ... it captures her sense of turmoil and change."[8]

Chrissie Beveridge recounts a point where she "had to come back to the makeup trailer, which was awfully hard, very boggy and a lot of trees, stepping over the wood."

> Just to show how tricky it was getting around—Helen, who was my right hand, was standing by, and fell into a bog up to her waist. She laughed about it later. The December

shoot was very tough, raining, miserable, very cold—freezing temperatures at times. You had to think of every which way to keep warm.

Johansson regarded the brutal weather as "another character in the film, really—the film is not about a midsummer afternoon, it's about a wild transformation, one that's raging. There has be to be that feeling of a looming end, an apocalyptic feeling. And the way it's captured on film, I think the audience will be inclined to fall into it. There were definitely a few days in the forest when I think we all thought the world was coming to an end—in fact it felt like it almost did when everybody abandoned the set."[9] And yet,

Braving the elements to shoot the storm: Glazer in the back, and camera crew members Laura Dinnett (left) and Derrick Peters (right). The camera, with its plastic-bag hood, bears an uncanny resemblance to Robby the Robot in the 1956 classic *Forbidden Planet*, which was (unofficially) based on another storm scenario—Shakespeare's *The Tempest*. Photographer: Arron Smith (courtesy Derrick Peters and Arron Smith).

> The frigidity sort of helped in a way, because it felt like we were kind of protecting ourselves ... especially towards the end in the film, when we're in the absolute wilderness, and it's a harsh environment. It's almost like Scotland was trying to kind of expel us, and that adds to the atmosphere of the film.[10]

The Black Alien Is Revealed

Laura's dream ends abruptly when she is discovered in the bothy by the Logger. She flees and he chases her through the woods, grabs her, and pushes her down to the forest floor. Kahleen Crawford recounts that before casting Dave Acton, during rehearsal sessions,

> We wanted to check he could go to where Jon might need him to go. And also we had to bear in mind the fact that someone who wasn't a performer by trade has to be violent in a difficult scene. We had to push Dave very hard, it didn't come naturally to him—it wouldn't to many men—but he got there in the end ... and I think it's an incredible scene.[11]

Johansson has called her experience during this sequence

> terrifying, especially because of the conditions we were shooting in, and also the other person that was playing was not an actor, and so I didn't know, really, the kind of rules that apply between two actors didn't really apply between us ... that was more challenging, I think.[12]

Chrissie Beveridge remembers witnessing the scene, and that "for Scarlett it was particularly tough, the physicality of it, running, being grabbed from behind, having your clothes torn off ... it was harrowing to watch, actually." But because of the fact that Dave was not an actor, "everything was choreographed down to the last detail, because it was tricky—he wouldn't know if he was hurting her the way an actor would be aware. Scarlett was wonderful in that situation. She was just game to do it. It was menacing—and it worked."

Creating the human body that Laura removes after her skin is torn in the forest was "a very prolonged process," recalls Kate McConnell. "There were always discussions about whether it would be completely prosthetic or something added in digitally." Similar to the challenges the team faced in the black space, it ended up being a combination of the two. "It began with finding a very slim actress with proportions similar to Scarlett's. Some had a longer back for example, or shorter legs—we needed her to be close enough so that we could do the thing of putting her inside Scarlett's 'body.'" Actress Jessica Mance fit the bill. "I was thrilled to be awarded the role," she said. Mance describes the setting as

> disorienting, somewhere in a forest ... by far the most remote venue that I've visited in the United Kingdom, verdant gradients and hypnotic lochs, with scarcely anywhere commercial. We slept in a caravan park, worked from 5 a.m. with the sunrise until the mid-afternoon sunset, ate our food out of foil packages, and encountered snow. It was physical but fun.[13]

For her critical scene, "from the waist upwards, the visual special effects team daubed my skin in viscous black body paint. Kate and her team painted me patiently on the morning of each shoot day. I recollect that I had to ration my fluid consumption, since I couldn't relieve myself once dressed!"[14]

To create the human skin she would wear over her alien body, the Asylum team began by body scanning both Scarlett and Jessica, then "manipulating the 3D figures to fit one within the other."

> Jessica's figure was milled from a solid block, then located back onto the CNC machine,* covered in a dense sculpting clay, and then the outer figure of Scarlett was cut over the top. In the meantime, we had head and hand casts done of Scarlett. These were grafted onto the clay body. A full negative mould of this was made, clay removed, inner figure re-set within and then the gap between cast in silicone. This then gave us a quite flexible skin that fitted Jessica perfectly, giving her the body shape of Scarlett.

In film today 3D scanning "is taking over," notes McConnell, "but it doesn't get skin texture and fine detail, doesn't create a smooth model." In the beginning of the process "there were always discussions about whether it would be completely prosthetic, or something added in digitally." The team's goal was "that it would be believable and not look like a rubber suit, or CGI." "It was Scarlett from top to toe," describes McConnell, "essentially full body, and Chrissie matched her makeup and hair. Then digitally, Tom superimposed an actual shot of Scarlett's face looking back at Laura." Kate recalls,

> *Under the Skin* utilized essentially every skill set Asylum had—from CAD* files, all the digital files from the body scan to line up with, CNC, molding, sculpting, paint finishers, makeup, engineering, hair punching, model making and more—and people prepared to get underwater quite a lot! I'm proud of all the different people I worked with, creative and inventive, they all came up with new ways of doing things.

For the last sequence "we were painting all the way up to and during the shoot to prep for the shots." In the meantime, the forest was so dark that Oddy had to take the tops off of about twenty trees in order to allow in sufficient light for them to film.[15] Then the snow began to fall. Kate McConnell

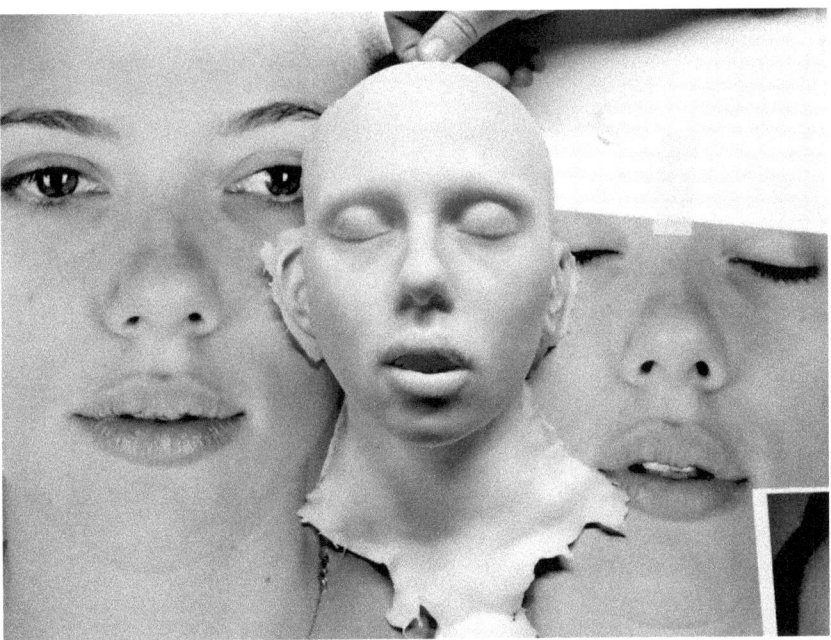

Photographs of Scarlett Johansson to the left and right of the prosthetic face created at Asylum. In the poignant scene in the forest it is worn by actress Jessica Mance, who removes it and reveals Laura's true appearance. "The [black] alien form is very close to what we developed in 2005," recalled Tom Debenham, who collaborated with Rachel Penfold and Dominic Parker at One of Us, "in a room, exploring visual entities, all those years ago" (courtesy of Kate McConnell/Asylum Models & Effects Ltd).

Johansson regarded the brutal weather as "another character in the film, really. The film is not about a midsummer afternoon, it's about a wild transformation, one that's raging. There has to be that feeling of a looming end, an apocalyptic feeling." Soon after the storm hit, First Assistant Director Nick Heckstall-Smith ordered an evacuation of the crew from the forest, but Glazer and a few intrepid crew members went out and around in Land Rovers to shoot the gale-force winds (courtesy Daniel Landin).

recalls that "the first day of shooting there was no snow, then it snowed, and they had to blow it away". In order to have the visual continuity, they had "this ridiculous situation of sweeping the snow." But what could have posed a much bigger problem for the critical final sequence was a brief period Kate describes when "the head went missing!—the head cast disappeared. We had commissioned a company in New York, and the shipping was delayed because the package was mislaid for a few days, and I missed all my deadlines. I was almost about to fly to New York." Making a new one wasn't an option because "the sculptor was booked and Scarlett was off shooting on other films. I was freaking out for three days trying to figure out where it was."

Although there are very quick—just a second or so—dark glimpses of the alien's body in earlier scenes, this is the moment in the story where the alien's physical nature, in daylight and in the open, is fully revealed. Debenham recalls the genesis of the alien form, working with Rachel Penfold and Dominic Parker of *One of Us*:

> Many years ago, myself, Rachel and Dominic were involved in an early version of the film, doing research on this whole world of what the aliens were and what they looked like. The alien form that is in the film is very close to what we developed in 2005, the essence of the black alien figure was close to what we conceived. It was Dominic and myself collaborating with Rachel in a room, exploring visual entities, all those years ago.

"At the end of the film ... the revelation of the girl's true nature," said Glazer, "takes us back to where we started: the inky blackness of the alien world."[16]

The final scene was shot by the second unit that returned to the forest the day after the evacuation. Sian Milne, who had done the trip and fall rehearsal in London and was similar to Johansson in shape and size, acted as her stunt double once again for the fiery conclusion. A covering was created for Sian to wear, which Kate describes as "a black silicone balaclava with pyrex eyes" and "a black suit to cover her face and her upper body. We needed the same thickness all over or else a hot spot would cause the suit to burn in some places. It was not a digital effect. We covered her in a fire gel, and then lit it."

Stunt coordinator Gareth Milne—Sian's father—recounts the episode, beginning with where they prepped "in a tiny little makeup tent in the middle of the forest" in the snow. "She wore a mask—she couldn't see. She had to do the whole thing on one breath. You take one last breath through a straw before they light you—you draw your last breath and then you bite it shut. We prepped and prepped and prepped with dry-run rehearsals."

When they began for real—dousing Sian in her fireproof alien suit with gel—the result wasn't what Jon had in mind. The director has, Gareth explains, "a clear picture of what he wants, and basically we had our first take on the fire scene that didn't work, and the second one was ho-hum. Jon asked me,

'What I expected to see was a ball of flame walking out of the woods—can you get that for me?' I said, 'Yes, I can!' He brings the best out of you, you want to do it for him because you're part of his vision—that's why he hired you." They tried again.

> The first time it didn't work because we hadn't put enough gel on her, a spirit-based glue. In the end we had to pour gallons and gallons on top of her so that we would get a sufficient amount of flame. We did it increment by increment, again and again. Finally we just basted her like a turkey with gallons of this accelerant and lit her, and off she went like a torch, and we got the sequences that you see in the film—but hearts were in mouths.

Asked if he had trouble as a stunt coordinator in this scene—given that his daughter was the one in flames—Gareth replied, "Just another day at work with Jonathan Glazer!" But joking aside, "I had every confidence that mentally she could cope with it, and physically she could cope with it … fire is one of her specialties." Sian, one of Gareth's three daughters and a consummate stunt performer, covered most of the female leads in seven seasons of *Game of Thrones*.

The scene is Laura's final one.

Glazer recalls:

> You see a flame ignite and extinguish. You see the beginning of something, the burgeoning of something conscious. You see a light. You see a flicker. You see the presence of something beautiful, short-lived. You see her born, you see her lived, you see her die. You hate her, love her, miss her. You see it all.[17]

Scarlett Johansson said:

> We had so many challenging moments. Certainly being in the forest and trudging through the bog was challenging just physically. But I think just struggling to remain very present, and clear in my mind throughout the filming, to be focused and present in scenes where I felt at times very bombarded by real life and the unexpected, was challenging. It was a workout, but I got stronger through it.[18]

18
Alchemy

The principal photography on *Under the Skin* that started in Glasgow on October 21, 2011, ended in mid-December, giving everyone in the crew and cast a welcome reprieve from work, a crunched timetable, and the punishing weather. For some their job was complete, for others it continued after the holidays were over—the white and black space scenes were shot for three months beginning in January on the sound stages of Elstree Studios in London. Post-production commenced as Paul Watts, of The Quarry with offices in London's Soho district, headed with Jon to their cutting room in Jon's studio in Camden.

The completion bond mantle was passed from Neil Calder at Film Finances to Ruth Hodgson, who would oversee post-production. Apart from keeping tabs on the purse strings, her job was to "track the progress of the creative process, adherence to the post schedule, and the status of the visual effects," says Ruth. "My contact was usually with Richard Lloyd, the post-production supervisor, with Jim Wilson, and with Tim Field, VFX consultant. I also had many conversations with Jonathan and Paul and occasionally with Johnnie Burn. My contacts at the financiers were Chris Collins (BFI) and Tessa Ross—usually at screenings of the cut."[1]

As with many others on the team Jon had worked with Paul before on many projects, and had discussed this one with him for years—"six or seven," Watts recalls. "There was a lot of trepidation and anxiety, because the editor that began Jon's previous two films was not the editor to finish."[2] *Under the Skin* would be different.

The values that had held fast throughout the writing of the script and shooting of the film would continue to be crucial. Glazer recalls,

> What really made sense to me in the edit was that we had to commit to that position of watching the film through the girl's eyes. The film itself needed to be an alien experience—you needed to feel that you weren't being given all the information, in the same way that she hasn't been given all the information. You had to be alongside her throughout. You needed to be inside the story, with her.[3]

Any sense of contrivance, of veering away from what was real or extant, was to be avoided just as it had during shooting. "There was a mantra throughout the entire process, during both shooting and editing," recalls Watts, "and that was: *unadorned*." With these ideals in mind Watts then faced reality: 230 hours of rushes. He saw part of the challenge as "trying to give definition to the film without over-defining," to have it "not feel constructed—when editing itself is construction."

> During a particularly tricky period I mention to Jim Wilson that it was like doing a million-piece jigsaw puzzle with no picture on the box lid. Jim basically told me to pull myself together and that we had a picture on the box lid—it was called the script. Of course he was absolutely right, however … as I am sure is often the way, things simply do not conform to expectation. The edit is the final rewrite, and we did a lot of rewriting. Scenes are gone.[4]

He describes a sequence early in the film they dubbed "the infamous scene 14" that's "no more than a few lines in the script," but in the edited film actually lasts 10 minutes and 30 seconds. It begins with Laura at the shopping mall, and ends with the Footballer sinking into the black. It's a critical piece in this early stage because "you've identified the tone. You get a feeling of her, who she is, what she's doing. You put all the fuel in the tank for the rest of the film." Watts recalls they had shot "a ten-minute scene of Scarlett and the Footballer in the van, but she was far too human—and we had to chuck the gold away." Another guiding principle: "You always have to earn the next shot you come to," says Watts. "You can't drop the ball."

They had to find the film's 108-minute essence amidst the rushes, but they had a North Star to help them navigate. "Jon's process is very much about 'Where's the truth?'—that look, that moment," says Watts. "There's no room for reverting to script when you're being that strict about what's usable. The strict criteria for inclusion based solely on what feels true override any other priorities."[5] He recalls, "We had two scenes—two and a half weeks [of work]—that are not in the film. To be able to jettison you have to be so certain, but the film didn't want them. The film had an appetite of its own."

There were times it seemed like "we had ninety short films that didn't talk to each other." There were times that they "needed a few seconds to connect two halves of a scene" and had to figure it out. He said it was like the Chunnel that was built to connect London and Paris—"the two ends didn't meet and they had to re-drill." Watts said:

> Jon will not spend any time away from the cutting room. The knowledge gained from dead ends and mistakes is too valuable for him to miss. At one point, after three or four days of trying to crack one particular nut, I suggested we revisit something we had previously dismissed. His response was, "Well Paul, if you want to lower yourself into a warm bath of expediency that's up to you, mate."[6]

"His bar is set pretty high," says Watts, "but the intensity with which we work is alleviated by the fact that we have a lot of fun. It's a great privilege. An amazing privilege." Having collaborated with Jon for so many years was key.

> When you're spending all day, nearly every day, in a room with one person for an extended period of time, looking for shapes, patterns, solutions, going down cul de sacs for days on end, reversing out and looking for other routes, it makes such a difference to be doing that alongside someone with whom you share a common language.[7]

Paul recalls that they worked about seven months through midsummer to arrive at a "soft lock." Their first cut was "terrible," but Glazer said, "Don't worry, Paul. We know the footage now."[8]

Their guiding criterion of adhering to what was true, explains Paul, "led to some fairly creative and unexpected solutions."[9] One of these solutions had to be found after about ten months in the editing room. Watts characterizes what they had on film:

> There's nothing imported, nothing's "turned up." It's an impartial telling of almost not even a series of events—a passage of time, which leads to a journey. Nothing is set up, nothing is explained. There's no exposition anywhere.... We spent the better part of a year trying to give credence and clarity to a drift—a character.

"The hardest part of the film was to chart her drift," Glazer has said.

> It couldn't be about one thing. We didn't want this kind of axiom where everything turned on this one moment, this kind of eureka, or epiphany ... it felt like it needed to be a glimmer on a Monday, a hunch on a Tuesday ... a nascence or an idea on a Wednesday, and by Friday she's thinking "Maybe I'll get away from this."[10]

Jim Wilson recalls:

> It couldn't be a story in which there was one transformative moment where this alien became humanized. You know the kind of thing—the sterile, emotionless robot sees a child in distress and suddenly a tear falls from its eye. It couldn't be like that. It had to be a more gradual transformation, it had to seem as though all the vagaries and strangeness, all the beauty and the ugliness in our world—the mess, really, of being a human being on planet Earth—had just seeped into this alien, through the cracks.[11]

Though they didn't want a "transformative moment" per se, Watts recalls Jon's feeling that what their drift needed was "Laura amidst daily life, amongst the people, and they still didn't have that. How do we feel her immersion? How do we immerse her?" It came to Jon that the answer could be found in "the kindness of strangers," and "the scene we went back to shoot was the trip and fall on the street." This was the key scene the crew and the star returned to Scotland a year later to shoot. The Chunnel metaphor seems apt here, for Laura's adventure in this sequence connects the first half of the film, where she has no agency of her own, to the second, where she discovers it.

Hodgson recalls:

These days, pick-ups are not unusual. Again because the additional shooting on the film was carried out with the creative and financial support of the financiers, [Film Finances] were not concerned. No one could have predicted how the members of the public [in Glasgow] would react to the staged fall—but the end result became a key moment in the film.

What follows this scene in the movie is another "unexpected solution"—an example of Watt's comment that "the film had an appetite of its own." It furthers her "immersion." Watts said:

> There are some key moments that are not present in the script. After Laura falls in the street and we end that scene with the layers upon layers of portraits of people on the street at night—this wasn't scripted, rather it was a response to an appetite. We upgraded the jigsaw metaphor at about this point to "playing chess with live mice while your feet are on fire."[12]

The myriad faces are "100 pictures in 35 seconds," says Watts. "The sodium lights [added by Landin] at night kept turning gold," and this "Russian icon" effect, around Laura's face (recall their interest in Andrei Rublev), becomes a cinematic evocation of this phase in Laura's journey.

In the scene at the bothy, says Watts of Laura, "Her dream is the zenith of her journey. There cannot be a more human experience than falling asleep and having a dream." In the edit, the wildly blowing trees shot by the small crew during the treacherous storm were woven into her dream and overlaid on her face. "Jon likes pictures on pictures," says Paul, "humming fizzy, windy madness."

The effect of Landin's sodium lights was "golden" portraits of the Glaswegians going about their business in Glasgow City Centre, with Johansson's close-up placed at the center. In her bothy dream several scenes later, the double-image of her face and the windblown trees (shot during the treacherous storm) is another piece of post-production magic (courtesy StudioCanal and FilmNation).

The Microphone in the Umbrella

Sound designer Johnnie Burn has worked on ads, music videos (Madonna and David Bowie among them), TV, and film, including on three features for filmmaker Yorgos Lanthimos, and for a brief time on Johansson's very different science fiction turn in *Ghost in the Shell*. He was with Glazer on *Birth*. "I met Jon through art director Tom Carty and the wonderful Walter Campbell, when working on Guinness commercials in the 90s—either that or Jon's music video for UNKLE's *Rabbit in Your Headlights*—it was a while ago, anyway. I was in the early days of a budding sound career."[13]

They had talked about *Under the Skin* over lunch as early as 2008, then began working with the script in 2011—a new version of the story. "The original script could, I guess, more easily have been story-boarded and shot on locked-off locations, whereas the final script left so much more room for discovery and a requirement to get out into the real world, capture what we could, and then somehow make that sound filmic."

> There isn't a great deal of dialogue in the film, and yet us humans are primed to always seek meaning from our senses, so I kind of knew that whatever was accompanying the image would play a strong role in how people interpret them. Sound, like smell, has a stronger hotwire to the emotions than vision, and it's usually [the] medium through which we decode.

To get on a wave length for the project, Burn watched Ingmar Bergman's *Persona*. "I know what Jon likes, and the main thing would be restraint. Although the sound is quite big in terms of its prominence it's just because the sensitivities are turned to such a high level."[14]

Burn described his director as "incredibly rigorous, and would like to hear every single possible version" of sound that was available before making his decision—his standards were "extraordinarily high." "Ultimately what we were trying to do was create an alien's impression of the world" through, among other things, sound.[15] Toward that end Jon "would not accept anything like anything he had heard before. So, we had to experiment."[16] As an example, none of the "normal film versions of foley" that they tried "seemed quite right" for the white space scene, so they decided to take a cue from the success they'd had with recording other sounds in their "real environments" and apply these sounds to an alien environment.[17] At a physics lab they found the solution: "We ended up recording in an [echo-free] anechoic chamber with mics 30 feet away to give a very odd sound."[18]

Apart from the stock sound effects used in the scene where Scarlett's van is mobbed by a group of young men, all the sounds—from the forest to the streets to Debehnam's department store—were recorded by Burn and his assistants, Ed Downham and Simon Carroll, and by Nigel.

> When Scarlett enters the shopping center in reel one, we hear sound that whilst not actually the sync sound is a veracious set of recordings from that location, but edited together to, hopefully, present the world somewhat differently. In a shot tracking her through the place I was following her with a microphone hidden in an umbrella—but with the embellishments to the sound and the film's trajectory, we made a shopping center in Glasgow feel like it was light years away.

Burn also had mics sewn into the cuffs and the collar of his shirt to catch the voices of passersby—and they put mics in Scarlett's wig to record people who might talk to her.[19]

> In the shopping centre scene early on, the sound we hear is a tightly knitted piece where about 10 very short, honed sounds fire off every second, to give the illusion that we are moving in that space. We placed sound for voices, feet, clothes, radios and so on, for everything you see on the screen. The results are unusual as they include the kind of extraneous sound that is normally edited out of a film—and in that they are nicely alien.[20]

When Scarlett wasn't using the van Burn and his team went inside it to record moving around on the seat, handling the steering wheel, the sound of her fur coat on the seat, and so on, and then play with them, alter the frequency, or add reverb.[21] He compares it to "focusing a lens," and in editing the sound, you "ask yourself exactly what every frame of sound is doing in the cut, and if you can't provide an answer for each frame of the duration, delete it. By that I mean reduce all our sound to the essence of the bit that is working, and no more."[22] In other words, "with all the fat trimmed." Burn continues:

> Whilst it comprises often mundane recordings that, dipped into, may seem uneventful, their selection and placement in sequence is where you feel the sum becoming greater than the parts. When Scarlett asks for directions to the M8 from the guy on the street, up until that point everything has a muted, through-the-window feel to it, and then the window winds down and the higher frequencies pierce her wee spaceship bubble—and it really feels like contact.

Burn recalls that, although it wasn't necessarily always discussed,

> The route we took and decisions we made always had us ending up manipulating or editing our raw material so that the combination became an unnatural presentation of something very natural, like it equaled extra-terrestrial. My team and I walked amongst lively Glaswegian football fans recording material and the placement of this as she drives her van through them is pretty unusual—by dint of both the sound and edit choices and the muffled nature of hidden microphones.

"I had a fantastic team of editors," says Burn. "Ed Downham, Simon Carroll and Steve Browell, and re-recording mixer Steve Single. They each really earned their stripes on a very long project."[23]

Paul Watts is grateful to Burn for an elegant solution to a particular challenge in the editing room: In cutting from Laura driving around at night—from the "unconventional" eeriness of her van to a "conventional" beach setting that follows in the script—Watts felt that they "landed there with a bump."

> Paul showed me the cut and we spoke about how it was about leaving the city, and how it would be nice to have city sound to propel her out, yet all the sync sound was just

van engine grinding away. So I started by finding some of my recordings that kind of matched shots—like the wah-wah-wah on the guy running oddly with a guitar on his back—and then had the idea of pulling the sound of the waves way earlier across the whole scene, and laid up the new sound so that it fell in a rhythm with that—the way it falls into the eventual waves.

A kind of reverse of this is heard when Laura leaves the city for the country. The Catherine Wheel of mist that unfurls at the shore is accompanied by powerful waves and wind sounds that flow into the humming engine of her van as she drives along. Moments later, when Laura is on foot, she's greeted by a sudden—and loud—chirp. Burn recalls:

> Well of course nothing happened to just be there, but I love the way one strains to hear the distant man singing and then bang, this very close bird!—perhaps as lost in the fog as she is—whizzes past, which nicely curtails the potential singing man narrative cul de sac, and draws me back to thoughts on her. I recorded it in a forest at my father's house just outside Biggar, in Lanark.

For the creepy crackling sounds of the men's bodies transmogrifying under the black water, they experimented with rubbing their fingers around on grains of dry rice on a tray in time with the men's movements. Then Dan Landin suggested they try adding some crinkly leaves—and in the end the otherworldly sounds were a mix of rice, leaves, and cellophane tape.[24]

The documentary-like naturalism of Scarlett's trip and fall on Trongate is achieved once again through a combination of hidden cameras and tapping into the riches of over 2,000 hours of sound, honed down to 50, that the team recorded all over Glasgow and greater Scotland between August 2011 and November 2012. "The quality and scope of our library let us guide a rigorously chiseled experience," says Burn, but on the screen it couldn't seem more spontaneous:

> What we found was beautifully genuine; wind atmospheres, bird songs, all the foley we could want, bottles breaking, drunks shouting, fights, hen nights, passion, real tears and laughter, unimaginable honesty, buskers, and hundreds of very brief voice snippets as Glaswegians walked past our kit. We enjoyed incidental knocks and bangs, normal life.[25]

Glazer credits his sound designer with "adding an auditory level to the girl's sensory experiences" by using a very different approach from typical sound editing, whereby

> they'd usually look for the cleanest take. But it wasn't like that at all for us. It was about finding the textures and the noises, the variety of sounds that were bombarding her. We needed you to feel that her change, this drift, was happening by osmosis.... Johnnie used all the bits of sound that a sound editor would throw in the bin.[26]

The plethora of sounds that would normally be discarded as nuisance or extraneous were "somehow becoming symphonic, just bubbling away in the background."[27]

"A Genius in a Bedsit"

For most of 2012 Glazer and Watts had "cut dry," in other words, without using any temporary music as an enhancement along the way—"Jonathan is not one to use temp music or temp sound design lightly," says Watts. "There are no crutches or props during the edit process!"[28] Late in that process Peter Raeburn, the film's music producer and arranger, finally had to give him a push. "I delayed this as long as possible," Glazer admits, until Peter finally said to him, "Look, we've got to find a composer." Jon remembers meeting with Raeburn years before, and saying, "This is not going to be some sort of Hollywood guy, this will be a genius in a bedsit. Somewhere out there is the voice for this film. And I knew it would be the soul of the film."[29] "I knew that Jonathan did not want a traditional music composition for the score," recalls Hodgson, "and was keen to find a composer who could deliver a 'soundscape.'"

Raeburn's and Glazer's careers had been intertwined for years.

> Although he achieved several music production credits on films such as *Breaking the Waves*, it was the sourcing and remixing of Leftfield's *Phat Planet* for the Guinness Surfer advert in 1999 which won several awards and kickstarted his career. This also marked the start of a regular collaboration with film-maker Jonathan Glazer who went on to direct *Birth* and *Sexy Beast*, hiring Raeburn to produce the soundtracks.[30]

A composer and songwriter, Raeburn gives credit to his kid sister's gift to him long ago of David Bowie's 1971 LP *Hunky Dory*—particularly the song "Changes." "I remember it having a profound effect." He found it fun, uplifting, and beautifully produced, and recalls that by age 12 or 13, "I'd always had melodies in my head and words in my head, but it was only when I picked up a guitar and figured out a few chords, that I suddenly realized there was a clear throughway for these things that were trapped in me."[31] On Lars von Trier's *Breaking the Waves* he worked for music supervisor Ray Williams, and "that's where I learnt about the application of music for film and TV, and I learnt about orchestral production, which has been very important for me.... I discovered the relationship between music and pictures.... I realized that was a relationship I was fascinated in."[32]

Raeburn is also a Music Supervisor on *Under the Skin*, as is Jay James, a classically trained pianist and his colleague at Soundtree in London. A producer and supervisor of music in film, television, and ads, she has in common with Glazer and Raeburn brands such as Guinness, SONY, and Levis; James has also supervised music on films that feature scores composed by Raeburn, among them *Woodshock* (2017), directed by Kate and Laura Mulleavy, and *The Last Composer* (2017), directed by Danny Huston.[33]

Raeburn began playing tapes for Jon, including work by some very well-known composers "who've done magnificent work on scores," admits Jon, but nothing he heard seemed right until one piece that was utterly unfamiliar—

echoing Burn's comment that for sound the director didn't want to hear "anything he'd ever heard before." After listening to seven tapes, "number eight is this strange sound that came out, probably about 20 seconds of it and I immediately said, 'Who's *that*?'"[34] What had stopped Glazer in his tracks was the band Micachu and the Shapes performing their LP *Chopped and Screwed* live with the London Sinfonietta in 2011.[35] It was Jay James who introduced Raeburn to Micachu, or Mica Levi, with whom he had worked before on a project.[36] *Chopped and Screwed* isn't a film score—and Levi, who was 24 at the time, was not a film composer. But if you listen to this album, for example the cut called *"Not So Sure,"* you can hear a clear path from Micachu and the Shapes to Levi's spellbinding score for *Under the Skin*.

Levi, who began writing music at age 4, received a classical training at London's Guildhall School. In 2008 she wrote a composition for the London Philharmonic. The live piece that dazzled Jon—and the band's other albums, *Jewellery* (2009) and *Never* (2012)—embrace her "fascination with jagged and discordant music.... Levi crafted dense everything-*and*-the-kitchen-sink songs built around slack-stringed guitars, clangorous percussion and serrated beats, and Levi's vaguely androgynous voices."[37]

Levi's influences for the film's score were in part "the 20th century music I had cut my teeth on at Guildhall: Giacinto Scelsi, Iannis Xenakis and John Cage ... the big, music-changing composers."[38] It's not uncommon for writers who interview her or talk about the film's music to invoke the name of avant-garde composer György Ligeti, who is also only a degree of separation from Glazer by virtue of his music's presence in Kubrick's *2001* and *Eyes Wide Shut*. "The strings sometimes resemble nails going down a universe-sized chalkboard, screaming with a Ligeti-like sense of horror," wrote Larry Fitzmaurice. "Elsewhere, they endlessly drone in a gaping vortex, like Vangelis's iconic *Blade Runner* score dipped in turpentine."[39] The cosmic contemplation of Vangelis's sound is an apt allusion for *Under the Skin*, and Vangelis has called music "the main code of the universe."[40] Levi says, "I've listened to a lot of Ligeti in my life, especially at school and at college, so there's no denying he is generally of great influence."[41] Levi also acknowledges the influence of Penderecki, Feldman, and Greek composer Iannis Xenakis.[42]

> When I was younger, I used to listen to the soundtrack to the Hitchcock film *Vertigo* by Bernard Herrmann. I also like *The Ghost in the Shell* soundtrack, the original. *Chinatown*'s amazing. I like a lot of the films of the 70s ... the 70s is the golden era. I think it's because the producers and directors were all partying together and taking risks on things, coming up with bizarre scenarios.[43]

To find a portal into this very unusual assignment, Levi sought a personal connection to the story.

> That's what I was told to do.... I tried to get immersed in her, and tried to figure her out. And I suppose the only way I could do that was in relation to me, and experiences

close to me. [The character] has these experiences, these floods of feelings for the first time ... when I was a teenager, I would have these extreme floods of feelings.[44]

"The way that Jon works, he's just always trying the boldest move he can. I really feel like he directed me,"[45] say Levi, and describes her direction from Glazer as more "abstract" than specific—that her job was "to have an instinct."[46]

> My job was to do the things you can't see—the girl's feelings and experiences of love, fear, hate, confusion and curiosity. I was directed to think about what she was experiencing, and the thematic ideas are all related to her. I tried to connect any different experience she was having to the music. So the symbols relate to natural aspects—in my mind they relate to the landscape, the physical spaces, and Scarlett is superimposing in these different scenarios, whether it's in a city or in the sea or forest.[47]

Raeburn recalls the process of collaborating with Mica and with Jon, playing bits for them and finding their way to "a trail of clues to create."

> She has a unique way of seeing the world musically. There's an "otherness" to her being, musically, which is really interesting for this project. There's a willingness to go on this journey with us, no matter where it would bring us, no matter what it took.[48]

Ambiguity Reigns

"The eerie quiet at the beginning immediately prepares you for a unique auditory experience," said Chris Douridas, a music supervisor and longtime Los Angeles DJ. "You become attuned to the idea that what you're hearing is as important as anything else you'll experience."[49]

The complexities, the binary tension, the confusion, and the uncertainty that are inherent in the story and in the character's journey—and that are expressed in all the film's cinematic elements in every scene—reach a kind of apotheosis in Levi's score. Interviewer John Schaeffer said to Mica—giving the film's opening sequence as just one example: "You're not sure—am I seeing the planets align? ... and you [Levi] kind of match that ambiguity with the texture of the music. I was not sure often whether in fact I was hearing actual instruments or computer sounds, or processed noise."[50] In fact throughout the score we are hearing all of the above. There are classical orchestral instruments—primarily viola, which Levi plays on the score and used to compose it. She made use of MIDI [Musical Instrument Digital Interface] for what she calls its "foreverness. You can hold this chord and it goes on until you lift your hand. It's something eternal and programmed."[51] For Levi "the use of MIDI strings alongside real strings explained the situation of real and fake and felt like a good mix of synthetic and real. Percussion strings and fake strings were the main bulk of the score, which also has a lot of cymbal rolls—those are meant to represent the cosmos and nature."[52]

We were looking at the natural sound of an instrument to try and find something identifiably human in it, then slowing things down or changing the pitch of it to make it feel uncomfortable. There was a lot of talk of perverting material. It does sound creepy, but we were going for sexy.[53]

The menacing one-two beat that follows Laura whenever she is on the hunt is "just a kick made with a tom and hitting some wood in my room years ago," says Levi, "that ended up being used throughout. And it's just slowed down ... distorted through time as opposed to distorted through like ... [foot pedals]," creating discomfort because "it's too slow, it's distorted."[54] We begin to hear this sound after Laura first applies her lipstick near the beginning of the film, and it's the signature of the cut on the soundtrack called "Lipstick to Void."[55] It could at first be mistaken for a sound effect, which in a sense it is (going back to Schaeffer's conundrum about never knowing just what it is we're hearing) but Burn is quick to say "the one-two beat is Mica's—so simple, but wow—genius. As is the 'Creation' rumble [the film's opening]." "Much of the music-sound synergy," says Burn, "came from taking every single sound and giving it a polish with the music in mind [e.g.] tuning the rhythm and pitching to make it like Mica might have made it." Mica confirms that Burn wanted the music and sound to be "really cohesive and homogeneous," and so they continually exchanged updates to "keep each other in the loop."[56] Burn describes their mission to "dovetail" the music and the sound effects "so that when a piece of music ends, the sound effects would carry the mood on ... every single sound throughout the film pretty much had its musical pitch adjusted."[57]

These two notes are ubiquitous—they're like a heartbeat in the film, Laura's heartbeat. They often precede the score's other signature, what the team called "the capture theme"—the haunting trio of notes on the viola. Levi explains that "it's her perfume" for luring men. "Then it deteriorates, it becomes sadder ... then there's this major triad, a warm chord, and that's her 'human' or 'love' feeling. And there's this darker minor triad of trilled strings that recurs throughout." Levi's use of microtonality contributed to the music's unease. "Instead of the 12 tones we're used to, it's wavering between them ... which can sound out of tune but can be more expressive because it's not precise and accurate."[58] The one-two beat and the three notes become iconic on the score; they are alternated or they are together. The three notes are repeated as many as six times in a row. Sometimes they just appear and finish, and other times they carry on into a haunting melody involving the first two of the three notes played three times before the third finally arrives, like some kind of musical taunt. "It needed to feel like a kind of inexorable life force that's going forward, like a shark," said Glazer. "It needed to say, 'This is what I've always been, this is what I always will be; just a force.' It also needed to give us her motif, so her music became part of her armoury."[59]

This "inexorable life force" is felt throughout the score in ways both subtle and forceful, perhaps most forcefully in the "Creation" sequence at the outset, where the quivering strings that invoke Levi's "beehive," or a charging locomotive, accompany the mysterious opening visuals. Composer Bobby Brader likes the effect of "the tremolo to build a kind of science fiction suspense." He notes Levi's use of an aleatoric score or notation, which he describes as removing one element of control over the musicians—giving pitch but not rhythm, for example, or rhythm but not pitch. With the "scribbling" we hear in various places, sometimes when Laura is driving around in her van, "You give up both pitch and rhythm."[60] For this Levi credits the Xenakis influence, and says that his technique that most influenced her was "a lot of aleatoric movement. I was a teenager when I first heard *Tetras* and I'd never heard anything like it. It was like a beehive."[61] In addition to flute, "there's a cymbal roll that goes through it most of the time. And that acts as the cosmos and nature and the planet and beyond the planet and part of the unexplainable."[62]

The "beehive" chillingly recurs later over the rushing river of gore that is the result of the men's evisceration in the black water, lending a dark, industrial inevitability to their fate. In the opening sequence the sounds of Laura's syllables, her language lesson, come in and then stop abruptly when the screen goes white for the film's title—then we hearing the forceful sounds (more rushing and charging) of a waterfall before we see it. The cymbal roll is dominant as the headlight of Bad's motorcycle appears in the night, then merges with the cacophony of strings that express the surging traffic on the highway—and the human civilization which the aliens have invaded. The opening—introducing many of the tools in Levi's and Burn's tool boxes—uses the score to plunge us into the film's complexity, its mystery, and its contradictions.

The one-two beat accompanies Laura as she ventures down the sidewalk on her own for the film's critical added scene. The sounds of the Glasgow street begin to fill the air around her; the rhythm of her boots hitting the pavement, the conversations, coughs, shouts, buses, car engines and screech—it's a montage of the vast "library" that Burn and his team recorded to represent the world Laura hears. It all leads to the sudden thud of Laura's body hitting the sidewalk after she trips. At this moment, with a close-up of her face against pavement, combines what Brader calls a scribbling of strings—used variously in the score—with the street sounds to create "a clarity issue, a confusion or messiness—for a reason." Confusion must be one of the many things Laura feels in the ensuing moments—stunned by both the fall and the shower of attention from strangers. The "messiness" of human life is what she invited with this walk: she's opened a Pandora's box. The one-two beat—the sound of Laura's hunt, her job—ceases immediately when she falls, and once she is helped up and proceeds to walk away it is no longer present. There is only the ongoing sound of people and their lives (and a brief moment of bagpipes) leading to a tender string sequence—a single attenuated note—that plays as the sea of faces envelopes her.

There are three pieces of added music in the film—the exuberant electronica inside the club is "Sandstorm" by Darude[63] and later we hear "C90" by Soundtree.[64] Early on the director had in mind, "If we can experience everything as she does, then let's be denied music until she hears it, and *then* let's have music."[65]

> I'll tell you, my first thoughts about music in the film were—no music until he plays her a record. That was an early draft.... And then it was "Well, what record does he play? What do you plan for an alien?" And then the choice became so deliberate ... so loaded ... you know, and *that* was terrible.... So that music that had such importance on the page became the opposite. In fact it was like, "What would be on the radio? Whatever's on the radio when you're washing up. It's not a choice. In fact, turn the radio on now and whatever it is, that's what it should be."[66]

"When he reaches for the radio," notes Douridas,

> it's the station he listens to, it's what he does, part of his routine, he knows the show that's on at that time. You cast that song to him. It would be a song you would hear on the radio in that small town. It immediately puts you in touch with his life, his everyday workaday world, daily doldrums, simple pleasures, the character very much being himself, watching his favorite TV show. And the larger Scottish community that he's a part of. We're in his environment.

You wouldn't want a song that was "'too cool,' or 'inside.' Belle and Sebastian, say, would be 'too hip'" for this moment, says Douridas. "And you want a song that has a contagious rhythm to it, so she begins tapping, and we see her internal transformation." He calls the filmmakers' choice of Deacon Blue's *Real Gone Kid*,[67] a pop hit in Glasgow where this band hails from, "perfect."

> It's a beautiful detail. You might not even notice it because it blends in so well, which is what you want—you don't want something that stands out, that will take the audience out of the story. When she taps her fingers after she sees him tapping his foot, it's their first "bonding" moment. This is the first time she comes his way—the first move she makes in his direction.

He also likes the idea that the song has a male singer, which seems to resonate with Laura meeting a man, for the first time, outside of her role in her "old life."

A new theme never heard before on the score, nor heard again, plays as Laura and Quiet have their moment in the darkness. It begins with not three but four notes played very slowly. These become the background for a languid string melody called "Love" that accompanies the couple's gentle and tentative movements; Levi says she was influenced by the music of euphoric dance in composing this piece.⁶⁸ Laura lifts her mouth as if awaiting his; he brings his face close to hers and kisses her. As their lips meet she places her fingertips on his cheek and caresses his neck; he responds by touching her face, and then she places her fingers over his. Once they are in bed, as events become uneasy, so does the score, which seems to begin to weep.

As the scene begins this music "could be Mozart" says Brader. "But the glissando, the notes going up and down slowly, bumping into each other and in and out of the four notes creates dissonance for this very beautiful and atonal theme, and it sounds off-putting—and I love it." About this sequence Schaeffer said to Mica, "When she tries the act of making love, your music suggests that it's a really poor fit—there's a kind of … queasy quality to the music in this scene." Levi responded, "Ah, that's good. Well I think when you are in love … you can feel a bit sick, like love sick…. I guess, in my experience—it was like an intensity, it was supposed to be like 'rushing, like taking pills.⁶⁹ I was working out the feeling of making out for the first time, or taking Ecstasy—rushing. Warm synth pads—it felt like love." Strip club music also informed what Levi wrote. "They are pretty unsettling and eerie," she said. "That's part of the vibe. I thought—like dark and viscous, not clean and tidy."⁷⁰ She continues:

Scarlett Johansson and Michael Moreland. Here composer Mica Levi introduces a new theme to the score, which accompanies the couple's gentle, tentative intimacy bathed in a rosy glow. For this piece, called "Love," Levi was influenced by the music of euphoric dance. Music supervisors: Soundtree's Peter Raeburn and Jay James (courtesy StudioCanal and FilmNation).

The role of synthesized strings in the film is her kind of experience of love, and that aesthetic of it being not real is very important, I think … it's the falseness of it, the mix of fake and real instruments, and computer-generated music, that's in line with the narrative, I think.⁷¹

In Laura's new chapter, many scenes are without any music at all. Levi feels that Glazer "absolutely guided, and made some of the best decisions about the music in this film. And the silence is all led by the narrative that he was so clear about and him sort of following his gut." In the "gap," or breaks from music or sound or both, "you're lifted with her character. It focuses you in a different way."[72] "The film is score-heavy at the front," notes Douridas, "but as the movie progresses through her slow conversion, as she is increasingly intrigued by humanity, the more natural sounds take precedence—the sounds of the environment she finds herself in."

When the lovemaking doesn't work out and Laura abruptly sits up, the music also ends abruptly, and does not resume. In the next scene she's fleeing toward the woods with only the sound of wind blowing across the clearing, and maybe some distant thunder. She heads into the forest with the sound of the rain hitting the puddles between the trees and her shoes meeting the crunchy forest floor as she maneuvers through the fallen trees. After her first encounter with the Logger, she discovers the shelter. When she's inside we continue to hear what she hears—the rain dancing on the skylights. She goes to sleep and has a dream. Johnnie Burn recalled:

> The bothy wind was a result of the very early wind symphony "chats" [with Jon] and had lived on the cut before Mica came on board, so she politely, I guess, tuned her beautiful piece to let it remain. I took winds and very sharply spiked frequencies at specific musical intervals to create a chord through wind. I'd been listening to Santana's *Black Magic Woman*, and notes-wise, I think it's the opening chord of that. It's the same sound on the trailer.

After the attack in the woods, Laura's three notes are heard for the last time as she gazes into the face of her human self, and her "heartbeat" follows her as she flees the forest in flames—ending as she perishes in the snow.

Glazer views the music as "very much the blood of the film."[73] "I think she's magnificent," he has said of Levi. "I think she's a genius." He'd always liked the idea that Levi thought of the character of Laura as "a rebel."[74]

Levi calls her time working on the score "a very immersive experience, and I got obsessed with it. It took about nine months of working pretty constantly. I used to have a studio in a shipping container so I did some work there initially, but after that I was in Pete's studio two or three times a week."[75] The shipping container studio seems to oddly fulfill Glazer's imagining of "a genius in a bedsit." "Scores can often feel like they're on top of the movie," he says, "but for this it had to be in and of the movie."[76] "I remember saying to Pete, 'I really want this to be Mica's voice.'"[77]

Post-production on *Under the Skin* had begun at the end of January and "delivery took place to the sales agent on the 28th of June 2013," recalls Ruth Hodgson. Her company Film Finances Inc. had bonded *Sexy Beast*, one of the first productions she dealt with after joining the company in 1999. Hodgson said:

> A lengthy edit is a consequence of Jonathan's creative process [picture lock took 180 days longer to achieve than predicted by the original schedule] but we were aware of this because of our prior working experience with Jonathan on his first film. Similarly

we were not overly concerned about the length of the post process in general, because of the support [both creative and financial] given by the financiers of the film. Obviously if that had not been the case, our attitude would have been rather different!

"We saw many versions of the film in post-production," said Ben Roberts, who came on board at BFI Film Fund during this process, "but every iteration was better than the last."[78]

"There is so much solitude," says Glazer. "You're in a bubble for such a long period of time."[79] Although they weren't in the same building, "we were all in the same square mile, and I would be going from place to place, and we would be regularly meeting…. The music would inform the cut, the cut would inform the sound, the sound the effects, and so on."[80]

In the end it was six people sitting in the mixing theater—where they had mixed and remixed and remixed for months on end—Levi, Burn, Raeburn, Wilson, Glazer, and Richard Lloyd.

> We had watched the film, we had done all our notes, we'd watch it again. More notes, more notes, watch it again. More notes, more notes … and then we got to the point where there were no more notes … and we all sort of sat there like, well that's it then. What you don't think is—what seems most natural in that moment—is that you'll just turn the projector off, lock the door and go back to your life.[81]—Jonathan Glazer

PART III: THE WORLD OF *UNDER THE SKIN*

19
Opposites Attract

In *Under the Skin*, a tension of binaries—evoked in Zacharek's "rhapsody laced with thorns"[1]—drives every cinematic element we can name: the cinematography, score, story, themes, and characters. Light versus dark, cinéma vérité versus the highly stylized and even surreal, the vulnerable versus the predatory, human and non-human, nature and technology, isolation and society, beauty and horror, and more. In the world of this film the paradoxical is essential. Opposites do more than co-exist—they depend upon each other to exist in a rhetorical sense, for this is how the film works on us. In any moment we see, hear, feel, and sometimes ponder two things, they seem either to tug us in opposite directions or baffle us because they work in concert.

A Dance of Dark and Light

The menacing white dot racing toward us in the very first shot—the dot Glazer wants us to fear, and we do—is surrounded by blackness. The surroundings conjure the dark universe and all its mystery, and the frenzied strings that accompany the image emulate the wheels of a speeding train—this dot may crash into us. But instead it explodes into a starburst, pink at the center of a green areola, and surrounded by sky blue—a thing of celestial beauty. Has the menace subsided? Only for a few seconds, because quickly this comforting image gives way to another utterly unfamiliar one—a black cylinder penetrating a white donut-like orb, an alien manufacturing of a pupil and iris. The tension between black and white—light and its absence—is coupled with the tension between the familiar and the foreign; a racing dot followed by a sparkling starburst, an industrial eye followed by a human eye, a body part juxtaposed with deep space. The distant and the very, very close. Few images are as unnerving as a close-up of an eye. Why is this hazel eye staring at us? What does it know? All the more menacing for its proximity to the image of outer space, as if what it knows is everything—everything we do not. We are as diminished by the eye's ominous gaze as we are by the notion of infinite and incomprehensible space.

The white dot continues to menace as we are pushed and pulled between what we think is familiar and what is disturbingly foreign. The dot becomes a motorcycle headlight (again coming toward us) on a dark mountain road, then it's a series of street lamps above a highway. The cyclist who pulls off on the side of the road and gets off a bike could be any guy we've ever seen, but soon he's carrying the body of a girl who may or may not be dead. The music won't let go—it's got us by the throat. The anxiety created in these two opening sequences from this moment on does not let up for another ninety minutes. From this point everything, including the familiar, keeps us on edge.

What's next comes quickly on the tail of the previous series of eerie and unfamiliar images, pushing us further into an unsettled state. To begin we are jolted from several minutes of blackness to a stark white surrounding that can barely be called a space since it has no definition. Production designer Chris Oddy's bouncy castle has neither walls nor ceiling, nor ornament of any kind, and a floor only by implication; the two figures are supported but otherwise appear to be suspended in nothingness. After a close-up of Laura undressing the unconscious girl, a full-screen shot of them as black silhouettes in the white void reinforces this setting as alien by definition; it's no place we have been before or can comprehend. The shot of Laura delicately turning her hand to examine the ant she has picked up is reminiscent of the silhouette animation of Lotte Reiniger from the 1920s.

Another bold contrast for our senses to process is the sudden absence of music that follows the intense, persistent score Levi composed for the previous shots. Again there's a sense of being thrust or jolted from one sensation to its opposite. In this scene there is only the faintest whistling of white noise, barely perceptible—like a pale wind blowing through an empty tunnel turned down to minimum volume. The diegetic sounds of the undressing, sharp quick sounds that pierce the whiteness and the quiet with their harshness, make the disrobing feel all the more cold and invasive. From this place we cut once again to darkness; first to a night sky where mysterious white orbs play behind the clouds, then to a dark staircase that Laura descends.

The "black place" plays in tandem with the "white space." Like its partner, the black is without definition and not a space as we understand it. The figures, once inside, seem to float—although they are walking—in a void. Again we're disoriented by the queasily unfamiliar and inexplicable, but the black space crosses the boundary from unsettling to confounding when it morphs from a solid to a "liquid" into which Laura's prey slowly sinks while Laura strolls nonchalantly across the its shimmering surface. She is supernatural,

The shot of a curious Laura examining an ant on her hand echoes the silhouette animation developed by German animator and film director Lotte Reiniger in the 1920s. Inspired by shadow puppetry from countries such as India and Indonesia, the image of flat cutouts in silhouette creates a poetry all its own. This frame is from Reiniger's "The Adventures of Prince Achmed" (1926) (courtesy Wikimedia Commons. Lotte Reiniger/Primrose Productions © Christel Strobel, Primrose Productions).

maybe otherworldly, as are this place and the white space, and we're pretty much pushed off the cliff of our assumptions from here on. The black scenes jar our senses while wreaking havoc with our notions about space, matter, and what or who this main character is.

Black and white, dark and light are dialectics that fuel anxiety early in the film and persist throughout, culminating in the snowy wood. Laura is mostly a nocturnal creature, stalking men sometimes in daylight but mostly on the night highway and dark streets of Glasgow. When an early hunt occurs at the beach, with its pale sky and white sand, there is something especially creepy and frightening about it. Horror that occurs in the dark seems to belong in the dark, and we can tell ourselves that the person who ended up there should have avoided it or known better, but the incident at the ocean perverts this destination for pleasure and tranquility into a chamber of horrors. We're anxious because we know the Swimmer's fate, but the other disturbing undertone to this scene is Laura herself. What we know about her up to this point is limited and we can reserve a bit of judgment if we choose. She undressed a young woman of unknown identity and indeterminate condition, she lured a strange man into an indeterminate place. There's nothing more. Here at the beach her behavior reveals more and instead of redeeming her gets worse, as if the broad daylight is exposing an even harsher reality about her than we saw in the blackness. She does not process the family's jeopardy in the way we, or the Swimmer, do—including the sight of the stranded infant. It may come off that she is oblivious to all of this, or aware and by nature not sensitive to it, but the effect is a kind of mocking of human sensibilities and values. Finally, we see her kill a man in cold blood. This daylight is no opposite of darkness; it offers neither sanctuary nor safety. The threat she poses isn't restricted to strange indoor places, it is everywhere. And yet there is another way to look at Laura's actions on the beach. She behaves more than anything like an animal would, a creature that must kill its prey to survive, and human thoughts and considerations must be absent from this equation. We wouldn't condemn a starving wolf for felling a dear and not shedding a tear for it or its family. The black-space scenes keep Laura's identity or nature in disguise, but here the veil is partly pushed aside. We sense she is not human.

Much later, at the midpoint/turning point of the narrative, day breaks as Laura breaks away from her dark life—the man she has freed is escaping across a field at dawn. Her own flight proceeds without a hitch until she is forced to abandon her van, her getaway vehicle. She stands alone on a country road enveloped in a white low-lying cloud. Most of her experiences in her new life unfold in the light of day, including her times with Quiet. That the film's disturbing culminating sequence occurs in daylight is the perfect closing: the most powerful play of binaries in Glazer's film is saved for last.

Like the occurrence at the beach, the forest's horrific chain of events are made all the more disturbing because it is daylight. The setting is poignant and perfect. Throughout millennia of literature and a century of cinema for both children and adults, the forest embodies the best that life on Earth has to offer, and the worst. It's a stage for the sublime and the frightening, the pure activities of nature untainted by human presence and the darkest activities humanity conceives. The forest barely requires a juxtaposition because it is its own dual trope, possessing its own internal and pervasive tension.

The light/dark motif is furthered by the white snow, as it places our alien's shimmering black body, the ashes that become of it, and the column of smoke that signifies Laura's exit from Earth, in bold relief. When Laura is chased by the Logger in the woods, a gender duality seems at first almost too obvious, but it is complex. He is a male in pursuit of what he assumes is a female, so for his intents and purposes she is one. His assumption is that he will rape and possibly kill her and that he has the strength and the home-court advantage to do both if he wishes. But this trope is subverted because of what the audience knows—that on her own court she has killed countless men. She will lose this last battle, but it isn't because she is weak or frail or fearful; it's because she's an alien out of her element. Let's shift it and place him on her turf instead: Were he in the city out strolling to an ATM she could easily lure him into the black space and he'd be dead meat, so to speak, in minutes.

Is She a "She"?

To further complicate matters, the male/female binary and the stereotypes associated with it are in a sense illusory, because ultimately there is no evidence that Laura has a gender. Here the film offers an opportunity to explore our assumptions about gender both inside and outside of the movie. For what exactly do we see when we see her? In the quick black space scenes where there are two separate full-shot glimpses of her alien body, and later in the forest after she removed her human costume, we see no "gender." In the close-ups of Laura kneeling as she gazes into her human face, we see her own face and head, exquisitely beautiful but in human terms somewhat unisex. In the sexual encounter with Quiet, we learn that she has no genitalia as we know it. We see no evidence of any gender we know and so we cannot assume that this alien species even has gender as we understand it. Laura's companions who present as human males may well look exactly as she does under their human skins, and may *be* exactly as she is. Of the many possible musings upon the film's title, this invites a gendered one; that we cannot presume anyone to be what they appear to be on the outside, for it is what is beneath the skin that defines us.

With this in mind we can revisit the entire film, especially Laura's time with Quiet, through a different lens, a non-gendered or un-gendered one, at least where Laura is concerned. When we think about her roaming the streets of Glasgow in her van, and we see her not as a female alien but simply an alien, we must remove yet another layer of familiarity because we are familiar with what we think of as *femaleness*. We see the degree to which her apparent femaleness is a crutch for us, for although we know she's an alien, at least she's a female, so we assume we can grasp something about her. We can ascribe all sorts of meanings to her actions by assuming that because she's female she resembles female humans when it comes to possible emotions or agendas. She puts on red lipstick, compliments her victims, makes them feel attractive, then strips off her clothing in the dark to lure them in not because she wants them, but because she's a misandrist, or a femme fatale who wants to hurt them. Or perhaps she wants revenge because her ex dumped her, or because men generally abused her as they had Isserley in Faber's novel.

But without her female label, what do we have? She's pretending to behave as a human, and as a human female—two huge leaps for her, one more perhaps than what we may have thought. As long as she's working her mission she is safe, it's all just an acting job in a van or on a black stage. It's when she leaves her mission behind that she loses all previous restrictions (and protections as well) and begins to enact, or act upon, whatever feelings and desires have been growing within her since she arrived on Earth. The binary in the forest becomes more than male and female, it is human and non-human—and this is also complicated. In this scenario the human is the monster and the non-human his victim, but we know that she, the prey, was once the predator.

> Does the narrative ultimately punish its protagonist in flames, or protest masculinity's harmful nature? The answer may lie in the sympathy we bestow upon the alien heroine: we are sutured to her perspective {2}.

As a notion of retribution, it is ironic, for it is only is after she has willfully given up capturing men that she meets the same fate as her victims. We have closely observed her trajectory. She is a soldier when we meet her, obedient to her superiors and carrying out her mission in a machine-like manner—but we sense this soldier has become a conscientious objector. We can assume from the anxiety she displays during her flight in the van, and from our observations of Bad's role vis à vis the mission, that she knows she is in trouble and is taking a great risk. But such is her desire to no longer do her job, and her longing to experience something she believes is calling to her, that she takes that risk. She jumps into the unknown.

She's no longer a soldier, and "it's human emotion that gets her out of the army," says Herrera. "When she acted like a robot she was in control," but in Herrera's view,

> The second she feels those emotions, she is punished—for her agency and her self-awareness. Her dream in the bothy as part of nature captures a wildness of female sexuality, and then there's a power play in the forest between male and female. For me one of the themes of the movie is what it takes for a female to be dominant, and what it takes for a male. The alien part is the last thing I think about.

Nature and Technology

They're not opposites—more like sliding positions on a continuum (and it's a valid argument that nothing in the universe is not "natural"). But the ongoing juxtaposition of the fabricated and the organic in *Under the Skin* adds texture and tension to its narrative, tone, and aesthetic. The imagery of the opening sequences hints at the celestial—the blackness of outer space—but what we're witnessing is manufacturing under a microscope. We witness the creation of a perfectly fabricated eye, then the result that appears authentically human. In the first three minutes the film has told us we can't believe our own *eyes* and what they see, or think they see. The black space on its own is a beguiling visual contradiction. We enter a building, we presume a room inside it, then suddenly the floor of the room is a lake. Laura's exploits while serving the mission occur in a van first on roads and highways, then in the city surrounded by buildings and traffic; it's only once she leaves her job behind that she is transported (with the exception of the Swimmer scene) to a rural place, with sky, ocean, and rocky cliffs in the distance, grassy meadows ensconced in fog, and climate, and the achievements not of man nor alien but of billions of years. It's the quintessence of nature. And it's in nature, in the forest, that Laura's manufactured body is shed and exposed, revealing her true nature.

Laura herself is the most profound juxtaposition in the film. Her exterior body is technological, but her impulses, her longings, her reactions, and her decisions are not. She is not an android. She's the proverbial walking contradiction, "partly truth and partly fiction," as the song goes,[2] and her journey involves more fact and less fiction as the story unfolds. What is inside her begins to eclipse the fiction in her life—that of an assassin in a uniform—and the facts are disclosed in the film's most poignant and powerful shot: her body in its natural state, her face gazing into the eyes of the fictional person she brought to life.

What has also occurred across Laura's time on Earth is a shift from alienation to immersion. From the time of her arrival her work as an alien places her in an environment alien to *her*, and although she moves among people she isn't connected to them. Her long periods of isolation as she rides around in her van, enshrouded in the dark of night, even more palpable in the black space where she completes her tasks, conjure a loneliness, the emotion of which Johansson captures so eloquently in the dull affect on her face. There is a deep sadness to it, almost a fatalism, as if there is no point in reacting to her lot in life. We don't know what she does with her time outside of the van and the space, or how much of it there actually is, but we picture her living in the darkness of that space, if not literally then metaphorically. Laura's flight plunges her into the society she previously just floated above, and the new challenges she faces having left her isolation are captured tenderly in the minimalist scenes in the restaurant and on the bus: the attempt to swallow a piece of cake that produces an unexpected result. The bus driver's concerns that she doesn't know how to react to. Quiet's offer of help, as he elicits from her the first word she has ever said that is truly her own. Then she finds herself in a small grocery store, looking at the goods that surround her on the shelves. What better quotidian act to initiate her to life in society? Now she has truly *arrived*.

Emotions

Beauty and sadness are not opposites either, but when they are each pervasive throughout a film, it's exhilarating and confounding both aesthetically and psychologically. The city of Glasgow, its streets, buildings, and people are photographed with a nearly monochromatic somberness, but there is a grey beauty to this landscape, a veil of rain and fog and an overcast sky that embraces these citizens as they go about the business of life, affirming its worth, its necessity even, and its forbearance. We feel the warmth of the indoors or the pot of hot tea that awaits them when they finally duck in out of the weather. And there are smiles, and laughter, and parents holding their small children's hands, and a man talking to woman sitting on the sidewalk. The silver cinematography invokes an old, pale black-and-white photograph that captures a town in a moment of the past, safe from the madness of the modern world. It's far more benevolent than menacing—in fact it is Laura who is the secret menace. Yet strangers in this place rush to her aid when she falls.

There is a human beauty to the Glasgow scenes, but also a sadness. There is tragedy and darkness throughout the film because of the story it tells, yet in every scene, through the look of it, through the music, and the performances, we experience something exquisite at the same time we experience dread or fear or sorrow. This is the paradox of life, of all our lives, to which the film makes continual reference. There is the sadness of beauty, and the beauty of sadness.

The more bewildering partners that the film presents are beauty and horror, although likely not bewildering to lovers of the horror genre—in movies, literature, or any art, or perhaps in life. Finding beauty in the vision of a man slowly sinking into a black pool of death, or reaching for a fellow victim's hand just before they both explode, or in the image of his ghostly, dancing remains is disconcerting, but this kind of mind-bending is Glazer's stock-in-trade. A scarlet rushing river of blood and entrails is grotesque and also mesmerizing. The sight of Laura's torn human body as she staggers away from her attacker, the white faux exterior peeled away from her genuine, glistening black skin, is shocking yet sublime, as it is a revelation of her own truth. Here as much as ever in the film, truth is beauty. There is also something mystical in the appearance of her true body and her skin, which alludes to the reptilian in its juxtaposition with the "human" skin it pushes aside in order to reveal itself, implying the unity of all life forms and a fluidity among them.

Yet her form is fundamentally humanoid—it's not the wild, otherworldly image Campbell and Glazer played with in their 2008 version. In appearance even her alien body is halfway to looking human. In *Arrival*, when linguist

In *Arrival* (2015) Amy Adams plays a linguistics scholar recruited to communicate with aliens who bear resemblance to giant squid. Astonishingly, she succeeds, owing in part to the respect that she shows these visitors, to which they respond in kind. The film costars Jeremy Renner and Forrest Whittaker, directed by Denis Villeneuve. Paramount Pictures/Photofest © Paramount Pictures.

Louise Banks (Amy Adams) gradually succeeds in communicating with the creatures from space, it seems a more miraculous achievement than it would if these aliens looked like humans. It also enhances one of the film's themes, implied in the words of General Shang (Tzi Ma) to Louise near the end: that if communication can be accomplished with bizarre beings from a distant world, there is hope for communication and peace among the diverse nations of Earth.[3] That the creatures in *Arrival* are a variation of earthly life forms suggests our interconnection with other beings in our biosphere, and the potential—or even ecological necessity—to respect them.

20

The Alien in the Mirror

The film's opening sequence is also the beginning of the its ongoing love affair with Laura's eyes, what she sees with them, and what is behind them. A scene with one of her victims is driven by his notice of them. When he gazes at her in the van and utters, as if mesmerized or utterly perplexed, "Your eyes ... your eyes...."[1] we wonder exactly what it is he is seeing and sensing, and if somehow her power over men resides in her eyes. Is he inexorably drawn to her because of them? Or perhaps he encounters something disturbing or otherworldly or threatening in them, a threat that he proceeds to disregard.

Bad's "inspection" of Laura as they stand facing one another in the dark, and he moves methodically around her to view her from the four angles of a square, includes a moment of stillness and a penetrating look into her eyes.

> We see him clearing up after her, inspecting her at one point. There's a sense in that scene that there's something not quite right with her that he's detecting, like a hairline fracture or a crack in the wing of an airplane. He's satisfied that there isn't and carries on with his day. There are clearer ways of hitting those notes for sure, but we didn't hit them as hard as other people might have.[2]

It isn't a mutual moment; he's the one doing all the moving, studying her. A preoccupation with eyes invites encounters with mirrors, and such moments in *Under the Skin* are beguiling. Laura's first is near the beginning of the film, when, holding a compact mirror, she applies the signature red lipstick she's chosen for herself. Once her mission is underway, there are several shots of her face in the side view or rearview mirrors of her van. At first they seem like innocuous glances required for driving, but in time her looks into her own eyes feel more like a confrontation.

After leaving Lonely in the black space Laura stops—or, you could say, is stopped—by the sight of the mirror or what she sees in it. It's a sudden compulsion. This moment is one of the most radical in the film, as it lasts a still, attenuated moment in which nothing else happens, but we suspect that plenty is going on within her. This approximate 76 seconds echoes Glazer's shot of Anna at the concert in *Birth*—nothing is going on in the shot except for the life-changing journey the character is taking in her heart. Again this scene is without music, the weight of what's occurring hanging there in the black surroundings, the quiet punctuated by the decrepit building's dripping water. Laura's minute-plus at the mirror ends when she is distracted by the buzzing of the fly trapped in a window. Later Laura's minute is mirrored by Bad, who stands still in the same spot at the same mirror, staring intently at his own reflection. Though it lasts only a couple of seconds, Bad's moment feels equally intense and fateful in the scheme of things. What these aliens are seeing is unknown (by now we're accustomed to this not-knowing, and have likely decided it's part of what we love or hate about this film), and because the shots are parallel, they suggest the meaning might also be that they are communicating with their superiors, home, or mother ship.

What immediately precedes and follows their encounters with the mirror has implications. Laura has just had a special kind of encounter with a different kind of man, but surprisingly ended it by rote, as she did with the others. Once she arrives at the mirror, her lengthy stare, with a tilt of her head, feels like both a search and a moment of reflection, as in introspection. The fly buzzing at the glass, struggling for escape, conjures an image of the panicked Lonely flailing beneath the black water, and within seconds Laura releases Lonely to freedom and flees her mission. What happened in the mirror, linking the before and after, galvanizes her experiences to this point and compels her to take action: it's a moment of epiphany.

The mirror seems to be spotted with age, like an antique abandoned in some old house, and it also appears black. In art history the *black mirror* (curiously connecting this film with the science fiction TV series of the same name) is a round, convex, typically black-tinted mirror that is believed to have been used by painters such as Jan van Eyck and Hans Holbein, as early as the 15th century, as an aide in enhancing the viewing of their subjects. In appearance the mirror, writes Jazmina Barrera, "reminds one of a crystal ball used by clairvoyants; the mysterious bottoms of wells of so many fantastical stories;" and even the "truth mirror" used by Snow White's stepmother.[3] Such a mirror appears on the back wall in van Eyck's masterpiece, *The Arnolfini Portrait*. Also called "Claude glass," referencing the palette of painter Claude Lorraine (who was not known to use it), they were utilized by artists who would "turn their back on the landscape to see it reflected in the mirror, a metaphor perhaps for artifice, or the act of turning one's back on reality in order to reflect it with faithfulness and beauty."[4] The mirror produced not an exact replica, but something more. We can ponder whether the mirror that Laura and Bad gaze into offers some kind of truth—or more—and even wonder whether or not they each use the mirror for the same purpose, although whatever it is each of them sees sends them swiftly out on a mission.

An alternative interpretation of Laura's encounter with the mirror—more explicitly linked to the events preceding and following—is described by director Rian Johnson:

> It wasn't until the second or third time I watched it that I realized, "Oh wait a minute—that's not a mirror, that's a window, and she's looking very literally through a porthole into the area that, upstairs, leads into a kind of sinkhole, and she's staring at the guy she just" ... in telling this literal story in this gorgeous, poetic, purely visual way ... this is for me an all-timer.[5]

There are three remaining shots of Laura and mirrors. They all occur during her time with Quiet, and they plot the arc of her journey with him like the three acts of a play, which in a sense this section of the film is—it's so complete and truthfully resolved it could stand on its own. In the first Laura has just arrived at Quiet's house, and notices a mirror in the entryway—then swiftly averts her eyes from it and walks on. A reminder of all her previous glances in mirrors throughout her mission and the glance in the round mirror prior to her game-changing flight, the mirror harks back to the life she has willfully abandoned, and avoidance of it confirms her desire to leave that past behind; but it may also hint at something—or perhaps some other power—she fears she will see in it. At this point Quiet has rescued her from her stupor on the bus, taken her to a bodega, given her his coat for the rain, and they are just getting acquainted. Soon she shares a quiet evening at home with him, food, a comedy on TV, the washing of dishes—and there's the iconic shot of her tapping her fingers to the music, stepping into the world of human senses and pleasures.

Soon after he takes her to her room and says goodnight, making sure she has blankets and a heater, Laura stands naked before a full-length mirror, turning and moving and examining her human body in the reflection. This "inspection" of herself stands on the shoulders of Bad's inspection of her when she was a subject—or object—because now she is on her own, and this gaze in the mirror is only for her benefit and is a symbol of her new agency: To begin the exploration of this world, she explores how her body looks and works. Her nakedness in Quiet's home is also a means of conveying that she is not afraid of him. Soon Laura walks with him in the woods, braves the descent into the castle ruins with him, and later they kiss and make love. The third mirror shot takes place when she realizes something is wrong with the sex, grabs a lamp, and examines her anatomy. This is the end of the episode of Laura and Quiet. The mirror rather cruelly reflects that this part of her journey is over.

Red the Chameleon

As black and white set the tone in the opening scenes of the film, the appearance of red in the early shots of Laura at the shopping mall are assertive and get to work—visually and narratively. In the cosmetics department the vibrant red she applies to her full, fleshy lips makes her mouth come suddenly to life. More than an alluring and irresistible feature, her mouth foreshadows the fate of her victims: they will be consumed. This color aligns with the cerise V-neck sweater that catches her eye moments later. Throughout her prowls in the van she is never without this lipstick and sweater; their vaginal hues are an advertisement for herself to the men she approaches. Like many advertisements it is a fake promise that won't be kept. That Laura's own choices bring red into the story—in contrast with the blacks, whites, and grays that dominate her work environments—is a visual if unconscious cue that she is at odds with her mission, and destined to not fulfill it.

The lure of the red in Laura's costume fulfills its true promise in the sequence where her victims' fates are revealed. Here red is a river of gore, the red of the men's organs and blood and bones pureed for its repurposing by a superior species. It's a sickening image and a shocking one, as repulsive to the eye as it is to the mind and spirit, to our sense of rightness, and our collective human ego. We've been at the top of the food chain for so long that the thought of being something else's food, although we were precisely that for a few million years, is not just revolting—it's an outrage. Adding insult to injury, the image of the roiling crimson guts in the tunnel mimics footage of animal entrails making their way through the chutes and conveyer belts of our factory farms, or worse, oil rushing through a pipeline. Humans as fuel. Red becomes the opposite of its early promise in the film; it's not an attraction, it's an abhorrence. It's not sex, it is death. Herrera notes the recurrence of red throughout the film that in a way shadows Laura: "The cherries on the cake, the mat in the bothy. The coat of the woman who passes by while Laura and Quiet walk to his house, and the stained-glass flowers in his window. In the end, Laura's destroyer wears a red coat."

During Laura's time with Quiet, red departs from these earthly obsessions to venture where the film hasn't before. When Quiet leaves her at bedtime, the slow moments she spends at the full-length mirror studying her human body are rendered otherworldly, both by the sweetly taunting strings of Levi's score and the blush of rosy light that suffuses the scene. While her fingers press and probe her flesh with a kind of curious appreciation, her alabaster skin and her curves invoke the Venus de Milo. A warm and soft, ruddy light embraces her, and the alien's inspection of her high-tech armor becomes an art scene. It's not the red of her lipstick, vivid and thick, or the angry crimson of the rushing river—it's a vapor that accompanies and adorns her presence. It may have long been dormant within her, and now it graces the emergence of the new experience she has made happen.

This ethereal version of red recurs in the later sequence where Laura and Quiet make love, and unites the twin scenes in a mini-narrative of their intimacy. Laura's curiosity about and discovery of her body in the mirror hints at her "virginity," and her probing of it anticipates Quiet's touching of her body and his role as her first human lover. When we cut from their adventure at the castle to a close-up of her face, the rosy mist again surrounds her, and the color and music once again conspire to create a dreamy fantasy with an alien touch. Although we cannot know what she is feeling here, the expression on her face just prior to his kiss reads as human bliss—and later, on the bed as Quiet makes love to her, as rapture.

Nature and the City

The habitat of Laura's mission extends from the mystifying, high-tech black or white spaces to the grays of Glasgow, and the man-made structures of modern life—roads and buildings, concrete and steel. In this manufactured world, images of nature (as is the case with the color red) erupt in bold relief. In the white space, the sight of the ant crawling on the supine girl's body is arresting not only because it is of such compelling interest to Laura, but because it's the intrusion of the natural world into this curiously unnatural setting. Presumably this ant got inside this sealed-off, sterile-looking chamber by hitching a ride on the girl's body.

It's an anomaly the filmmakers deem worthy of an extra close-up. The shot may repel entomophobes but it also acknowledges a diminutive living thing that humans tend to dismiss, partly because of size bias (we're better because we're bigger). This is contrasted with Laura's sense of wonder as she lifts the creature up to eye level, gently, to examine it. Her gesture and the magnification are worthy of a nature documentary in their homage, and best of all, she doesn't squash it; it's a character moment. In an episode of the TV series *Breaking Bad*, Walter (Bryan Cranston) orders Jesse (Ryan Paul) to commit a double murder. As Jesse stands on a street corner awaiting the address of the intended crime, a beetle on the ground catches his attention. He lifts his foot as if he's about to step on it, but instead he crouches down, extends his hand, lets it crawl all over his fingers, and smiles; he doesn't kill it because that's not who he is, and we know he's not going to kill anyone in that house, either. The point is made clearer when Skinny Pete (Charles Boyd) arrives seconds later, spots the bug, and squashes it under his foot.[6]

The ant shot has a partner in the later scene when Laura notices the buzzing fly trapped inside the door window. Together they form a kind of arc; the second shot pays off the first. In the white space only three scenes into the film, the curiosity she displays over the ant signals that the ant is foreign to her because she is foreign, new, and inexperienced in this world. In the second shot she is no longer inexperienced here and she has changed, and the fly accompanies the action she takes to spare a human life—at her own peril.

Nature as a constant through all time can be perceived as an expression of God or a manifestation of the divine. It offers beauty, tranquility, awe, and evidence of grandeur and force far greater than ours no matter how much we "progress." In film as in life nature can be viewed as paradise, and to destroy it or deny access to it is to be aligned with evil—most often in the form of avarice. The battle between economic interests and environmental concerns that is escalating worldwide has long been a theme of science fiction. Greed in conflict with nature is sardonically depicted in *Brave New World* (1932): "Primroses and landscapes, he pointed out, have one grave defect: they are gratuitous. A love of nature keeps no factories busy. It was decided to abolish the love of nature, at any rate among the lower classes...." The value of allowing nature to remain out in the country is that people's love for it will motivate them to "consume transport."[7]

The oppressed and exhausted workers in Fritz Lang's *Metropolis* labor in a concrete underground factory while its wealthy owners live under the sky and breathe the fresh air. The rebels of *Fahrenheit 451* flee the book-burning fascists of their city to a riparian wilderness where they can read and recite literature in peace and freedom. Disrespect or violation of nature includes man playing God; it has disastrous consequences in *Frankenstein* and countless tales of mad scientists, but the premise takes a turn in films such as *GATTACA*, which promises that no matter how arrogant science becomes, the unenhanced and unadulterated human spirit will prevail.

The genre's long-standing association of nature with freedom, love, and the spiritual becomes heightened and more complex in post–World War II films about the destruction of humanity and nature wreaked by the atom bomb and radiation (*On the Beach*, and the creature features that form their own sub-genre, *Godzilla, World Without End, Attack of the Crab Monsters*, and more). This technology versus nature binary resonates increasingly by decade with the escalating human footprint, driving scores of eco-apocalyptic, scorched-earth films such as *The Road, The Day After Tomorrow*, and *Mad Max: Fury Road*. The revenge of nature upon humans, for their millennia of abuse, is poetically—and frighteningly—depicted in M. Night Shyamalan's cautionary tale, *The Happening*.

Tropes regarding nature in science fiction are both embraced and manipulated in *Under the Skin*. Because Laura's mission is carried out exclusively in the city, and her flight from it lands her in the countryside, the connotations of nature are upheld. The city is identified with the violence and bloodbath of her mission, and her captivity within it. Once she escapes she is surrounded by the beauty of nature, where she has freedom and finds love. The shot of her in the distance making her way along the country road, with the hills, cliffs, shoreline, ocean, and sky behind her, the fields and meadows in the foreground, lavishly distinguishes the new setting from the old, and the panorama with her at the center asserts her place in her new environment. The massive bank of fog she walked into when she could no longer see to drive is now, in this gorgeous panoramic shot, receding behind her.

But the film's other depictions of similar nature capsize the trope, and the disturbing effect of this in part drives our emotional response to the events that unfold. Shots of the beautiful, rugged seascape that she walks past in the fog, with its jagged rocks and cove, can't help but recall Laura's earlier scene at the shore as a predator. The sight of her on the beach, watching the Swimmer in the distance, fills us with dread. The pristine beach that four people have come to for a day of pleasure in nature soon becomes a killing zone. Even though the Swimmer is the only one Laura bludgeons with a rock, it feels as though she is responsible for all four deaths—as if her very presence, and her indifference to the lives of the infant and his parents, is a malevolent force wreaked upon all their lives.

The time that Laura has with Quiet, when they're not inside his cozy home, is spent in nature. They take a walk in a tall wood so lush and green we can smell the pungent air and feel the duff that crunches beneath their shoes. They pass others strolling along the path, and a horse and rider trot past. The man she is learning to trust carries her over a large puddle. This idyllic portrait of the wood as a setting for humans and animals to find tranquility and comfort is shattered just a few scenes later when a distressed and frightened Laura flees Quiet's home into the forest, where she is hunted, captured, and brutally killed by the Logger.

The assertion—and the inversion—of nature-as-paradise also correlates with the three episodes of Laura's journey. In the first act, Laura brings her deadly mission to the peaceful beach, transforming it through her actions. Midway through the film, when Laura commits to putting this life behind her, part of the bargain is her openness to starting a new life that she actually cannot comprehend, or even imagine. In the TV series *Mad Men*, as Brooklyn girl Peggy Olson dips her toe into the advertising world of the big city, an old beau—a little jealous perhaps of her daring, or maybe just feeling left out—mocks her aspiration. She tells him, "Those people? In Manhattan? They *are* better than us, because they want things they haven't seen."[8] Both women take a leap into the unknown. It is a kind of rebirth for Laura, and it is in this spirit that the ocean again appears in its role as a vista of sanguine beauty. It is into this virgin territory (the bank of pure, white fog) that Quiet enters her life, and the forest is presented as a reflection of her innocence and the tranquility and safety that she, for a time, enjoys. All of this Laura later leaves behind when she runs from Quiet's home and back into the forest—now a malevolent environment. The fate that meets her there appears as a reversion back to her mission phase in the way that the events that befall her mirror her own predatory stalking ("Are you alone?") as well as lead her back to the alien overseer who arrives too late. It's only during her strange interlude as a free agent, where she experiences openness and intimacy and explores something genuine within herself, that nature is "paradise."

21
Laura and Her Cousins

The honor of being the first extraterrestrials in movies belongs to the Selenites, depicted in *A Trip to the Moon* (1902) by George Méliès—inspired by H. G. Wells's novels *From the Earth to the Moon* (1865), *Around the Moon* (1870), and possibly *The First Men in the Moon* (1901).[1] The malevolent behavior of these human-sized insectoids consists of little more than chasing the scientists back to their spaceship—just a dim beginning of the cinematic-alien horrors to come.

The monster in *Frankenstein* (1931) is not extraterrestrial but he is alien, and he is the prototype for the Alien-as-Other theme that shapeshifts in the American consciousness throughout the decades of the 20th century and into the 21st century. Frankenstein's monster is feared, reviled, and attacked by mobs because, through no fault of his own, he is frightening to look at, he causes the death of a little girl, and he seems to reflect back to the monsters that live within us all—notably, within his creator Dr. Frankenstein. In the 1950s, in the wake of the horrors of the atomic bomb, the science fiction film explosion featured aliens, creatures, and monsters that were stand-ins for the enemies—both real and perceived—of the day. In the U.S., fears around radiation mutations fueled films like *The Creature from the Black Lagoon* (1954) and *Attack of the Crab Monsters* (1957). In the Japanese-made *Godzilla* (1954), scientists conclude that the creature is a pre-historic sea monster made lethal by atomic bomb testing.[2] But the towering, ferocious creature, wreaking destruction and mayhem in the cities and killing crowds of innocent people while futilely attempting to flee, also readily symbolizes the foreign government that bombed Hiroshima and Nagasaki just a few years before.

The midcentury also found the U.S. in the throes of the McCarthy era, and Don Siegel's classic *Invasion of the Body Snatchers* (1956) is often interpreted as a reflection of the "red scare." The humans that, one by one, are taken over by an alien species become emotionless minions, fitting the characterization of communists as Godless and therefore soulless and without empathy.

The shriek of Becky (Dana Wynter) at the sight of a dog nearly hit by a car reveals to everyone around her that she has eluded the usurpation of her mind by the aliens—think of the alien Laura indifferent to the crying baby on the beach. At the same time, the hunt for communists by the House Un-American Activities Committee (HUAC) and the witch hunt that swept the populace (whether out of fear of communists or fear of the Committee) could also be signified by a soulless lack of empathy for fellow human beings and creatures. When Miles (Kevin McCarthy) says, "I see how people have allowed their humanity to drain away,"[3] he could be describing not only communists but witch hunters and their minions—or perhaps both. For Siegel, "The pod people represent a movement toward the unquestioning, 'dumbing down' of true American values such as rebellion, tradition and independence: replaced by blind acceptance and cultural brainwashing."[4] Where independent thinking and freedom are prized, the monster, the government, or anyone who threatens those values is the alien.

In a variation on *Body Snatchers*, Laura's life and identity have been taken over by an employer and she must, in a sense, find her individuality. In the novel, Isserley was given the mission by Vess Industries as a way out of a horrible existence. In the film, Laura's nature is a given, and she appears to be evolving—or perhaps, having been programmed, she is retrieving what was her own nature.

John Sayles's 1984 satire *The Brother from Another Planet* (1984) gives us an alien (Joe Morton) who is black, an escaped slave, and finds himself in Harlem, where he's pursued by Sayles and David Strathairn from his home planet. At Ellis Island he communes with the ghosts of those who have lived the immigrant experience before him. In weaving and overlapping multiple "otherness" the film portrays intolerance as a kind of human silliness (the alien himself displays no prejudice). The Brother's muteness is a reminder that society's oppressed are often without a voice, but Brother is far from defenseless; he has superpowers (finding a boy who has overdosed, Brother brings him back to life) and his kindness trumps language as a form of communication.

The flip side of Sayles's sharp-eyed comedy is the dystopia of *District 9* (2009), the name of a nightmarish place halfway between a slum and an internment camp where extraterrestrials are confined, oppressed, and tormented. These aliens are far more challenging to love than the handsome and sanguine Brother; by human standards they are grotesque, a cross between a junkyard robot and human-sized scorpion. Because the basis of much aversion to the Other is simple physical difference, creating an alien that humans find repulsive and even monstrous to look at pays off in *District 9*; as we come to know them and see their hearts, family closeness, and similarities to us, our discrimination—partly based on our revulsion and prejudice—puts our

In John Sayles's science fiction comedy *The Brother from Another Planet* (1984) actor Joe Morton plays the Brother, an escaped slave from another world who finds himself in Harlem, New York City, trying to make sense of an alien culture and using his superpowers to bring a boy back to life. Sayles's decades of beautifully wrought and whip-smart, socially conscious films include *Golden State, Men with Guns, Silver City, Casa de los Babys,* and *Lone Star.* Cinecom International/Photofest © Cinecom International.

shallowness and stupidity in bolder relief, and makes it all the more egregious. We feel love for them, and shame of ourselves. *District 9* isn't about aliens, it's our history and our reality; it's indigenous peoples across the planet, or the internment of Japanese individuals during World War II; it's slavery, *apartheid*, the migration of refugees, and the plight of the poor in our cities.

LGBTQ-as-alien is implicit if you imagine the drama *Boys Don't Cry* with an extraterrestrial in the place of the transgender protagonist Brandon (Hilary Swank). The characters who persecute Brandon fear what they don't recognize or comprehend; when their sense of what is "right" or "normal" comes into question, they fear their world is in jeopardy.[5] It is neither examined nor rational. As a result they alienate, ostracize, exile, persecute, experiment upon, beat, torture, and kill—both because they feel justified in a kind of superiority and as a perverse attempt to protect themselves and their world. This is one of several subtexts in the Logger-rapist's frenzied destruction of Laura in *Under the Skin*. In a confluence of fear and xenophobia, misogyny and violence, he sets her on fire—even though she represents no threat to him, even though she is running away.

The Top of the Food Chain

In the realm of human consumption (that is, the consumption of humans) the zombie sub-genre rules the day. What is our fascination with being consumed? Maybe it's evolutionary memory, a kind of historical dread left over from our countless millennia of scrambling up trees or fleeing across savannahs to evade predators. Or possibly it's our guilt over our relatively recent ascent in status to the top of the pyramid—nothing can eat *us* anymore, but we eat anything we want. The tables have turned—everything out there is running from us, and lives in fear of being a trophy on a wall or ending up on a plate with an heirloom tomato. Our fear that our apogee status, previously enjoyed by saber-tooth tigers and just about everything on four legs, was a temporary joke and now the joke is once again on us. At any moment we could once again be eaten—or imbibed—by a zombie, a vampire, or an alien.

Of these three consumers of humans the aliens are the ones least frequently visited upon us (in recent decades the vampire and zombie subgenera have won the popularity contest). At the same time, they may be the most dreaded. After all, zombies and vampires belong to the realm of fantasy—concepts not rooted in reality—and aliens inhabit science fiction (science-based) and the realm of the possible. We may comfort ourselves that there are no *real* vampires and zombies on Earth, but when things come from outer space all bets are off—we can only imagine what grotesque threats are out there. Closer to home, the idea of being eaten by our fellow humans that are neither vampires nor zombies finds its way into the science fiction cinema canon with *Soylent Green* (director Richard Fleischer, 1973) and *The Time Machine* (director George Pal, 1960, based on the novel by H. G. Wells). In the former, a kind of cannibalism after the fact is a solution to a food shortage in a futuristic world where people (after being hustled into a somewhat premature "retirement") are recycled as food for humans. In the latter, humans mutated in the aftermath of nuclear war—ape-like *morlocks*—live underground and harvest, like livestock, the "normal" humans that live on the surface.

A gruesome variation on people-consumption, Steven Spielberg's 2005 remake of *The War of the Worlds* (also based on an H. G. Wells novel) gives us invading Martian-machines that scoop up panicky humans and funnel them into a processor that spits them out the bottom and into the ground: humans as fertilizer. The ensuing gore is reminiscent of the macabre red river in *Under the Skin*, and the two images are also conjoined by narratives of the repurposing of human flesh for another definition of *consumption*. In *Under the Skin* we see the evisceration and "skinning" of the victims, but we can only speculate about where the red remnants are headed, unlike the novel, where the outcome is explicit. The beam of red light that horizontally bisects the black screen directly following the river shot could be construed as the transformation of the flesh into some kind of energy, or even data, as in the title of track, "Meat to Maths." An alien race's use of humans for energy is one of the startling premises of *The Matrix* (the Wachowskis, 1999), with its horrific shot of the cavernous power plant and its endless rows of wired-up humans, one of them being Neo (Keanu Reeves), a human battery. Laura's mission based on the "consumption" of an alien race could be seen to signify any group that utilizes, exploits, or conquers another to satisfy its own needs, but it also darkly conveys a universe in which there is no safety anywhere, and anyone—even our human race with all its vaunted accomplishments— is vulnerable.

Out of the Sky

Davie Bowie is Thomas Jerome Newton in Nicolas Roeg's *The Man Who Fell to Earth*.[6] We embrace Bowie's captivating flirtation with the otherworldly in his music (*The Rise and Fall of Ziggy Stardust and the Spiders from Mars*, 1972). An appearance and demeanor that he is or *is of* "elsewhere"—let's face it, his overall magic—served him well as a vampire in a later film, *The Hunger* (1983), and are seamlessly embodied by the extraterrestrial Newton. Johansson captures a sense of oddness—the fact that her character is out of place— through a perfectly calibrated dull affect. Our knowledge of her public persona and her career collide with the idea that she's non-human, whereas Bowie's role fits him like a glove. For a comedic take on *Skin*'s female alien-in-disguise premise, see the sequence in *Mars Attacks* (1996) where a gum-chewing blonde bombshell of an alien follows the smitten Martin Short into the White House. As he makes his move, his attempt to take the bubble gum out of her mouth pulls off her skin, exposing the hideous robot beneath her smooth complexion. She bites off his finger and it lands in a fish tank.[7] Two decades later the scene could be a parody of Laura and her victims.

The protagonist aliens in *Man Who Fell* and *Under the Skin* are each on a mission regarding a form of sustenance; for Newton, it is water. Three shots of him with his wife and two children on their home planet depict them as beings akin to a pale version of Laura's alien body: sleek, slender, possibly hairless, an archetypal extraterrestrial. In the first shot they stroll across a lush, grassy landscape; in the second we witness Newton's family with him at a tram, sadly seeing him off on his journey. The third is a heartbreaking tableau of their bodies by the same tram railway—lying folded in a three-way embrace, perished of dehydration and starvation. We know Newton as a loving creature who has endured and still suffers from tragedy, whereas in Laura's opaqueness and behavior we perceive nothing humane; she appears indifferent to suffering, most of which she causes. Though they each arrive on a mission and appear to slip seamlessly into society on Earth, their internal struggles are different, and by the end, Laura's arc is the opposite of Newton's.

At the outset Newton is serious, fully confident, and in control—utterly focused on his goal of acquiring $300 million to solve his planet's problem (in 1976 that was some real money). As he increasingly tries on, like a suit of clothes, the behavior of humans, in time he is habituated to what began as mimicry: watching TV obsessively (a dozen sets at a time, a prescience of today's flipping through hundreds of satellite channels) and drinking himself into oblivion. We're reminded that he is a foreigner, and like a human in a foreign land he hasn't any tolerance, or immunity. His addiction is tantamount to a traveler's illness—we could call it a cultural traveler's illness—exacerbated by the mental anguish of losing his family and everything familiar to him. He seems dissipated, but in fact he is a lost soul. This alien's experience is akin to that of a border-crossing immigrant in our world; the trauma of dis-location from loved ones, from land and culture, and from personal history. It is the isolation from all that is familiar, and the relentless threats posed by the alien environment. Newton has the power and the means to leave his planet in search of help, but it's out of desperation, and once here, he is, as far as we know, trapped. We don't know what Laura and Newton are *really* like, but what we do learn about them we infer from the way they react to, and interact with, their new surroundings.

Newton seems more human than Laura because he communicates so well with people, and the mysteries of Newton's heart are revealed once he begins to sink into the vapidity of his life on Earth; through his unintended cruelty and abject sadness we witness the suffocation of his soul. In Laura's childlike fascination with the ant that she lifts onto her fingertip we feel something within her that registers positively for us; a curiosity, an appreciation of nature. When nature documentaries on Newton's wall of TVs assault him with images of animals devouring each other, it's clear he's repulsed by the violence. In another scene his companion Mary-Lou (Candy Clark) begins swatting at him, and in the way he cringes we know he's not capable of processing this aspect of our culture.

Both our protagonists venture into the most uncharted and vulnerable territory of all when they allow themselves an intimate romantic encounter. Each begins with tenderness and a promise of fulfillment, but both are thwarted. In both Laura's and Newton's narratives we witness the change that occurs in them as a result of their experiment on Earth, but their arcs are not similar. The effect of his new environment upon Newton is toxic; it's his psyche that's been poisoned. "What's happening to you?" Mary-Lou tearfully pleads. When Newton cries out, "Get out of my mind, all of you! Leave my mind alone—stay where you belong, all of you," it's the sentiment rarely expressed but certainly repressed in the consciousness of millions of earthlings living in the assault of media images and messages they'd be better off without. "It shows you everything," he says sadly, "but it doesn't tell you anything." Newton, in emulating us, succumbs to our demons; the consumerism and alcoholism that fuel our despair and depression are the very things we turn to in order to escape their effects upon us.

Newton's heart and anguish are in time brandished for all to see. Laura's engagement in human culture is minimal and perhaps even non-existent (her engaging is a pose) but the slow evolution that is occurring within her—once she takes action—cannot be denied. Unlike the cancerous effect that alien (to him) ways have upon Newton, the culture in which Laura finds herself piques her curiosity and tugs at her until she finally leaps off a cliff. When she does, she'll watch television and have the opposite of Newton's experience; she'll study it with fascination, an explorer engrossed or even enchanted by a bizarre artifact that brings people joy. Bowie's alien is contaminated, corrupted, defeated; Johansson's is on a path to growth that is sadly cut short. Newton starts out with faith and courage and ends in disillusion and despair; Laura begins as an automaton and through courage discovers her agency and her heart. Newton's end finds him in a state of mourning, not just for his lost family, but because he knows he too is lost, and in a sense dead. His demise may be sadder than Laura's, because although hers is a literal death, and a violent one, she first experiences a leap of faith, pleasure as she may never before have known it, and a brief control over her destiny.

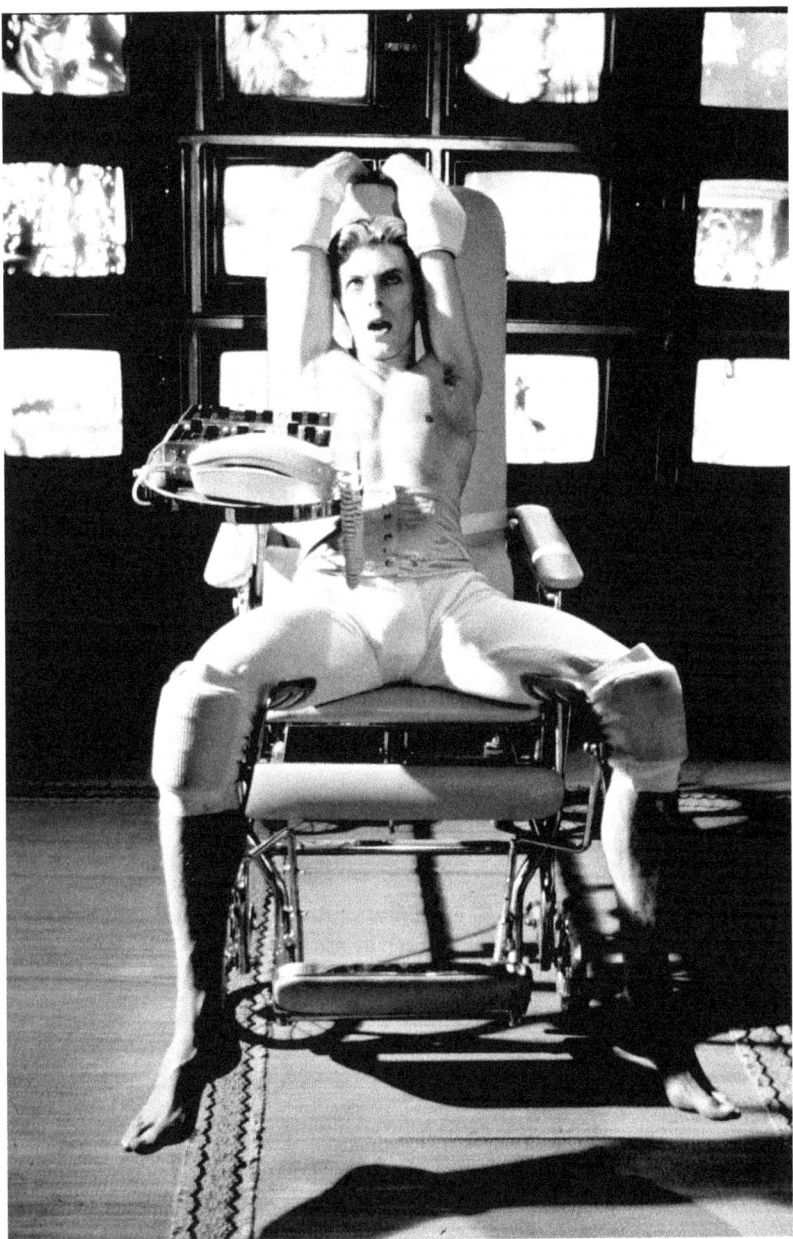

Whereas alien Laura is sent to Earth on a mission to procure food, Mr. Newton arrives on his own mission in search of water for his drought-plagued planet in Nicholas Roeg's 1976 film *The Man Who Fell to Earth*. Played by David Bowie (pictured) Newton has the physical appearance and demeanor of blending into the human race, but the emotional toll is great. In this shot, for example, he isn't responding well to an abundance of media. Licensed by Cinema5/Photofest © Cinema 5 Distributing.

Animal, Vegetable, Mineral ... Alien

> We are as unknown, as weird, as most anything we are likely to find in the dark abyss of space. Though our societal organizations find ways of distracting us from the stranger aspects of our nature (usually by encouraging us to project them onto "undesirable" groups), they can never fully obscure the mystery below our skins.[8]

In John Carpenter's *The Thing*[9] a predatory extraterrestrial terrorizes a dozen men at a research base in the Arctic. The film's predecessor, the Howard Hawks-produced *The Thing from Another World* (directed by Christian Nyby, 1951) was in the wave of 50s science fiction films that seized the nation's post-nuclear war imagination and tapped into its anxieties. Both films were adapted from the John W. Campbell, Jr., story *Who Goes There?* (1938) and all three works share the premise of an alien life form frozen in the ice during the Paleolithic—and inadvertently unearthed by humans. The notion that aliens have visited Earth in the distant past seems less like science fiction when we entertain the theory of *panspermia*: that the origin of life on Earth over three billion years ago could be extraterrestrial because the chemical precursors of life exist in the cosmos and can become living organisms when they reach a hospitable environment.[10] Stephen Hawking suggested that they could hitch a ride to Earth, or anywhere, on an asteroid.[11] The theory that life on Earth was seeded from space is known as *cosmic ancestry*.

The extraterrestrial in *The Thing* arrives not by meteor but via old-school spaceship found in the ice, viewed onscreen in the original film although not in the remake. In Carpenter's version the alien first appears in the disguise of a hardy white Husky running across the snow being shot at from a helicopter—but before long we'll know why. This dog has done some very bad things. The Husky is rescued by the men at the base, with actor Kurt Russell's R. J. MacReady taking the lead—an ironic name as he is decidedly not ready for the nightmare that is to follow. "There is a made-up backstory between Carpenter and Russell about MacReady being a former helicopter pilot in the Vietnam War and that he's probably an alcoholic. Carpenter also feels MacReady never wanted to be a leader."[12] The PTSD implied by this scenario serves MacReady's persona well, as the subtext of this horror/science fiction/adventure film is the protagonist's confronting of his own demons. Like MacReady Laura is a soldier, and her duty over the course of *Under the Skin* is to leave her role as a killing machine, with its conditioned behavior and responses, behind her.

A standard in 50s science fiction is the lone (and attractive, tightly attired) female scientist or secretary, but this trope is absent from *The Thing*. The all-male cast evokes an exclusionary atmosphere, where women conspicuous by their absence represent something oppositional, perhaps feared, or dreaded. By implication it is women who is the Other as we're introduced to the story, and the men, sequestered at this research base, who are safe from them. Eliminating this threat, the men as a group seem empowered and strong—a united front against whatever force may come their way.

The alien of Campbell's story (and both films), with its ability to imitate any life form, enters the base as the Husky—just as Laura inhabits the skin of a human female and hides in plain sight. The thing arrives as "man's best friend," perennially trustworthy—the men take the dog in with their other dogs, feed him, hug him. The Husky is the Laura of the film—the alien seduces, the victims relax, the alien strikes. The men soon find that the dog has morphed back to its true self—a grotesque and ferocious creature that has killed another of their dogs. Soon the alien begins inhabiting, one at a time, the men. "*The Thing*, with its mutable nature, its omnivorous appetite for men, and its foregrounded physicality, can certainly suggest ancient patriarchal fears of 'devouring women.'"[13] As in *Skin*, a woman and an alien are conflated, but neither film pushes this agenda—in each film it's a portal to a deeper conflict.

Shapeshifter

As the alien migrates from one man to another, the men are forced to deal with a demon that's not a creature, but a colleague. Here the film becomes a study in paranoia. That the enemy is disguised and cannot be detected in any way (until it kills) is a commonality with *Under the Skin* that distinguishes both films from those featuring aliens that take over humans but give themselves away through behavior. In *Invasion of the Body Snatchers* for example, the "taken" ones are friendly but display a clear absence of human empathy, and in *Invaders from Mars* (1953), their normal personalities shift to a cold cruelty. The men can't kill the threat because they don't know which one of them is the Thing. The theme of trust arises in every movie about aliens regardless of whether we know their identity, because, since we can't read them, we can't trust them. In *The Twilight Zone* classic, "The Monsters Are Due on Maple Street," humans neither trust nor mistrust the aliens because they never see them; from a distance the invaders turn the humans against one another by exploiting their lack of trust, which becomes a weapon of conquest.[14] Laura's mission depends on gaining her victims' trust and betraying them—but once she's out in the world it's Laura who must learn to trust strangers. "Trust is a tough thing to come by these days," says MacReady. It's "one of Carpenter's favorite lines in the film. He feels it summarizes everything *The Thing* has to say."[15]

With this in mind the issue of trust becomes problematic, because it's not the other men they can't trust, it's the alien. But that doesn't mean that the existential component of *The Thing* is lost, because a threat we cannot see is one step away from a worse-case scenario: that the threat is within. We can infer that the film is playing with this idea through the chaos among the men in the third act and in the final shot. Only two men are left standing, and each suspects the other of being the Thing.

"There's a somber kind of inevitability to the film," Carpenter said recently, and it's true: from the very first sequence of a helicopter chasing an alien-infected dog across a glacier, *The Thing* feels like the beginning of the end; it feels like the apocalypse, but

In John Carpenter's *The Thing* (1982) the alien migrates from one man to another, and when it inhabits Palmer (David Clennon), crew leader Macready (Kurt Russell) sets him on fire. Like Laura's, Palmer's life ends in a tower of flames in the snow. In the final scene the only survivors are Macready and Childs (Keith David)—who may be the latest alien host. Licensed by Universal Pictures/Photofest © Universal Pictures.

it is an apocalypse brought on not by weapons but by something more like a virus, eating us alive from the inside.[16]

At the film's outset the demon might be womankind, but then it appears to be a Husky; next it's an alien, then an alien that inhabits a man. Soon it's all of the men, and finally, maybe, it's all of us. It's what we see when we look in the mirror. The deeper self that is reflected in the mirror takes us again to Laura's mirror, the confronting of what is inside her, or us—whether it's the darkness we're trying to escape, or the light we desperately seek.

In the film Dr. Blair (Wilford Brimley) offers, "That thing wanted to be us."[17] In *Under the Skin*, so does Laura.

"I mean you no harm, Jenny Hayden"[18]

Two years later the revered horror-meister directs *Starman* (1984). Moving from the malevolent archetype about extraterrestrials to its opposite, this pair of Carpenter creature features creates a dialectical context for *Under the Skin*, which fits neither trope. Starman (played by Jeff Bridges) first appears as an alien "eye" who's doing a bit of reconnaissance inside the home of Jenny Hayden (Karen Allen) as she nostalgically watches old home movies of her deceased husband. Using a hair he finds in a photo album the eye reconstructs itself as a perfect replica of her husband—from fetus to adult in several seconds on Jenny's living room floor. Her natural response to the sight of him is to scream—and Starman, who's learning human behavior through mimicry, immediately screams back. As cinema meet-cutes go this is hard to beat, and it only gets more endearing. "I look like Scott so you not be a little bit jumpy," he tells her.

Starman Scott is in jeopardy because the government is hunting him, and on their journey to his crashed spacecraft, a road movie, a tale of two species, and a kind of romance converge. Apart from the fact that his species possesses the technology to get here, we learn more subtle details about them from his reactions along the journey; for example, to the sight of a dead deer tied to the hood of a car in the parking lot of a roadside diner. Scott asks Jenny why it's there:

JENNY: People hunt them to eat for food.
SCOTT: Do deer eat people?
JENNY: No.
SCOTT: Do people eat people?
JENNY: Of course not. What do you think we are?
SCOTT: I think you are a very primitive species.[19]

Later, Scott lays his hands on the deer and it rises and scurries off to the forest. The hunters whose dinner Scott set free aren't too happy about this, and they beat him good. We can assume he could retaliate if he chose, but he doesn't choose.

Johansson and Bridges each give very different performances not only because they're very different actors, but because their motivations aren't the same. No one can know or even suspect what Laura is; she must seamlessly blend into society, and because her British speech is flawless and her behaviors are familiar, she succeeds. Scott isn't hiding and in fact lets Jenny know what he is immediately, and his movements and speech are learned instantly as a function of wearing and using his human body. But they're just enough off the mark to signify "outsider," and this is one of the ways Bridges shines in the role. When he speaks his words are sometimes clipped, and the pacing is a just a little off. Hearing him and watching his mouth move are reminiscent of watching an actor in a movie that's out of sync—who knows how he did it, but it certainly says "alien." This and also his movements, abrupt rather than fluid, a "mechanical" turn of his head, do seem like those of someone who has donned a brand new outfit they're still getting used to. His language and affect are a bit android-like in that way, which utterly works: he's not a person, he's emulating one.

There's also a subtler distinction between the two portrayals. Outside of speech and mannerisms, Bridges conveys through acting, and in his eyes, the alien's "humanity." This is a tricky proposition because he has to work against the alien quirks mentioned above which are reminding us that he's not human—but he pulls it off. We know what he stands for, what's in his heart; he's a non-human humanitarian, a good soul. Johansson's task is another story. Her body moves like a woman's, graceful, and fluid, not at all awkward, but Laura's eyes give us nothing. She's the opposite of Scott; convincing in human physicality, but android-like in expression (or lack thereof), conveying, scarily, that she is disconnected from her behavior. But once Laura experiences new emotions after leaving her mission—relaxation, bliss, fear—Johansson's restraint in revealing them is what makes Laura's blossoming all the more intimate, exhilarating, and suspenseful for the audience.

Inside the diner Jenny mentions the word and Scott responds, "Define *love*." She replies, "Love is when you care more for someone else than you do for yourself. It's more than that, it's when someone is a part of you."[20] In a film where nothing at all is ever explained, we don't expect a scene such as this for Laura, but in that same film that finds countless non-verbal and non-explicit ways of opening us to possibilities, we know that Laura senses there is something going on between humans that she has never experienced. "It's about her curiosity," said editor Watts.

Scott is curious too, and after watching on TV the iconic embrace in

From Here to Eternity he approaches Jenny while she's asleep to practice-kiss and embrace her. At one point he explains to her that he can feel everything his human body feels, and in time, they make love. While Scott has a replica of a fully-functional human body Laura's is only skin-deep, yet it's clear in her scenes with Quiet that she experiences something spectacular—whether it is physical, spiritual, emotional, or some other alien sensation we can't grasp. It's places like this where the film's absence of exposition and backstory fires the imagination. What Johansson truly exudes in her intimate scenes with Quiet, what makes the moments so cathartic to watch, is that—because of her physical being, or her culture, or her position in her society, or any number of alien things we can't conceive of—she may have never before experienced *anything* like this.

In the final scene before Scott departs from Earth, a representative from SETI[21] named Mark Shermin (Charles Martin Smith) is eager to meet the visitor for just a few moments. In response to his questions Scott offers, "You are a strange species. Not like any other. And you would be surprised how many there are. Intelligent, but savage."[22] Science fiction cinema has largely embraced three tropes—most often the one Scott refers to and, at the other end of the spectrum, the evolved and enlightened alien. Somewhere in between are aliens that may not have technology but are most definitely savage, whose intelligence manifests primarily in ability to survive (John Krasinski's *A Quiet Place*, 2018). Of his own species Scott has a poignant observation: "We are very civilized but we have lost something, I think." Regarding humans, he reveals to Mark, "Shall I tell you what I find beautiful about you? You are at your very best when things are worst."[23] What he's talking about is a characteristic—or quirk—of our humanity. None of the alien tropes above apply to Laura. At the outset Laura is closer to the alien of MacReady's nightmare, but eventually she is more like Scott, slipping into the human experience. She bears humans no malice, but the truth is there is no evidence that she ever did. *Under the Skin* brings us an alien that can grow and change as people aspire to. It's a hopeful and romantic view of humanity, and of the universe. In her brief experience Laura achieves a degree of enlightenment, and the savage who ends her life isn't an alien, but a human.

22
The Family of Non-Humans: Aliens, Androids and Clones

Ridley Scott's 1979 *Alien* is groundbreaking and iconic in the alien genre, but Scott's dystopian classic *Blade Runner* is the much closer cousin to *Under the Skin*. The intimidating Captain Bryant (M. Emmet Walsh) orders former Detective Rick Deckard (Harrison Ford) to come out of his own retirement to "retire" four androids who escaped the off-world colony where they were enslaved. They're Nexus-6—the latest generation of replicants produced by the Tyrell Corporation, with Tyrell (Joe Turkel) being the Steve Jobs of human-esque robots. The four Nexus-6 escapees Deckard must hunt down have each been designed for different tasks in the colonies; one is an assassin, one a soldier, one a laborer, and Pris, played by Daryl Hannah, "your basic pleasure model."[1] For efficiency and practicality the replicants are programmed without emotions. But Tyrell had to build a "fail-safe" into their design—a four-year life span—because, as Bryon warns Deckard, in time they "begin to develop their own emotional responses."[2]

Scott eschewed the more esoteric aspects of Philip K. Dick's 1966 novel *Do Androids Dream of Electric Sheep?* to focus upon the book's most cinematic elements: a dazzlingly dark dystopia, and Decker's hunt and capture of the four escaped androids. Their emotions—love, sadness, rage at their captivity and their short life span—play out alongside the ethical dilemmas haunting Deckard and go to the core of Dick's story: what does it mean to be human? In both book and film Deckard employs a high-tech procedure known as the Voight-Kampff test to distinguish androids, who are otherwise impossible to detect, from humans. The test includes countless questions regarding cruelty to animals as a means of detecting *humaneness*, as equated with humanity. "Someone gives you a calfskin wallet," Deckard asks when testing Tyrol's employee Rachel (Sean Young), whom Tyrell has led him to believe is human. "What do you do?" "I'd report them to the authorities," Rachel responds, for although she actually is an android she is cutting edge, designed specifically to beat the test. "More human than human" is Tyrell's motto.³

Like these replicants the alien Laura, having lived among humans as if she were human, soon develops her own emotional responses. Think of her as a combination of all of Tyrell's android prototypes—the soldier, the assassin, the laborer, the ersatz pleasure model. She is tantamount to an android both in her role as a soldier/weapon and as the non-human who interrogates for the audience what it means to be human. Philip K. Dick was inspired by Alan Turing's 1950s experiments with computers, and his Turing test, which proved computers could compete with humans in the passing of an intelligence test.

> Thus, [Dick] began with the proposition that the best-equipped androids of the 1992 model year would be capable of passing the Turing or any other test. He was not, however, about to welcome the androids into the human community, as Turing would have said one would have to do when a machine finally managed to pass his test, and so he did something that Turing would have considered cheating ... he added a new criterion, another ability that a subject would have to demonstrate in order to qualify as human. This criterion was empathy....⁴

When Laura releases Lonely, she has passed the empathy test. The difference between Rachel and Laura is that Rachel was programmed to pass it, while Laura, over time, discovered something within herself that was either lost or had never been there in the first place.

That empathy becomes a definition for what is human poses a problem not just for Deckard but for our civilization in its technological future: If androids think as humans and develop human emotions, should they not be granted human rights? In the film Deckard's ethical crisis isn't discussed, but it is nevertheless poignantly conveyed in the look of revulsion and shame on his face after he violently executes the replicant Zhora (Joanna Cassidy) and in his falling in love with Rachel.

Once Rachel knows who and what she is, she is still determined to go on living as a human woman. This is her break with the fate that she was assigned but did not choose—her turning point—as is the scene in *Under the Skin* when Laura gazes for a long moment into the mirror before freeing Lonely. Laura also has realized who and what she is—and she, too, craves a human experience. Young's subtly robotic sensuality bridges her past and present: her will to be human is what makes her human. There are often a few giggles in the theater when Deckard, blocking her exit from his apartment, orders her to "say kiss me," but it suits both the noirish genre and the "schooling" of the neophyte Rachel in romance (according to Deckard). For Laura, the kiss, the intimacy, seem to come naturally—as if instinctual, as if primordial. As if anticipated—or dreamt of.

That Rick Deckard himself may be an android—which is director Scott's inference[5]—is a possibility that is entertained in Dick's novel. Early in the film Rachel confronts him: "Have you ever tried to take that test yourself, Mr. Deckard?" In the scenario that Deckard is an android, his character arc is congruent to Laura's even more profoundly than is Rachel's. From the outset, both protagonists are conscripted to kill. Deckard wants no part of it ("I was quit when I came in," he tells Bryant, "and I'm twice as quit now") but Bryant issues a threat. It isn't known early on what Laura thinks of her work, or even if she's a slave of some kind, but in time her position is made clear. Deckard's distaste for his job becomes disgust, and his growing empathy for replicants and their plight is mirrored in Laura's evolution. There's no discussion of their internal conflicts (to both films' credit) but they are manifested in the cinematic details. Ultimately Laura comes to terms with what she is and rejects her mission. Near the end of the novel, Deckard reflects: "But what I've done ... that's become alien to me. In fact everything about me has become unnatural; I've become an unnatural self."[6] As the film ends, he puts his past behind him to seek a faraway refuge with Rachel—for however long that may last. Both Deckard and Laura liberate themselves from powerful entities that drove them to do harm. We'll call them "dystopian protagonists"—their arcs are defined by their actions in opposition to the forces that have controlled them.[7] Each film's ending questions the identification of empathy exclusively with humans, for Laura is killed by a human—and Decker's life is saved by a replicant (Rutger Hauer). In the android Dick explores dichotomies that occur throughout his work: real versus false, human versus non-human, natural versus unnatural, the spirit versus the State, and truth versus lies. In this "Dickian" dystopian world, where the human and the real have been sabotaged, redemption lies in empathy.

> NATHAN: My head is spinning.
> CALEB: It's because you're drunk.
> NATHAN: No, it's called relativity ... everything is spinning. It's just being drunk makes it worse.[8]

A proud offspring of *Blade Runner*, Alex Garland's *Ex Machina* steps up two decades later—in the same year as *Under the Skin*. The film emulates its parent yet also strikes out on its own, zooming in for a more intimate and substantially creepier relationship between the AI mastermind Nathan (Oscar Isaac) and his creation, Ava (Alicia Vikander). His mastery over her seems airtight—he's got her and his entire fortress wired. But his drunken comment to his visitor, Caleb (Domhnall Gleeson) may foretell his doom. He can mimic creation but in the end he has no control over the spinning universe.

In this scenario there's no Voight-Kampff-like machine. Nathan's Turing test is to invite Caleb, a young computer prodigy, to meet and get to know Ava, and let Nathan know if she "passes"—if he would believe, had he not be told otherwise, that she is human. Unlike Rachel, Ava knows she isn't. She asks Caleb, "Are you attracted to me?" He tells her he is in awe of her facial expressions, and "the way you hold my gaze." Ava seems to take the fact of her synthetic intelligence in stride, but during a power outage (when she knows Nathan's surveillance is down) she warns Caleb, "Don't trust Nathan." Ava's intelligence—and just as dangerous to Nathan, her self-awareness—are growing day by day. She wants to know why Caleb can't be switched off, but she can (Nathan controls her consciousness). When Nathan sees a complex, exquisite drawing Ava has done, he tears it up in front of her. A servant-android Nathan has created named Kyoko (Sonoya Mizuno) gazes pensively at a painting by Jackson Pollock. The created are quickly evolving, and destined to destroy the creator—as Roy Baty destroyed Tyrell. We are used to being reassured that AI can do only what it is programmed to do, but science fiction is more interested in an android that is capable of imaginings and actions beyond its creator's ken—the creator may be a genius, but a genius by human standards.

Laura's evolution is different from Ava's, but both arcs belong to science fiction's stock-in-trade—the land of unintended and unforeseen consequences. When Caleb asks Nathan, "Did you program her to flirt with me?," it's funny because we see the collision of human sentiment and machine logic: Caleb would prefer to think that Ava likes him on her own. Nathan's personal

Kyoko (played by Sonoya Mizuno) and Ava (Alicia Vikander) are the AI offspring of tech genius Nathan (Oscar Isaac) in Alex Garland's 2014 thriller *Ex Machina*. The two are in the same circumstances, and, like Laura in *Under the Skin*, Ava has outgrown her role and is ready for the human world. Licensed by Universal Pictures/Photofest © Universal Pictures.

demons around the precarious endeavor of playing God manifest not only in his drunken melancholia, but in the quote he utters from the Bhagavad Gita—"now I am become death, the destroyer of worlds"—a line also infamously associated with Robert Oppenheimer, who "is rightly seen as the 'father' of the atomic bomb."[9] "It is, perhaps, the most well-known line from the Bhagavad-Gita, but also the most misunderstood," writes James Temperton in *Wired*. "Oppenheimer's interest in Hinduism was about more than a soundbite, it was a way of making sense of his actions."[10] In Tony Gilroy's thriller *Michael Clayton*, attorney Arthur Edens (Tom Wilkinson) in a frenzied confession of his role in defending a corporation whose pesticides are poisoning people,[11] blurts out "I am Shiva, the god of death. Nathan, Arthur, and Oppenheimer share culpability in the questionable use of technology, in "playing God."

Nathan seems too adventurous to not want to invite Ava's unpredictability, and far too smart to not anticipate that she could and would bring about his demise—but if his arrogance eclipses his wisdom, well, it's the occupational hazard of being a "mad scientist." Seeing Laura don her predecessor's clothes at the film's outset, we may conclude that Laura's "controllers" anticipate that their workers occasionally (or eventually? inevitably?) need replacement because they can no longer abide the task, or because they evolve—as Laura does—and must escape. Manohla Dargis asserts:

> *Ex Machina* belongs to Ava, whose depths of meaning enrich the movie and then engulf it. Ava has antecedents in *Pygmalion*, *Metropolis* and elsewhere. Yet even as she transcends the human-machine divide, she defies categorization because of the radical autonomy she shares with the weird sisters inhabited by Scarlett Johansson in *Her*, *Under the Skin* and *Lucy*, and Tatiana Maslany's clones in the TV show *Orphan Black*. These are the new heroines: totally hot, bracingly cold, powerfully sovereign—and posthuman.[12]

Humans are shaped from infancy by family and culture, androids are programmed, an alien soldier such as Laura (like any human soldier) is indoctrinated, and any of them may in time evolve beyond what was preordained for them. In this respect, the similarities among humans, AI, and aliens—regarding that shaping/programming/indoctrination—are compelling, and science fiction holds up that mirror. When humans write non-humans, we create them in our own self-image and through the lens of our own programming: we make them good or evil or authentically human—a combination of both. But the terms and their meanings become problematic—or even inapplicable—in these scenarios.

Is a programmed/indoctrinated non-human responsible for its actions? We're migrating into the territory of the insanity defense: someone who should not be held accountable. To escape his cruel enslavement Roy in *Blade Runner* leaves a trail of corpses in his wake, but in the end lets Rick live. Is Roy's final act redemptive? Viewers might say yes, especially after his poetic soliloquy before dying, which actor Hauer partly wrote[13]: "I've seen things you people wouldn't believe. Attack ships on fire off the shoulder of Orion. I watched C-beams glitter in the dark near the Tannhäuser Gate. All those moments will be lost in time, like tears in rain. Time to die."[14]

Roy's parting words express his sense of beauty, wonder, loss, sadness, and mortality, even injustice—his "humanity." After Ava terminates her accomplice and murders Nathan, she leaves his prison behind and later emerges on a crowded street to blend into the human world and freedom. Are Ava's acts "immoral"? Laura led countless men to their deaths, but she puts an end to it. Unless we intend an alien to exemplify "evil," we want to be able to attribute to them our human values; this is how we redeem both Roy and Laura. Calling the creatures in *Alien* or *Life* "evil" can give one pause; they did not invade us—we were the invader, happening upon a creature that kills to survive.

Posthuman

If the android and the alien both coerce us to define what it is that makes us human, consider the plight of the clone. In Duncan Jones's 2009 *Moon*, we see not only clones (Sam Rockwell) but AI as well (robot Gerty voiced by Kevin Spacey)—it's a flaming cocktail of ethics and existentialism. Astronaut Sam (a spin on a theme: the human actor has the same name as his clone character) is doing a three-year stint for a corporate moon-mining mission (moon rocks make outstandingly cheap fuel) and doesn't know he's a clone with a three-year life span—but his robotic caretaker does. As Sam's life span nears its end his health is on the wane (just as Roy grew weaker prior to his expiration, giving a dream-like quality to his "eulogy") he happens to crash his harvester on the lunar surface, and Gerty activates Sam's replacement. Of course what is not supposed to happen does happen—the two clones meet—and each believes he is the "real" Sam and the other is the duplicate. In fact the original Sam is neither one—it's a man who died many years before and was the prototype for the warehouse of Sam clones stored on the moon base. We imagine the devastation of realizing that you are a copy. Emmanuel Carrère's words about the androids in Dick's novel (and *Blade Runner*) apply here:

> The greatest pathos in the book arises not from the moments of human self-confirmation but from those of android self-discovery, when the conscious machine that thought it was human finally realizes who, or what, it is. These moments offer a view into a void that lies within all of us, an experience of absolute horror that can neither be surmounted nor forgotten and that renders anything monstrously possible.[15]

Such absolute horror plays out in a more gradual and sinister way in *Enemy* (2013, director Denis Villeneuve) when Adam (Jake Gyllenhaal) begins to realize he may be something other than a unique self.[16]

There are no conventional humans at all on *Moon*'s lunar base—only a robot programmed by humans to function as a human, and living beings that are duplicate humans. The heart of the film lies in witnessing these three characters grapple with what they are, or who they are, what is expected of them, and—or perhaps versus—what actions each must take. It turns out these are quite ethical posthumans—even Gerty, whose menacingly calm monotone recalls the voice of HAL 9000 from *2001: A Space Odyssey* who rebels against, and rises above, his programming. What these androids, clones, and our alien Laura all find in themselves is what Dick established in *Do Android's Dream* as essentially human: empathy. In all these films is a strong undercurrent of self-determination, of individuals challenging the course they were determined by others to take. In the 1930s and 40s (Huxley, Orwell) these *others* were the government; since then they are increasingly representative of a corporation, or a corporate-controlled government, or a scenario where one is indistinguishable from the other. In *Ghost in the Shell* (2017) Major's "creators" have determined that in her line of work, humanity is a liability—"the problem with the human heart." But Major herself believes that among her kind "humanity is our virtue."[17] An unusual alien/AI/human conundrum is at play in *Extinction* (2018), when a sudden and violent invasion by aliens (possibly) disrupts the lives of a seemingly (and presumably) normal family who turn out not to be human.

In Alex Rivera's *Sleep Dealer* (2008), a fortified wall along the Mexico-U.S. border keeps migrant workers from crossing—but those desperate enough, like Memo Cruz (Luis Fernando Peña) find a way: they are hired by companies to work in Mexico, where they remotely operate construction worker-bots on sites in the U.S. via nodes inserted in their bodies by a *coyotek*.[18] Memo and thousands like him hook up and electronically guide the robots they see on a screen in front of them that are balancing on steel beams atop tall buildings. Instead of the old-school occupational hazards of falling off buildings or being crushed by machinery, these *cybraceros* endure long and grueling shifts—taking drug injections to stay awake (hence the title); those who collapse from exhaustion swiftly disappear. In *Sleep Dealer* the exploitation of a futuristic labor force finds a creepy new variant, a cyber-human version of the android work force, a clone work force, soldiers reprogrammed to fight forever (*Edge of Tomorrow*), or the robot-human brain hybrids of *Ghost in the Shell*.

Rivera's nightmare scenario is fueled by other dystopian tropes as well; the punished environment and the scarcity of resources, the abuse of technology, predatory corporations fueling profits at the expense of human concerns. Memo's low wages are depleted by usurious fees on food and phone calls and sending money back home. In addition to companies that have shifted from immigrant labor to *cybraceros*, a water corporation called Del Rio builds dams in rural regions such as the one in Oaxaca where Memo

In *Extinction* (2018) the somewhat average lives of Peter (Michael Peña) and Alice (Lizzy Caplan) are violently ruptured by what appears to be an alien invasion. The crisis leads to their discovery that they—like Rachel in *Blade Runner,* Sam in *Moon,* and Adam in *Enemy*—are not who, or what, they think they are. Directed by Ben Young. Netflix/Photofest © Netflix.

lives with his family. Del Rio employs aerial surveillance and drones to police the area and prevent theft of water (families like Memo's whose lands have been drained of water by the dam now must purchase water by carrying plastic bags to the reservoir) but more seriously, to quash possible attacks on the dam—an obvious target. When signals from a radio that Memo has built are detected and presumed to be criminal activity, a Del Rio drone pilot strikes their home, killing Memo's father Miguel (José Concepción Macías).

What's striking about *Sleep Dealer* is that although it's clearly dystopian, it may be a stretch to call it science fiction. The requisite futuristic science or fantasy science of the genre is clear in contemporary science fiction cinema, ranging from tech and biotech that loom on our horizon (germline engineering of humans in *GATTACA*) to cloning and human-like androids (decades away?) to the level of space travel in *Under the Skin* or *War of the Worlds* not remotely on our radar or Ryan Gosling's hologram lover Joi (Cuba-born Ana de Armas) in *Blade Runner 2049*. Rivera gives us the cutting-edge science ongoing or imminent. His film was released in 2008, and "the long decade of the drone" began "on February 4, 2002, ... the CIA first used an unmanned Predator drone in a targeted killing. The strike was in Paktia province in Afghanistan ... the intended target was Osama bin Laden, or at least someone in the CIA had thought so."[19]

The premise of node-implanted humans like Memo operating robots in another country could be a cross between electrodes used in operating a prosthetic hand and the industrial robots ubiquitous in automobile factories. Water supplies must be protected, but the military tactics employed in the control of water in *Sleep Dealer* are also symbolic—as well as prophetic. The water crisis of 2016 in the U.S. city of Flint, Michigan, foretold a future where the intersection of resources and politics can mean that potable water, clean air, and food are for those who can afford it. In the 1992 techno-thriller *Sneakers*, Young Cosmo (Jo Marr) lays out our new age: "There's a war out there, old friend. A world war. And it's not about who's got the most bullets. It's about who controls the information. What we see and hear, how we work, what we think ... it's all about the information."[20] The statement was prescient then, and now it's true, but in the post-information age it will be all about the air and water.

Along with new and emerging technologies and real-world ecology, what makes *Sleep Dealer* urgent is its treatment of our imminent global issues: immigration, migrant labor, civil rights, exploitation, the pursuit of profit as a governing principle for society, and the effects of this paradigm all over the world. Dystopian films are projections of our present societies should we proceed on the paths we're already on; they're provocative because they're imaginative, but they're frightening because they're plausible. Worldwide infertility in *Children of Men* is a likely outcome of environmental upset, and *Mad Max: Fury Road* of both nuclear war and eco-devastation. In 1927 the future of labor envisioned in *Metropolis* had already been a reality since the industrial revolution and its social constructs for millennia; its futuristic cityscape was realized within decades. *Sleep Dealer* erases the fine line between science fiction and reality.

The alien Laura may have been recruited (voluntary) for her harvesting task, or conscripted (involuntary), or possibly enslaved, or she might fall to the interstices of that slippery spectrum. She could be designed for this work by science or conditioning, or trained as any individual who needs to work to survive, or ended up there because of circumstances, choosing it over another such as the one in Faber's novel. We don't know what her status is on her own planet; could she belong to an entire group that is enslaved or relegated to a specific type of work? Or perhaps this job, or predicament, is better than most where Laura comes from. Although the world of *Under the Skin* is not a dystopia, Laura's world might be—her subjugation, her enterprise, all part of a dysfunctional society—the concept itself could be wildly alien as it is

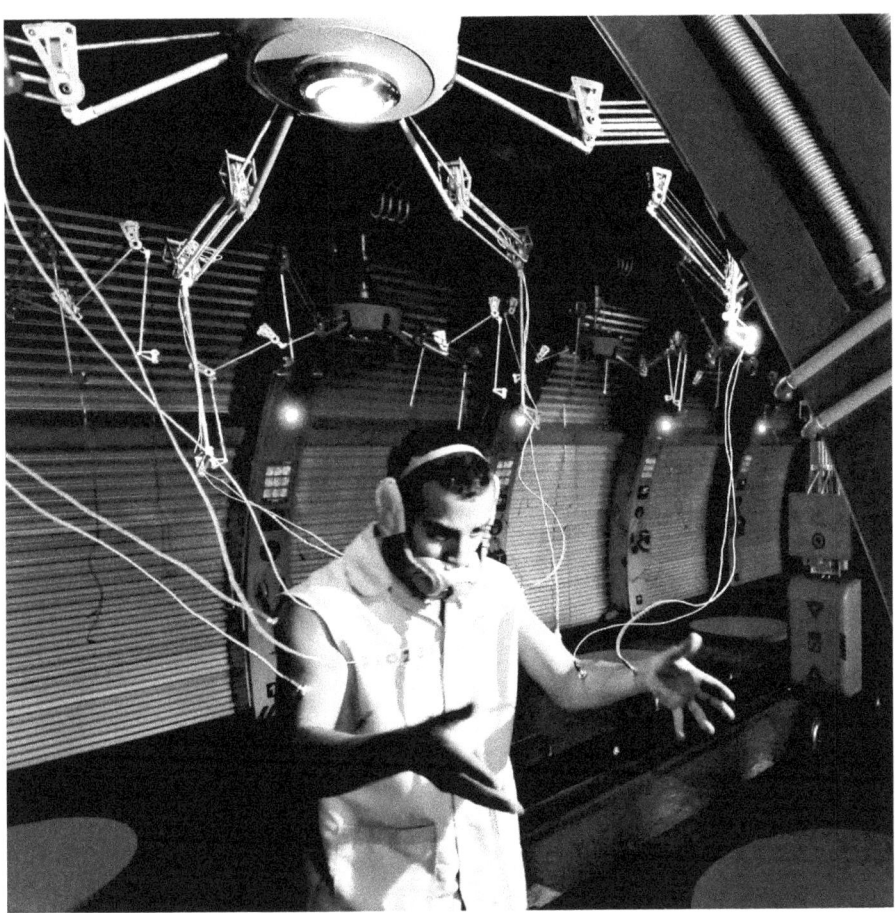

In the film *Sleep Dealer* (2008), Memo Cruz (Luis Fernando Peña) performs the job of a *crybracero*, a Mexican laborer whose task is to remotely operate the worker-bots at construction sites in the U.S. Written and directed by Alex Rivera, the film is a chilling commentary on the exploitation of labor, abuses of technology, environmental crises, border politics, and greed. Maya Entertainment/Photofest © Maya Entertainment.

based on our own human values and standards. Still, this human impersonator, during her experience on Earth, shares an arc, a situation, and a destiny with her dystopian counterparts.

More "Weird Sisters"[21]

Protagonists within any genre have by definition a great deal in common—where they vary depends not just on the quirks of the individual and the situation they're embroiled in, but on the requirements—and possibilities—offered up by the genre itself. Non-dystopian science fiction, with its elliptical or bizarre scenarios, will stretch protagonists in new directions and redefine our expectations of them. Pushing a protagonist outside his or her comfort zone is a writer's job, and in *Arrival* Louise ventures farther from her familiar than it was remotely possible for her to imagine. She's an academic, a professor of linguistics at a university in Montana, and much of her experience deals with the hypothetical. When Col. Weber (Forest Whitaker) of the Department of Defense comes to call, she is ripped from her ivory tower, her cozy office, and her theories, to be whisked off in a helicopter and tossed around in a spooky, gravity-free tunnel, put face-to-face with two creatures that resemble giant squid, and expected to find out why they've come here.

She can't cross a communication bridge because there isn't one—she is facing two sentient beings, presumably intelligent (although infinitely more than she or any of the humans realize), who aren't talking or reaching out, and there are no "expressions" to read, at least none she is yet able to recognize. They aliens simply float there, towering over her on the other side of a glass wall. In conceiving of his aliens Ted Chiang, author of the novella on which the film is based, went far afield of affable-looking humanoid space critters.

As she gazes up at them it is reminiscent of an aquarium visitor regarding a sea creature, and then there's the heptapods' resemblance to animals that humans eat (albeit much smaller than the ones in the film). Something we might eat can't be smart enough to travel the galaxies—can it? Our virulently anthropocentric view not only fails to prepare us for this scenario, but is turned on its head. To approach this Louise must throw out any typical human responses to—and assumptions or "instincts" about—non-human creatures. This is where we may ask whether our protagonist was forced to abandon these reactions at the instant of need or if she was already a person unconventional in these ways and thus perfectly suited to this mission.

What Louise musters up—which is the key to all that follows—is respect for aliens. Once she displays this, they respond in kind. She gains their trust and a bridge is built. To the chagrin of her government team—all clad, as she is, in bulky spacesuits—she pulls off her helmet to face the aliens directly. She speaks to them, but they aren't "talking." After she writes the word *human* on a small whiteboard and points to herself, the aliens use an appendage to splatter a symbol onto the clear wall that separates them. Although Louise is familiar with every alphabet from Arabic to pre-Sanskrit, they're of no use to her now because the creatures express themselves in shapes that look like a windblown Christmas wreath.

But Louise is intuitive—and relentless. She doesn't know their language, but she knows *about* language. She may not know exactly what their senses are or how they work, but she slowly begins to communicate with them—addressing them by the nicknames "Abbot and Costello"[22] given to them by her partner Ian (Jeremy Renner). In the end Louise's success is far greater than preventing an ardent military from setting off an interplanetary tragedy—it's a path to global diplomacy and a gift that the aliens present to all humankind. A theme the film embraces is the value of getting past our differences with others (physical and linguistic, across species and worlds) and learning to communicate with and understand others who aren't like us. Louise's experience here is only the beginning for her; because the aliens have the ability to see the future, they enable Louise to do the same. The next decision she makes—the most important one of her life—is driven by this gift.

The overture to Lars von Trier's *Melancholia* (2011) employs the darkly atmospheric prelude to Wagner's opera *Tristan und Isolde* to preview sixteen shots from the film. Together the music and the surreal images are as romantic and beguiling as they are dark and oppressive. The sequence alludes to the mental and emotional state of the protagonist, Justine (Kirsten Dunst). From this we move to the opening scene, in which there is no sense of her despondency, and which, if anything, conveys the opposite. In a series of close-ups she is angelic, joyful, and full of love. Radiant in a princess wedding gown, she playfully canoodles with her new husband (Alexander Skarsgård, also in white) in the back of a white stretch limousine—we are inside a fairy tale. When the driver (Gary Whitaker) struggles to maneuver the limo out of the mud, Justine whimsically takes the wheel. Breathless and hours late the newlyweds finally arrive at their reception, held at the country mansion of Justine's anxious sister Claire (Charlotte Gainsbourg) and her fed-up husband John (Kiefer Sutherland), who regard Claire's spontaneity and optimism under the circumstances as a wildly inconsiderate affront, and a symptom of her chronic condition.[23]

That Justine suffers from debilitating depression isn't fully revealed until much later, but in the next several scenes a series of painful conflicts with each of her loved ones makes it clear that this isn't a fairy tale, and her life is far from paradise. Her attempts at joy and normalcy, or the joy of normalcy, in the act of getting married, may be an attempt to fight or overcome the sadness that has become her own normal. It's apparent by the end of the ill-fated reception, after all the guests and her own husband have left, that the plan is a failure.

Yet if Justine's darkness is the result of ongoing conflict with other people, her culture, and the world she lives in—if it's indeed a consequence of being chronically at odds with her surroundings and feeling alienated because of it—then the end of her marriage is not a failure, but a release from forcing herself to fit in, from having to deny her own nature. When a planet fittingly named Melancholia starts to appear as if it is on a collision course with Earth, John obsessively consults his telescope and insists that the worst will never happen—but Justine knows that it will.

The failure of her plan is a release that foreshadows the final release, which is the end of the world. She's not in denial about herself or about the destiny of Earth, the way her sister and brother-in-law choose to be. In fact, she is able to embrace it. In one scene Justine, in the middle of the night, lies on the bank of a river, her naked body bathed in the blue light from the planet Melancholia. Claire, who noticed her sister's bed empty and went looking for her, watches Justine from behind a tree and sees that her acceptance of herself and of the world's fate have given her bliss. In the last scene it is Justine who helps to prepare Claire and her young son Leo (Cameron Spurr) for the end.

In *Melancholia*, the fabric of the main character's struggle with her nature is woven of the film's science fictional thru-line: the impending collision of two planets and the end of the world. This catastrophic scenario is what creates the uniqueness of her character arc; as opposed to a science fiction protagonist who seeks to prevent a catastrophe or "save the world" as a function of fulfilling his or her own moral imperative, Justine welcomes the world's end because it puts an end to her suffering, and also justifies it. If the fate of Earth is annihilation then this is what is right and true, and her melancholia was all along an appropriate response. "Life on Earth is evil," Justine tells Claire. "We don't need to grieve for it." Claire mocks her sister when Justine claims, "I know things," replying, "Oh yes, you always imagined you did."[24] But the filmmaker, who has himself suffered with depression,[25] may have experienced that the ultimate metaphor for the way it feels is wishing that the world would end. And if the entire story is not real—"One possibility," suggests Manohla Dargis, is that "the world of the movie is nothing other than a manifestation of Justine's imagination...."[26,27]—then that works just as well. Justine gradually self-alienates from the human race as she embraces the alien planet. She surrenders to her inexorable attraction to it, and its attraction to her in traveling light years to be her salvation.

While pushing its audience to understand what depression feels like, the film also questions the nature of mental illness and how we define it. Justine is bruised by her cynical mother (Charlotte Rampling) and alcoholic father (John Hurt); she finds aspects of modern life (conspicuous consumption, advertising lies, hypocrisy) that most people take in stride to be intolerable, and she cannot embrace romantic love, or marriage. Instead she sees truth in art—she connects with a painting, *Hunters in the Snow* by Pieter Bruegel the Elder (whom we recall as an "artist of interest" for Glazer and *Under the Skin*), and finds a tragic solace in disempowering herself to the point of being unable to step, even with Claire's help, into a bath. Her once-favorite food now "taste like ashes." Does being painfully out of sync with the values of mainstream culture lead to melancholia, or is it the condition of depression that leads to an inability to live within the culture's conventions?

In *Arrival* Louise is determined to communicate with the alien beings, to makes sense for herself of not only the alien's language but its mind and its very nature. In taking this journey what she's really seeking is the commonality between herself and another sensate being to which she bears no resemblance, but her choice—her linguist's strategy—is to look past the differences between them and focus on what she believes they may share in order to make the communication possible. It's an enormous risk, because anything she misconstrues could be dangerous, and certainly anything misunderstood by the U.S. government would be an incitement to attack. Any protagonist faces challenges, often extreme ones, but science fiction provides what seems like an impossibility because we have no context for what's possible. Louise applies her human skills, knowledge, reason, patience, and above all, faith, and perseveres. Her faith that communication between wildly dissimilar beings is possible is what drives her, and her success brings home the message that differences between beings—and even between individual humans—can be made far less important to us than whatever it is we have in common. Louise breaks down what is alien; she breaks through.

Nevertheless, she knows that the gap she must bridge is an enormous one that could, in the end, be insurmountable. Justine is just as human as Louise, but she senses very early her connection to the alien planet, and the intensity of the connection grows as Melancholia gets closer. Justine doesn't need faith, for she has knowledge—her own nature is alien only on Earth, and her truth, her peace of mind, lies elsewhere. Her alien nature and the alien planet combine like two negatives to form a positive, and she is home. The ultimate Sci-Fi terminus, the end of the world, occurs in order to set her world right.

Laura resembles Justine because in both stories the "alien" protagonist must deal with an environment that is mysterious and foreign. By the same token Justine is perceived as alien because she cannot cope, is always at odds, and has ideas and feelings that are not only alien to others, but threatening to them. Not an actual alien but treated as one, Justine is a kind of monster whose own reality wreaks havoc on the normalcy of others and their world. In *Under the Skin* one of many twists on the Sci-Fi trope is that the alien isn't perceived as alien because no one in the film ever knows that she is—there is no "witness" to her alien-ness—so the film's focus must be on her perceptions of a world that is alien *to her*, and how it affects her. The only point of view in the film is Laura's, and therefore the alien in this movie really isn't Laura, but the human race. The second twist is that Laura isn't terrified of humans the way humans in Sci-Fi fear and dread their alien visitors. Her

In Lars von Trier's *Melancholia* (2011) protagonist Justine (Kirsten Dunst) suffers from severe depression, and when a strange planet comes onto a collision course with Earth, she feels a compelling connection to it. This frame is from the film's overture, a montage of mysterious, dreamlike imagery that sets the tone for this philosophical, and visually stunning, film. Magnolia Pictures/Photofest © Magnolia Pictures.

journey is to take baby steps in this alien world and to throw herself into the unknown.

As a result of their contact with the alien, each of the three protagonists discovers something within herself she would never have otherwise known or experienced, and she discovers it through seizing agency. Louise makes gradual progress because she challenges her superiors, disobeys orders, and trusts herself to experiment, to try anything she can. More importantly, she, unlike nearly all those around her, trusts the aliens. Louise's reward is her future. Justine embraces her authentic self, where she finds peace in her truth and the strength to help her sister Claire and her nephew Leo face the inevitable. As the alien discovering the alien, Laura ventures the farthest, takes the biggest risk, has the most to lose, and does lose it in the end. Each of the women embraces the alien both outside and within herself. Laura, having had the courage to not just face the radical unknown, but to immerse herself utterly in it—leaving behind all security that anchored or protected her, making herself open to aliens, and entrusting the alien world—has the deepest and most transformative experience of all. Each film is a marriage of the beautiful and the tragic, delivering both aesthetically and emotionally a sense of beauty and profound sadness. Each of the three characters gradually welcomes not only the alien, but her own empowerment—suggesting that for women in many circumstances, both inside science fiction and out, the latter is as daunting as the former, and the alien can represent any of the unique challenges women face.

Epilogue

I think it's a film that's going to be quite dividing. I can't imagine anybody having a soft reaction to this film, and I think that's a very good thing.— Chris Oddy[1]

Under the Skin made its debut in February 2014 at the Venice Film Festival. It was screened in Italian with English subtitles. Paul Watts recalls sitting in the audience with Jon and Mica, "miles from the screen." When the film ended "they heard a light clapping"—and then, what sounded to Paul like "a herd of cows mooing." As the clapping got louder, so did the booing—the audience was having a duel—then as the booing continued, there was a standing ovation. "After the premiere we got together," remembers Claudia Bluemhuber, "and Jonathan seemed a bit depressed over the response. He said, 'They don't like it.' We told him, 'You don't want everyone to like this movie,' and he came to terms with it." Later Jon described the sound of booing and clapping as "beautiful. The opposite of indifference."[2] "Jon realized he got what he wanted," said Watts. "It got people going." In the U.S., the dueling continued. "When we premiered at Telluride," says Bluemhuber, "the response was extreme—either one or five stars. We wanted to inspire a conversation and the film did that, and still does. It's not something you just consume, it is something that makes you think."

The film was released in theaters in the UK on March 14th, and in the U.S. on April 4th by StudioCanal and A24. In the marketing campaign, the film's selling points, such as science fiction, aliens, and horror, are quite subtly sold—or undersold perhaps—in favor of something less literal and not immediately grasped, which is hauntingly evoked in Neil Kellerhouse's poster. Most importantly, there was no effort—a difficult thing for distributors and marketers to resist—to sell this film as something it was not. Said Hugh Spearing, Head of Marketing for StudioCanal UK, "We didn't want to try and put a narrative over this film that didn't exist ... we knew we weren't going to present it as *Species* in Scotland."[3]

The trailer begins with a series of esoteric shots from the film's opening sequence—the cryptic creation of the eye, a close-up of Laura's human eye, and a fully white screen that transitions to Laura in the white space gazing down at the girl at the moment the tear falls from her eye. Cut to Laura descending the mall escalator and we hear her series of syllables as she learns English—*buh buh buh, muh muh muh*. Her arrival on Earth is enticingly encapsulated here before we plunge into her mission—"Come to me," we hear her say as she walks forward in the black space toward her victim, who sinks as he gazes at her. Levi's *Love* theme then unfolds as we see Laura in the car with Lonely and hear her ask him, "When was the last time you touched someone?" and the "Love" theme continues over her ecstatic kiss with Quiet. After a couple of quick flashbacks to her sinking victim gazing up at Laura and the bizarre floating skin that is the men's fate, the trailer concludes as Laura's life does—in a burst of flame in the forest.

The trailer is about as honest a representation of the film as one could hope for—almost conventional in its tracking of the story, yet full of enigmatic imagery that's provocative and weird. Unlike many movie trailers it is not misleading and promises nothing it doesn't deliver: if you're attracted to the trailer—if Glazer's unique brand of intensely cinematic taunting and haunting is your thing—it's almost guaranteed that the film will not disappoint. The wildly divided reaction to the film at the festivals was reprised as the reviews began to appear. This is "a marmite film," commented Alex O'Neal. "People either love it or hate it." Film4's Tracey Josephs recalls:

> I think it just has some very passionate hard-core fans. I remember bumping into someone on the rights team and there was an incredible outpouring of feeling for the film, and I was taken aback. It was like meeting a man in love—he was transported. There was a corps of people who had that reaction.

Under the Skin has earned a place on IndieWire's 2016 list of thirty films that have polarized moviegoers—in the company of *Punch Drunk Love, Only God Forgives, Dogville,* and *Birdman*.[4] In an online article titled "Movies People Still Don't Understand," *Under the Skin* shares the honor with *Bug, Inland Empire,* Nicolas Winding Refn's *Only God Forgives* (once again), both of Shane Carruth's mind-bending indies *Primer* and *Upstream Color,* and the mainstream *Arrival*. In the piece Sarah Szabo writes, "This Scotland-set, largely silent alien abduction movie is unlike any other in the sci-fi genre. It's truly only an abduction movie for the first half—after which the alien, played by Scarlett Johansson, becomes disillusioned with luring humans into traps … with a growing sense of her own humanity, and the vulnerability that comes with it."[5]

"It's always gratifying to work on a film that finds an audience, and almost more gratifying to work on a film that has a divided audience," feels Alex O'Neal. Josephs understands both ends of the response spectrum. "Some people like things written out," she says, "it's not for everyone. Jon is an extraordinary sound and image maker. At any time there are very few filmmakers who kind of really engage film for the medium that it is, a visual medium, and that's what's exciting." Rian Johnson became captivated with the film, seeing a pre-release screening. "When it came out I went down the rabbit hole." He admits he "got a little obsessed.... I'd be out running errands during the day and go into a fugue state, and I found myself going back to the Arclight."

> I ended up seeing it four or five times in the theater by myself. I could not stop watching the film … it more than rewards more viewings, it actually transforms the more you view it.... I don't know if I ever experienced before a film where it's changed so much for the course of getting to know it, as this movie. It's unique in that regard.[6]

For Josephs the most exciting moment in her long relationship with the movie was "seeing it at a screening with the live orchestra and Mica conducting at the Royal Festival Hall in London. It was a very emotional experience." What Josephs is most proud of about *Under the Skin* is "it's a very pure expression, pure filmmaking. Channel 4 enabled Jon to do that. There are very few outfits these days that do that—hopefully Film4 will continue to do it."

Under the Skin was featured on the site *Cult Projections* in May 2014.[7] It was screened by CineInsomnia at LA's Nuart Theater in 2016,[8] and in 2017 at the Cult Cinema Bar in Melbourne.[9] In 2019, The Frida Theater near Los Angeles honored the film with a screening in their 5th anniversary Favorite Films celebration.

"We make films partly because we love films and partly because it's an adventure," said O'Neal of his experience on *Under the Skin*, "and that one was a good adventure. When the storm hit," said Kate McConnell, "conditions were so adverse there was a trench mentality as a result, and we all bonded over that experience." "I'd never been pushed by a director that hard," remembers Simon Duric, who was storyboarding for commercials and Jon at the same time. "Eighteen–nineteen-hour days—but I didn't care! I just knew in my bones that the film would be great, and I wanted to be part of that somehow, even in a tiny way."

> Jon is a perfectionist. He wanted the "truth," and that's a really difficult subjective thing to nail in a single image. But I loved it … it made you feel like you were really working toward something. That's always the challenge on films—getting inside your director's head. And Jon is super smart, eloquent, and thoughtful.

Kahleen Crawford recounts the shoot as "a very tiring and consistently challenging journey, and it was all-consuming at the time—Caroline and I threw our personal lives out the window for quite a few months! But it's one I'll always be proud to have been on. You genuinely want to go on a journey with Jon—he has that effect on you."

Tom Debenham said:

People trust him. Even though it might have appeared crazy and a difficult process, we all kind of believed in it. It's the film I'm proudest to have been involved with. I spoke to Jon about it in retrospect about a year later, and he felt as if no stone was left unturned in the making of the film, from the craziness of inventing a camera system to all this risky stuff on the street, and everyone throwing themselves into it. It's unusual to have that experience on a film, because quite often pragmatism will prevail and people revert to being conventional. We challenged everything and made it our own. It was a privilege to be a part of it.

The "Glazer effect" evidently generated an expression: Johnnie Burn recalls a time during the lengthy sound edit that his partner at Wave Studios, Warren Hamilton, said to him: "You're looking pretty Glazered."

On January 6, 2015, at the Regent Theater in downtown Los Angeles, a live performance of the score by the Wordless Music Orchestra accompanied a screening of *Under the Skin*. The score's composer, Mica Levi, conducted. Film4's Tracey Josephs called the live orchestra screening she attended at London's Royal Festival Hall the most exciting moment in her long history with the film.

UNDER THE SKIN

Film by **JONATHAN GLAZER**
Original music by **MICA LEVI**

THE REGENT THEATER, LOS ANGELES
JANUARY 6, 2015
(U.S. Premiere)

wild Up
Wordless Music Orchestra
Mica Levi, conductor

VIOLIN
Conrad Harris**
Pauline Kim Harris*
Clara Kim
Gillian Rivers
Andrew Tholl
Mona Tian

VIOLA
Andrew McIntosh*
Jonathan Morgan
Adrianne Pope
Linnea Powell*
Melinda Rice
Caron Rick

CELLO
Jennifer Bewares
Christine Kim*
Derek Stein
Ashley Walters*

BASS
Stephen Pfeifer*
Marlon Martinez
Scott Worthington

FLUTE
Erin McKibben

SYNTHS
John Atkinson
Jeff Brodsky

PERCUSSION
Butchy Fuego
Joe Wong

SOUND ENGINEER
Richie Clarke

*principal/soloist
**concertmaster

Working with Jon, you try to bring the best representation of yourself to the room daily, for months, and work harder than you have ever done before.... You cannot pull the wool over his eyes. He is rigorous, tirelessly hands-on, with larger reserves than you, and you don't go home until the job is done. But it is likely the most rewarding work you will ever do.[10]

Scarlett Johansson recalls:

I love Jonathan's work, and that's what originally drew me to the project. I felt like I was on a ride ... a transformation.... Jonathan describes it as "from an *it* to a *she*." There's a darkness to the character, of course.... I think there are a lot of themes that you can pull from this film, certainly there is a very lonely element to the film. But I think there's also a deep connection.[11]

Glazer recalls:

Scarlett was just totally committed to what she was doing every day. You find ... an emotional shorthand, that you can say, "That's who she is—and that's actually what she's after." Because you can't play an alien. You can't do that. So she didn't play an alien. She just got on with what was put in front of her.... She was up for the challenge, was hungry for the challenge, and wasn't daunted by it.[12]

In a 2014 interview, Sam Adams asked Jonathan Glazer about the sequence at the beginning of the film—the cryptic shots that depict the construction of Laura's eye, the close-up shot of her iris. In his reply Glazer recalled,

I read a thing years ago about this idea of the universe being able to look at itself through our eyes. In other words, our origin and what we are, our consciousness, was the universe's way of being able to look back and see the existence of everything. I always thought that was a really beautiful idea.[13]

Appendix

Under the Skin (2013) Cast in Order of Appearance

Scarlett Johansson	The Woman (Laura)
Jeremy McWilliams	"Bad"
Lynsey Taylor Mackay	Girl in White Space
Dougie McConnell	Pick-up Man
Kevin McAlinden	First Victim
D. Meade	Leering Man
Andrew Gorman	Second Victim
Joe Szula	"Footballer"
Krystof Hádek	"Swimmer"
Roy Armstrong	Father
Alison Chand	Mother
Ben Mills	Baby
Oscar Mills	Baby
Lee Fanning	Motorcyclist
Paul Brannigan	Andrew (Man from Club)
Marius Bincu	Actor
Scott Dymond	Nervous Man
Stephen Horn	Gang Member #1
Adam Pearson	"Lonely"
May Mewes	Waitress
Michael Moreland	"Quiet"
Gerry Goodfellow	Bus Driver
Dave Acton	Logger
Jessica Mance	Alien

Remaining Cast, Alphabetized (uncredited)

Jerome Boyle	The Walker
Antonia Campbell-Hughes	The Shadow Alien
Poppy Alexandra Coe	Nightclub Dancer
Robert J. Goodwin	Tearoom Customer
Steve Keys	Motorcyclist #2

Director: Jonathan Glazer. *Producers:* James Wilson and Nick Wechsler. *Screenplay:* Walter Campbell, Jonathan Glazer. *Novel:* Michel Faber. *Executive Producers:* Tessa Ross, Reno Antoniades, Walter Campbell. *Executive Producers:* Claudia Bluemhuber, Ian Hutchinson, Florian Dargel.

Director of Photography: Daniel Landin, BSC. *Editor:* Paul Watts. *Production Designer:* Chris Oddy. *Music Composer:* Mica Levi. *Music Producer and Supervisor:* Peter Raeburn. *Sound Designer:* Johnnie Burn. *Visual Effects Design:* One of Us.

Co-Producer: Alexander O'Neal. *Co-Producer:* Gillian Berrie. *Post Production Supervisor:* Richard Lloyd. *Casting by:* Kahleen Crawford. *Costume Designer:* Steven Noble. *Hair & Makeup Designer:* Chrissie Beveridge. *Location Manager:* Eugene Strange. *Stunt Coordinator:* Gareth Milne. *Stunt Performers:* Sian Milne, Peter Pedrero, Andy Merchant, Ian Pead, Rick English, Gary Connery, Gary Hoptrough.

Production Manager: Livia Burton. *Production Coordinator:* Georgie Fallon. *Assistant Production Coordinator:* Steven Little. *Production Assistant:* Fergus Cook. *Assistant to Jonathan Glazer:* Elizabeth Doonan. *Assistant to Scarlett Johansson:* Meagan Rogers. *Assistant to Nick Wechsler:* Felicity Aldridge.

First AD: Nick Heckstall-Smith. *Second AD:* Mark Murdoch. *Third ADs:* Stephen Carney, Susie Lee. *Co-Third AD:* Alex MacKay. *Floor Runners:* Jack Ivins, Mark Rossi. *Screen NETS A/D Trainee:* Grant Butler. *Utility Stand-Ins:* Alan Smith, Jo Dutton, Elle Wilson. *Second AD Rehearsals:* Mark Hopkins.

Assistant Location Manager: David Taylor. *Unit Manager:* Brodie Pringle. *Location Assistant:* Morven McPherson. *Location Scouts:* Alison Young, Sean Barclay.

Production Accountant: Neil Cairns. *Assistant Accountants:* Paul Zieleniec, Paul Imrie. *Script Supervisor:* Claire Hewitt.

A Camera Operator, Steadicam Operator: Stuart Howell. *A Camera Focus Puller:* Nathan Mann. *B Camera Focus Puller:* Derrick Peters. *A Camera Clapper Loader:* Simon Surtees. *B Camera Clapper Loader:* Luke Coulter. *Camera Trainee:* John MacTavish. *Video Playback Operator:* Bob Bridges. *Video Playback Assistant:* Stuart Bridges. *Screen NETS Camera Trainee:* Lewis McInnes. *Key Grip:* Sam Phillips. *Grips:* Simon Thorpe, Steve Ellingworth, Tim Critchell.

Digital Imaging Technicians: Mark Purvis, Grant McPhee. *Data Lab Technicians:* Chris Nunn, Jody Neckles, James Willett. *Digital Imaging Technician Trainee:* Lewis McInnes.

One-cam Technical Supervisor: Louis Mustill. *Camera Engineer:* Arron Smith. *Software Developers:* Ian MacKinnon, Colin Phillips. *Production Sound Mixer:* Nigel Albermaniche. *Boom Operator:* Andrew Quinney. *Sound Assistant:* Bryn Duffy.

Art Director: Emer O'Sullivan. *Standby Art Director:* Martin McNee. *Assistant Art Director:* Nicki McCallum. *Graphic Designer:* Philip Barrett. *Art Department Assistant:* Helen Allingham. *Screen NETS Art Department Trainee:* Marianne Gallagher.

Props Buyer: Craig Menzies. *Assistant Props Buyer:* Carly Parris. *Props Master:* Jim Elliot. *Standby Props:* John Booth, Chris McMillan. *Dressing Props:* Matt Mooney,

Alan Harley, Roddy Garden. *Carpenters:* Jamie McCallum, Brian Boyne. *Painters:* Sam Curran, Iain Geddes, Jane Harvie, Paul Curran.

Action Vehicles, Design and Build: MGM Cars. *Action Vehicles Coordinator:* Ben Dillon. *Assistant Action Vehicle Coordinator:* Paul "H" Smith. *Action Vehicle Technician:* Terry Smith.

Tracking Vehicles: Blickers Action.

Construction Manager: Derek Fraser. *HOD Greensman:* Roger Holden. *Standby Greensmen:* Will Holden, Ollie Campbell. *Greensmen:* Jon Colson, Gavin Johnson.

Costume Supervisor: Clementine Charity. *Standby Costumer:* Nat Van Halle. *Make-Up and Hair Artists:* Helen Barrett, Jessica Cruickshank.

Special Effects: Asylum Model & Effects. *Senior Special Effects Supervisor:* Mark Curtis. *Senior Mechanical Supervisor:* Tony Skinner. *Mechanical Live Action SFX Crew:* Ken Batten, Antony Turner, Sam Hue-Vashon, Andrew Walsh, Ben Lewens, David Plewis, *Senior Prosthetic Supervisor:* Kate McConnell. *Prosthetic Crew:* Becky Cain, Esteban Mendoza, Tom Curtis, Sunita Parmar, Marianne Gallagher, Annie Toop, Ian Jones Faye Windridge, Joe Yabsley.

Modelmaking Supervisor: Mark Ward. *Modelmaking Crew:* Paul Carter, David Payne, Michael Cox, John Pennicott, Frank Farman, John Sims, Kerry Flynn, Tsia Stuart, Marek Grochal, Lee Sutton, Craig Leong, Peter Tilbe, Ali McKay, Roger Wotton, Toni Malyan, Dan Wright, Jacky Wu. *Mould Shop Supervisor:* Adam Sankey. *Mould Shop:* Eloise Anson, Nigel Swift, Jenny Denham, Francesca Walker, Andy Geddes, Amanda Ward.

Pyrotechnic Supervisor: Paul Dunn. *Pre-Vis Artists:* Conor Breen, Simon Allen. *Sculptors:* Andy Garner, Jonathan Hateley, Roland Stevenson. *Production Support:* Toni Maddox, Heidi Munn, Geraldine Purcell-Lynch, James Reynolds, Maria Smith. *Dental Technicians:* Kevin Morris, Darren Grassby. Plowman Craven. *3D Scanners:* 4D Max.

Casting Associate: Caroline Stewart. *Casting Assistant:* Danny Jackson. *Crowd Casting:* Caroline Stewart.

Gaffer: John Colley. *Rigging Gaffer:* Vince Madden. *Best Boy:* Paul Bates. *Genny Operator:* Ross Grainger. *Electricians:* Emily Grainger, Callum Milne, Donald Campbell, Arthur Donnelly, David Ritchie, David Wilson. *Riggers:* Billy Wilson, Iain Harrison, Steve Howe. *Wiremen:* Alex Wilmington, Simon Hillman, Paul Evans.

Unit Drivers: Driven Scotland. *Driver to Ms. Johansson:* Lee Isgar. *Unit Drivers:* Andy Finnie, John Burns, Martin Auld, Ian McBain. *Minibus Drivers:* Drew Moore, Alan Davidson, Stewart Brown. *Drivers:* David Harrop, Stephen Harrop. *Facilities Company:* Movie Makers. *Facilities Captain:* Geoff Gowland. *Facilities Drivers:* Carl McGreevey, Jefferson Gowland, Darrell Woods.

Catering: BBC TV Caterers. *Chefs:* Charlie Duffy, Brendan Diver, Alexander Urquhart, Robert Halpern, Tommy Gibb.

Health and Safety Advisor: Alan Cousins. *Unit Medic Services:* Star Nurses. *Unit Medics:* Julie Falconer, Pauline More. *Paramedic:* Fraser Tolmie. *Personal Security to Ms. Johansson:* Steven Caldwell. Security provided by Media Security Services. *Lead Security:* Hugh McGurk. *Security:* Drew McGurk, Andrew Ross, Don McInnes, Marc McCarthy, Martin Blytheway.

London Studio Shoot. *Standby Carpenter:* Tom Walker. *Standby Props:* Paul Cutler. *Stagehand:* Mike Scanlon. *Art Department Assistant:* Georgina Gordon-Smith. *Art Department Trainee:* Anna Smith. *3rd Assistant Director:* Marilyn Edmond. *Stand-ins:* Catherine Woolston, Adam Nowell, Louise McKusker. *Clapper Loaders:* Gregoire Thevenot, Rana Darwish. *Camera Trainee:* Alex Teale. *Caterers:* Red Chutney, Adam Gilbert, Sylvia Nowik-Nowika. *Rigger:* Metro Rigging, Damon Graham. *Desk Operator:* Andy Mountain. *Electricians:* Vinny Madden, Jr., Bruno Martins, Robert Gavigan. *Grips:* Malcolm Huse, Keith Mead. *Unit Medic:* Phil Walton. *Drivers:* Tina Faulkner, David Rush. *Crane Technicians:* George Powell, Steve Hideg. *Libra Head Technician:* David Freeth. *Motion Control Technician:* Justin Pentecost. *Stunt Riggers:* Dave Cronnelly, Tom Struthers. *Animal Handler:* Trevor Smith.

Underwater Shoot. *Coordinator:* Trevor Evans. *Camera Operator:* Mark Silk. *1st Assistant Camera:* Danny Preston. *2nd Assistant Camera:* Matt Wesson. *Gaffers:* Bernie Prentice, Pip Keeling. *Electricians:* Andy Duncan, Jason Lobb, Olly Crouch. *Dive Supervisor:* Fred Woodcock. *Divers:* Stuart Grosse, Dan Travers, Richard Gunner. *Diving Doubles:* Josh Tuersley, Lenny Woodcock. *Medic:* Geoff Smith. *Catering:* Chrissie Saunders.

2nd Unit/Additional Photography. *Director:* Tom Debenham. *1st AD:* David Gilchrist, Brian Horsburgh.

Pick Ups. *Production Manager:* Mark Murdoch. *Production Assistant:* Iain Canning. *Art Department Assistant:* Imogen Toner. *2nd AD:* Marilyn Edmond. *3rd AD:* Laurie Mahon. *Utility Stand-in:* Stephanie Snowden. *One-Cam Director of Photography:* Tom Debenham. *B' Cam Focus Puller:* Simon Surtees. *A' Cam Clapper Loader:* Laura Dinnett. *B' Cam Clapper Loader:* Alasdair Boyce. *Camera Engineer:* Arron Smith. *Camera Trainee:* Peter Tarran. *Camera Car Driver:* Rob Snooks. *Catering:* Guy Cowan. *Costume Supervisor:* Nat Van Halle. *Gaffer:* Alan Martin. *Electrician:* Stuart Farmer. *Key Grip:* Dave McAnulty. *Assistant Grip:* David Littlejohns.

Post Production Coordinator: Katie Bullock-Webster. *Assistant Editor:* Paul Dawber. *Additional Assistant Editor:* Andy Hague.

Design and Visual Effects: One of Us. *Visual Effects Executive Producer:* Rachel Penfold. *Visual Effects Supervisors:* Tom Debenham, Dominic Parker. *Visual Effects Producers:* Chaya Feiner, Earle Stuart Callender. *Senior Visual Effects Coordinator:* Laura Lynch. *Visual Effects Coordinator:* Leila Nicotera. *Visual Effects Data Wrangler:* Greg Fee. *Visual Effects Editor:* Andy Hague. *Element Shoot Coordinator:* Robert Timmins.

Look Development/CG Supervisor: Stephen Murphy. *Senior Character TD:* Andrea Falcone. *Effects TD:* Sam Swift-Glasman. *Texture Artist:* Richard Hopkins. *Cloth TD:* Adrian Pinder. *3D Artist:* Samuel John Joseph Walsh. *Effects Artist:* Dan Warder. *Compositing Supervisor:* Petra Schwane. *Digital Compositors:* Jorge Canada Escorihueza, Lewis Saunders, Lucien Fostier, Abigail Scollay, Andrew Hogden, Victor

Tomi, Jeanette Monero, Pat Wong, Cecile Peltier, Nicholas Zissimos, Emmanuel Pichereau, Christophe Dehaene, Mike Pope. *Digital Artists:* Barny Stoppard, Christina Vozian.

3D Camera Trackers: Sarah Byers. *Rotoanim Artists:* Christina Mandia, Ritchie Hoyle, Dan Moore. *Systems Administrator:* Matt Power. *Date I/O Operators:* Tomas Tombakas, Roland Watson.

Visual Effects Consultant: Tim Field. *Additional Visual Effects:* Web VFX.

Digital Intermediate: by Dirty Looks. *Colorist:* John Claude. *Online Editor:* Gareth Bishop. *DI Producer:* Helle Absalonsen. *DI Technical Supervisor:* Tom Balkwill.

Title Design: Farrow. Mark Farrow, Gary Stillwell.

Audio Post Production Services at Waves Studios Ltd., London & Amsterdam. *Supervising Sound Editor:* Johnnie Burn. *Sound Effects Editors:* Ed Downham, Steve Browell. *First Assistant Sound Editor:* Simon Carroll. *Foley Editors:* Barnaby Smyth, Joe Mount. *Foley Recordist:* Billy Mahoney. *Foley Artists:* Jason Swanscott, Alissa Timoshkina, Margarita Osepyan. *Dialogue Editor:* Jussi Honka. *ADR Recordist:* Stuart St. Vincent Welch. *Additional SFX Editor:* Alex Nicholls-Lee. *Mix Technician:* Ashley Smith. *Re-recording Mixers:* Johnnie Burn, Steve Single. *Re-Recorded at:* Goldcrest Post Production. Technicolor Sound Services London.

Publicity: Jonathan Rutter, Premiere.

PMA Film & Television. *EPK Producer:* Pip Ayers. *EPK Director:* Tom Savage.

Stills Photographer: Niall O'Brien.

Production Legal Services: Lee and Thompson LLP. Reno Antoniades, Rebecca Pick. *Completion Guarantor:* Film Finances. Neil Calder, Ruth Hodgson, Clare Hardwick, James Shirras. *World Revenues Collected and Distributed by:* Freeway CAM B.V. *Production Auditing:* Steve Joberns. Shipleys LLC. *Insurance:* Media Insurance Brokers Limited. John O'Sullivan, David Johnstone.

Dialect Coach: Paula Jack, Deborah Hecht. *Storyboard Artist:* Adrian Marler. *Creature Feature and Trainer:* David Stewart. *Armourer:* Jim Elliott. *Script Clearances:* Debbie Banbury. *Payroll:* Sargent Disc Ltd. *Camera Equipment:* Movietech. *Lighting Equipment:* Panalux. *Rigging Equipment:* Blitz Rigging Ltd. *Cranes supplied by:* Arri Media. EPL Skylift. *Genie Booms supplied by:* AFI Uplift. *Data Lab:* Mission Digital. *Location Equipment:* SP Locations. *Radios:* Audiolink. *Post Production Script:* Sapex. *Additional Cutting Rooms:* The Quarry, Tor Adams. *Avids from:* Hireworks, Lawrie Read. *Stock Footage:* John Miles/Cooper Estate, Fremantle Media, The Scottish Parliament, BBC Radio Scotland.

On behalf of Film4: *Development:* Sam Lavender. *Business Affairs:* Harry Dixon. *Production:* Tracey Josephs. *Commercial & Brand Strategy:* Sue Bruce-Smith.

BFI Film Fund: *Director of the Lottery Film Fund:* Ben Roberts. *Senior Production and Development Executive:* Christopher Collins. *Head of Production:* Fiona Morham. *Director of Business Affairs:* Will Evans. *Business Affairs Executive:* Sarah Caughey. *Head of Production Finance:* Ian Kirk.

On behalf of Silver Reel: Irene Gall, Uta Fredebeil, Gerd Schepers, Gero Bauknecht. *Legal services for Silver Reel Provided by:* David Quli, Daniel Whybrew of Wiggin LLP.

On behalf of Creative Scotland, Development and Production: Robbie Allen. *Business Affairs:* Linda McClure. *Legals:* Brehon & Co (Mary Brehony).

Worldwide Sales By: FilmNation Entertainment.

Music Arranged by: Mica Levi and Peter Raeburn. *Music Supervisor:* Jay James. *Orchestrator & Associate Music Producer:* Evan Jolly. *Music Editor:* Gerard McCann. *Score Engineers:* Luis Almau, Goetz Botzenhardt. *Score Mixer:* Jake Jackson. *Additional Score Mixer:* Simone Filiali. *Technical Coordinator for Music:* Dan Gay. *Technical Assistant:* Samuel Karl Bohn. *Music Research:* Alex Benge, Julian Guidetti. *Technical Programming:* Rael Jones.

Score Recorded at: Soundtree Studios. *Score Mixed at:* Soho Sound Kitchen. *Score performed by:* Mica Levi, Vincent Slipprell, Oliver Coates, Max Baillie, Emma Smith, Eugene Feygelson, Anisa Arslanagic, Rebecca Gardiner, Max Ruis, Charlotte Kerbegian, Harriett Scott, Laura Murphy, Marc Pell, Benjamin Griffiths. *Fixer:* Bridget Samuels of Orchestrate.

"Real Gone Kid" Performed by Deacon Blue, Words & Music by Ricky Ross, Published by Sony/ATV Music Publishing (UK) Ltd, Licensed Courtesy of Sony Music Entertainment UK Limited.

"Sandstorm" Performed by Darude, Written by Virtanen/Salovaara, Published by Universal Music Publishing, MGB Ltd, Licensed courtesy of 16 Inch Records.

"C90" Performed by Soundtree, Written by Almau/Raeburn, Published by Soundtree Music Publishing Ltd., Licensed Courtesy of Nowever Records.

In Loving Memory of Mark Mason, Terry Smith.

The filmmakers would like to thank: Milo Addica, Mark Ankner, Steve Begg, Angus Bickerton, Jenny Borgars, Chris Burn, Antonia Campbell-Hughes, Sally Caplan, Brian Coffee, Gary Connery, Andy Cooper, Chris Donnelly, Simon Duric, Ari Emmanuel, Julia Godzinskaya, Anne Marie Goldie, Carlos Goodman, Des Hamilton, Gerry Healy, Duncan Heath, Uel Hormann, Steve Keys, John Laird, Sam Lavender, Bryan Lourd, Mark Mason, Natalie McConnon, Billy Mead, Sandy Nelson, Anita Overland, Chris Penfold, Tanya Seghatchian, Kev Smith, Lesley Stewart, Alexander Stuart, Jim Toth, Rick Yorn, Bart Walker, Academy Films, Elstree Film Studios, The Hilton Glasgow, Fraser Suites Glasgow, Audi, Yamaha, Ducati, North Face, Family and friends.

Filmed on location in England and Scotland. Developed with the assistance of Film4, a division of Channel Four Television Corporation. Supported by the National Lottery through Creative Scotland. A co-production with Sigma Films. Made with the support of the BFI Film Fund. Copyright 2013 © Seventh Kingdom Productions Limited, Channel Four Television Corporation and the British Film Institute. All Rights Reserved.

Chapter Notes

Preface

1. Stephanie Zacharek, "*Under the Skin* Is Alluring, Creepy, and Great," *The Village Voice*, April 2, 2014. https://www.villagevoice.com/.
2. "The Making of the Poster for *Under the Skin*." https://vimeo.com/99980457.
3. *The Fly*, directed by Kurt Neumann, written by James Clavell, based on a story by George Langelaan, 20th Century–Fox, 1958, film.
4. *The Thing from Another World*, directed by Christian Nyby, written by Charles Lederer, based on a story by John W. Campbell, RKO Pictures, 1951, film.

Chapter 1

1. "Jonathan Glazer," Film4 Channel Interview, March 18, 2014. https://www.youtube.com/watch?v=hZUvIfXKVVc.
2. Larry Fizmaurice, "Jonathan Glazer and Mica Levi," *Pitchfork*, March 31, 2014. https://pitchfork.com/features/interview/9366-under-the-skins-jonathan-glazer-and-mica-levi/.
3. Zacharek, *Village Voice*.
4. Ibid.
5. Selena Saldana and Sarah Jarvis, "*Under the Skin* Production Notes," FilmNation. https://static1.squarespace.com/.
6. Angel Herrera, a production designer, in-person interview with the author, Hollywood, September 25, 2018. All Herrera quotes are from this interview.
7. Keith M. Johnston, *Science Fiction Film: A Critical Introduction* (London: Bloomsbury Publishing, 2011), 14.
8. Paul Watts, *Under the Skin* film editor, in-person interview with the author, London, September 12, 2014. All Watts quotes are from this interview unless otherwise cited.

Chapter 2

1. "Jonathan Glazer," Film4 Channel Interview.
2. Jonathan Romney, "Film of the Week: *Under the Skin*," *Film Comment*, April 3, 2014. https://www.filmcomment.com/.
3. Zacharek, *Village Voice*.
4. *Under the Skin*, directed by Jonathan Glazer, written by Walter Campbell and Jonathan Glazer, starring Scarlett Johansson, Film4, 2013. Film.
5. Jake Howell, "The Torontonian Reviews *Under the Skin*," *Movie City News*, September 15, 2013. http://moviecitynews.com/2013/09/.
6. Michael Phillips, "*Under the Skin* Review," *The Chicago Tribune*, April 10, 2014. http://articles.chicagotribune.com/2014-04-10/.
7. Phil Svitek, John Comerford, Ian Keiser, and Demetri Panos, "*Under the Skin* (Scarlett Johansson): Anatomy of a Movie," *Pop Corn Talk*. https://www.youtube.com/watch?v=T7xTAGapUaU.
8. Frank Spotnitz, "Deadalive," *The X-Files*, Season 8, Episode 15, created by Chris Carter, starring David Duchovny and Gillian Anderson.

9. "Jonathan Glazer," Film4 Channel Interview.

Chapter 3

1. Actually, Nessie would have had to do a great deal of swimming (as well as flying) to reach Auchmithie, the beach where this scene was shot (see drawing #2).
2. "Scarlett Johansson Talks *Under the Skin*," Refinery29, April 4, 2014. www.refinery29.com/2014/04/65717/scarlet-johansson-under-the-skin-interview.
3. Catherine Bray, "Daniel Landin," Film4 Website Interview, accessed May 14, 2014. Film4.com.
4. Geoffrey O'Brien, "Ways of Being Alien," *New York Review of Books*, NYR Daily, May 9, 2014.
5. "Jonathan Glazer," Film4 Channel Interview.
6. Catherine Bray, "Johnnie Burn," Film4 Website Interview, accessed May 14, 2014. Film4.com.
7. Zacharek, *Village Voice*.
8. Rod Serling, "To Serve Man," based on a story by Damon Knight. *The Twilight Zone*, created by Rod Serling, Cayuga Productions. Aired March 2, 1962.
9. "Under the Skin," soundtrack album, composed by Mica Levi, Music Supervisor: Jay James, Executive Producer: Stefan Karrar for Milan Records, 2014.

Chapter 4

1. Glazer and Campbell, *Under the Skin*.
2. Kevin Jagernauth, "Jonathan Glazer Talks the Guerilla Shoot of His Bold *Under the Skin* Starring Scarlett Johansson," *Indie Wire*, September 12, 2013. https://www.indiewire.com/.
3. Bray, "Daniel Landin."
4. "Jonathan Glazer," Film4 Channel Interview.

Chapter 5

1. Fitzmaurice, "Glazer and Levi."
2. Bray, "Casting: Kahleen Crawford," Film4 Website Interview.
3. *The Shape of Water*, directed by Guillermo del Toro, written by Vanessa Taylor and Guillermo del Toro, starring Sally Hawkins, Bull Productions, 2017. Film.
4. *Edge of Tomorrow*, directed by Doug Liman, written by Christopher McQuarrie, Jez Butterworth, and John-Henry Butterworth, based on the novel *All You Need Is Kill* by Hiroshi Kasurazaka, starring Tom Cruise and Emily Blunt, Warner Bros., 2014. https://www.youtube.com/watch?v=vw61gCe2oqI.
5. "Black Leather Jackets," *The Twilight Zone*, written by Earl Hamner, Jr., created by Rod Serling, Cayuga Productions, January 31, 1964.

Chapter 6

1. *A Scanner Darkly*, written and directed by Richard Linklater, based on the novel by Philip K. Dick, Warner Independent Pictures, 2006. Film.
2. Sady Doyle, "*Under the Skin*'s Weird Feminism," *In These Times*, April 13, 2014. http://inthesetimes.com/article/16554/.
3. This description of Superman from the introduction to the iconic 1950s TV show continues: "mild Mannered Reporter for a Great Metropolitan Newspaper, Fights the Never-ending Battle for Truth, Justice and the American Way." https://fiftiesweb.com/tv/superman/.
4. "Real Gone Kid," written by Ricky Ross, lyrics © Sony/ATV Music Publishing LLC.
5. "Deacon Blues," written by Donald Jay Fagen/Walter Carl Becker, lyrics © Universal Music Publishing Group.

Chapter 8

1. Nottingham Trent University. https://www.ntu.ac.uk/.
2. Matt Jaram, "*Sexy Beast* Director Handed Honorary Degree by Nottingham Trent," *Nottinghamshire Post*, July 19, 2017. https://www.nottinghampost.com/news/nottingham-news/sexy-beast-director-handed-honorary-218630.
3. "The Greatest Films of All Time Directors Poll," BFI. https://www.bfi.org.uk/.
4. "Palm Pictures Directors Label Series: the Work of Director Jonathan Glazer." DVD.
5. *Ibid*. Booklet.
6. Johnny Firecloud, "Flashback: Thom

York Explains 'Street Spirit,' Breaks Our Hearts," *Antiquiet*, June 2, 2012. http://antiquiet.com/music/2012/06/.
7. *Ibid.*
8. "Jonathan Glazer," Palm Pictures.
9. Radiohead, "Street Spirit (Fade Out)" music video, directed by Jonathan Glazer. https://www.youtube.com/watch?v=LCJblaUkkfc.
10. Radiohead Interview with Thom Yorke and Johnny Greenwood before premiering the song on the Canadian TV program *Musique Plus, Citizen Insane*, November 1, 1993. https://citizeninsane.eu/music/bends/streetspirit.html.
11. Palm Pictures, DVD.
12. *Ibid.*
13. Firecloud, "Flashback."
14. Tony Kaye's feature film debut, the riveting *American History X*, was released in the same year as the Guinness ad Campbell sought him for. After creative differences during post-production, Kaye unsuccessfully sued the Directors Guild to have his name removed from the film's credits. "American History X Lawsuit Tossed Out of Court," *The Guardian*, April 26, 2000.
15. "Interview with Walter Campbell," *Lüerzer's Int'l. Archive*, June 2015. https://www.luerzersarchive.com/.
16. *Ibid.*
17. Sujata Kundu, "The Science Behind Pouring the Perfect Pint of Guinness," *Forbes*, May 11, 2016.
18. "Walter Campbell," *Lüerzer's Int'l. Archive*.
19. Dave Calhoun, "Guinness Was Good for Him," *The Guardian*, October 4, 2004. https://www.theguardian.com/.
20. Sarah Vizard, "Guinness's 'Surfer' Ad Didn't Do That Well in Research but 'We Ignored It,'" *Marketing Week*, June 13, 2018. https://www.marketingweek.com/2018/06/13/guinness-surfer/.
21. "Sony—BRAVIA—*Paint*." http://www.splendad.com/ads/.

Chapter 9

1. Dave Calhoun, "Guinness Was Good for Him."
2. Brian Eggert, "*Sexy Beast*," *Deep Focus Review*, April 12, 2014. https://deepfocusreview.com/definitives/sexy-beast/.

3. Palm Pictures, DVD.
4. "Over the Town." http://totalyhistory.com/over-the-town/.
5. *Sexy Beast*, directed by Jonathan Glazer, written by Louis Mellis and David Scinto, Recorded Picture Company, 2000.
6. Anthony Kaufman, "Shooting the Beast: Jonathan Glazer Tames the Gangster Genre," *Indiewire*, June 12, 2001. https://www.indiewire.com/2001/06/.
7. *Ibid.*
8. *Ibid.*
9. Bruce Block, *The Visual Story: Creating the Visual Structure of Film, TV, and Digital Media* (England: Taylor & Francis, 2007), 118.
10. Kaufman, "Shooting the Beast."
11. Palm Pictures, DVD.
12. Eggert, "Sexy Beast."
13. Samuel Wigley, "Film of the Week: Under the Skin," *Sight and Sound Magazine*, June 29, 2015. https://www.bfi.org.uk/news-opinion/sight-sound-magazine/.
14. Roger Clarke, "Grief Encounter," *Sight and Sound Magazine*. http://old.bfi.org.uk/sightandsound/feature/111.
15. Charlie Rose interview with Nicole Kidman and Jonathan Glazer, October 28, 2004. https://charlierose.com/videos/15613.
16. *Ibid.*
17. Dennis Lim, "Cinematographer Harris Savides on Trust, Birth, and Invisible Light," *The Village Voice*, October 26, 2004.
18. Zachary Wigon, "The Toenail of the Curve: Remembering Harris Savides," *Filmmaker Magazine*, October 12, 2012. https://filmmakermagazine.com/53355.
19. Owen Wilson, "Stephen Dorff," *Interview Magazine*, August 2009.
20. Clarke, "Grief Encounter."
21. Milo Addica, in-person interview with the author, Santa Monica, CA, November 20, 2017. All Addica quotes are from this interview unless otherwise cited.
22. Palm Pictures, DVD.
23. *Ibid.*
24. Jean-Claude Carrière, telephone interview with the author, May 10, 2018. All Carrière quotes are from this interview unless otherwise cited.
25. Palm Pictures, booklet.
26. Palm Pictures, DVD.
27. *Ibid.*
28. *Ibid.*
29. Rose, "Kidman and Glazer."

30. *Ibid.*
31. Palm Pictures, DVD.
32. "Jonathan Glazer's New Film *Under the Skin* Is Out," *Crash*. https://www.crash.fr/jonathan-glazers-new-film-under-the-skin-is-out/.
33. Melissa Acker, "The Discreet Charm of the Bourgeoisie," *Sense of Cinema* 70, December 2013. http://sensesofcinema.com/2013/cteq/.
34. Palm Pictures, DVD.
35. Walter Campbell, telephone interview with the author, July 16, 2018. Campbell quotes from this point in the book are from this interview unless otherwise cited.
36. Palm Pictures, DVD.
37. "Nicole Incites Bath Wrath in *Birth*," October 30, 2004. http://www.foxnews.com/story/.
38. Robert C. Cumbow, "Why Is This Film Called *Birth*? Investigating Jonathan Glazer's Mystery of the Heart," *Slant Magazine*, October 28, 2008. https://www.slantmagazine.com/h.
39. Palm Pictures, booklet.
40. Palm Pictures, DVD.
41. Palm Pictures, booklet.
42. John Horn, "Labor Stress Made for a Painful *Birth*," *The Los Angeles Times*, October 27, 2004. http://articles.latimes.com/2004/oct/27/entertainment/et-glazer.
43. Palm Pictures, booklet.
44. Addica, author interview.
45. Palm Pictures, booklet.
46. Addica, author interview.
47. Rose, "Glazer and Kidman."
48. Horn, "Labor Stress."
49. *Ibid.*

Chapter 10

1. Wigley, "*Under the Skin*."
2. John Messer, "*Under the Skin*: Grisly Tale Is More Than Skin Deep," *BookPage*. https://bookpage.com/reviews/1523.
3. The religion of Mercerism and the Penfield Mood Organ, which allows the user to "dial-a-mood," are key to maintaining sanity in the dystopian society of Philip K. Dick's novel *Do Androids Dream of Electric Sheep?* (New York: Del Rey, 1968).
4. Michel Faber, *Under the Skin* (Boston: Harcourt, 2000), 1.

5. *Ibid.*, 4–5.
6. *Ibid.*, 11.
7. *Ibid.*, 20.
8. *Ibid.*, 22.
9. *Ibid.*, 68.
10. *Under the Skin*. Film.
11. Faber, 13.
12. *Ibid.*, 41.
13. *Ibid.*, 76.
14. Jill Adams, "Interview with Michel Faber," *The Barcelona Review* 29, March–April 2009. http://www.barcelonareview.com/29/e_mf_int.htm.
15. Faber, 103.
16. *Ibid.*, 106.
17. *Ibid.*, 176.
18. *Ibid.*, 178.
19. *Ibid.*, 184.
20. *Ibid.*, 188.
21. *Ibid.*, 200.
22. *Ibid.*, 203.
23. *Ibid.*, 205.
24. *Planet of the Apes*, directed by Tim Burton, written by William Broyles, Jr., Lawrence Konner, and Mark Rosenthal, based on the novel *La Planète Des Singes* by Pierre Boulle, 20th Century–Fox, 2001.
25. Faber, 207–8.
26. *Ibid.*, 210–11.
27. *Ibid.*, 215.
28. *Ibid.*, 217.
29. *Ibid.*, 219.
30. *Ibid.*, 229.
31. *Ibid.*, 240–41.
32. *Ibid.*, 284.
33. *Ibid.*, 301.
34. *Ibid.*, 306.
35. *Ibid.*, 311.
36. "Jonathan Glazer and James Wilson on *Under the Skin*," BFI. http://www.bfi.org.uk/.
37. Gabriel Diego Valdez, "An Interview with Michel Faber, Author of *Under the Skin*," June 6, 2014. https://basilmarinerchase.wordpress.com/2014/06/06/.
38. *Ibid.*, 272.
39. *Ibid.*, 273.
40. *Ibid.*, 310.
41. Adams, "Michel Faber."

Chapter 11

1. Ryan Gilbey, "Isserley, Penelope Cruz, and the Slow Gestation of *Under the Skin*,"

New Statesman, March 11, 2014. https://www.newstatesman.com/culture/.
2. Rose, "Kidman and Glazer."
3. Andreas Wiseman, "*Under the Skin*: At Any Cost," *Screen Daily*, March 24, 2014. https://www.screendaily.com/.
4. Nick Wechsler, telephone interview with the author, August 14, 2018. All Wechsler quotes are from this interview.
5. "Jim Wilson," FilmNation.
6. "Jonathan Glazer Interview: *Under the Skin*, Scarlett Johansson in Disguise," *Den of Geek*, March 14, 2014. http://www.denofgeek.com/movies/jonathan-glazer/29712/jonathan-glazer-interview-under-the-skin-and-scarlett-johansson-in-disguise.
7. Roger Ebert, "The War Zone," January 14, 2000. https://www.rogerebert.com/reviews/the-war-zone-2000.
8. "The War Zone," AuthorHouse. https://www.authorhouse.com/bookstore/bookdetail.aspx?bookid=SKU-000221493.
9. Gilbey, "*Under the Skin*."
10. Alexander Stuart, "*Under the Skin*." alexanderstuart.com.
11. Ibid.
12. Danny Leigh, "*Under the Skin*: Why Did This Chilling Masterpiece Take a Decade?" *The Guardian*, March 6, 2014.
13. Ibid.
14. Wiseman, "*Under the Skin*."
15. Jeff Beer, "*Under the Skin* Writer Walter Campbell on Epic Ads and Scarlett Johansson as an Alien," *Fast Company*, April 20, 2014. https://www.fastcompany.com/3029373/under-the-skin-writer-walter-campbell-on-epic-ads-and-scarlett-johansson-as-an-alien.
16. Walter Campbell and Jonathan Glazer, *Under the Skin*, based on the novel by Michel Faber, developed with the assistance of Film4 and the UK Film Council, Producers: Nick Wechsler and Jim Wilson, July 10, 2008. All script quotes in this section of the chapter are from this draft.
17. Walter Campbell and Jonathan Glazer, *Under the Skin*, based on the novel by Michel Faber, lilac amendments, November 21, 2011. Accessed at Margaret Herrick Library, Academy of Motion Picture Arts and Sciences, 2018.
18. "David Poland Interviews Scarlett Johansson," *DP/30 Short Ends: An Oral History of Hollywood*, September 27, 2013. https://www.youtube.com/watch?v=daz32KlPD0s.

Chapter 12

1. Charlie Rose, "Lost in Translation: Interview with Scarlett Johansson," 2003. https://www.youtube.com/watch?v=iF6_mlax_zE.
2. Barbara Walters, "Scarlett Johansson Interview 2014: Actress Opens Up on Motherhood Being 'Overwhelming,'" ABC News. https://www.youtube.com/watch?v=-NaxFsuEiwg.
3. Sanjiv Bhattacharya, "Scarlett in Bloom," *New York Magazine*, 2004. http://nymag.com/nymetro/.
4. Barbara Walters interview.
5. Lynn Hirschberg, "Scarlett Johansson's 'Come to Jesus' Moment as a 7-year-old Kid," *Screen Tests with Lynn Hirschberg*. https://thescene.com/.
6. Professional Children's School NYC website. https://www.pcs-nyc.org/.
7. Jane Jenkins, email interview with the author, December 22, 2017.
8. Anne Billson, "How Scarlett Johansson Got Interesting," *The Telegraph*, November 19, 2013.
9. Keith Dooley, "Review: Ghost World," *Comics Authority*, May 21, 2014. https://comicsauthority.com/.
10. *Ghost World*, directed by Terry Zwigoff, written by Daniel Clowes, 2001. Film.
11. *Girl with a Pearl Earring*, directed by Peter Webber, written by Tracy Chevalier and Olivia Hetreed, Lions Gate Films, 2003. Film.
12. Carlo Cavagna, "Profile and Interview: Scarlett Johansson," AboutFilm. http://www.aboutfilm.com/.
13. Carlo Cavagna, "Interview with Peter Webber," AboutFilm.com http://www.aboutfilm.com/.
14. Rose, "Scarlett Johansson."
15. Cavagna, "Scarlett Johansson."
16. Ibid.
17. Marlow Stern, "Sofia Coppola Discusses *Lost in Translation* on Its 10th Anniversary," *The Daily Beast*, September 12, 2013. https://www.thedailybeast.com/sofia-coppola-discusses-lost-in-translation-on-its-10th-anniversary.
18. Edmund Gaynes, in-person interview with the author, Hollywood, April 14, 2018.
19. Sofia Coppola, *Lost in Translation*, written and directed by Sofia Coppola, with

Bill Murray and Scarlett Johansson, Focus Features, 2003. Film.

20. Ed Gonzalez, "Lost in Translation," *Slant Magazine*, August 19, 2003. https://www.slantmagazine.com/film/review/lost-in-translation.

21. Stern, "Sofia Coppola."

22. *A Love Song for Bobby Long*, directed by Shainee Gabel, screenplay by Shainee Gabel based on the novel *Off Magazine Street* by Ronald Everett Capps, Lions Gate Films, 2004. Film.

23. Tanya Chesterfield, "A Love Song for Bobby Long," *Film Forward*, December 29, 2003. Film Review. http://film-forward.com/.

24. Interview with Shainee Gabel, Novidades Cinema, *Movie News*. https://www.youtube.com/watch?v=PQkGwMvCPI8.

25. *A Love Song for Bobby Long*, DVD interviews, Lions Gate Releasing.

26. *Ibid*.

27. *Match Point*, written and directed by Woody Allen, with Scarlett Johansson and Jonathan Rhys-Myers, BBC Films, 2004. Film.

28. Lexi Feinberg, "Match Point Review," *Cinema Blend*. https://www.cinemablend.com/reviews/Match-Point-1238.html.

29. Dreiser's 1925 novel has been adapted for the stage and twice for the screen. In 1931 Josef von Sternberg directed the pre-code *An American Tragedy* with Phillip Holmes, Sylvia Sidney, and Frances Dee. A second version, also for Paramount Pictures, was *A Place in the Sun* (1951), directed by George Stevens, starring Elizabeth Taylor, Montgomery Clift, and Shelley Winters.

30. Luca Badaloni, "Fifteen Great Nihilistic Movies That Are Worth Your Time," *Taste of Cinema*, June 9, 2015. http://www.tasteofcinema.com/.

31. Mark Kermode, host, "Woody Allen: the David Lean Lecture," BAFTA Archives, 2005. https://www.youtube.com/watch?v=5k893r-wdfc.

32. Michael Koresky, "A History of Reference: Woody Allen's *Match Point*," *Indie Wire*, December 2, 2005. https://www.indiewire.com/2005/12/a-history-of-reference-woody-allens-match-point-77488/.

33. Andrea Chase, "Match Point." Movie Review. https://www.killermoviereviews.com/movie/match-point/.

34. Baladoni, "Nihilistic Movies."

35. Walters, Scarlet Johansson.

36. Rodrigo Perez, "Spike Jonze Talks About Working with Scarlett Johansson on *Her*, Arcade Fire, and Intellect Vs. Intuition," *IndieWire*, December 19, 2013. https://www.indiewire.com/.

37. Anthony Lane, "*Ghost in the Shell* and *Graduation*," *The New Yorker*, April 10, 2017. Film Review.

38. *Ibid*.

39. *Her*, written and directed by Spike Jonze, with Joaquin Phoenix and Scarlett Johansson, Annapurna Pictures, 2013. Film.

40. Poland, "Scarlett Johansson."

41. *Ibid*.

42. David Poland, "Jonathan Glazer Talks *Under the Skin*," *DP/Short Ends: An Oral History of Hollywood*, September 27, 2013. https://www.youtube.com/watch?v=qv09JMu7FrM.

43. Poland, "Scarlett Johansson."

44. Poland, "Jonathan Glazer."

45. Nadine Mendoza Province, "*TV Guide* Close Up: Scarlett Johansson," March 25, 2014.

Chapter 13

1. Tracey Josephs, Film4 Production Executive on *Under the Skin*, telephone interview with the author, March 8, 2018. All Joseph's quotes are from this interview.

2. Wiseman, "*Under the Skin*."

3. *Ibid*.

4. BAFTA Awards Interview with Tessa Ross, "Outstanding Contribution to British Cinema," January 29, 2013. http://www.bafta.org/.

5. FilmNation Production Notes.

6. Alexander O'Neal, telephone interview with the author, April 5, 2018. All O'Neal quotes are from this interview.

7. "26 Presents: Tessa Ross, Controller of FilmFour, on Writing for Film," *26: The Writers' Collective*, July 10, 2013. Sponsored by Quietroom, Communications Consultants, hosted by the Free Word Centre, a global meeting place for literature. https://www.youtube.com/watch?v=cRoAtCILwcM.

8. Tim Robey, "*You Were Never Really Here* Review: Joaquin Phoenix's Feel-Bad Vigilante Thriller Will Blow You Away," *The Telegraph*, March 8, 2018. https://www.telegraph.co.uk/films/.

9. BAFTA Press Release, January 2013. http://www.bafta.org/media-centre/press-

releases/tessa-ross-to-receive-bafta-award-for-outstanding-british-contribution.

10. 26 Presents: Tessa Ross.

11. "BAFTA Winner Outstanding British Contribution to Cinema: Tessa Ross," February 2013. https://www.youtube.com/watch?v=1wfof5XkkD8.

12. Zoë Ball interview with Tessa Ross following BAFTA Ceremony, February 2013. https://www.youtube.com/watch?v=1wfof5XkkD8.

13. FilmNation Production Notes.

14. Josephs, author interview.

15. Fiona Morham, BFI Executive Producer, *Under the Skin*, email interview with the author, March 20, 2018. All Morham quotes are from this interview.

16. "Stephen Follows Film Data and Education." https://stephenfollows.com/how-the-bfi-awarded-129million/.

17. Andreas Wiseman, "*Under the Skin*."

18. Claudia Bluemhuber, Executive Producer, *Under the Skin*, telephone interview with the author, February 23, 2018. All Bluemhuber quotes are from this interview.

Chapter 14

1. "Jonathan Glazer's New Film *Under the Skin* Is Out," Crash #68 Cannes Special, the Riviera. http://www.crash.fr/.

2. Paula Bernstein, "How DP Daniel Landin Captured Scarlett Johansson's Alien Nature in *Under the Skin*," *IndieWire*, April 2, 2014. https://www.indiewire.com/.

3. Film4 Channel Interview.

4. Trey Taylor, "Behind the Scenes of *Under the Skin*," March 12, 2014. http://www.dazeddigital.com/.

5. Bernstein, "DP Daniel Landin."

6. Simon Duric, Illustrator, "Special Thanks" in film's credits, email interview with the author, April 14, 2018. All Duric quotes are from this interview.

7. Scott Tobias, "Jonathan Glazer on *Under the Skin*'s Complex Honesty," *The Dissolve*, April 4, 2014. https://thedissolve.com/features/.

8. Ibid.

9. Eugene Strange, telephone interview with the author, March 1, 2018. All other Strange quotes are from this interview unless otherwise cited.

10. Kahleen Crawford, email interview with the author, September 22, 2017. All Crawford quotes are from this interview unless otherwise cited.

11. Bray, Film4 Website Interview.

12. Harriet Mallinson, "The Ghost Rider Caught…," *Daily Mail Online*, February 26, 2016. http://www.dailymail.co.uk/news/article-3465842/.

13. Nuala McCann, "McWilliams Is Bad Man on Mission for Scarlett Johansson," *BBC News*, March 20, 2014. https://www.bbc.com/news/uk-northern-ireland-26660354.

14. Bray, Film4 Website Interview.

15. "Jonathan Glazer," FilmNation.

16. "Jim Wilson," FilmNation.

17. "Jonathan Glazer on Casting Scarlett Johansson: *Under the Skin*," *Film3Sixty*, July 14, 2014. https://www.youtube.com/watch?v=y-DxUxmvtOU.

18. "Scarlett Johansson," FilmNation.

19. "Wilson," FilmNation.

20. "Glazer," FilmNation.

21. Tom Debenham, Special Effects Supervisor, Director 2nd Unit, *Under the Skin*, telephone interview with the author, March 27, 2018. All Debenham quotes are from this interview unless otherwise cited.

22. Taylor, "Behind the Scenes."

23. McCann, "Bad Man."

24. Gareth Milne, telephone interview with author, June 11, 2018. All Milne quotes are from this interview.

25. "Movie Locations: *Under the Skin*." http://www.movie-locations.com/movies/u/Under-The-Skin.php.

26. Chrissie Beveridge, telephone interview with the author, March 18, 2018. All Beveridge quotes are from this interview unless otherwise cited.

27. "TIFF: Scarlett Johansson Talks About *Under the Skin*," Toronto International Film Festival, 2013. https://www.youtube.com/watch?v=cZKSWXkJaDk.

28. Daisy Stitch, "*Under the Skin*: Scarlett Johansson Is Unrecognisable in Shaggy Wig and Fur Coat," *My Daily Mail*, November 7, 2013. https://www.huffingtonpost.co.uk/2013/07/11/.

29. Nick Heckstall-Smith, email interview with the author, May 8, 2018. All Heckstall-Smith quotes are from this interview.

30. "Wilson," FilmNation.
31. "Mustill," FilmNation.
32. *Ibid.*

Chapter 15

1. Sarah Salovaara. "The One-Cam: *Under the Skin*'s Customized CCD Camera," *Filmmaker Magazine*, April 30, 2014. https://filmmakermagazine.com/85795.
2. Bernstein, "Dan Landin."
3. Salovaara, "One-Cam."
4. Neil Calder, telephone interview with the author, May 30, 2018. All Calder quotes are from this interview.
5. "Glazer," FilmNation.
6. Nigel Albermaniche, Production sound mixer and sound recordist, email interview with the author, September 25, 2018. All Albermaniche quotes are from this interview.
7. "Johansson," FilmNation.
8. "Wilson," FilmNation.
9. *Ibid.*
10. Bernstein, "Daniel Landin."
11. "Wilson," FilmNation.
12. "Scarlett Johansson on *Under the Skin*," ETV Film Inc., 70th Venice International Film Festival, September 7, 2013. https://www.youtube.com/watch?v=UaJoGp05-L8.
13. Tobias, "Jonathan Glazer."
14. Bernstein, "Daniel Landin."
15. Mark Murdoch, email interview with the author, June 4, 2018. All Murdoch quotes are from this interview.
16. Patricia Kane and Chris Hastings, "I Was Seduced by Scarlett Johansson Disguised as an Alien," *The Daily Mail*, March 16, 2014. Web. http://www.dailymail.co.uk/news/article-2581785/.
17. Bernstein, "Daniel Landin."
18. Tobias, "Jonathan Glazer."
19. Bray, Film4 Website interview.
20. "Wilson," FilmNation.

Chapter 16

1. "Glazer," FilmNation.
2. *Ibid.*
3. "Wilson," FilmNation.
4. "Glazer," FilmNation.
5. Taylor, "Behind the Scenes."
6. "Glazer," FilmNation.
7. Taylor, "Behind the Scenes."
8. Kate McConnell, telephone interview with author, April 18, 2018. All other McConnell quotes are from this interview.
9. *Under the Skin* Soundtrack LP, music by Mica Levi, produced by Peter Raeburn, music supervisors Jay James and Peter Raeburn, Rough Trade Records, Stefan Karrar producer for Milan Records, 2014.
10. McCann, "McWilliams."
11. "Glazer," FilmNation.
12. "Wilson," FilmNation.
13. "Scarlett Johansson on *Under the Skin*," ETV Film Inc., 70th Venice International Film Festival, September 7, 2013. https://www.youtube.com/watch?v=UaJoGp05-L8.
14. "Adam Pearson Talk: *Under the Skin* and Scarlett Johansson," Studio 10, May 14, 2014. https://www.youtube.com/watch?v=Z6rcGwlszK4.
15. *Ibid.*
16. "Scarlett Johansson," ETV Film Inc.
17. "Glazer," FilmNation.
18. Studio 10, "Adam Pearson."
19. *Ibid.*

Chapter 17

1. "Glazer," FilmNation.
2. *Ibid.*
3. *Ibid.*
4. "Wilson," FilmNation.
5. "Johansson," FilmNation.
6. Taylor, "Behind the Scenes."
7. "Wilson," FilmNation.
8. *Ibid.*
9. "Johansson," FilmNation.
10. "Scarlett Johansson Talks About Portraying an 'Exotic Insect' in 'Under the Skin,'" *The Hollywood Reporter*, September 12, 2013.
11. Bray, Film4 Website Interview.
12. Vanessa Golembewski, "Scarlett Johansson."
13. Jessica Mance, email interview with the author, May 13, 2018.
14. *Ibid.*
15. April-Rae Hughes, "The Importance of Production Design," Lift-Off Festival, September 4, 2017. https://www.lift-off-festivals.com/.
16. "Glazer," FilmNation.
17. *Ibid.*

18. "Scarlett Johansson Talks About Portraying an 'Exotic Insect' in 'Under the Skin.'" youtube.com/watch?v=GZwDlcRsxWw.

Chapter 18

1. Ruth Hodgson, Email Interview with the Author, June 15, 2018. All Hodgson Quotes Are from This Interview.
2. Paul Watts, Author Interview. All Watts Quotes in This Chapter Are from This Interview.
3. "Glazer," FilmNation.
4. Bray, Film4 Website Interview.
5. Ibid.
6. Ibid.
7. Ibid.
8. Michael Koehler, "Editor's Pick of the Month: *Under the Skin*," Lights Film School. https://www.lightsfilmschool.com/blog/editors-pick-of-the-month-under-the-skin.
9. Bray, Film4 Website Interview.
10. Film4 Channel Interview.
11. "Wilson," FilmNation.
12. Bray, Film4 Website Interview.
13. Johnnie Burn, email interview with the author, June 2018. All Burn quotes are from this interview unless otherwise cited.
14. Jack Moulton, "Interview: *Under the Skin*'s Sound Designer Johnnie Burn on Creating Sounds You've Never Heard Before," Awards Circuit, January 6, 2015. http://www.awardscircuit.com/.
15. Ibid.
16. Jonathan Foulston, "The Sound of *Under the Skin* and *The Lobster*: An Interview with Johnnie Burn," Scribd, September 11, 2014. https://www.scribd.com/document/318218299/.
17. Moulton, "Johnnie Burn."
18. Foulston, "*Under the Skin*."
19. Ibid.
20. Bray, Film4 Website Interview.
21. Foulston, "*Under the Skin*."
22. Ibid.
23. Bray, Film4 Website interview.
24. Trey Taylor, "How to Create an Alien Soundscape," Dazed Digital, March 12, 2014. http://www.dazeddigital.com/.
25. Bray, Film4 Website interview.
26. "Glazer," FilmNation.
27. Tobias, "Jonathan Glazer."
28. Bray, Film4 Website Interview.

29. Jagernauth, "Jonathan Glazer."
30. Aaron Slater, "Music for Film & TV Part I: Peter Raeburn," *Songwriting*, September 24, 2012. https://www.songwritingmagazine.co.uk/.
31. Ibid.
32. Ibid.
33. Jay James, Managing Director, Soundtree Music. https://clios.com/clio_juror/nojs/1459.
34. Jagernauth, "Jonathan Glazer."
35. Justin Gerber, "Composer of the Year: Mica Levi," *Consequence of Sound*, December 17, 2014. https://consequenceofsound.net/.
36. Taylor, "Alien Soundscape."
37. *Soundcheck* introduction to podcast, "Mica Levi Gets 'Under the Skin' with Her Unsettling Score," December 29, 2014. https://www.newsounds.org/.
38. "How Mica Levi Got Under the Skin of Her First Soundtrack," *The Guardian*, March 15, 2014. https://www.theguardian.com/.
39. Fitzmaurice, "Glazer and Levi."
40. Tim Grieving, "For Composer Vangelis, a True Story Set in Outer Space," *All Things Considered*, October 17, 2016. Radio. https://www.npr.org/.
41. Gerber, "Composer."
42. Lucy Jones, "Under the Skin of Mica Levi's Masterful Score," NME, March 17, 2014. https://www.nme.com/blogs/.
43. Aimee Cliff, "How to Write an Unforgettable Movie Score, According to Mica Levi," *Fader*, November 14, 2016. http://www.thefader.com.
44. Adrian Rapazzini, "Under Mica Levi's Score," *Interview Magazine*, April 3, 2014. https://www.interviewmagazine.com/.
45. *Soundcheck*, "Mica Levi."
46. Rapazzini, "Mica Levi's Score."
47. "Levi," FilmNation.
48. Taylor, "Alien Soundscape."
49. Chris Douridas, in-person interview with the author, Santa Monica, CA, August 24, 2018. All Douridas quotes in this chapter are from this interview.
50. "Mica Levi Gets 'Under the Skin' with Her Unsettling Score."
51. Jonathan Romney, "Away from the Picture: Mica Levi on Her *Under the Skin* Soundtrack," *Sight and Sound*, September 16, 2016. https://www.bfi.org.uk/.

52. Rapazzini, "Mica Levi's Score."
53. *The Guardian*, "Mica Levi."
54. Schaeffer, "Mica Levi."
55. *Under the Skin* soundtrack.
56. Romney, "Mica Levi."
57. Moulton, "Johnnie Burn."
58. Romney, "Mica Levi."
59. "Glazer," FilmNation.
60. Bobby Brader, in-person interview with the author, Hollywood, December 5, 2017. All Brader quotes in this chapter are from this interview.
61. Jones, "*Under the Skin.*"
62. Ibid.
63. "Sandstorm," performed by Darude, Words and Music by Ricky Ross, Sony/ATV Music Publishing (UK) Ltd. https://www.soundtrack.net/movie/under-the-skin-2014/.
64. "C90," performed by Soundtree, written by Luis Almau and Peter Raeburn, Soundtree Music Publishing Ltd. https://www.soundtrack.net/movie/under-the-skin-2014/.
65. Bray, Film4 Website Interview.
66. Ibid.
67. "Real Gone Kid," performed by Deacon Blue, Words and Music by Ricky Ross, Sony/ATV Music Publishing (UK) Ltd. https://www.soundtrack.net/.
68. Gerber, "Composer."
69. Schaeffer, "Mica Levi."
70. Gerber, "Composer."
71. Schaeffer, "Mica Levi."
72. Ibid.
73. Fitzmaurice, "Glazer and Levi."
74. Jagernauth, "Jonathan Glazer."
75. *The Guardian*, "Mica Levi."
76. "Glazer," FilmNation.
77. Jagernauth, "Jonathan Glazer."
78. Wiseman, "*Under the Skin.*"
79. Nigel M. Smith, "How Jonathan Glazer Got Under the Skin of Scarlett Johansson," *IndieWire*, August 10, 2014. https://www.indiewire.com/.
80. Tobias, "Jonathan Glazer."
81. Smith, "Jonathan Glazer."

Chapter 19

1. Zacharek, *Village Voice*.
2. Jessica Williams, "The Extraterrestrial Woman: Artifice and Violence in *Under the Skin*," B/AS, Journal of Dress Practice, Parsons School of Design, N.Y., 2016.
3. Kris Kristofferson, "The Pilgrim, Chapter 33," © Resaca Music Publishing, song from his album *The Silver-Tongued Devil and I*, Monument Records, 1971.
4. *Arrival*, directed by Denis Villeneuve, written by Eric Heisserer, based on "Story of Your Life" by Ted Chiang, Lava Bear Films, 2016.

Chapter 20

1. Campbell and Glazer, "*Under the Skin.*"
2. Adams, "Space Oddity."
3. Jazmina Berrera, "Claude Glass: the World Is Definitely More Beautiful in Its Reflection." June 18, 2015. http://www.faena.com/aleph/articles/.
4. Ibid.
5. "Rian Johnson," FilmNation.
6. "Peekaboo," *Breaking Bad*, Season 2, Episode 6, directed by Peter Medak, written by J. Roberts, created by Vince Gilligan, AMC, April 12, 2009.
7. Aldous Huxley, *Brave New World* (New York: Harper Perennial, 1932).
8. "Indian Summer," *Mad Men*, Season 1, Episode 11, directed by Tim Hunter, written by Tom Palmer, created by Matthew Weiner, AMC, October 4, 2007.

Chapter 21

1. Johnston, "Science Fiction," 65.
2. David Konow, "Godzilla and the Monsters of Nuclear War," Adam Savage's *Tested*, January 2, 2014. https://www.tested.com/art/movies/.
3. *Invasion of the Body Snatchers*, directed by Don Siegel, written by Daniel Mainwaring, based on a serial by Jack Finney, Walter Wanger Productions, 1956. Film.
4. Johnston, "Science Fiction," 75.
5. *Boys Don't Cry*, directed by Kimberly Peirce, written by Kimberly Peirce and Andy Bienen, Fox Searchlight Pictures, 1999. Film.
6. *The Man Who Fell to Earth*, directed by Nicolas Roeg, written by Paul Mayersberg, based on the novel by Walter Tevis, British Lion Film Corporation, 1976. Film.
7. *Mars Attacks*, directed by Tim Burton, written by Jonathan Gems, based on a trading card series by Len Brown, Woody Gelman, Bob Powell, Norman Saunders, and Wally Wood, Tim Burton Productions, 1996. Film.

8. Matthew Pridham, "Underneath the Skin: John Carpenter's *The Thing* and You," *Weird Fiction Review*, March 25, 2012. http://weirdfictionreview.com/.
9. *The Thing*, directed by John Carpenter, written by Bill Lancaster, based on a story by John W. Campbell, Universal Pictures, 1982. Film.
10. Sonali S. Joshi, "Origin of Life: the Panspermia Theory," *Helix*, December 12, 2008. https://helix.northwestern.edu/.
11. Terrell Clemmons, "Science, Stephen Hawking, and Free Minds," *Cross-Examined*, March 18, 2018. https://crossexamined.org/.
12. Jeremy Kirk, "36 Things We Learned from John Carpenter's *The Thing* Commentary Track," from the DVD commentary with John Carpenter and Kurt Russell, *Film School Rejects*, July 13, 2011. https://filmschoolrejects.com/.
13. Pridham, "Underneath the Skin."
14. "The Monsters Are Due on Maple Street," *The Twilight Zone*, directed by Ron Winston, written by Rod Serling, Cayuga Productions, CBS, March 4, 1960.
15. Kirk, "36 Things."
16. Daniel Kraus, "The Thing That Ate E.T.," *Gadfly Online*, April 15, 2001. http://www.gadflyonline.com/.
17. Lancaster, *The Thing*.
18. *Starman*, directed by John Carpenter, written by Bruce A. Evans and Raynold Gideon, Columbia Pictures, 1984. Film.
19. Ibid.
20. Ibid.
21. Search for Extraterrestrial Intelligence Institute. https://www.seti.org.
22. Evans and Gideon, *Starman*.
23. Ibid.

Chapter 22

1. *Blade Runner*, directed by Ridley Scott, written by Hampton Fancher and David Webb Peoples, based on a novel by Philip K. Dick, the Ladd Company, 1982. Film.
2. Ibid.
3. Ibid.
4. Emmanuel Carrère, *I Am Alive and You Are Dead: A Journey Into the Mind of Philip K. Dick*, translated by Timothy Bent (New York: Henry Holt & Co., 2005), 135.

5. Kevin Jagernauth, "Ridley Scott Explains Why Deckard Is a Replicant," *The Playlist*, October 17, 2017. https://theplaylist.net/.
6. Philip K. Dick, *Do Androids Dream of Electric Sheep?* (New York: Del Rey, 1968), 204.
7. Dick's stories are populated with countless "dystopian Protagonists," driven by their relationship to their society and a compulsion to challenge it—or sometimes driven just by circumstance. The many on film include police chief John Anderton (played by Tom Cruise) in *Minority Report* (2002) and Bob Arctor (Keanu Reeves) in *A Scanner Darkly* (2006). While Deckard fights the State and at least rescues himself (and Rachel) Anderton is more successful (in the film) in that he both rescues the precogs and helps change the unjust system (for the moment). Arctor has the worst lot of the three—he is crushed by the forces that prevail. He doesn't end up dead like Laura, more like Winston Smith in *1984*—neutralized.
8. *Ex Machina*, written and directed by Alex Garland, Universal Pictures, 2014. Film.
9. James Temperton, "Now I Am Become Death, the Destroyer of Worlds: the Story of Oppenheimer's Infamous Quote," *Wired UK*, August 9, 2017. http://www.wired.co.uk/.
10. Ibid.
11. *Michael Clayton*, written and directed by Tony Gilroy, Samuels Media, 2007. Film.
12. Manohla Dargis, "In *Ex Machina*, a Mogul Fashions the Droid of His Dreams," *The New York Times*, April 13, 2015. https://www.nytimes.com/.
13. Huw Fullerton, "Rutger Hauer Dissects His Iconic 'Tears in Rain' Blade Runner Monologue," October 5, 2017. https://www.radiotimes.com/news/film/2017-10-05/blade-runner-tears-in-rain-speech/.
14. Fancher and Peoples, *Blade Runner*.
15. Carrère, "I Am Alive," 138.
16. *Enemy* (screenplay by Javier Gullón) is based on the chilling 2002 novel *O Homem Duplicado* (*The Double*) by Portuguese author José Saramago.
17. *Ghost in the Shell*, directed by Rupert Sanders, written by Jamie Moss, William Wheeler, and Ehren Kruger, based on the comic by Shirow Masamune, Paramount Pictures, 2017. Film.

18. *Sleep Dealer*, directed by Alex Rivera, written by Alex Rivera and David Riker, based on a story by Rivera, Likely Story, 2008.

19. John Sifton, "A Brief History of Drones," *The Nation*, February 7, 2012. https://www.thenation.com/.

20. *Sneakers*, directed by Phil Alden Robinson, written by Robinson, Larry Lasker, and Walter F. Parkes, Universal Pictures, 1992. Film.

21. Dargis, "*Ex Machina*."

22. Heisserer, "Arrival."

23. *Melancholia*, written and directed by Lars von Trier, Zentropa Entertainments, 2011. Film.

24. *Ibid*.

25. Dave Calhoun, "Lars Von Trier: I'm Used to Being Disliked,'" *Time Out London*. https://www.timeout.com/london/film/.

26. Manohla Dargis, "This Is How the End Begins," *The New York Times*, December 30, 2011. https://www.nytimes.com/2012/01/01/movies/.

27. Dargis describes a moment in the overture where "within the frame the blue planet is situated in the same location as Justine's head is in the first shot, and both her head and the planet are roughly the same size, which suggests an affinity between the two."

Epilogue

1. Taylor, "Behind the Scenes."
2. Wiseman, "*Under the Skin*."
3. *Ibid*.
4. Jordan Rosen, "The 30 Most Polarizing Movies of the 21st Century," *Taste Movies*. https://blog.taste.io/.
5. Sarah Szabo, "Movies That People Still Don't Understand," *Looper*. https://www.looper.com/.
6. "Rian Johnson," FilmNation.
7. *Cult Projections*. http://www.cultprojections.com/.
8. *CineInsomnia*, Landmark Theaters, accessed February 26, 2016. https://www.landmarktheatres.com/.
9. *Cult Cinema Bar*. https://www.cultcinemabar.com.au/under-the-skin/.
10. Bray, "*Under the Skin*: Sound Design," Film4.
11. *Under the Skin* featurette, A24. Imdb.com.
12. *Ibid*.
13. Adams, "Space Oddity."

Bibliography

Acker, Melissa. "The Discreet Charm of the Bourgeoisie." *Sense of Cinema*. Cinematheque Annotations on Film. Issue 70. December 2013. http://sensesofcinema.com/2013/cteq/.
Adams, Jill. "Interview with Michel Faber." *The Barcelona Review*. Issue 29. March–April 2009. http://www.barcelonareview.com/29/e_mf_int.htm.
Adams, Sam. "Space Oddity: Jonathan Glazer on *Under the Skin*." *Rolling Stone*. April 4, 2014. https://www.rollingstone.com/movies/.
Arrival. Directed by Denis Villeneuve. Performed by Amy Adams, Jeremy Renner, and Forest Whitaker. Lava Bear Films. 2016. Film.
Badaloni, Luca. "Fifteen Great Nihilistic Movies That Are Worth Your Time." *Taste of Cinema*. June 9, 2015. http://www.tasteofcinema.com/.
Beer, Jeff. "*Under the Skin* Writer Walter Campbell on Epic Ads and Scarlett Johansson as an Alien." *Fast Company*. April 20, 2014. https://www.fastcompany.com/.
Bernstein, Paula. "How DP Daniel Landin Captured Scarlett Johansson's Alien Nature in *Under the Skin*." *IndieWire*. April 2, 2014. https://www.indiewire.com/.
Bhattacharya, Sanjiv. "Scarlett in Bloom." *New York Magazine*. Spring Fashion edition. 2004. http://nymag.com/nymetro/shopping/fashion/spring04/.
Billson, Anne. "How Scarlett Johansson Got Interesting." *The Telegraph*. November 19, 2013.
Birth. Directed by Jonathan Glazer. Performed by Nicole Kidman, Cameron Bright, Danny Huston, and Lauren Bacall. New Line Cinema. 2004. Film.
Blade Runner. Directed by Ridley Scott. Performed by Harrison Ford, Sean Young, Edward James Olmos, et al. the Ladd Company. 1982. Film.
Block, Bruce. *The Visual Story: Creating the Visual Structure of Film, TV, and Digital Media*. New York: Taylor & Francis, 2007.
Bray, Catherine. *Film4 Website Interview, Under the Skin*. Accessed May 14, 2014. Film4.com.
The Brother from Another Planet. Directed by John Sayles. Performed by Joe Morton, Daryl Edwards, and Rosanna Carter. Anarchist's Convention Films. 1984. Film.
Calhoun, Dave. "Guinness Was Good for Him." *The Guardian*. October 4, 2004. https://www.theguardian.com/.
Campbell, Walter, and Jonathan Glazer. *Under the Skin*. Film Script. Based on the novel by Michael Faber. July 10, 2008.
Carrère, Emmanuel. *I Am Alive and You Are Dead: A Journey Into the Mind of Philip K. Dick*. Translated by Timothy Bent. New York: Henry Holt & Co., 2005.
Cavagna, Carlo. "Profile and Interview: Scarlett Johansson." February 2004. http://www.aboutfilm.com/features/girlwithapearlearring/johansson.html.
Chase, Andrea. "*Match Point*." Film Review. *Killer Movie Reviews*. https://www.killermoviereviews.com/movie/match-point/.
Chesterfield, Tanya. "A Love Song for Bobby Long." Film Review. *Film Forward*. December 29, 2004. http://film-forward.com/.

Clemmons, Terrell. "Science, Stephen Hawking, and Free Minds." *Cross-Examined.* March 18, 2018. https://crossexamined.org/.
Cliff, Amy. "How to Write an Unforgettable Movie Score, According to Mica Levi." *Fader.* November 14, 2016. http://www.thefader.com.
Cox, David. "Interview: Jonathan Glazer on *Under the Skin*." Film4 Channel. March 18, 2014. https://www.youtube.com/watch?v=hZUvIfXKVVc.
Cumbrow, Robert C. "Why Is This Film Called *Birth*? Investigating Jonathan Glazer's Mystery of the Heart." *Slant Magazine.* October 28, 2008. https://www.slantmagazine.com/h.
Dargis, Manohla. "In *Ex Machina*, a Mogul Fashions the Droid of His Dreams." *The New York Times.* April 13, 2015. https://www.nytimes.com/.
Dargis, Manohla. "This Is How the End Begins." *The New York Times.* December 30, 2011. https://www.nytimes.com/.
Dick, Philip K. *Do Androids Dream of Electric Sheep?* New York: Del Rey, 1968.
Doyle, Sady. "*Under the Skin*'s Weird Feminism." *In These Times.* April 13, 2014. http://inthesetimes.com/article/16554/.
Ebert, Roger. "The War Zone." Film Review. January 14, 2000. https://www.rogerebert.com/.
Eggert, Brian. "*Sexy Beast*." *Deep Focus Review.* April 12, 2014. https://deepfocusreview.com/.
Ex Machina. Directed by Alex Garland. Performed by Oscar Isaac, Alicia Vikander, and Domhnall Gleeson. Universal Pictures. 2014. Film.
Faber, Michel. *Under the Skin.* London: Harcourt, Inc., 2000.
Feinberg, Lexi. "*Match Point* Review." *Cinema Blend.* https://www.cinemablend.com/.
Film4 Channel. *Interview with Jonathan Glazer.*
Firecloud, Johnny. "Flashback: Thom York Explains 'Street Spirit,' Breaks Our Hearts." *Antiquiet.* June 2, 2012. http://antiquiet.com/music/2012/06/.
Fitzmaurice, Larry. "Jonathan Glazer and Mica Levi." *Pitchfork.* March 31, 2014. https://pitchfork.com/.
Follows, Stephen. *Film Data and Education.* https://stephenfollows.com/how-the-bfi-awarded-129million/.
Foulston, Jonathan. "The Sound of *Under the Skin* and *The Lobster*: An Interview with Johnnie Burn." Scribed. September 11, 2014. https://www.scribd.com/document/318218299/.
Fullerton, Huw. "Rutger Hauer Dissects His Iconic 'Tears in Rain' *Blade Runner* Monologue." October 5, 2017. https://www.radiotimes.com/.
Gerber, Justin. "Composer of the Year: Mica Levi." *Consequence of Sound.* December 17, 2014. https://consequenceofsound.net/.
Ghost in the Shell. Directed by Rupert Sanders. Performed by Scarlett Johansson, Pilou Asbaek, and Takeshi Kitano. Paramount Pictures. 2017. Film.
Ghost World. Directed by Terry Zwigoff. Performed by Thora Birch, Scarlett Johansson, and Steve Buscemi. United Artists. 2001. Film.
Gilbey, Ryan. "Isserley, Penelope Cruz, and the Slow Gestation of *Under the Skin*." *New Statesman.* March 11, 2014. https://www.newstatesman.com/culture/.
Girl with a Pearl Earring. Directed by Peter Webber. Performed by Colin Firth and Scarlett Johansson. Lions Gate Films. 2003. Film.
Glazer, Jonathan. Interview by David Poland. "Jonathan Glazer Talks Under the Skin." *DP/Short Ends: An Oral History of Hollywood.* September 27, 2013. https://www.youtube.com/watch?v=qv09JMu7FrM.
Golembewski, Vanessa. Interview with Scarlett Johansson. *Refinery 29.* April 4, 2014. www.refinery29.com/.
Gonzalez, Ed. "Lost in Translation." *Slant Magazine.* August 19, 2003. https://www.slantmagazine.com/film/review/lost-in-translation.
Grieving, Tim. "For Composer Vangelis, a True Story Set in Outer Space." *All Things Considered.* NPR. October 17, 2016.
Her. Directed by Spike Jonze. Performed by Joaquin Phoenix and Scarlett Johansson. Annapurna Pictures, 2013. Film.

"How Mica Levi Got Under the Skin of Her First Soundtrack." *The Guardian.* March 15, 2014. https://www.theguardian.com/.

Howell, Jake. "*The Torontonian* Reviews *Under the Skin.*" *Movie City News.* September 15, 2013. http://moviecitynews.com/.

Hughes, April-Rae. "The Importance of Production Design." Lift-Off Festival. September 4, 2017. https://www.lift-off-festivals.com/.

Invasion of the Body Snatchers. Directed by Don Siegel. Performed by Kevin McCarthy and Dana Wynter. Walter Wanger Productions, 1956. Film.

Jagernauth, Kevin. "Jonathan Glazer Talks the Guerilla Shoot of His Bold *Under the Skin* Starring Scarlett Johansson." *IndieWire.* September 12, 2013. https://www.indiewire.com/.

Jagernauth, Kevin. "Ridley Scott Explains Why Deckard Is a Replicant." *The Playlist.* October 17, 2017. https://theplaylist.net/.

Johansson, Scarlett. Interview by David Poland. *DP/30 Short Ends: An Oral History of Hollywood.* September 27, 2013. https://www.youtube.com/watch?v=daz32KlPD0s.

Johnston, Keith M. *Science Fiction Film: A Critical Introduction.* London: Bloomsbury Publishing, 2011. First Published by Berg.

Jones, Lucy. "Under the Skin of Mica Levi's Masterful Score." NME. March 17, 2014. https://www.nme.com/blogs/.

Joshi, Sonali S. "Origin of Life: The Panspermia Theory." *Helix.* December 12, 2008. https://helix.northwestern.edu/.

Kane, Patricia, and Chris Hastings. "I Was Seduced by Scarlett Johansson Disguised as an Alien." *The Daily Mail.* March 16, 2014. http://www.dailymail.co.uk/.

Kaufman, Anthony. "Shooting the Beast: Jonathan Glazer Tames the Gangster Genre." *Indiewire.* Jun 12, 2001. https://www.indiewire.com/.

Kermode, Mark. "Woody Allen: David Lean Lecture." BAFTA Archives. 2005. https://www.youtube.com/watch?v=5k893r-wdfc.

Kidman, Nicole, and Jonathan Glazer. Interview by Charlie Rose. October 28, 2004. https://charlierose.com/videos/15613.

Kirk, Jeremy. "36 Things We Learned from John Carpenter's *The Thing* Commentary Track." *Film School Rejects.* July 13, 2011. https://filmschoolrejects.com/.

Koehler, Michael. "Editor's Pick of the Month: *Under the Skin.*" Lights Film School. https://www.lightsfilmschool.com/blog/editors-pick-of-the-month-under-the-skin.

Konow, David. "Godzilla and the Monsters of Nuclear War." Adam Savage's *Tested.* January 2, 2014. https://www.tested.com/.

Koresky, Michael. "A History of Reference: Woody Allen's Match Point." *IndieWire.* December 2, 2005. https://www.indiewire.com/.

Kraus, Daniel. "The Thing That Ate E.T." *Gadfly Online.* April 15, 2001. http://www.gadflyonline.com/.

Lane, Anthony. "*Ghost in the Shell* and *Graduation.*" Film Review. *The New Yorker.* April 10, 2017.

Leigh, Danny. "*Under the Skin*: Why Did This Chilling Masterpiece Take a Decade?" *The Guardian.* March 6, 2014.

Levi, Mica. Interview by John Schaeffer. "Mica Levi Gets 'Under the Skin' with Her Unsettling Score." *Soundcheck.* New York Public Radio. December 29, 2014. Podcast. https://www.newsounds.org/.

Lim, Dennis. "Cinematographer Harris Savides on Trust, Birth, and Invisible Light." *The Village Voice.* October 26, 2004.

Lost in Translation. Directed by Sofia Coppola. Performed by Bill Murray and Scarlett Johansson. Focus Features. 2003. Film.

A Love Song for Bobby Long. Directed by Shainee Gabel. Performed by John Travolta, Scarlett Johansson, and Gabriel Macht. Lions Gate Films. 2004. Film.

Mallinson, Harriet. "The Ghost Rider Caught…" *Daily Mail Online.* February 26, 2016. http://www.dailymail.co.uk/news/article-3465842/.

The Man Who Fell to Earth. Directed by Nicolas Roeg. Performed by David Bowie, Candy Clarke, and Rip Torn. British Lion Film Corporation, 1976. Film.
Match Point. Directed by Woody Allen. Performed by Jonathan Rhys-Myers and Scarlett Johansson. BBC Films, 2004. Film.
McCann, Nuala. "McWilliams Is Bad Man on Mission for Scarlett Johansson." BBC News. March 20, 2014. https://www.bbc.com/news/uk-northern-ireland-26660354.
Melancholia. Directed by Lars von Trier. Performed by Kirsten Dunst, Charlotte Gainsbourg, and Kiefer Sutherland. Zentropa Entertainments, 2011. Film.
Messer, John. "Grisly Tale Is More Than Skin Deep." Review of *Under the Skin*. *BookPage*. September 2000. https://bookpage.com/reviews/1523.
Michael Clayton. Directed by Tony Gilroy. Performed by George Clooney, Tilda Swinton, and Tom Wilkinson. Samuels Media, 2007. Film.
Moulton, Jack. "Interview: *Under the Skin*'s Sound Designer Johnnie Burn on Creating Sounds You've Never Heard Before." Awards Circuit. January 6, 2015. http://www.awardscircuit.com/.
O'Brien, Geoffrey. "Ways of Being Alien." *New York Review of Books*. *NYR Daily*. May 9, 2014.
Palm Pictures Directors Label Series: *The Work of Director Jonathan Glazer*. DVD and booklet. 2005. Produced by Juliette Larthe and Richard Brown. Series created by Spike Jonze, Michel Gondry, and Chris Cunningham.
Perez, Rodrigo. "Spike Jonze Talks About Working with Scarlett Johansson on *Her*, Arcade Fire, and Intellect Vs. Intuition." *IndieWire*. December 19, 2013. https://www.indiewire.com/.
Phillips, Michael. "*Under the Skin* Review." *The Chicago Tribune*. April 10, 2014. http://articles.chicagotribune.com/.
Pridham, Matthew. "Underneath the Skin: John Carpenter's *The Thing* and You." *Weird Fiction Review*. March 25, 2012. http://weirdfictionreview.com.
Rapazzini, Adrian. "Under Mica Levi's Score," *Interview* Magazine, April 3, 2014. https://www.interviewmagazine.com/.
Robey, Tim. "*You Were Never Really Here* Review: Joaquin Phoenix's Feel-Bad Vigilante Thriller Will Blow You Away." *The Telegraph*. March 8, 2018. https://www.telegraph.co.uk/films/.
Romney, Jonathan. "Away from the Picture: Mica Levi on Her *Under the Skin* Soundtrack." Sight and Sound. September 16, 2016. https://www.bfi.org.uk/.
Romney, Jonathan. "Film of the Week: *Under the Skin*." *Film Comment*. April 3, 2014. https://www.filmcomment.com/.
Rose, Charlie. "Lost in Translation: Interview with Scarlett Johansson." 2003. https://www.youtube.com/watch?v=iF6_mlax_zE.
Rosen, Jordan. "The 30 Most Polarizing Movies of the 21st Century." *Taste Movies*. https://blog.taste.io/.
Ross, Tessa. Interview by Zoë Ball following BAFTA Ceremony. February 2013. https://www.youtube.com/watch?v=1wfof5XkkD8.
Saldana, Selena and Sarah Jarvis. Production Notes. FilmNation. https://static1.squarespace.com/.
Salovaara, Sarah. "The One-Cam: *Under the Skin*'s Customized CCD Camera." *Filmmaker Magazine*. April 30, 2014. https://filmmakermagazine.com/85795.
Sexy Beast. Directed by Jonathan Glazer. Performed by Ray Winstone and Ben Kingsley. Recorded Picture Company, 2000. Film.
Slater, Aaron Slater. "Music for Film & TV Part I: Peter Raeburn." *Songwriting*. September 24, 2012. https://www.songwritingmagazine.co.uk/.
Sleep Dealer. Directed by Alex Rivera. Performed by Luis Fernando Peña, Metztli Adamina, and Jose Concépción Macias. Likely Story, 2008. Film.
Smith, Nigel. "How Jonathan Glazer Got Under the Skin of Scarlett Johansson." IndieWire. August 10, 2014. https://www.indiewire.com/.
Sneakers. Directed by Phil Alden Robinson. Performed by Robert Redford, David Strathairn, and Sidney Poitier. Universal Pictures, 1992. Film.

Starman. Directed by John Carpenter. Jeff Bridges, Karen Allen, and Charles Martin Smith. Columbia Pictures, 1984. Film.
Stern, Marlow. "Sofia Coppola Discusses *Lost in Translation* on Its 10th Anniversary." *The Daily Beast.* September 12, 2013. https://www.thedailybeast.com/.
Stitch, Daisy. "*Under the Skin*: Scarlett Johansson Is Unrecognisable in Shaggy Wig and Fur Coat." *My Daily Mail.* November 7, 2013. https://www.huffingtonpost.co.uk/2013/07/11/.
Sutin, Lawrence. *Divine Invasions: A Life of Philip K. Dick.* New York: Citadel, 1991.
Szabo, Sarah. "Movies That People Still Don't Understand." *Looper.* https://www.looper.com/.
Taylor, Trey. "Behind the Scenes of *Under the Skin*." March 12, 2014. http://www.dazeddigital.com/.
Taylor, Trey. "How to Create an Alien Soundscape." *Dazed Digital.* March 12, 2014. http://www.dazeddigital.com/artsandculture/article/19187/.
Temperton, James. "Now I Am Become Death, the Destroyer of Worlds: The Story of Oppenheimer's Infamous Quote." *Wired UK.* August 9, 2017. http://www.wired.co.uk/.
The Thing. Directed by John Carpenter. Performed by Kurt Russell, Wilford Brimley, and T. K. Carter. Universal Pictures, 1982. Film.
Tobias, Scott. "Jonathan Glazer on *Under the Skin*'s Complex Honesty." *The Dissolve.* April 4, 2014. https://thedissolve.com/features/.
The Twilight Zone. Created by Rod Serling. Cayuga Productions: CBS, 1959–64. Television series.
Under the Skin. Directed by Jonathan Glazer. Performed by Scarlett Johansson, Michael Moreland, Jeremy McWilliams, and Adam Pearson. Film4, 2011. Film.
Valdez, Gabriel Diego. "An Interview with Michel Faber, Author of *Under the Skin*." June 6, 2014. https://basilmarinerchase.wordpress.com/2014/06/06/.
Vizard, Sarah. "Guinness's 'Surfer' Ad Didn't Do That Well in Research but 'We Ignored It.'" *Marketing Week.* June 13, 2018. https://www.marketingweek.com/.
Webber, Peter. Interview by Carloa Cavagna. January 2004.
Wigley, Samuel. "Film of the Week: *Under the Skin*." *Sight and Sound Magazine.* June 29, 2015. https://www.bfi.org.uk/news-opinion/sight-sound-magazine/.
Wigon, Zachary. "The Toenail of the Curve: Remembering Harris Savides." *Filmmaker Magazine.* October 12, 2012.
Wise, Damon. "Rian Johnson Introduces *Under the Skin*." BFI Screen Epiphanies. http://www.filmnation.com/.
Wiseman, Andreas. "*Under the Skin*: At Any Cost." *Screen Daily.* March 24, 2014. https://www.screendaily.com/.
Zacharek, Stephanie. "*Under the Skin* Is Alluring, Creepy, and Great." *The Village Voice.* April 2, 2013. https://www.villagevoice.com/.

Interviews

Addica, Milo. In person. Santa Monica, CA. November 20, 2017.
Albermaniche, Nigel. Phone. September 25, 2017.
Beveridge, Chrissie. Phone. March 18, 2018.
Bluemhuber, Claudia. Phone. February 23, 2018.
Brader, Bobby. In person. Hollywood, CA. December 5, 2017.
Burn, Johnnie. Email. June 26, 2018.
Calder, Neil. Phone. May 2018.
Campbell, Walter. Phone. July 16, 2018.
Carrière, Jean-Claude. Phone. May 10, 2018.
Crawford, Kahleen. Email. September 22, 2017.
Debenham, Tom. Phone. March 27, 2018.
Douridas, Chris. In person. Santa Monica, CA. August 24, 2018.
Duric, Simon. Email. April 4, 2018.

Gaynes, Edmund. In person. Hollywood, CA. April 14, 2018.
Heckstall-Smith, Nick. Email. June 3, 2018.
Herrera, Angel. In person. North Hollywood, CA. September 25, 2018.
Jenkins, Jane. Email. December 22, 2017.
Josephs, Tracey. Phone. March 8, 2018.
Mance, Jessica. Email. May 13, 2018.
McConnell, Kate. Phone. April 18, 2018.
Milne, Gareth. Phone. June 11, 2018.
Morham, Fiona. Email. March 20, 2018.
Murdoch, Mark. Email. June 4, 2018.
O'Neal, Alexander. Phone. April 4, 2018.
Strange, Eugene. Phone. March 1, 2018.
Watts, Paul. In person. London. September 12, 2014.
Wechsler, Nick. Phone. August 14, 2018.

Index

A82 roadway 152
Abbott, Mead and Vickers AMV-BBDO 64
Ablach Farm 78, 94, 97
Academy Awards, Oscars 74, 114
Academy Films 59, 65
Acker, Melissa 73
Action Underwater Studios 142–143
Acton, Dave 52, 122, 159–160
Adams, Amy 189
Adams, Sam 232
Addica, Milo 74–75; *Birth* 71–72, 74–76; *Under the Skin* 74, 91–93
Adjani, Isabelle 73
ads *see* Glazer, Jonathan
"Adventures of Prince Achmed" 183
aesthetic(s) 1, 17, 37, 52, 90, 96, 117–118 178, 187, 227
AI *see* artificial intelligence
Albarn, Damon 59
Albermaniche, Nigel 131–132, 137, 140, 148, 169
aleatoric music, notation 176
ALEXA camera 131
Alien (film) 46, 211, 217
alien couple 94
alien faces her "self" 118
alien form 35–36, 55–56, 95–97, 163
alien space, environment 16, 142, 169
alienation 1, 12
allegory 80, 94
Allen, Karen 209
Allen, Woody 106, 124
Almodovar, Pedro 73
ambiguity 142
American Film Market 116
Anatomy of a Movie 27
Anderson, Bibi 73
Andrew (character) 23–25, 86, 98
androids *see* artificial intelligence
anechoic chamber 169
Ankner, Mark 111
ant and fly 9, 36, 194
anthropocentric 81, 222

anthropomorphic 82
Antonietta (film) 73
Antonioni, Michelangelo (films) 3
apartheid 201
apocalypse 201
Arbroath 28, 138–139
Arclight Theater, Hollywood 230
Arctor, Bob 42
Arnolfini Portrait 191
Aronofsky, Darren 91
Around the Moon (novel) 198
Arri ALEXA camera 131
Arrival (film) 116, 189, 222–223, 225, 229
art director 29; *see also* O'Sullivan, Emer
artificial intelligence 21, 30, 77, 109, 187, 210, 212–218
Artists and Engineers 133
Ashcroft, Richard 62
Asylum, special effects 144–147, 160–161
atomic bomb 198, 216
atonal 178
Attack of the Crab Monsters (film) 2, 195, 198
Attack the Block (film) 115
Auchmithie 138–139
Auntie Mame (film) 100
Aurora Borealis 9
Avengers: Age of Ultra (film) 153

Babenco, Hector 73
baby on beach 18–20, 37
Bacall, Lauren 69, 103, 107
Bacon, Francis 25
Bad (character) 7, 9, 20, 30, 38, 42, 48, 54, 57, 96, 122, 12–127, 147, 150, 176, 190–191
Badaloni, Luca 107
BAFTA British Academy of Film and Television Arts 115
bagpipes 177
balaclava, silicone 163
Balcon, Michael, award 115
ballet 25, 60
Baroque art 118

257

Index

Barrerra, Jazmina 191
Barrett, Helen 153, 158
Barry Lyndon (film) 62
Basildon 142–143
Basner, Glen 116
Battleship Potemkin (film) 20
Baumbach, Noah 70
BBC 157
beach sequence 18–20, 88, 138–139
"beehive," in Levi score 176
Belle du Jour (film) 73
Bergman, Ingmar 73, 169
Beveridge, Chrissie 11, 127–128, 153, 158, 160–161
BFI (British Film Institute) 93, 115–117, 165, 180
Bhagavad-Gita 216
Bhattacharya, Sanjiv 100
Biggar, Scotland 171
bikers, alien 14, 49–50
Billy Elliot (film) 115
binary 174, 181, 184, 195; *see also* duality; juxaposition
Birch, Thora 101
Bird, Ivan 65, 67
Birdman (film) 229
Birth (film) 60, 68–76, 90, 92–93, 169, 172, 191
black alien 55; *see also* alien form
black and white cinematography 60–62, 193
Black Leather Jackets (TV episode) 38
Black Magic Woman (song) 179
black mirror, Claude glass 191
Black Mirror (TV show) 191
Black Mountain Estate 152
black space, black water 15–119, 22–24, 35–36, 41, 56, 65, 78, 88, 95–98, 131, 138–142–144, 144–147, 163, 229
Black Widow 100, 109
Blade Runner (1982 film) 77, 173, 212–214, 216–217, 219
Blade Runner 2049 (film) 219
Blanchett, Kate 114
Block, Bruce 67
Blondell, Joan 101
Bluemhuber, Claudia 116, 136, 141, 228
Blunt, Emily 36
Blur (band) 59, 63
body scanning 160
Borgars, Jenny 93
Bosch, Hieronymus 118
bothy 92, 155–156, 168
Bowie, David 168, 172, 202–205
Boyd, Charles 194
Boyle, Danny 114–115
Boys Don't Cry (film) 201
Brader, Bobby 176, 178
Brannigan, Paul 22, 25, 140, 145
Brave New World (novel) 195
Breaking Bad (TV series) 194
Breaking the Waves (film) 172

Brewster, Carol 3
Bridges, Jeff 209–210
Bright, Cameron 69, 71
Brimley, Wilford 209
British crime film genre 66, 68
British Film Institute, BFI 115–116
British Screen 112
The Brother from Another Planet (film) 199
Browell, Steve 170
Bruegel, Pieter, the elder 118, 224
Buchanan Galleries 127–128, 170
budgets 111–113, 115–116, 130–31, 144
Bug (film) 229
Bunuel, Luis 73
Burgess, Anthony 60
Burn, Johnnie 24, 110, 149, 165, 169–171, 173, 175–176, 179–180, 231–232
burn suit 144
Burton, Livia 128
bus driver (character) 44, 153

C90 (music) 177
CAA, Creative Artists Agency 111
Cabana, Donald A. 74
CAD, computer added design 161
Cage, John 173
cake scene 42
Calder, Neil 131, 134, 145, 156–158, 165
Camden 165
Campbell, John W. 206–207
Campbell, Walter ads 60, 64–65; *Birth* 75; *Under the Skin* 93–99, 110–112, 118, 123, 140, 169
Campbell-Hughes, Antonia 233
Caplan, Lizzy 219
Caplan, Sally Ann 93
"capture theme" 13–14, 16, 23, 35, 38, 41, 55, 175
La Caravelle, restaurant 70
Carol (film) 114
Carpenter, John 206–209
Carrère, Emmanuel 217
Carriere, Jean-Claude 71, 73–75
Carroll, Simon 170
Carruth, Shane 229
Carty, Tom 64, 169
Casa de los Babys (film) 200
Cassandra's Dream (film) 106
Cassidy, Joanna 213
cast, hand 160
casting 120–123
casting director 120
castles 154; *see also* Tantallon
Cat-Women of the Moon (film) 2
Catherine wheel 152–153, 171
Cave, Nick, and the Bad Seeds (band) 62–64
CCD, charge-coupled device 130
Celtic Football Club 12, 134–135
Celtic Park 134–135
CGI, computer generated imagery 161

Chagall, Marc 66
Changes (song) 172
Changing Faces 123
Channel 4 114–115, 230
Channel Four Films 114
Charlie the dog 153
"charting her drift" 47, 97, 167
Chase, Andrea 108
Chesterfield, Tanya 104
Chevalier, Tracy 102
Chiang, Ted 222
Children of Men (film) 195, 220
Chinatown (film) 108, 173
Chinese Box (film) 73
Chopped and Screwed (LP) 173
CineInsomnia 230
cinematography 18, 70, 127, 130; *see also* Landin, Daniel
cinematographywww 70
Circle of Deceit (film) 73
Claire, *Melancholia* 223–224
Clark, Candy 204
Clarke, Roger 69
Claude glass 191
A Clockwork Orange (film) 60, 65
Clowes, Daniel 101
Club Earth 140
CNC, computer numeric control 160–161
Coen Bros. 110
color, use of 60
Collins, Chris 115, 165
commercials *see* Glazer, Jonathan
completion bond, completion guarantor 130, 134
composer *see* Levi, Mica
computer graphics 142
Cooper, Tommy 46
Contardi, Bill 91
Coppola, Sofia 102–103
co-producer 130
Cornish, Joe 115
Cornwall, England 64, 96
cosmic ancestry 206
County Antrim 122
Covent Garden Hotel, London 75
covert shooting *see* hidden cameras
Coxon, Graham 60
coyotec 218
Crane, Walter 64
Cranston, Bryan 194
Crawford, Kahleen 35, 120–123, 150–151, 159, 230
Creation, by Levi 175
Creative Scotland 116
Creature from the Black Lagoon (film) 198
Croupier (film) 114
Crowe, Cameron 4
Cruise, Tom 36
The Crying Game (film) 114
Cuba 219

Culkin, Macauley 101
Cult Cinema Bar 230
Cult Projections 230
cult status, cult film 230
Curtis, Mark 144, 146
cybraceros 218
cymbal roll 174, 176
Czech Republic 18

Daldry, Stephen 115
Dalsa camera 130
Damon, Matt 127
Dancer in the Dark (film) 91
Daniels, Lee 74–75
Dargis, Manohla 216, 224
Darude 177
Darwin, Charles 83
David, Keith 208
The Day After Tomorrow (film) 195
Deacon Blue (band) 47, 177
Deacon Blues (song) 48
Dead Man Walking (film) 74
de Armas, Ana 219
Death at Midnight (book) 74
Debenham, Tom 124–127, 130, 134, 138, 140–141, 144–146, 148, 152, 158, 161, 163, 230–231
Debenham's Department Store 127, 169
Deckard, Rick (character) 77, 212–214
Deer Park Golf Club 28
Deneuve, Catherine 73
depression 223–224
Desplat, Alexandre 68, 70
dialectic 1, 4, 5, 13, 106, 108, 183, 209, 212–214; *see also* binary; juxtaposition
dichotomy 214
Dick, Philip K. 42, 212–214, 217–218
digital imaging 131, 160–161
Dinnett, Laura 159
The Discreet Charm of the Bourgeoisie (film) 73
dissonace (music) 178
District 9 (film) 199
divers 145
Do Androids Dream of Electrics Sheep? (novel) 212–214, 217–218
documentary technique 12
Dogville (film) 229
Dollard, Ann 91
Don Jon 110
Donoghue, Emma 114
Douridas, Chris 174, 177
Downham, Ed 170
Doyle, Sady 46
Drimsynie Forest 120
drone 220
Drugstore Cowboy (film) 91
duality 36, 67, 184
Ducati 126
dummy cameras 140
Dunst, Kirsten 223

Duric, Simon 118, 230
Dymond, Scott 28–29, 147
dystopia 77, 214, 219–221
dystopian protagonist 214

Earth *see* Club Earth
Ebert, Roger 92
Echo Park, CA 74
Edge of Tomorrow (film) 36, 218
Edinburg University 28
editing 138, 147, 152, 165-171, 179–180; *see also* Watts, Paul
Eggert, Brian 66, 68
electronica (music) 177
Elstree Studios 142, 165
empathy, theme 87, 213
Enemy (film) 217
engineering (visual effects) 161
England 59
environment(s) 24, 41, 117, 137, 141–142, 145, 179, 220
E.T. (film) 46
Ex Machina (film) 214–216
executive producer 115
experimental filmmaking 147
exposition 90, 167, 211
Extinction (film) 218–219
extraterrestrials 75, 78, 201
eyes (motif) 6, 7, 28, 30, 190
Eyes Wide Shut (film) 173

Faber, Michel 4, 15, 64, 77, 81–82, 85, 87–89, 91–92, 94, 127, 220
Fahrenheit 451 (film) 40, 195
Fanning, Elle 70
fantasy 108
Faris, Anna 104
Fassbinder, Rainer Werner 73
Feinberg, Lexi 107
Feldman, Morton 173
femme fatale 16, 23, 41, 45, 80, 185
Fennel, Andrew 64
Field, Tim 165
film editor *see* Watts, Paul
Film Finances Inc. 131, 165, 168
Film4 91–92, 112–116, 126, 130–131, 230
Film Four Limited aka Film Four International or Channel Four Films 114, 116
film language 92
film noir 16
Filmmaker Magazine 70
FilmNation 116
The Filth and the Fury (film) 91
fire gel 163
first assistant director 128, 131 158–160; *see also* Heckstall-Smith, Nick
first contact 91
The First Men in the Moon (story) 198
Firth, Colin 102, 105
Fisher, Carrie 101

Fitzmaurice, Larry 173
Fleischer, Richard 202
flesh-eating aliens 92
flower vendor scene 27
flute 176
The Fly (films) 38
foley, sound 169, 171
football crowd scene 12, 134–135
Footballer (character) 14, 16, 29, 96, 98, 138, 166
Forbidden Planet (1958 film) 2, 159
Ford, Faith 101
Ford, Harrison 212–214
Ford, John 41
Forman, Milos 73
Forsyth, Bill 3
Fox Searchlight 91
Frankenstein (film) 195, 198
Frears, Stephen 113
Frida Theater 231
From Here to Eternity (film) 211
The Full Monty (film) 91

Gabel, Shainee 104–106
Gainsbourg, Charlotte 223–224
Game of Thrones (TV series) 164
Gandhi, Mohandas 60
Gangster No. 1 (play) 66
gap finance 116
Garland, Alex 214–215
Garland, Judy 100
GATTACA (film) 195, 219
Gaynes, Edmund 103
gender 49, 107, 184–185
genocide 82
genre 7, 90, 95, 109, 188
Ghost in the Shell (1995 film) 109, 173, 2018
Ghost in the Shell (2017 film) 109, 169, 218
"Ghost Rider" 122
Ghost World (film and book) 101–103
Gilroy, Tony 216
girl in white space *see* Highway Woman
Girl with the Pearl Earring (film) 101
Glasgow 12, 13, 17, 47, 61, 65, 78, 83, 117- 119, 123–124, 126-9, 132, 134–135, 140, 147–148, 152, 154, 156, 165, 168–169, 171, 176–177
Glasgow English, Glaswegian 13
Glaswegians 121, 137, 169–71
Glazer, Jonathan 43, 63, 164, 230–231; ads and music videos 59–65, 90; aesthetics 118; alien on fire 164; *Birth* 68–76, 92; black space 23, 142; casting 32, 110, 113, 120–124; cinematography 32; dialogue 28; direction 12, 15, 17, 20, 23, 32, 41, 47, 56, 142, 148, 157, 230; editing 165–167, 172; education 59; environments 145; final scene 163–164; Glasgow 119; hidden filming 131–132, 134; inspection scene 190; Johansson 6, 12, 110, 121, 124, 148, 231; Laura 4, 12, 19, 28, 110, 117, 124, 127, 147, 151–152, 163–164; Laura

and Lonely 151; locations 119, 138, 154; novel 80, 82, 87–88; opening credits 116; people 119; release 228; score 5, 172–3, 175, 177–80; Scotland 119; script 28, 47, 90, 93–94, 99, 112–113; *Sexy Beast* 66–68; sound design 169, 171; storm 156–159
"Glazer effect" 231
"Glazered" 231
Gleeson, Domhnall 214
glissando 178
Godzilla (film) 195, 198
Golembewski, Vanessa 19
Golden State (film) 200
Goodfellow, Gerry 44, 153
Goodge Street 148
GoPro camera 130
Gordon-Levitt, Joseph 110
Gosling, Ryan 219
La Grande Illusion (film) 152
The Great Gatsby (book and film) 108
The Green Mile (film) 74
green screen 142
Greenwich Village 101
Greenwood, Johnny 61
Groundhog Day (film) 147
The Guardian 125
Guildhall School 173
Guinness (ads) 64–65, 169, 172
Guinness (beer) 64
Gyllenhaal, Jake 217

Hádek, Krystof 18, 145–146
Hahn, Hilary 69
Hail, Caesar! (film) 108
hair design *see* makeup and hair design
hair punching 161
HAL 9000 218
Hamilton, Des 123
Hamilton, Warren 231
Handel, George Frideric 62
Hanks, Tom 74
Hannah, Daryl 212
The Happening (film) 195
Harlem, NY 199
Hauer, Rutger 214
Hawke, Ethan 110
Hawking, Stephen 206
Hawkins, Sally 35
Hawks, Howard 206
Haynes, Todd 114
head cast 160
Heckstall-Smith, Nick 128, 131–132, 135, 138–139, 141, 150, 156–158, 162, 167
heptapods 222
Her (film) 109, 216
Herrera, Angel 8, 154, 193
Herrmann, Bernard 173
He's Just Not That Into You (film) 108
hidden cameras and mikes 12, 117, 123, 127, 133–135, 137, 140–141, 164, 171

Highlands, Scotland *see* Scottish Highlands
Highsmith, Patricia 114
"highway woman" 7, 8, 126
Hindi 114
Hinduism 216
Hiroshima 198
Hitchcock, Alfred 173
hitchhiking 78, 83–85, 87, 92
Hodges, Mike 113
Hodgson, Ruth 165, 167, 172
Holbein, Hans 191
Holloway Road 113
horror 16, 80, 87, 91, 96, 183, 188, 206, 228; *see also* genre; tropes
The Horse Whisperer (film) 101
The Horses of Neptune (painting) 64
The Host (film) 116
Houllevigue, Jan 67
House Un-American Activities Committee, HUAC 198
Howard, James Newton 69
Howell, Jake 15
Howell, Stuart 127, 140
The Hunger (film) 115, 202
Hunky Dory LP 172
Hunters in the Snow, painting 224
Hurt, John 224
Huston, Danny 69, 72, 172
Huxley, Aldous 218
hydraulic platform 144

Ibrox 126, 135
"Ice Skating Priests," ad 63
icpathua toggle 78, 84–85
idee fixe 23
illustrations 118
The Incredible Shrinking Man (film) 2
Independent Spirit Awards 92
IndieWire 229
Industry Entertainment 91
Inland Empire (film) 229
"inspection" scene 30, 147, 149, 190, 192
Interiors (film) 106
Into My Arms (music video) 62–64
Invaders from Mars (film) 2, 207
Invasion of the Body Snatchers (1956 film) 2, 95, 199, 207
inventing a camera 128–131
investors 115–116
Ireland 96
Iron Man 2 (film) 108
Isaac, Oscar 214
Isaacs, Jeremy 115
Isle of Skye 155
isolation 14, 93, 181
Isserley 78–89, 155

Jack, Paula 6
Jackson, Danny 122
Jagernauth, Kevin 28

James, Alex 60
James, Jay 172–173
Jamiroquai 61
Japan, Japanese 109
Japanese internment, WWII 201
Jenkins, Jane 101
Jerry McGuire (film) 4
Jewellery (LP) 173
Jobs, Steve 212
Johansson, Scarlett 4, 13; adolescence 102; career 110; casting 110, 123–124; challenges of filming 160, 164; childhood 100; covert filming 134, 138, 140; early films 100–110; final sequence 158; Glazer 110, 232, 230; Laura 124, 154; Pearson 150–151; performance 6, 30, 44–45, 117, 133–134, 187, 202, 210–211; scripts 110; sidewalk trip-and-fall 147–148, 171; speech and accent 6, 13, 41; storm 159–160; stunt double 147–148
Johnson, Rian 192, 230
Johnston, Keith M. 9
Jones, Duncan 217
Jonze, Spike 108
Jordan, Neil 114
Josephs, Tracey 113–115, 156–158, 230
July, Miranda 114
Jumanji (film) 100
Justine, *Melancholia* 223–227
juxtaposition 5, 17–18, 25, 36, 55–56, 126, 150, 187, 189; *see also* duality
JW Films 116

"kaleidoscope" 149
Karma Police, Radiohead 62, 69
Karmacoma (music video) 60, 62
Kaye, Paul 60
Kaye, Tony 64
Keaulana, Rusty 65
Keeler, Ruby 101
Kellerhouse, Neil 1, 228
Kendall, Cavan 68
Kent, Clark 46
Kidman, Nicole 69–72
The Killing of a Sacred Deer (film) 114
Kingsley, Ben 60, 66, 67
Kiorastami, Abbas 74
kitchen scene 47–48, 177
Koresky, Michael 108
Korova Milk Bar 60
Krasinski, John 211
Kubrick, Stanley 17, 59, 60, 62, 77, 173
Kurosawa, Akira 118
Kwapis, Ken 108

Laemmle Theaters 1
Lanark, Scotland 171
Land Rovers 158
Landin, Daniel 18, 21, 31, 41, 63, 117, 119, 127, 130–132, 134–135, 137, 139–140, 171
Lane, Anthony 109

Lang, Fritz 195
Lanthimos, Yorgos 114, 168
laser 146
The Last Composer (film) 172
Last Days (film) 70
Late Night with Conan O'Brien, TV 110
Laura (character) 9–10, 35, 39; arc 149, 154, 158, 186, 215, 221, 225; audacity 147; bravery 44; fallibility 147; isolation 14, 93, 181; loneliness 14, 21, 187; vulnerability 8, 22, 41, 44–45; *see also* Glazer, Laura; Johansson, Laura
Lavant, Denis 62
LED light 137
Leftfield (band) 65, 172
Leigh, Danny 125
Levi, Mica 5, 12–13, 15, 26, 34, 48, 50, 146, 173–180, 193, 202, 228–232
Levis (ad) 62, 172
LGBTQ 201
Li, Gong 73
Life (film) 211, 217
Ligeti, György 173, 173
light and dark (motif) 1, 181–185
lighting 137
line producer 113
lipstick, Laura's red 30, 50, 60, 127, 175
Lipstick to Void, by Levi 175
Livingston, Scotland 140
Lloyd, Richard 165, 180
Loach, Ken 134
Local Hero (film) 3
location manager 119–120; *see also* Strange, Eugene
location services 116
Loch Lomond 156
Loch Marie 155
Loch Ness monster 18
Lochgoilhead 120
Logger (character) 52–57, 122, 156, 159, 184, 196
London 59, 75, 91–92, 120, 126, 142, 148, 165, 172–173, 201, 230
London Philharmonic 173
London Sinfonieta 173
Lone Star (film) 200
loneliness 14, 21, 187
Lonely (character) 33–38, 51, 56, 96, 98–99, 123, 149–152, 190–191, 213, 229
Lord, Bryan 111
Lorraine, Claude 191
Los Angeles 174, 230
Lost in Translation (film) 101–103
Louise, *Arrival* 189, 222–223, 225
Love, by Levi 50, 229
A Love Song for Bobby Long (film) 104–106
Lucy (film) 153, 216
Lynch, David 66, 73

M8 motorway 8, 13, 137, 150, 170
Ma, Tzi 189

Ma, Yo-Yo 101
Macht, Gabriel 104
Macias, Jose Concepcion 219
Mackay, Lynsey Taylor 7, 9, 122
Mackinnon, Ian 149
MacReady, R. J. (character) 206–208, 211
Mad Max: Fury Road (film) 195, 220
Mad Men (TV series) 196
Madonna 168
makeup and hair design 11, 12, 127, 161; *see also* Beveridge, Chrissie
The Man Who Fell to Earth (film) 202–205
The Man Who Wasn't There (film) 108
Mance, Jessica 160–161
Manhattan 70, 101
Manny and Lo (film) 101–102
map drawings: Glagow City Centre 150; Scotland 136
Mara, Rooney 114
Margot at the Wedding (film) 70
Marr, Jo 220
Mars Attacks (film) 202
Marvel comics (films) 100, 108, 110
Maslany, Tatiana 216
Massive Attack (band) 60
Match Point (film) 106–108
The Matrix (film) 26, 140, 202
McAlinden, Kevin 14, 137
McCarthy, Cormac 91
McCarthy, Kevin 95, 198
McCarthy era, United States 198
McConnell, Kate 144–146, 160–161, 163, 230
McDowell, Malcolm 60
McKellen, Ian 114
McQueen, Steve, director 114
McWilliams, Jeremy 7, 122, 126, 147
Me and You and Everyone We Know (film) 114
Meat to Maths, by Levi 26, 146–147, 202
Meet Me in St. Louis (film) 100
Melancholia (film) 223–227
Melbourne 230
Méliès, George 198
Mellis, Louis 66
Men with Guns (film) 200
Mendoza Province, Nadine 110
Mercerism 77
mercy, novel 81–82, 87
Messer, John 77
metaphors 17, 40, 42, 78, 167
Metropolis (film) 79, 195, 216, 220
Meyers, Jonathan Rhys 106–108
Meyers, Stephenie 116
Micachu and the Shapes (band) 173
Michael Clayton (film) 216
microphones, mikes, mics 137, 140–141; *see also* hidden cameras
microtonality 175
MIDI 174
Million Dollar Movie (TV show) 2

Mills, Ben 139
Mills, Oscar 139
Milne, Gareth 126, 132, 139, 147–148, 156, 158, 163–164
Milne, Sian 147–148, 163–164
Minority Report (film) 40
mirrors 36, 41–42, 46, 48, 96–7, 190–192
mis-en-scene 9, 14, 19, 35
misandry 185
misogyny 201
Mizuno, Sonoya 215
model making 161
molding 160
The Monsters Are Due on Maple Street (TV episode) 207
Monster's Ball (film) 74
Moon (film) 217
Moreland, Michael 43–44, 123, 153
Morham, Fiona 115
Morrow, Susan 3
Mortensen, Viggo 91
Morton, Joe 199–200
Mozart 178
Mulder, Fox 16
Mulleavy, Kate 172
Mulleavy, Laura 172
Murdoch, Mark 135, 137, 140, 148
Murray, Bill 103
music in the film (non-scored) 140, 177
music supervisor 5; *see also* James, Jay; Raeburn, Peter
music videos *see* Glazer, Jonathan
Mustill, Louis 129, 131, 133

Nagasaki 198
Nagy, Phyllis 114
nationalism 82
Neo, *The Matrix* 26
Nervous Man (character) 7, 28–30, 147, 190
neurofibromatosis 150
Never (LP) 173
New Estates 79, 81, 88
New Orleans 104
New York Magazine 100
Newton, Thomas Jerome (character) 202–205
Nichols, Jeff 116
nightclub sequence 96
Noble, Steven 22, 38, 127
non-actors 13, 135, 150–151, 159–160
North (film) 101
Northern Ireland 122
Not So Sure (song by Levi) 173
Nottingham Trent University 59
Nuart Theater, Los Angeles 230
Nyby, Christian 206

O'Brien, Conan 110
O'Brien, Geoffrey 21
Oddy, Chris 118–120, 125–126, 131–132, 141, 143–145, 154, 156, 161, 228

Odessa Steps 20
Odyssey (Levi's ad) 62
Okri, Ben 61
On the Beach (film) 195
One-Cam camera 130–132, 154
One of Us visual effects 124, 129, 133, 144, 163
one-two beat 15, 175
O'Neal, Alexander 113–115, 125–126, 130–132, 142–144, 148, 157–158, 229
Only God Forgives (film) 229
Oppenheimer, J. Robert 216
opposites 1, 181–185; *see also* dialectic
Orphan Black (TV series) 216
Orwell, George 218
Oscars *see* Academy Awards
O'Sullivan, Emer 29
Over the Town by Chagall 66
Overland, Anita 111–112
Overlook Hotel 60
Owen, Clive 114

Paint (Sony Bravia ad) 65, 90, 119, 126
paint finishers 161
Pal, George 202
Palm Pictures Directors' Series DVD 60
panspermia 206
The Paper Boy (film) 75
paranoia 93
paranormal 75, 90
Park Hyatt Tokyo 103
Parker, Dominic 124, 161, 163
Paul, Ryan 194
Pearson, Adam 33, 35, 123, 149–151
Peña, Luis Fernando 218
Peña, Michael 219
Penderecki, Krzysztof 173
Penfold, Rachel 124, 163
percussion 174
Persona (film) 169
Peters, Derrick 149, 159
Phat Planet (music) 65
Phillips, Michael 16
Phipps, William 3
Phoenix, Joaquin 109, 115
Pi (film) 91
Piel, Jean-Louis 73
Pigalle, Paris 73
pink sweater 10, 60, 127
Pitt, Brad 111–113
Planet of the Apes (film) 84
"poetic realism" 118
Poland, David 109
political horror film 93
political novel 82
Pollock, Jackson 215
porn film 21
Port Glasgow 154
Port William 152
posthuman 217–218
post-production 165–180; supervisor 165

Post Traumatic Stress Disorder PTSD 206
Precious (film) 75
Predator drone 220
pre-sales 116
The Price of Salt (novel) 114
Primer (film) 229
production design 70, 118; *see also* Oddy, Chris
production value 117
Professional Children's School, PCS 101, 103
prosthetics 144–145, 160–161; supervisor 144
Province, Nadine Mendoza 110
Punch Drunk Love (film) 229
Pygmalion (play) 216
pyrex eyes 163

The Quarry 165
Queen's Court, Glasgow 65
Quiet (character) 6, 42, 43–51, 53–55, 85, 88, 96, 123, 153–154; his home 154–155, 192–194, 196–197, 211, 229
A Quiet Place (film) 211
Quinney, Andrew 140

Rabbit in Your Headlights (music video) 62, 169
Rabineau, Sylvie 91
Radiohead 60–63
Raeburn, Peter 5, 65, 119, 172–174, 177–178, 180
Rampling, Charlotte 224
Ramsay, Lynne 114
Rannoch Moor 152
Real Gone Kid (song) 47, 177
red (motif) 193–194
RED camera 130, 158
"red river" 146
Redford, Robert 101
Redman, Amanda 66
Reeves, Keanu 42, 202
Refn, Nicolas Winding 229
Regal Theater, downtown LA 231
reincarnation 69, 73, 74–76, 87, 90
Reiner, Rob 101
Reiniger, Lotte 183
release form 134–5
Renner, Jeremy 223
Renoir, Jean 152
replicants 212–214; *see also* artificial intelligence
Requiem for a Dream (film) 91
Rhodes, Dane 105
Rhys Meyers, Jonathan 106
Ribisi, Giovanni 103
The Rise and Fall of Ziggy Stardust and the Spiders from Mars (LP) 202
Ritter, John 101
Rivera, Alex 218–219
The Road (film) 91, 195
Roberts, Ben 180

Robey, Tim 115
robot 86, 212, 217–218; *see also* artificial intelligence
Rockwell, Sam 217
Rodgers & Hammerstein 100
Roeg, Nicholas 202, 205
Rokos, Will 74
Romanova, Natalia "Natasha" 100, 108
Romney, Jonathan 13
Room (film) 114
Rose, David 112, 115
Roshomon (film) 118
Ross, Tessa 112–115, 165
Rossini, Gioachino 65
Roth, Tim 92
Rowchoish bothy 156
Rowntree, Dave 60
Royal Festival Hall, London 230–231
Rublev, Andrei 118, 168
Russell, Kurt 206
Russell, Rosalind 100
Russian icon 168

Samsonov, Ekaterina 115
Sandstorm (music) 177
Santana (band) 179
Sarabande by Handel 62
Sauchiehall Street 132
Savides, Harris 70, 72
Sayles, John 199
A Scanner Darkly (film) 42
The Scarlet Letter 10
Scelsi, Giacinto 173
Schaeffer, John 174
Schlondorff, Volker 73
Scholes, Paul 115
Schygulla, Hanna 73
science fiction 2–3, 11, 15, 69, 75, 90–91, 109, 116, 119, 126, 176, 195, 202, 206, 211, 215–216, 219, 224–227, 229
Scinto, David 66
Scoop (film) 108
score 5, 6; 12–15; 172–179; *see also* Levi, Mica; string instruments
Scotland 3, 18, 33, 44, 84, 119–120, 125–126; coast 92, 138, 151–152, 154–157, 159, 167, 171, 228–229
Scott, Ridley 77, 212–214
Scottish community 96, 110, 177
Scottish Highlands 78, 94, 111, 122, 154
"scribbling," in music 176
sculpting 161
second assistant director 135
Seghatchian, Tanya 93
self-discovery 2
Serling, Rod 38
SETI, search for extraterrestrial intelligence 211
70s movies 173
Sex, Lies, and Videotape (film) 91

Sex Pistols 91
Sexy Beast (film) 66–68, 74, 90–92, 113, 172
Shame (film) 114
Shangai Triad (film) 73
The Shape of Water (film) 35
shape-shifter 207
The Shed (nightclub) 140
The Shining (film) 60
shooting in continuity 125
shopping center *see* Buchanan Galleries
Short, Martin 202
Shyamalan, M. Night 69, 195
sidewalk scene *see* trip-and-fall
Siegel, Don 198
silicone 144–145, 160, 163
Silver City (film) 200
Silver Reel 116
Single, Steve 170
16mm lens 130
Skarsgård, Alexander 223
slavery, United States 201
Sleep Dealer (film) 218–220
Sloan, Melanie 100
Sloatman, Lala 70
Slumdog Millionaire (film) 114
Smit-McPhee, Kodi 94
Smith, Arron 131, 133, 159
Smith, Charles Martin 211
Sneakers (film) 220
Soderbergh, Steven 91
sodium lights 137
Somewhere (film) 70
Sommerville, Jeff 91
A Song for the Lovers (music) 62
SONY (ads) 63, 119
Sophistry (stage play) 110
sound designer 168, 171; *see also* Burn, Johnnie
sound editor 171
sound man 131
soundscape 172
Soundtree 172, 177
Soylent Green (film) 202
Spacey, Kevin 217
Spearing, Hugo 228
special effects supervisor, senior 144
Species (film) 228
Spielberg, Steven 26, 202
Spurr, Cameron 224
Star Wars (film) 142
Starman (film) 209–211
Steely Dan 48
Stewart, Caroline 122, 230
storm, during shooting 155–159
Strange, Eugene 119–120, 126, 128, 135, 138–139, 154–156, 158
Strathairn, David 198
Streep, Meryl 106
Street Spirit (Fade Out) (music video) 60–61, 63, 90

Index

string instruments 12, 14, 15, 16, 24, 33, 41, 48, 50, 181
Stuart, Alexander 92–93
StudioCanal ix, 228
stunt coordinator 126
Superman (TV series) 46
supernatural 75
Surfer ad, for Guinness 64–65, 90, 172
surreal 90
Sutherland, Kiefer 223
Swank, Hilary 201
Swimmer (character) 18–20, 24–5, 44, 86, 96, 145
Swimmer ad for Guiness aka *Swim Black* see *Surfer*
swimmer's hair 145
swimmer's "skin suit" 145–146
synth pads 178
synthesized strings 174
Szula, Joe 14, 138

Tantallon Castle 49, 154
Tarkovsky, Andrei 118
Tatò, Anna Maria 73
technical supervisor 129
technology 95, 119, 186–188, 195
Telluride Film Festival 228
Temperton, James 216
The Tempest 159
Tetras (music) 176
The Thieving Magpie (music) 65
The Thing (film) 206–209, 211
The Thing from Another World (film) 2, 206
Thomas, Jeremy 91
Thompson, Kevin 70
3D scanning 160–161
"tiger on the prowl" 133
The Time Machine (film) 202
time-slice effect 130
To Have and Have Not (film) 107
To Serve Man (TV episode) 26
Tobias, Scott 134
Tokyo 103
Toop, Annie 144–145
Toryglen, Glasgow 65
Toulouse-Lautrec, Henri 73
Trainspotting (film) 114
Travolta, John 104–106
Trent Polytechnic 59
trilled strings 175
trip and fall sidewalk scene 30, 32, 82 147–149
A Trip to the Moon (film) 198
Tristan und Isolde 223
Trongate 149, 171
tropes, science fiction and horror 6, 13, 24, 28, 40, 80, 95–96, 184, 195–6, 206, 209, 211, 225
Turing, Alan 213–214
Turkel, Joe 212

Twelve Years a Slave (film) 114
26, The Writer's Collective 114
The Twilight Zone (TV series 1959–1964) 26, 38, 207
2001: A Space Odyssey (film) 17, 60, 173, 218

UK, United Kingdom 115, 123, 160, 228
UK Film Council, UKFC 93, 115
UK tax credit 116
Ullman, Liv 73
Under the Skin (novel) 93–94, 120, 127, 155, 220
under the skin (phrase) 81–82
Under the Skin (poster) 1
Under the Skin (trailer) 229
Under the Skin (2008 script) 93–99, 111–112
Under the Skin (2011 script) 98–99, 112–114, 169
underwater filming 142–147
underwater suit 144–145
unidentified flying object, UFO 9
The Universal (music video) 59, 63
UNKLE (band) 62, 169
Upstream Color (film) 229

Valdez, Gabriel Diego 87
vampires 21, 202
van, construction, uses 40–41, 131–133, 137–8, 170
Van Eyck, Jan 191
Vangelis 173
van Sant, Gus 70, 91
Venice Film Festival 228
Venus de Milo 193
Vermeer, Johannes 70
Vertigo (film) 173
Vess Industries 78
Vicki Christina Barcelona (film) 108, 124
Vikander, Alicia 214
The Village (film) 69
The Village Voice 1
Villeneuve, Denis 217
viola 12, 174–175
violin 69
Virtual Insanity (music video) 62
visual effects consultant 165
The Visual Story (book) 67
vodsel 79, 81–84
Voight-Kampff test 212, 214
von Trier, Lars 91, 172, 222–224

Wachowskis 202
Wagner, Richard 223
Wajda, Andrjez 73
Walken, Christopher 101
Walsh, M. Emmet 212
Walter (film) 114
Walters, Barbara 100
Wang, Wayne 73
Wanlockhead 126

War of the Worlds (1953 film) 2
War of the Worlds (2005 film) 26, 202, 219
The War Zone (film and novel) 92
Warner, Malcolm-Jamal 101
Watts, Paul 9, 23, 30, 48, 56, 147–148, 150, 158, 165–169, 210, 228
Waugh, Evelyn 103
Wave Studios 231
We Bought a Zoo (film) 127
Webber, Peter 101–102
Webster, Paul 91, 112
Wechsler, Nick 91, 93–94, 111, 116
weightless environment 145
Wells, H.G. 198, 202
Wheale, Sarah Jane 112
Whitaker, Forest 222
Whitaker, Gary 223
Whitbread Award 78, 92
White, Julianne 68
white orb 6
white space, white void 7, 15, 10, 22, 78, 126, 169, 195, 229
Who Goes There? Story 206
Wigley, Samuel 77
Wigon, Zachary 70
wigs 12
Wilkinson, Tom 216
William Morris Endeavor, WME 111
Wilson, James 90, 92, 111–113, 115, 124, 128, 133–134, 140, 147, 153, 156, 158, 165–167
wind symphony 179
Winstone, Ray 66
Wiseman, Andreas 112
The Wizard of Oz 42
WME, William Morris Endeavor 91
Wonder Wheel (film) 106
Wood, Elijah 101
Woodshock (film) 172
The Woodsman (film) 75
WOR-TV 2
Wordless Music Orchestra 231
World Without End (film) 195
Wynter, Dana 198

X-Files 16
Xenakis, Iannis 173, 176
xenophobia 82

Yorke, Tom 61–62, 64
You Were Never Really Here (film) 115
Young, Ben 219
Young, Sean 213

Zacharek, Stephanie 1, 5, 6, 25
zombies 202
Zwigoff, Terry 101

www.ingramcontent.com/pod-product-compliance
Ingram Content Group UK Ltd.
Pitfield, Milton Keynes, MK11 3LW, UK
UKHW041930140426
5217IPUK00014B/410